KT-489-852

BRIEF THERAPY
Myths, Methods, and Metaphors

EDITED BY

Jeffrey K. Zeig, Ph.D.

AND

Stephen G. Gilligan, Ph.D.

BRUNNER/MAZEL *Publishers* · *NEW YORK*

All royalties from this book are the property of The Milton H. Erickson Foundation, Inc., 3606 North 24th Street, Phoenix, Arizona
85016. Royalties will be used to foster educational and scientific efforts that pertain to psychotherapy and hypnosis.

Library of Congress Cataloging-in-Publication Data

Brief therapy : myths, methods, and metaphors / edited by Jeffrey K.
  Zeig and Stephen G. Gilligan.
       p.   cm.
  Proceedings of the Fourth International Congress on Ericksonian
Approaches to Hypnosis and Psychotherapy, held in San Francisco,
Calif., Dec. 7-11, 1988, and sponsored by the Erickson Foundation.
  Includes bibliographical references.
  ISBN 0-87630-577-X
  1. Brief psychotherapy—Congresses.   2. Metaphors—Therapeutic
use—Congresses.   3. Mythology—Therapeutic use—Congresses.
I. Zeig, Jeffrey K.   .   II. Gilligan, Stephen G.   .
III. Milton H. Erickson Foundation.   IV. International Congress on
Ericksonian Approaches to Hypnosis and Psychotherapy (4th : 1988 :
San Francisco, Calif.)
  [DNLM: 1. Psychotherapy, Brief—congresses.   WM420 B8536 1988]
RC480.55.B75   1990
616.89'14—dc20
DNLM/DLC
for Library of Congress   90-1498
                                                                   CIP

Published by
BRUNNER/MAZEL, INC.
19 Union Square
New York, New York 10003

Designed by M. Franklin-Plympton
Manufactured in the United States of America
10   9   8   7   6   5   4   3   2

*This book is dedicated
to Kristina K. Erickson*

Contents

III. FAMILY THERAPY

IV. THE TEMPORAL FACTOR IN BRIEF THERAPY

V. TECHNIQUES OF BRIEF THERAPY

Preface

A number of months ago, a middle-aged woman requested a therapy appointment for a long-standing flying phobia. She proclaimed with conviction her belief that "long-term" therapy was necessary. I replied that the therapy would take as long as was needed, noting that for some this meant a few sessions, for others a longer period, and for her "just that amount of time to comfortably make the satisfying changes" she was capable of making. While I assured her that she could continue to elaborate any changes after the therapy was concluded, I also emphasized that any work we might do together would likely be active, experiential, collaborative, and solution-oriented.

As we continued to talk, her initial skepticism about brief therapy gave way to her intense desire for change, and we agreed to a therapy contract consisting of a maximum of 10 sessions, with the primary goal being dissolution of the phobia. Hypnosis was effectively employed during the first several sessions to develop confidence and access resources, so that by the third session we were focusing on which flight she would take as a "test case." When she took a flight with relative comfort during the following week, we were both delighted. During a fourth and final session, we agreed that the therapy contract had been fulfilled, and so no further sessions were scheduled. A later follow-up revealed that several additional flights had been successfully taken, and she considered the problem solved and the therapy successful.

This case illustrates a reality that has slowly been gaining recognition during the past 25 years: Therapy need not be lengthy to be effective. Today, the idea that effective therapy can be brief is central to a growing number of therapists, many of whom are eager to learn more efficient ways of practicing this type of approach. It is thus not too surprising that more than 2,300 therapists attended the Brief Therapy Congress sponsored by the Erickson Foundation in San Francisco on December 7–11, 1988. The Congress brought together the leading authorities in the burgeoning field of brief therapy and provided exposure to the cutting edge of current thought and practice in the field. A rich array of viewpoints and methods was presented, each demonstrating a different way of doing effective brief therapy.

This book is a record of the Congress. It contains each of the keynote addresses and the invited presentations. The presentations have been organized around key issues and major themes in contemporary brief therapy. While there is no unquestioned party line for describing, or fixed recipe for doing, brief therapy, the reader will discover that most of the authors harbor a deep confidence in clients' abilities to change, as well as an emphasis on action, resources, pragmatism, solutions, future orientation, context, and therapist flexibility. However, the way in which these values are implemented is surprisingly variable. Some authors advocate conscious change processes, while others favor unconscious processes; some focus on the individual, others on the family; and some think of therapy as a "one-shot" venture, while others suggest thinking of therapy as intermittent throughout the life cycle. Thus, a strength of the book is that it challenges therapists to discover the style of doing brief therapy that is most efficacious for them and their clients.

Taken as a whole, the book constitutes a state-of-the-art report on brief therapy, one that both experienced and novice therapists will benefit from reading. As its title promises, it examines brief therapy's myths, describes its methods, and elucidates its metaphors. Most important, it effectively addresses the key issue in any therapy, namely, how to help people successfully meet the challenges of living.

STEPHEN G. GILLIGAN, Ph.D.

Introduction

Contained in this volume are the proceedings of the Fourth International Congress on Ericksonian Approaches to Hypnosis and Psychotherapy, entitled *Brief Therapy: Myths, Methods and Metaphors*, held in San Francisco, California, December 7–11, 1988. Some 2,200 professionals from around the world attended the event. These proceedings consist of the keynote speeches and invited addresses.

ERICKSONIAN CONGRESSES

The First International Congress on Ericksonian Approaches to Hypnosis and Psychotherapy was held December 4–8, 1980, in Phoenix, Arizona. Milton H. Erickson, M.D., was a member of the organizing committee of that Congress. One of the purposes of the first meeting was to give him an opportunity to see the impact of his work. He did not have that chance; Dr. Erickson died eight and one-half months prior to the meeting. Doubtless, though, Dr. Erickson would have been pleased by the meeting. Approximately 2,000 professionals interested in his work attended the meeting.

The Second International Congress, also held in Phoenix, helped to broaden and advance Ericksonian methodology. The event was held November 30–December 4, 1983. Attendance at the second meeting surpassed 2,000, probably making it the largest professional meeting held on the topic of hypnosis.

The Third International Congress brought new people to the Erickson movement. About 1,800 people attended, and Dr. Erickson's psychotherapeutic legacy continued to thrive.

The meeting theme was expanded for the Fourth Congress, and more than 2,200 professionals from the United States and 24 countries met to learn various aspects of Brief Therapy. Dr. Erickson was a strong advocate of brief psychotherapy, and his work is a foundation for many therapists' work in that direction today.

CONGRESS FORMAT

The program for the Congress was designed so attendees could select from a wide variety of training courses. Registrants picked the format that best suited their needs; there was an academic and experiential component to the meeting.

The academic program consisted of keynote addresses and invited addresses. There were three keynote presentations: Cloé Madanes' "Strategies and Metaphors of Brief Therapy," Jay Haley's "Why Not Long-Term Therapy," and Arnold Lazarus' presentation, "Brief Psychotherapy: Tautology or Oxymoron" (with Allen Fay). There were 33 invited addresses. It is the academic portion of the Congress which appears in these proceedings.

The experiential component of the Congress consisted of two-hour workshops and practica, interactive events, and short courses. Fifty-five two-hour workshops were offered, plus small group practica. One of the features created in 1986 was carried over to 1988: Attendees were able to work in small group supervised practicum sessions on various topics of hypnosis and brief therapy. The two-hour small groups were limited to 12 participants and were led by faculty members. The entire faculty consisted of more than 160 members, including moderators, copresenters, and special faculty.

A format change the third day of the Congress gave attendees an opportunity to witness interactive events. One-hour clinical demonstrations, conversation hours, group discussions, and panels on special topics were featured that day.

Short courses also were presented during the Congress: These one-and-one-half hour miniworkshops covered a wide range of topics on Ericksonian methods, as well as brief therapy.

The evening events at the Congress included a welcome reception and an authors' hour. A special media program honoring the late Virginia Satir also was featured one evening.

The tone and content of the Congress resulted in a well-received meeting among practitioners of varying schools of psychotherapy.

San Francisco provided a beautiful backdrop to the meeting. Professionals who had attended previous Erickson Congresses missed Phoenix but agreed the City by the Bay was an excellent choice as a meeting site.

ACKNOWLEDGMENTS

The success of a meeting this size is due to the input of a great many individuals. I would like to take this opportunity to thank those people.

The following professionals reviewed proposals of short courses/symposia submitted for presentation at the Congress: Yvonne M. Dolan, M.A.; Jeffrey B. Feldman, Ph.D.; Stephen G. Gilligan, Ph.D.; Ronald A. Havens, Ph.D.; Melvin G. Hector, M.D.; Lynn D. Johnson, Ph.D.; Stephen Lankton, A.C.S.W.; R. Reid Wilson, Ph.D.; and Michael D. Yapko, Ph.D.

Stephen Gilligan shared equally all editorial decisions. This book illustrates the gift Gilligan has as an editor, and his diligence is the reader's reward.

On behalf of the Board of Directors, our heartfelt thanks again go to the distinguished faculty. The work provided by these professionals resulted in one of our most memorable meetings.

The Erickson Foundation staff worked tirelessly to ensure the success of the Congress. Under the direction of Executive Director Linda Carr McThrall, the following staff deserves special recognition: Chris Berger, office assistant; Theresa Cords, administrative assistant; Sylvia Cowen, bookkeeper; Greg Deniger, Congress registrar, computer operations manager; Mary Helen Kelly, executive secretary; Alice McAvoy, office assistant; and Judy Sachs, volunteer coordinator.

Michael Liebman, M.C., director of Clinical Services for the Milton H. Erickson Center for Hypnosis and Psychotherapy, provided additional assistance. His staff also should be specially recognized: William A. Cabianca, Ph.D.; Gordon Cuddeby, Ph.D.; Cari Ellis, R.N., M.S.; Larry Ettkin, Ph.D.; Brent B. Geary, M.S.; Mirta Ghiorzi-Volek, Ph.D.; Craig W. LeCroy, Ph.D.; Gary D. Lovejoy, Ph.D.; Frank C. Noble, Ph.D.; Peter J. Rennick, M.S.; Rebecca Rubin, M.C.; Andrea Scott, Ph.D.; Mark Treegoob, Ph.D.; Marti W. Waller, M.C.; and Neil C. Weiner, Ph.D.

A number of volunteers worked with Foundation staff members both prior to and at the Congress. Special thanks go to Ed Hancock, Phil "Mac" McAvoy, and Jaimie Andes, who provided enormous support throughout the planning stages of the Congress and during the event. Additionally, more than 75 graduate student volunteers served as monitors and staffed the registration and continuing education desks.

Special thanks go to Barry Shephard of SHR Communication Planning and Design of Phoenix. Barry designed the Erickson Foundation logo.

The Fourth International Congress was cosponsored by the Departments of Psychiatry and Psychology, the Veterans Administration Medical Center, Martinez, California; and the Department of Family Practice, University of California at Davis. Their efforts are gratefully acknowledged.

The Board of Directors provided great support during the planning of the Congress. Many thanks go to Sherron Peters, who worked on early plans prior to her resignation from the Board; Elizabeth M. Erickson; Kristina K. Erickson; and J. Charles Theisen.

JEFFREY K. ZEIG, Ph.D.
Director
The Milton H. Erickson Foundation
Phoenix, Arizona

Convocation Speech

When I look out the front window of my consulting office, which is attached to my home in Phoenix, Arizona, I see a maturing ironwood tree. Exactly eight years ago that same ironwood tree was in a wicker basket decorated with a purple ribbon. It sat on the stage of Symphony Hall in Phoenix, a much smaller, less mature version of its present self. I introduced that ironwood tree to the Convocation assembled at the December 1980 First International Congress on Ericksonian Approaches to Hypnosis and Psychotherapy.

I envisioned the first congress as a 79th birthday celebration for Milton H. Erickson, M.D. It was to be an opportunity for him to greet old friends and colleagues and to see the impact of his accomplishments on the field of psychotherapy. In my efforts to organize the meeting, a guiding personal vision was to introduce Dr. Erickson to the Congress. When he died less than nine months before the convention, I substituted the ironwood tree.

For those of you who don't know, Dr. Erickson fancied wood carvings. Toward the end of his life he collected carvings made of ironwood, a hardwood with lavender flowers, so dense it resists floating. These carvings were made by the Seri Indians, the Seris, who live in northwest Mexico in the Sonoran desert. They carved local sea and desert animals using primitive tools, and they stained their work with shoe polish. It seems that modern tools can be used only to initially cut ironwood logs. This wood is best worked slowly and by hand.

The wood utilized by the Seris is scrap. Freshly cut wood is uncarvable. Fallen wood must be used. The fallen wood does not rot. Rather it is cured by the desert climate. The Seris had the foresight to use something that others could not see how to use. And they used it to create art.

At one time, Dr. Erickson had one of the world's most extensive collections of Seri ironwood. Now that collection has dwindled. A number of pieces are gifts in the possession of colleagues and students, many of whom serve on the faculty of this meeting. My last Christmas gift from Dr. Erickson was an ironwood owl. I told him it was very wise gift indeed.

Now, the ironwood tree that I planted outside my office made a remarkable recovery. It lost all its leaves from the shock of standing on the stage of Symphony Hall at the 1980 meeting. It seemed as if it would never recover, but that was not the case. The leaves grew. The branches developed and continue to spread. The trunk remains solid.

Although it will take a while before there has been enough development, eventually woodworkers will be able to use the limbs from the tree to create sculptures—sculptures that will use modern forms and reflect modern culture. And, remember, it is only from the cured dead wood that the art can be created.

Now Dr. Erickson did get some of the intended honor from the first Congress. At the time he died, 750 people already had registered for the meeting. And this was a time before 750 people had ever previously convened for a "hypnosis meeting."

At the Erickson Foundation we continue a tradition by holding Congresses every three years, 1980, 1983, and 1986. Each of those meetings was attended by 1,800 to 2,000 people. This Brief Therapy meeting, with an attendance of 2,400, is the largest of any of the International Erickson Congresses.

Also, we continue to branch out. In 1985, the Foundation organized the Evolution of Psychotherapy Conference, which assembled 7,000 registrants in an attempt to promote concilience among different schools of therapy. Today's Congress continues that trend and brings together outstanding practitioners of brief therapy from many different schools. This meeting has been entitled, "Brief Therapy: Myths, Methods, and Metaphors." The Congress will examine brief therapy's history (myths), developments in technique (methods), and different models (metaphors).

Dr. Erickson was a man who championed a "utilization" approach to psychotherapy. He advised students to use whatever the patient brings —values, history, and even resistances. I think you will find many things to utilize among the diverse branches of brief therapy represented at this meeting. You might want to use this opportunity to learn from practitioners whose work may be less familiar to you and outside the realm of your preferred approach.

Now I wish I could introduce that ironwood tree to you today. But I can introduce some of the roots, and no tree grows without roots. The strong roots of the Foundation are its staff: Linda Carr McThrall, Executive Director; Theresa Cords, Administrative Assistant and Faculty Coordinator; Greg Deniger, Registrar; Sylvia Cowen, Bookkeeper; Mary Helen Kelly, Administrative Assistant and Institutes Coordinator; Judy Sachs, Volunteer Coordinator; Alice McAvoy, Assistant; Chris Berger, Assistant; and Michael Liebman, Director of the Milton H. Erickson

Center for Hypnosis and Psychotherapy. Some of the strongest roots of the Foundation have been the Erickson family members who have attended and lectured at these Congresses. The Erickson family members in attendance at this meeting are Mrs. Elizabeth Erickson; Kristina K. Erickson, M.D.; Lance Erickson, Ph.D.; Betty Alice Erickson Elliott, M.S.; Roxanna Erickson Klein, R.N., M.S.; and Robert Erickson, M.A.

I hope you have a great time at the meeting and that you acquire some of the knowledge and experience that you have come here for.

JEFFREY K. ZEIG, Ph.D.

"Each person is a unique individual. Hence, psychotherapy should be formulated to meet the uniqueness of the individual's needs, rather than tailoring the person to fit the Procrustean bed of a hypothetical theory of human behavior."

—MILTON H. ERICKSON, M.D.

PART I

Keynote Addresses

CHAPTER 1

Why Not Long-Term Therapy?
Jay Haley

It is curious how few meetings and training programs there are on how to do long-term therapy. Most of the announcements one sees are for seminars and workshops on brief therapy. The implication is that everyone knows how to engage clients in therapy for months or years. Yet long-term therapists are made, not born. Therapists do not have innate skills in committing clients to long-term contracts. Without training, they must learn by trial and error to do interminable therapy when they get into practice.

Often it is thought that long-term therapy occurs because the therapist does not know how to cure a person faster. A more respectful view is that it is a special ability. After all, many people do brief therapy because they lack the skill to keep clients coming for a long time. Little is written about long-term therapy techniques.

One of the few therapists with the courage to discuss how to keep a client in therapy and block him or her from going to someone else was Milton H. Erickson. For example, he proposed that a technique for preventing a client going elsewhere was to listen to him and respond, "I know how difficult it is for you to talk about this. If you had to go over it again with someone else, that would be even more painful." Erickson reported that such simple comments prevent clients from going to other therapists. More complicated techniques developed by Erickson to keep clients in therapy still remain secret.

The length of therapy is one of the most important issues in the field, and insurance companies now set the limits. Clinicians have some voice in this matter and should consider the issues. The first issue involves the needs of the therapist, and the second the needs of the client.

THE ISSUE FOR THE THERAPIST

Because therapy is both a calling and a business, the topic of how to keep someone in therapy can be embarrassing. The implication can be that the therapist wants to make money by seeing the client longer. It is best if we face facts. A therapist *does* make more money from a client who stays in therapy for years compared with a client who stays in therapy only a short time. The fact that more money is made should not be a reason to avoid workshops or instruction in long-term techniques.

If we accept the financial problem as something we must live with, what are the merits of long-term therapy for the therapist? Even if some therapists would rather not think about the positive side of interminable therapy, it should be discussed. Like having romantic affairs, many people would rather do it than talk about it at a public meeting.

At one time short-term therapists were on the defensive. Long-term therapists thought of themselves as "deep" and were confident, even arrogant. They liked to imply that brief therapy was a shallow, superficial endeavor. Brief therapists had to quote scientific outcome results to prove their success, pointing out that research did not show any correlation between length of therapy and successful outcome. Long-term therapists easily rejected such data as irrelevant. They pointed out that outcome results do not cause changes in therapy approaches in the field, which change only on the basis of fashion. Short-term therapy was simply condemned as not fashionable and not elegant in practice or theory. Now, with changes in insurance and HMO contracts setting limits on therapy length, the situation is reversed; long-term therapists are becoming defensive and brief therapists are bragging. One day we might even see long-term therapists desperately trying to bring science into the issue.

Young therapists won't recall the Golden Age of long-term therapy and might appreciate an example of a personal encounter to illustrate how it was in those days. I was once dining in a restaurant in Paris and began talking with an American couple who were sitting at the next table. When they asked what I did, I said I directed a therapy institute. The couple knew a lot about therapy since they were from New York. They were pleased to find we had something in common. The husband said he had been in therapy for 12 years, considering psychoanalysis to be therapy, and his wife had been in therapy for 8 years. Both of them had several sessions a week. I asked if therapy had solved their problems. They looked surprised at the question. "Of course not," said the gentleman, as if thinking the matter over for the first time. "We wouldn't still be going if it had." I asked them if they would recommend therapy to someone else. They said, "Of course we would. Everyone should be in therapy." I could see they had a therapist who knew his business.

In the discussion, I mentioned that 12 years seemed a long time to be in therapy. Rather defensively, the man asked me how long we did therapy at our Institute. I said, "We average about six interviews. With student therapists the average is about nine interviews." The couple looked at me, shocked, as if regretting they had begun this conversation. I found myself saying apologetically, "Well, that's only an average, we see some people a long time." I even added, to fill the silence, "Sometimes people come once a month, and so six sessions can take as long as six months." The couple became rather condescending and polite. The gentleman said that I must see a different class of clients than he was familiar with. I said defensively that we treated every wretch who knocked on our door. He said that I certainly could not be doing therapy with advertising executives like him and his wife. They are required to be in therapy for a long time because they feel so guilty about their work that they have to pay a lot of money to an analyst for years as a kind of penance. I had to agree that our therapy did not meet that special need because we did not have that size advertising industry in our area. The couple lost interest in me and began to look for an Italian to talk to.

I found myself defensive about doing effective therapy even though the people were saying their long-term therapy had not produced results. I also realized that I did not know how the therapists of this couple had kept them coming so many years without any improvement. There are thousands of therapists with that skill in the large cities. If they teach it, they do not do so in public workshops where all of us can learn. Perhaps it is secretly taught during personal therapy. I understand a training analysis in New York now averages seven years. That is quite a bit longer than the few months that Freud recommended. Perhaps the analysands are more obtuse these days and so require a longer analysis, but it might also be that they are being taught more secrets about how to contain people in therapy.

Now that fashions, and funding for therapy, have changed, people are beginning to be defensive about doing long-term therapy. The pendulum is swinging. As we examine therapy today, there have been remarkable changes in the last two decades. No longer do a few therapists deal with a few clients in distress. Therapy has become a major industry. Just as photocopying machines are flooding the world with paper, the universities are pouring out therapists of every species. There are psychologists, psychiatrists, social workers, educational psychologists, industrial psychologists, hypnotherapists, rational therapists, drug counselors, hospital therapists, marital therapists, family therapists of a dozen schools, and so on. These therapists rush out into offices and agencies everywhere. Part of the reason for this deluge is the publicity given to therapy in the mass media. In TV dramas the characters are in therapy and discuss it as part of life. Talk show hosts discuss their therapy, setting examples for the audience. Women's magazines have columns on the subject. TV and radio psychologists advise everyone to rush off and get therapy. "If only your husband will go into counseling, all will be well" is the cry of the radio psychologist heard by millions.

   With therapy such a way of life, is it proper for a therapist to talk about how briefly it can be done? Isn't that like General Motors bragging about how quickly they can build a Cadillac? Or surgeons bragging about how short a time it takes them to do bypass heart surgery? In the early days of therapy when people were less affluent and there was no insurance, it seemed appropriate to be brief. Now with what it costs to become a therapist, obviously it is only fair to get a return on the investment. Not only is an expensive undergraduate degree necessary, and an expensive graduate degree, but there is postgraduate training. There is also typically the personal therapy expense. It is hoped that a personal therapy will somehow make a therapist more successful. (It is also a way to provide clients for the training staff who might not otherwise have them. Four analysands and four guilty businessmen seen several days a week is all a long-term therapist needs to avoid having to get more referrals for several years.) Besides academic costs, therapists must go to private institutes to learn the therapy skills they were not taught in the university. Seminars and workshops are required to keep up with the continuing education requirements. A therapy practice these days represents a large financial investment, and we must accept that and count it in the fee.

   The therapist is not the only person who is being supported by the therapy fee. Just as there are 40 or 50 backup persons to support every soldier who is actually in combat, so the therapist is at the tip of a pyramid of support personnel. There are administrators of training institutes, supervisors, protective service personnel and judges, hospital and prison staffs, public agency case workers, teachers of abnormal psychology, systems theorists, journal editors, publishers, professional organization staff, licensing authorities, constructivists, and so on. Obviously, a therapy case must provide enough money to support not only the therapist and his family, but all the auxiliary personnel employed in the field.

Can the same income be made with short-term therapy as with lengthy therapy? Some brief therapists argue that it can be done but only if the therapist is willing to seek financial salvation through suffering. The effort required to keep the hours of the brief therapist filled is considerable. I once had a brief therapy private practice, and to equal the income of the long-term therapist required from three to four times as many referrals. A constant supply of clients is necessary because they are constantly changing. I can recall envying the long-term therapists who could schedule their hours a year in advance with confidence that the rent would be paid. In short-term therapy one recesses as soon as there is an improvement, and so a client is shifted to appointments every two weeks or once a month. What happens to that hour next week that must be filled? Perhaps a new referral will come in time, but perhaps it will not. Another talk to a PTA meeting might be necessary. Each decision about whether to have an interview becomes a moral decision, not a routine matter.

The style of short-term therapy is also more exhausting. A day is long, rather than leisurely. As an example, in a first interview the therapist must make the effort to clarify what is wrong and think of something relevant to do, all in an hour. He or she typically formulates a problem and gives a directive. The second interview reveals the response to the directive, which is then modified. By the third interview a positive improvement is taking place and sessions can be spaced more widely apart. The search for new clients begins. What a contrast that is to a long-term approach, where it takes three sessions to complete a history and three more to finish the genogram before one begins to think about what to do to solve the problem. How much easier it is to lean back and say, "Tell me more about that" or "Have you wondered why it upset you that I was late today?"

Long-term therapy can be leisurely because it lacks a goal, but brief therapy requires that something be done to achieve some end. One cannot create a method and try to fit everyone into it. The therapist must innovate a special directive for each person. The long-term therapist needs to learn only one method and apply it. The therapist does what he did with the last person. If the client does not fit the method, another one will. How much more demanding it is to come up with an innovation or a variation in each case. Some brief therapists try to use a method for all cases, such as always telling the clients to stay the same, but such simplicity only works with a few cases.

The long-term therapists have all the best theories to rationalize their techniques and the length of their therapy. Not only has there been a hundred years of talking and writing about psychodynamic theory, but new fashions in philosophy are always available. One can easily step from theorizing about the unconscious to turgid discussions of epistemology, aesthetics, constructivism, chaos, and so on. If the theory is heavy, the therapy can be light, particularly when the theories are about what is wrong with people rather than what to do about changing them. Brief therapists are usually stuck with talking about what to do, which does not lead to profound ideological discussions. There is also not much literature on brief therapy compared with the 70,000 books and articles written about psychodynamic theory.

As another issue, brief therapists tend not to have a theory of resistance. They believe one gets what one expects, and such a theory interferes with gaining cooperation from a client. Long-term therapy has a theory of resistance, which excuses therapy being done forever to overcome that resistance. They also have the potent theory that if the client wants to terminate, he is resisting change and has not really improved, obviously needing more therapy. Long-term ideology has the therapist be the one who decides when therapy is over, not the client, so the length of therapy is in safe hands. Therapy does not end until the therapist is satisfied that the client is as near perfect as can be achieved in one lifetime.

One must also not overlook the importance of the therapist's self-image when choosing the type of therapy to be done. The brief therapist tends to have an image of himself or herself as harried and under stress. The long-term therapist has a look of boredom at times, listening so much to so few people. Not even the marital contract requires that much togetherness. Yet the long-term therapist also has a positive image as a wise philosopher, one who could offer the best advice if he chose to, but clients must decide for themselves. In a comfortable chair in a well-decorated office, preferably with a fireplace, the therapist patiently listens like a good friend to the clients who come to him for many years. Sometimes confrontation is necessary, but if so it is gently done, so the person will continue in therapy. The long-term therapist is loved by his clients. Usually the short-term therapist is not. There is not enough time for a romance. This kindly, loving, philosophical image is particularly appealing as a target image for young people coming out of school. Graduates hope for a private practice, though more and more of them must settle for a salary in an agency or hospital where they must do brief therapy.

THE ISSUE FOR THE CLIENT

Besides the merits of long-term therapy for the therapist, there is the question whether the client benefits most from long- or short-term therapy. We must also consider not only the client but also his or her support personnel in the family network. A scientific case report might clarify the matter.

I recall a woman who became upset when she married. She went into therapy as a result. Eighteen years later she is still in therapy. At that point, she divorced her husband. She also divorced her therapist. The last time I saw her she was considering marriage to another man. She was also thinking of going back into therapy. Can we say that the two decades of therapy had a positive or a negative effect? Would short-term therapy have been preferable in her case? Only intensive research can resolve this question. However, a few ideas are evident. On one side, the woman never had a marriage that was a dyad. She was in a triangle with her husband and her therapist all during her marriage, as many men and women in individual therapy are today. What did the therapy cost her husband? Not only is the expense of therapy over the years a steady drain on a household budget, but what of the personal cost? This husband had a wife whose experiences and ideas, even her intimate thoughts, were more likely to be communicated to another man rather than to him. If communicated to him, it was often after she had spoken to her therapist about it and so it was a twice-told tale with second-hand emotion. Each major event in her life, including childbirth and crises with the children, was shared with her therapist. The husband was labeled as secondary as an advisor to his wife and a parent to the children, while the therapist was the authority and expert on human relations whom she consulted.

For a different perspective on this triangle, we can consider the fact that the husband lived 18 years with a wife while paying another man to listen to her complain. This relieved the husband of that task, which some husbands might consider a positive result and others might not. There was also the agreement, confirmed with each therapy visit, that the wife was defective and the husband was not, since he did not go to a therapist. Therefore, their relationship was defined by an expert as one where the husband was superior and took care of a wife who was not quite adequate. The long-term therapist was, of course, thinking of the wife as fragile and needing his support or he would not have continued with the therapy for so many years. By the act of seeing the wife in therapy, he communicated to the marital couple that the wife was not normal like other people.

How difficult it is to choose brief or long-term therapy in such a case. A positive aspect is that the therapist helped the marriage continue for those many years. An 18-year marriage is an accomplishment in this age of easy divorce. Many wives who get upset after marriage and have brief therapy rather than long-term might break up with their husbands. If the marriage was stabilized by therapy, should that not be considered a positive effect? One must also consider the fact that some wives and husbands do not seek therapy because they wish to change, but for consolation. Often they feel they must stay married for financial reasons, or for the children. They ask of the therapist only that a miserable marriage be made more tolerable by reframing aspects of it and offering suggestions. Perhaps it is wrong to help people stay in an unhappy marriage, but often they ask for that service. A brief intervention to make a change will not satisfy them.

THE STIGMA ISSUE

One important factor about long-term therapy is that the practitioners do not consider being in therapy a stigma. They consider therapy good for everyone and the fact of being in therapy does not mean one is defective, or inadequate, in the eyes of others. In this framework are the growth therapists, or those who seek to increase human potential. They do not find anything wrong with a client except the human condition, and all human beings can grow and improve. Yet the growth therapist might be aware that the client in therapy should not try to run for president. It is still the popular assumption that "therapy" means that a person is defective and unable to deal with life's problems like normal people, particularly if therapy goes on and on for years.

Long-term therapy is usually defended with the argument that the client is fragile and needs support in meeting life's problems. In contrast, the brief therapist tends to have the view that all the person needs to become normal like other people is a few sessions to straighten out some problems. The underlying premise of brief therapy is fundamentally different from the long-term therapy view of the human condition and how people cope with it. A brief therapist, for example, might turn down someone for therapy because the person does not need it. Long-term therapists consider therapy valuable for everyone and no one should be rejected if he or she can afford it.

AUXILIARY PERSONNEL

Only recently has the social context of a client been emphasized by therapists. The effect of the family organization is now more taken for granted. For example, suppose a kindly family member dies and the family becomes unstable. If a family member enters therapy with a kindly therapist, the family is stabilized. A problem only occurs when termination is considered. At that point the family will have to reorganize to adapt to the loss that they had not adjusted to. As the family becomes unstable, it is the client who will appear agitated, and the therapist will conclude he still has problems and must continue longer in therapy. As the years pass, the therapy has the function of stabilizing the family. Sometimes the same goal is achieved by regularly hospitalizing a family member, usually an expendable adolescent. The auxiliary personnel of the therapist, the hospital staff, and the auxiliary personnel of the client, the family, all benefit from the therapeutic arrangement. The family benefits by stability, the therapist and his auxiliary personnel benefit from the fee. Can we say that is not a proper function of therapy? Short-term therapy does not offer that function. In fact, short-term therapy tends to destabilize a family as part of inducing change. Long-term therapists tend to stabilize the organization the way it is.

There is another aspect of stabilization that involves symmetry in human relations. Just as human beings and other animals are symmetrical, having one eye above each side of the nose, one ear on each side of the head, and so on, there seems to be the same pattern in human interaction. This is called the 4th law of human relations. With a married couple, for example, if one spouse becomes attached to someone outside the family, the other may seek an attachment. That is, if one spouse begins an affair, the other spouse often seeks one also. Or the spouse might become overinvolved with people at work, or goes into therapy and attaches to a therapist. Similarly, if a spouse enters therapy, the other one can become attached to someone else as a way of balancing the symmetry of the family.

Within the family, if a mother becomes attached to her son, the husband is likely to become attached elsewhere, perhaps to his mother or a therapist. Obviously, if families need to balance symmetrically in this way, there must be therapists available to be paid to help correct the symmetry of the family. If the involvement of the family member with someone else is long-term, the spouse must have a long-term therapist to provide the needed stability for the system.

THE NEEDS OF THE INDIVIDUAL

Besides stabilizing an organization, what of the needs of the individual? Does long-term therapy meet those needs better than short-term therapy? Let us consider a basic human need: the need to hypothesize. Social psychologists have proposed for many years, and brain researchers are now suggesting, that a basic need of a person is to make hypotheses about himself and other people. One cannot *not* hypothesize. Whatever someone does, we must make a hypothesis about why the person did that. As this comment illustrates, we must even make hypotheses about why we hypothesize. In all our waking hours, if not in our dreams, we explain.

Does short-term therapy help with this need? Obviously it does not because it is not assumed that conversation about a problem will change the problem. Action must be taken. I recall years ago concluding that insight comes *after* a therapeutic change. When I did a brief intervention and got someone over a symptom, he or she wanted to tell me insightfully about all the functions of the symptom in the past and present. Even if I was not interested, the insight was imposed on me. I now realize that the person was fulfilling the need to hypothesize. People have to have an explanation of why they got over a symptom and so must rethink why they had it. Unaware of the hypothesizing need, I was impatient with them since the problem was over and they should go about their business.

When we examine long-term therapy from this view, obviously its greatest contribution is in the hypothesizing area. Hour after hour, week after week, month after month, year after year, the client has a therapist willing to sit and hypothesize. "I wonder why you are puzzled over what you did?" "Let us examine where that idea came from" or "Isn't it interesting that you . . . " Every hypothesis about the past and present is explored. The two people enjoy hypothesizing together, and each has needs satisfied. The therapist finds support for a theory that has as its foundation the need to hypothesize and explain. The clients must hypothesize to try to explain why their lives are always such a mess.

THE INTERPRETATION VERSUS THE DIRECTIVE

Long-term therapy primarily focuses on the interpretation, which is the tool of hypothesis making. Short-term therapy focuses on the directive, which is the tool for producing a change. Long-term therapy tends to be educative. Rather than focus on resolving a problem, the task is to help the person understand. With that emphasis, outcome research is not appropriate. There is nothing for the person to get over. In contrast, brief therapy usually focuses on a problem that is to be changed by the interventions. Whether the change occurs or not can more easily be determined. To put the matter in another way, long-term therapy tends to create an elite who have specialized knowledge about themselves that the average person does not have. The client learns to monitor himself and hypothesize why he does what he does within an ideological framework that is only learned in therapy. The short-term client tends to get over a problem and get back to being like other people rather than being special.

Long-term therapy ideas are easier to learn because they are part of the intellectual climate of the time and available in both professional and popular literature. Giving brief interventions, such as arranging an ordeal or a paradox, is more difficult to learn since the specialized techniques are largely confined to the practitioners of therapy and are unknown to intellectuals generally. Perhaps that is why few long-term therapy workshops are needed and many are necessary to learn brief-therapy techniques. They cannot be learned merely by living in an intellectual culture.

SPECIAL PROBLEMS REQUIRING LONG-TERM THERAPY

Rather than create an either/or situation for long-term or brief therapy, one might suggest that there are times for long-term therapy and other times for brief interventions. Let us consider some of the situations where long-term therapy seems appropriate.

Besides the need to stabilize a married couple or a family over time, there are special problems. One serious problem is that of sexual or physical abuse where therapy is usually mandated by the court. A brief intervention might stop those illegal or immoral acts. However, how can one be sure the acts have really stopped? The possibility of a relapse is not an academic matter but means a victim will be harmed. There is a need to monitor these clients over time to be sure the positive effect of therapy continues. If one follows the person in a serious way, it becomes long-term therapy and is compelled by the nature of the problems.

Another type of problem usually requiring long-term therapy is the chronic psychotic and his family. With a first episode of psychosis, therapy can be brief since it is focused on getting the person back to normal functioning as quickly as possible. A crisis therapy with the family is designed to get a young person diagnosed schizophrenic off medication and back to work or school. This can be accomplished relatively quickly. However, if a therapist is dealing with a case where the person has been hospitalized a half-dozen times, the need for long-term therapy is apparent. The client is chronic, the family is chronic in that it expects the person to be incurable, and the professionals dealing with the client are in a chronic expectation that medication will be needed forever and custody regularly. To change all the auxiliary personnel in such a situation is obviously not a short-term task.

Another special problem is the long-term therapy that is done reluctantly when a therapist wants to terminate a person and cannot. So the therapy goes on without enthusiasm and even with resentment. In the same way the client can wish to terminate and receives such a reaction from the therapist that he or she is unable to do so. One analogy in such a case is the addiction framework. Just as a person can become addicted to a lover, this can happen in therapy. The person might be hooked on a particular therapist or just on being in therapy with someone. A therapeutic goal is to successfully get the person free.

Perhaps it is in the nature of therapy that addiction occurs because of the kinds of sequences involved. In a typical addiction pattern there is a promise of feeling good and of intimacy, and this is followed by a rejection, which takes the form of not fulfilling the intimate promise. Yet it might still happen. It is like a mother encouraging her child to seek her out and then not responding because she is too busy. She invites the child and complains if he hangs on her. By the nature of the therapy contract, the situation is a relationship of an intimate nature. Yet the relationship cannot be consummated as an intimate relationship, and rejection is inevitable. The intimate rapport also lasts only as long as the person pays the bill; thus it is a paid friendship and so a rejection of intimacy while implicitly promising that. Often long-term therapists are caught up in such addictive relationships and cannot escape until a third party, such as a supervisor, helps detach them.

There are, of course, situations where long-term therapy is not appropriate and the therapist must work briefly. Therapy that is limited by an insurance company to a certain number of interviews is obviously not long-term, unless client or therapist decides to make a financial sacrifice and to continue the therapy. Another limited situation is the short-term hospitalization paid by insurance companies. The person is hospitalized for a few weeks and discharge will occur when the insurance runs out, no matter what. Usually the therapist who briefly sees the client inside the hospital cannot carry him or her outside and so continue the therapy.

FUTURE FINANCIAL ARRANGEMENTS

As we look over the field today and consider the long and the short of therapy, there are trends for which we must prepare. Obviously therapy is going to become shorter because of the ways it is financed. Just as it was discovered that hospitalization could be more brief when the insurance companies decided that, so therapy will become briefer as insurance companies limit the length of therapy. Certain changes are going to come in the basic financing of the therapy enterprise and so new opportunities arise.

When we look at the history of therapy, the most important decision ever made was to charge for therapy by the hour. Historians will someday reveal who thought of this idea. The ideology and practice of therapy was largely determined when therapists chose to sit with a client and be paid for durations of time rather than by results.

When one realizes that charging by the hour was an arbitrary decision, there is no reason why other ways of financing therapy could not be developed. Long-term therapists might continue to use the hourly charge for clients who can personally finance that, but other therapists can consider alternate ways of charging.

CHARGING BY THE RELIEF OF THE SYMPTOM

Of the many ways to set a fee, the most obvious is to charge for the cure of a symptom rather than the number of hours sitting in the presence of the client. Each problem can have a designated fee. There is a precedent for this in medicine, where a surgeon charges by an action, in contrast to a pediatrician, who charges by the hour or any portion thereof as an office visit.

In the field of therapy there are also precedents. Masters and Johnson charge a flat fee for sexual problems, with consultation for a period of time afterward. Milton Erickson was known to say to parents who brought in a problem child, "I'll send you a bill when he is over the problem."

There are also people charging a fee per phobia rather than charging by the hour. I understand a group is charging $300.00 to cure any phobia. Anticipating quick results, they will continue to see a person for that fee until the phobia is gone. Another way we are already charging by this method is when we accept time-limited therapy by insurance companies. To see a client for only 20 interviews at a set fee is to charge a set price for the relief of a symptom. The difference is that if the therapist resolves the symptom in only three sessions, he or she cannot collect for the remaining 17 hours, as might be done with a flat fee.

What are the problems in setting a fee for the successful relief of a symptom? First, the therapist has to be able to resolve the problem. That is what everyone attending brief therapy workshops is learning to do. If brief therapy can be successfully taught, as the teachers claim, there is no reason that payment cannot be made on the basis of success. There will also be the need to protect both client and therapist with any price arrangement. The client might be offered a choice: payment by the hour into an uncertain future, or a flat fee for getting over a specific problem. The contract would have to be precise in problem and goal. What if there is an ambiguous outcome? One way to protect therapist and client would be to have an escrow account. The fee could be put into it until the problem is over. On those occasions when client and therapist disagree, an arbitrator can be available.

Such procedures can be worked out since they are simply part of setting up a new system. A more important issue is setting the fee. How much for relieving a depression, if that category is used? How much for solving school avoidance? What is the price to stop an alcoholic from drinking? If a person has several problems, can priorities be listed? There might also be contingency fees for relapses. These are important issues, and resolving them will bring more precision into the therapy field. There will need to be a therapy manual rather different from the current DSM-III, which is irrelevant to therapy. Such a manual would essentially be a price-per-problem listing. One can hope that this arrangement will not lead to price cutting to compete for the insurance dollar. Obviously, the arrangement of payment per symptom will be met with enthusiasm by therapy contractors.

As this pricing system develops, most therapists will first think of correlating outcome with the number of hours to achieve the goal. In time it will be recognized that the issue is types of intervention rather than time. An example is the medication interview of a psychiatrist. Once they charged by the hour, sometimes regretting that they could not see more patients per hour, like other doctors. Then they discovered they could charge the same hourly fee for a medication interview and yet see clients for only 10 minutes. This increased their fee to six times the previous income per hour. Then the medication interview was set for a fee independent of hours. I know of one practitioner who has 60 medication interviews per day, charging what would once have been the fee for 60 hours. This can be a model for brief therapists. They might not achieve that large a number of clients per hour, but they can see clients for 10 or 15 minutes rather than an hour and so increase their incomes by several times.

Obviously there are a variety of ways of charging fees. The problem is complex, but it is solvable. A positive thought is that spontaneous remission is not uncommon and can be as high as 40% to 50%, according to waiting list studies. If that is so, therapists can be rather incompetent and still get a fee in almost half their cases, as they do now.

Once a few therapists have the confidence to charge on the basis of outcome, others will have to follow to stay in business. One important effect will occur in training programs as therapy requires more skill and becomes more brief and precise. It might ultimately be that teachers will be paid by particular therapy techniques successfully taught instead of being paid by the hour or the semester. Just as client fees can be determined by results, so can the fees for training.

At the moment it is the client who risks money and time by going to a therapist with no guarantee of change, with no limit on the length of time of therapy, and no way of knowing the ultimate cost. When a fee is charged for the successful resolution of a problem, it will be the therapist who takes that risk. The therapist must either change someone or continue to see him or her for unpaid interviews while more lucrative clients are waiting. With the past arrangement of pay by the hour, it was the client who could go broke or waste hours, months, or years of his or her time in therapy. With the fee-for-a-problem arrangement, it is the therapist who can go broke or waste time. Is that not something we are willing to risk rather than impose it on clients, since we therapists are kindly and helpful people?

CHAPTER 2

Strategies and Metaphors of Brief Therapy
Cloé Madanes

I will propose a way of thinking about therapy so it is organized and systematic. The ideas are part of a strategic approach to therapy where the therapist takes responsibility for what happens in the therapy room and plans a strategy for each particular case. The main therapeutic tool is the directive, which is to strategic therapy what the interpretation is to psychoanalysis. The therapist takes responsibility for change and practices respect—diagnostic labels are not used. No one is labeled chronic or hopeless. Only death is unsolvable and even that depends on one's spiritual orientation. Humor is frequently used because it helps to raise people to a higher level of being. An interactional view assumes that to solve a problem it is necessary to change the social context in which the problem takes place. This context is usually the family.

Metaphorical communication is central to therapy. If we did not express ourselves metaphorically, people would state their problems clearly and therapists would have no difficulty in understanding them. But things are not so simple. Messages are not always what they appear to be. We are all familiar with the idea that a message can be a metaphor for another message. For example, if I say, "You give me a headache," I may be referring to more than one kind of pain. A more unusual idea is that the interaction between two people can be a metaphor for another interaction. For example, a husband may come home upset and worried, and his wife may try to reassure and comfort him. If their child develops a recurrent pain, the father may come home and try to reassure and comfort the child in the same way that the wife was previously reassuring and comforting him. The father's involvement with the child is a metaphor for the wife's involvement with the husband. Also, one interaction replaces the other, because when the father is helping the son, the wife is not involved in helping the husband.

There are several interactional functions of metaphors. The first is to communicate: A son's violence, for example, may be expressing the mother's rage. A second function is to displace: A mother's frustration with her son may be a metaphor for her frustration with her husband and may replace that frustration. A third function is to promote closeness and attach people to one another: A quarrel between father and daughter, for example, may be a metaphor for the resentments between husband and wife which are expressed through the daughter, in this way bringing the couple together. When communication is metaphorical, problems are difficult to solve because messages do not refer to what they seem to say and people are caught in endless, repetitive sequences.

I will describe four different levels of family interaction and the metaphors characteristic of each level. Each level corresponds to specific types of problems. I also will present four strategies to use at each level and the therapeutic metaphors that apply to each strategy. Some of these strategies are classic; some are new and previously unpublished.

LEVEL I. TO DOMINATE AND TO CONTROL

At the lower level people are interested mainly in dominating each other and struggling for control and power over their own lives and over the lives of others. Typical problems are delinquency, some forms of drug abuse, behavioral problems, and bizarre behavior. Family members oppose each other in antagonistic ways, and the presenting problem can best be understood as an attempt to gain power over significant others. Power is used for personal advantage; relationships are mostly exploitative. Each individual's goal seems to be to dominate for his or her own benefit. The main emotion of family members is fear, since control and dominance are ensured through intimidation and exploitation. The therapist needs to redistribute power among family members and to change the way power is used.

Communication among family members centers around metaphors of crime, war, and punishment. Distance between relatives is presented as total separation when, in fact, there is intense involvement. Differences are seen as irreconcilable, when, in fact, personalities clash because they are similar.

For example, a family came to therapy because their 17-year-old son was spraying gasoline around the foundation of the house and playing with matches. He also threatened his mother with violence and was obnoxious in many ways. The parents too were loud and obnoxious and had been violent with each other in the past. It would have been possible to hypothesize that the son was worried about the many problems of the parents and was trying to help them by calling attention to himself. This was probably true, but not the most relevant way of thinking. What was urgent was to gain power over the young man's behavior so the family would not burn up in a fire.

The therapeutic strategies of choice for this first, most primitive level of family interaction are: correcting the hierarchy, negotiations and contracts, changing benefits, and rituals and ordeals.

1. Correcting the Hierarchy

When adolescents or young adults are antisocial, or out of control, and the parents are reasonably benevolent, they can be put in charge of establishing control over their offspring by agreeing on rules for them and on consequences if the rules are not followed. Likewise, grandparents and other relatives can be put in charge of the children. The idea is that the older relatives will provide the necessary kindly guidance to reorient the young person to socially acceptable behavior. In so doing, the older relatives will come together in agreement and resolve conflicts that may have caused the young person's outrage to begin with. The therapist introduces metaphors of the rules and regulations that ensure truce, peace, survival, and fair punishment and compensation.

Sometimes in order to put parents in charge of their children, it is necessary to take power away from professionals. A protective services worker may be intruding into a family and causing more strife and violence, a probation officer may be divesting parents of authority, or schoolteachers may oppress or discriminate against a child. The therapist needs to defend the family's rights—for example, by transferring power from a protective services worker to a grandmother or from a probation officer to a father—and to organize parents to protect a child and defend his or her integrity against the court system or the school system.

2. Negotiations and Contracts

Negotiations about money, children, relatives, leisure time, and sex are part of every marital and family therapy. The therapist helps family members express their preferences and compromise with each other. These negotiations are often written as contracts between family members. All the work of the therapy may consist of negotiating a contract and encouraging the family to respect the terms.

Negotiations are particularly important when violence is related to disagreements about money. One solution is to make a contract about money so that violence is discouraged. For example, in a case where a husband was abusing his wife, he was asked to put a thousand dollars in an escrow account. The husband then was asked to sign a contract with the therapist that if he hit the wife again, she would take all the money and give it to her mother, or to her children from a previous marriage. If he did not hit his wife, at the end of a year the couple would use the money to go on a vacation together. There are many possible variations of this strategy, but the principle is simple: to make the consequences of the violence more unpleasant to the victimizer than to the victim. Between husband and wife or parent and child agreements can be made so that confrontation is prevented. Arguments about money may be metaphorical of disagreements about sex; sexual unhappiness may be expressing conflicts with in-laws, and so on.

3. Changing Benefits

Sometimes hostile acts by a family member are rewarded with attention and concern. In these cases it is useful to reverse the situation so that hostility by one family member results in gratification rather than suffering for others. For example, when one brother is very good and another brother is very bad, the therapist can arrange that every time the bad one misbehaves, the good one will get a present or a special privilege. Instead of the bad brother being punished, the "goody-goody" brother is rewarded. Not only is the presenting problem solved, but the relationship between the siblings changes.

4. Rituals and Ordeals

Rituals are useful in marking the transition from one stage of family life to another or to indicate a transition in a relationship. The drama of the ritual should be commensurate with the severity of the problem presented to therapy. For minor problems, a birthday party or a trip to visit relatives may be appropriate. A serious transition may require, for example, a ceremony of renewal of marital vows.

Rituals are particularly indicated when people have to overcome bad things they have done to each other. In a therapy where the husband had abused the wife and she had attempted to murder him, the couple was asked to cut off their hair, put it in a jar, take the jar to the top of the mountain where George Washington took Martha when he was courting her, and bury the jar under a certain tree. Together with their hair they would be burying their past and all the horrible things they had done to one another. Yet knowing where their hair had been buried, they could return to that place under the tree when they needed to remember the past so that they would not repeat it. Cutting off people's hair might seem extreme, but when the problem is attempted murder, cutting off the hair is not very serious. The more extreme the problem, the more extreme the ritual that the therapist devises. Rituals are metaphors that bring people together in positive ways.

The ordeal is a strategy devised by Milton Erickson to make it more difficult for a person to have a symptom than not to have it (Haley, 1984). A man with insomnia, for example, may be told that if he does not fall asleep by a certain time he has to get up and scrub the floors. The ordeal should be more unpleasant than the symptom but beneficial to the symptomatic person.

Interactional ordeals are particularly interesting. An ordeal could be for a husband to give his wife, or better yet his mother-in-law, a present every time the undesirable behavior occurs. The ordeal is something that the person dislikes but that would improve his relationship with significant others.

LEVEL II.   TO BE LOVED

At the first level people are motivated by a desire to dominate one another. At the second, somewhat higher level, people are motivated by the desire to be loved. Typical problems are psychosomatic symptoms, depression, anxiety, phobias, eating disorders, and loneliness. Family members are involved in a struggle to be cared for that often leads to self-inflicted violence. A child might seek to be punished as a way of obtaining attention, even of a negative kind. A spouse may develop an incapacitating symptom in the hope of eliciting concern from the other spouse. Rivalry, discrimination, and antagonism often are based on a desire to be specially favored. The wish to be loved and appreciated can bring out the best qualities in people but it can also result in selfishness and destructiveness. The main emotion among family members is desire, since needs never seem to be fulfilled and there is always frustration and discomfort. Interactions are characterized by excessive demands and criticism. The therapist needs to redistribute love among family members.

Communication centers around metaphors of internal strife, pain, and emptiness. Characteristically, when one person is upset, another gets sick. Anger at others becomes internal pain. Family members intrude on each other's bodily functions, determining, for example, what another should or should not eat, or, at the other extreme, they are totally indifferent to basic needs for love and comfort. Boundaries are ill-defined and people feel for each other at a visceral level in symmetrical ways. There is not the complementarity that is necessary for an individual to feel loved. Metaphors are about being identical, about body parts and functions, and about physical illness. There is a preoccupation with sex and with material possessions. Blackmail and manipulation replace direct confrontation. Conversation is often about unsatisfied needs and desires.

The therapist's strategies of choice include introducing metaphors of make-believe and playfulness to move conflicts away from the concrete, physical level at which they are experienced and into a more abstract, mental and relational realm. Symbols are introduced as props and actions are performed symbolically. In one case, where a mother was asked to care for a sick child, she was given a nurse's uniform to wear as a symbol of giving love through action instead of through identification. A 12-year-old firesetter and his father set controlled prescribed fires, playing with make-believe danger instead of burning up with frustration and anger.

Spouses disagree, complain, and reassure each other in prescribed ways. Symptoms are acted out between family members instead of experienced internally. A bulimic, for example, mushes up food and flushes it down the toilet in the family's presence instead of secretly binging and vomiting. A depressed man pretends to be depressed and is comforted by his wife who cannot be certain whether or not he is pretending.

The therapist arranges for metaphors of contentment and reassurance to replace the metaphors of emptiness and desire. Reality and fantasy are deliberately confused. The message "This is pain" is replaced by the message "This is play."

At this level where people are seeking to be loved, the best strategies to use are: changing the way parents are involved with their children, prescribing the symptom or some aspect of the symptom, prescribing the symbolic act, and prescribing the pretending of the symptom.

1. Changing a Parent's Involvement

A therapist may observe that a child's disturbing behavior has the function of involving an otherwise distant father who interacts with the child by punishing him, but who is still otherwise indifferent. The strategy is to engage the father with the boy in positive ways, such as playing together, so the boy need not misbehave to maintain a relationship with his father.

Instead of being withdrawn, a parent may be overinvolved with a child in the sense that there may be an intense involvement around a symptom in a child and not around other areas of a child's life. A strategy is to keep parent and child intensely involved with each other but around other issues. For example, a bulimic daughter was intensely involved with her father, a physician who constantly criticized the young woman's eating habits. She constantly mortified him by eating junk foods and abusing her body through vomiting and laxatives. The strategy was to insist that every day father and daughter have a conversation about politics—the father was liberal and the daughter was a right-wing conservative. These conversations could take the form of heated arguments but there would no longer be any comments about food. The father would not criticize the daughter's habits and she would not tell him what she was doing to her body. The overinvolvement of father and daughter changed from food to politics, their relationship became more interesting, and she overcame her bulimia.

A related strategy is to change the memory of an adult's involvement with his or her parents in the past. This strategy is useful with people who are tormented with low self-esteem because of memories of being victimized by their parents. The strategy is to say that there must have been someone kindly in the person's childhood who has perhaps been forgotten but who must have existed and whose influence explains the good qualities that the person presents today. One can suggest that perhaps it was a grandmother, an uncle, or an aunt, maybe even a schoolteacher. Slowly the person will begin to remember someone and to build on this memory. Our childhood memories are no more than a few isolated episodes to which we attribute meaning and continuity. We assume that because we remember one episode, it is representative of many similar episodes that must have taken place. When a new memory of a kindly person is retrieved, the therapist can say that if one or two kindly actions, are remembered, there must have been many more. The therapist also can suggest that every time a bad memory comes to mind, it should be counteracted with the new-found memories of the kindly grandmother, for example, so that the person will carry inside himself the image of the good grandmother to counteract the image of the cruel father.

2. Prescribing the Symptom

This was the first paradoxical strategy described in the therapy literature. The idea was that if a person came to therapy to get over a symptom, the therapist asked him to have more of the problem he was trying to solve. For example, if it was stomachaches, he was asked to have more stomachaches, to have them at a certain time, in a certain place, and so on. A natural development of this strategy is to have parents prescribe the symptom to a child. For example, if the child is a firesetter, the father will have him setting fires under his supervision several times a day, so that setting fires becomes an obligation, like homework.

Another variation of this strategy is to prescribe where, when, and how the symptom will take place. A depressed man, for example, can be asked to get up early in the morning to sit in a special chair and be depressed. This strategy is particularly useful with couples who quarrel a great deal. They are instructed that every day at a specified time they are to meet in a room (e.g., the dining room) and for 10 minutes one spouse, looking the other in the eye, will complain, criticize, and express all of his or her resentments and disappointments. The other spouse is only to answer at the end of the 10 minutes: "I'm sorry, dear," and nothing more. Then it is the other one's turn to complain and the first one is to say only, "I'm sorry, dear." At no other time is either of them to complain or criticize the other except for those specific 20 minutes and in the manner prescribed. Under the guise of improving communication, communication is in fact blocked and negative sequences are discouraged.

3. Prescribing the Symbolic Act

When people are involved in compulsive self-destructive behaviors, a strategy is to ask them to perform repetitively an act that is symbolic of the self-destructive act but without the self-destructive consequences. Self-destructive behaviors are usually a misguided attempt to punish someone who does not provide enough love and attention. So the symbolic act should involve a certain punitiveness toward those whom the person is symbolically punishing. This strategy is particularly useful with bulimics and with people who engage in acts such as pulling out their hair or sticking pins in themselves. In the case of a bulimic, for example, the therapist can organize the family to buy all the junk food that she prefers for binging (fried chicken, Oreo cookies, cheap ice cream, French fries, etc.) and set it out on the kitchen counter. In the presence of the family, the bulimic is to mush up all the food with her hands in a way that symbolizes what goes on in the stomach when it digests food. When the food is all mushed, she is to throw it down the toilet. If the toilet clogs, the family member whom the bulimic loves or resents (for example, the father) is the only one allowed to unclog the toilet. The act symbolizes not only what the bulimic does to herself, but also what she puts her family through.

A different way of using symbols is the strategy of prescribing the metaphor. Here the therapist selects the most important elements of a situation, translates them to a metaphorical level, and presents them as the ingredients of a story, essay, or play for the couple or individual to develop. For example, in working with a couple the therapist can ask them to write an essay about how they would advise an imaginary organization to solve difficulties such as conflicts between the directors and threats to leave the organization. Each spouse is given an imaginary problem to resolve and each problem is metaphorical of the couple's own difficulties. Milton Erickson used to tell stories, based on the patient's situation, that would contain suggestions for solutions to the patient's dilemma. This is a similar strategy, but the clients create their own metaphors and find their own solution.

4. Prescribing the Pretending of the Symptom

A child may have a stomachache to obtain love and dedication from the parents. A husband may be depressed so that his wife will comfort him. In these cases the function of the symptom is a personal gain for the symptomatic person, and the benefit consists of receiving love. The therapist can arrange for the child to pretend to have the stomachache and for the parents to comfort him as if it were a real stomachache. The depressed husband can be asked to pretend to be depressed and the wife to take care of him as if his depression were real. When the benefit is obtained for the pretend symptom, the real symptom is no longer necessary.

LEVEL III.   TO LOVE AND TO PROTECT

At the first level people were motivated by the desire to dominate one another and at the second level they were motivated by the desire to be loved. At the third, still higher level, people are motivated by the desire to love and protect others. The wish to love and protect can bring out our highest qualities of compassion, generosity, and kindness. It also may elicit intrusiveness, possessiveness, domination, and violence. This intrusion and violence is often justified in the name of love.

The parent who punishes for the child's "own good," the lover who dominates to protect, and the teacher who criticizes to enlighten are all examples of love that leads to violence. When one is powerless to take care of the object of one's love, one resorts to indirect means of caring for others. A child, for example, might distract a parent from his problems by developing unreasonable fears or by ruthlessly attacking those around him. The parent, concerned about the child, may temporarily take respite from his own problems to take care of the child. The child, by arranging this respite, is offering love and protection to the parent. This love, however, is at the cost of the child's sacrifice and compromises his own desires, accomplishments, and fulfillment. This love is also violent toward the parent in that it manipulates him/her toward what the child has arranged. The main emotion among family members is despair, since the wish to love and protect others is the highest of man's inclinations, yet the seeds of violence are contained within that desire. Typical problems presented to therapy are suicide threats and attempts, abuse and neglect, guilt, obsessions, temper tantrums, and thought disorders. The therapist needs to change the way family members protect and love each other and who takes care of whom.

Communication between family members centers around death, hopelessness, exhaustion, loss of control, and guilt. Characteristically, when one person in the family is upset, another wants to die. Metaphors are of imprisonment, entrapment, and loss of freedom. People feel they have lost control of their own thoughts and their own lives since an individual's actions have life or death repercussions on other family members. There is competition among some family members for who is more guilty and more self-destructive, while other family members are idealized as kindly and worthy of love and protection. The therapist needs to introduce metaphors of togetherness, love, fun, and happiness, reversing who is helpful and who needs to be helped. Family members playfully enact situations where parents are helpless and children are helpful. Love is redirected and accepted. As children comfort and advise their parents, hopefulness replaces despair. The family members who are out of control or suicidal recover self-control as they advise and help the others.

At this level the best strategies are: to reunite family members; to orient people toward the future and to deeds of reparation; to change who is helpful to whom; and to empower children to be appropriately helpful to their parents.

1. Reuniting Family Members

When a problem brought to therapy is related to the pain of separation and exclusion from a loved person, the task of the therapist is to reconcile and reunite family members and to heal old wounds so that separation is no longer necessary. For example, a woman came to therapy because of anxiety attacks and panic that she thought were related to conflicts with her lover. However, she had three adult sons who for two years had disappeared from her life; they did not write or call, and she did not know whether they were dead or alive. The therapist assisted her, with the help of her separated husband, to find the sons through contacts with friends, relatives, and police. There was a family reconciliation where everybody came together at the mother's house and resumed communication from then on. The woman recovered from her anxiety attacks.

Sometimes one of the spouses in a couple loves the other and wants to stay in the marriage while the other spouse is rejecting, resentful, and refuses to come to therapy. In these cases, often the best strategy is to coach the loving spouse on how to win back the other one, how to understand the other spouse, how to respect his or her freedom, how to give the kind of love that the other one wants, etc. Similarly, sometimes it is necessary to coach a parent on how to deal with a child and sometimes it is necessary to coach a child on how to put up with, sympathize with, and take care of a parent.

When an individual is so alienated that self-inflicted violence has reached the point of a threat of suicide, and the therapist judges that the relatives truly want the person to live rather than secretly desire the person's death, hospitalization can be prevented by organizing a suicide watch in the home. All dangerous instruments, such as knives, scissors, and so forth, are removed from the house and family members take turns at watching the suicidal person 24 hours a day. The suicidal person, moved by this love and concern, eventually abandons the suicide threats.

2. Changing Who Is Helpful to Whom

Sometimes the benefit for the symptomatic person is altruistic and the function of the symptom is to help someone else. For example, the daughter of a depressed mother may make a suicide attempt, which forces the mother to come out of her depression to help her daughter. The girl's suicide attempt is helpful to the mother in that it makes her pull herself together and behave like a mother to a daughter who needs her. The strategy is to ask the mother to pretend to be depressed and the daughter to pretend to help the mother in age-appropriate ways, for example by saying reassuring things, entertaining her with games, expressing love directly, and so on. The hypothesis is that the depressed mother is covertly asking the daughter for help and the daughter is covertly helping the mother by attempting suicide. The pretending makes the mother's covert request overt and provides the daughter with appropriate and not self-destructive ways of helping her mother.

Another strategy is to change who has the symptom. This is an idea based on an important value of American culture: taking turns. In America people take turns at speaking and do not interrupt each other, they stand in line, and they take turns at playing, at chores, in love, and in sex. When a family presents with an adolescent or child who is very bad and other children who are very good, it is natural to suggest to the siblings that it is not fair that only one should be bad and ruin his or her life by being the focus of attention and providing thrills for the rest of the family. If the other children took their turn, the bad one could sometimes be good and get on with his life. This makes explicit an implicit family rule in a way that moves the good siblings to change so that the bad one need no longer be bad. The therapist appeals to the love between siblings and to their sense of fair play.

3. Reversing the Hierarchy

This strategy is useful when parents present as incompetent, helpless, physically ill, addicted to drugs or alcohol, abusive, or neglectful. The children love and protect the parents and the parents are not giving love and protection to the children. Nothing is asked of the parent or parents. The children are put in charge of one aspect of the parents' life, their happiness, and the therapist asks them how the parents could be happier. Should they go out more often? To a movie? To a restaurant? Perhaps they could go away for the weekend or have a candlelight dinner at home. Maybe the children could cook and serve the dinner. As the discussion proceeds, the therapist encourages the children to make concrete suggestions, for example, what movie the parents will see, what restaurant they will go to. Children may be put in charge of taking care of themselves and of the parent, of organizing the parents to get along better with each other so they can be happier, and of organizing the household and the family's good times. All this is done in age-appropriate and playful ways so that there is no burden to the children; on the contrary, they are relieved to be able to express their love and to take care of their parents. The children are not really in charge: The whole organization is in play, more in fantasy than in reality. The parents are moved as they experience their children's love for them and respond in kind, correcting the hierarchy and taking responsibility for themselves and for their children.

4. Memorable Actions

Sometimes people present to therapy with feelings of depression, worthlessness, and guilt. They are obsessed with thoughts about their failure and about the lack of meaning in their lives. Instead of arguing with them, the therapist can agree that they may be worthless and guilty but since they themselves are not important, they should give more of themselves to others for whom life, in contrast, is important. They should select a group of people, preferably those somehow related to their guilt feelings, and do anonymous good deeds for them. For example, a Vietnam war veteran haunted by visions of atrocities witnessed or committed, could be sent to do good deeds such as donating money, time, or work to organizations that care for Vietnamese orphans. The good deed should preferably be anonymous so that there is no question that it is not done for reward or recognition but purely for reparation and altruism. In one case of a religious black physician who came to therapy obsessed with guilt because he loved a woman more than he loved God, he was told that every time he had such thoughts of his own sinfulness, he was to do a good deed that would please God. For example, he had to find a homeless person and provide free medical care, or he had to go to a high school in a poor black neighborhood and talk to the students, particularly to the girls, to explain how they too could come out of poverty and become successful professionals like himself. Knowing that he had a way to counter his guilt, he was able to marry the woman he loved.

Another strategy for orienting people towards positive actions is creating good memories. Some couples come in bickering and fighting about every grim, menial detail of life. They quarrel about who will do the dishes, who will take out the garbage, who will clean the garage, who said what to whom. They focus on every sordid detail of life and ignore their love for each other. The strategy is carried out in steps. First, the therapist asks the couple to identify the best moments of their lives together. For example, what were the best moments of their courtship or their honeymoon? If the therapist insists, even the most sordid people will come up with wonderful stories about things they did many years before. Then the therapist emphasizes that 10 years from now, who did the dishes and who took out the garbage is not going to be remembered.

Only that which is special, unique, or unusual is remembered. So at the end of the session, the therapist directs the couple to do something in the next week or two that will be remembered positively 10 years from now. For a few sessions, every session, the therapist gives only this directive. This strategy brings out the best in people and raises them out of their grimness.

LEVEL IV.   TO REPENT AND TO FORGIVE

At the first level I described how people are motivated by the desire to dominate, at the second level people are motivated by the desire to be loved, and at the third level the motivation is to love and protect. At the fourth level the main issue between family members is to repent and to forgive. Typical problems are incest, sexual abuse, and sadistic acts. When people have inflicted trauma on each other and have suffered injustices and violence, interactions are characterized by grief, resentment, lies, secrecy, deceit, self-deprecation, isolation, and dissociation. The main emotion is shame because of what one has done, or because of what one has refrained from doing, or because one cannot forgive. If family members are to continue to relate to one another, the therapist needs to redistribute who in the family carries the shame since it is often the victims who are blamed.

Communication among family members is sparse and centers around secrecy. They are afraid of revelations that will bring on more shame, but secrecy maintains inappropriate coalitions and makes incest and abuse possible. Metaphors are of ignorance and lack of conscience, empathy, and responsibility. People behave like predator and victim.

The therapist introduces metaphors of spirituality and unity, emphasizing symbols of compassion and higher emotion. Family members are moved step by step from abuse to repentance, reparation, and protection of one another. Reality and responsibility are emphasized and secrecy and hypocrisy are replaced with open communication and sincerity.

At this level the best strategies are: to create an atmosphere of higher emotions; to find protectors for the victims in the family; and to elicit repentance, forgiveness, compassion, and a sense of unity with others.

1. Creating a Positive Framework

This includes improving the quality of life and creating an atmosphere of higher emotions. The therapist makes an effort to improve communication, assertiveness, and the ability to give and receive love.

Often a therapist needs to raise people away from the grimness of their situation into a better way of being. It is useful to start every session, and to remind people during the session, that they have come to therapy out of love and concern for each other and that they are seeking a better way of being and of relating to each other. These comments by the therapist prevent angry interactions and petty hostilities between family members.

Humor and the use of the absurd are an important part of this strategy. When people are irrationally grim, the introduction of playfulness can elicit new behaviors and bring about new alternatives. What makes change possible is the therapist's ability to be optimistic and to see what is funny or appealing in a grim situation.

2. Finding a Protector

In cases of abuse and neglect, the very existence of the family unit is threatened. The therapist needs to look for strong, responsible people in the extended family or in the community and transfer responsibility to them and away from professional helpers. The transfer needs to happen gradually and in stages, so that ultimately, under the care of the protector, family members will be able to forgive each other. For example, if an adolescent has been abused by a father, a responsible uncle or grandmother can be put in charge of supervising the family to make sure that this will not happen again. At first the family will be supervised by both the protective services worker and the uncle, then only by the uncle, who will report to the protective services worker, and finally by the uncle alone, with the worker remaining available to reopen the case if necessary.

3. Repentance and Reparation

This is a strategy designed for situations where there has been sexual abuse within the family, typically from an older brother to a younger sibling. However, it can be adapted to situations of incest between father and daughter, to physical abuse, and even to situations where the abuse happened a long time ago. The strategy is therapeutic for both the victim and the victimizer, and it can be modified for therapies that do not include the victimizer or the victim.

The therapy takes place in steps. First, the therapist gathers the whole family and obtains as detailed an account of the sexual offense as possible, in terms of who did what to whom, when, where, and so on. This is in itself therapeutic as it is usually the first time that the family discusses the events openly. This is an important step because it is essential in these cases to violate secrets in the family. Incest is possible because it is secret. Then the therapist asks the offender why what he did was wrong. The offender gives reasons such as that it was violent, it is against his or her religion and against the law. The therapist might ask the parents or other family members to help the offender and give reasons. Then the therapist says that it was wrong for all those reasons but also for another most important reason, that is that a sexual offense causes spiritual pain or a pain in the heart. The therapist explains that somehow sexuality and spirituality are linked and that is why a sexual attack is worse than other attacks. Also, a sexual attack causes a pain not only in the heart of the victim, but also in the heart of the victimizer because it is so horrible to do such a thing to another person, particularly one whom one loves, such as a family member. At this point, usually the family offers the information that the victimizer was also molested and perhaps that other people in the family have also been molested. The therapist listens sympathetically and emphasizes how they all understand this spiritual pain and adds that the sexual offense also caused a spiritual pain to the mother, to the father, and to the siblings, who would have wanted to protect the victim.

The therapist then asks the offender to get on his knees and express repentance and sorrow for what he has done. The victim can forgive him if she wants to, but she does not have to. After the family agrees that the offender's repentance and apology are sincere, the rest of the family gets on their knees in front of the victim to express sorrow for not having protected her. If the victim is not present, the offender can repent in front of the family. If the offender is the father, he can get on his knees in front of the mother also and express sorrow for what he did. If the offender is dead or disappeared, still the rest of the family must apologize to the victim.

After this, the therapist discusses with the family what will be the consequences should something like this ever happen again and encourages the family toward the most drastic consequences, such as expulsion from the family. Then the therapist discusses how to find one or several protectors for the victim. The offender is asked to do a deed of reparation, which should involve some sacrifice and usually has to do with working to set up a special fund for the education of the victim. Normal activities for both the victim and the victimizer are discussed and they are encouraged to each interact with their own peers. This includes discussions with the offender about proper sexual behavior and conversations with the victim about how all this will be forgotten and is not as important as other aspects of her life, such as her friends, her interests, and so on.

Before the therapy can be ended, the therapist needs to restore the mother's love for the offender, and to encourage an appropriate relationship between the offender and the victim where the offender becomes a protector and not a victimizer. Also, the therapist needs to help the offender to forgive himself. Throughout the therapy it is necessary to dispel implications of provocation and emphasize that the victim was not responsible for the acts of the victimizer.

4. Compassion and Unity

This strategy is useful for working with individuals who have been the victims of trauma and injustice and are obsessed with trying to remember and to understand why this happened to them. After spending the necessary time to understand the person and to help him recover his memories, it is important to reach closure and end the subject so that the person can move on to better things in life. The therapist accomplishes this by talking about how what really happened to that particular person is not so important. For example, if a woman is concerned about whether she was sexually molested, what matters is that so many millions of women have been abused through the centuries that each one carries within her the memory of all those women who suffered, and their pain is each woman's pain. If a man was abandoned by his mother when he was a child, what matters is that so many children suffer terrible injustice and torment without reason or explanation. What is important is for each one to make some contribution toward ending that pain. In fact, the adult person has more in common with the therapist or with a friend than with that child that he once was and who was abused or neglected. This appeal to separate from the past while at the same time developing a sense of unity with the rest of humanity helps to disengage people from past traumas and to get on with their lives.

CONCLUSION

To summarize, I have presented my favorite strategies for changing metaphors of strife and conflict to metaphors of love. All problems brought to therapy can be said to stem from the dilemma between love and violence. This dilemma appears at different levels as the fear of a struggle for power, as the desire to be loved, as the despair of not being able to love and protect, and as the shame of not repenting and not forgiving.

REFERENCE

Haley, J. (1984). *Ordeal Therapy: Unusual Ways to Change Behavior*. San Francisco: Jossey-Bass.

CHAPTER 3

Brief Psychotherapy: Tautology or Oxymoron?

Arnold A. Lazarus and Allen Fay

> *All pleasantries ought to be short—and for that matter, gravities too.*
>
> —Voltaire

In the classic little book *The Elements of Style*, E. B. White recounted how William Strunk, Jr., waxed eloquently on the beauty of brevity in the use of English, and how he recommended pruning deadwood from cumbersome sentences:

> Vigorous writing is concise. A sentence should contain no unnecessary words, a paragraph no unnecessary sentences, for the same reason that a drawing should have no unnecessary lines and a machine no unnecessary parts. This requires not that the writer make all his sentences short, or that he avoid all detail and treat his subject only in outline, but that every word tell. (Strunk & White, 1979, p. 23)

Analogizing from the elements of literary style to the fundamentals of effective psychotherapy, we contend that:

> Good therapy is precise. A session should contain no unnecessary psychological tests, no protracted or redundant methods, no needless techniques, no prolonged silence, and as

little dilatory rhetoric as possible. This requires not that the therapist gloss over important details, nor that he or she forgo thoroughness for the sake of brevity, but that every intervention tell.

While the foregoing is idealistic, from an ethical standpoint, why shouldn't treatment *always* be as brief as possible? Who would tack on additional sessions, administer needless tests, or create unfortunate dependencies, thereby keeping clients in therapy year after year? Only a small minority of exploitative therapists would knowingly and deliberately make prisoners of their patients. But there is an insidious force that compels many clinicians to view long-term treatment as necessary for most, and brief therapy as insufficient for nearly all. Such thinkers receive intermittent reinforcement because some clients do indeed seem to require considerable time to absorb different perspectives and manifest new behaviors. Even straightforward and relatively circumscribed problems sometimes necessitate the passage of time if sustained treatment gains are to ensue. For example, various social and interpersonal skill deficits may call for extended learning and unlearning processes before a degree of efficacy—let alone mastery—is accomplished. Nevertheless, it is important to note that treatment gains often do not require extensive contact with the therapist.

A case in point concerns an intelligent yet extremely unassertive and socially inept 26-year-old woman who nevertheless held a high-paying job as a computer programmer. She was the only child of two alcoholic parents: her father died of cirrhosis of the liver when she was 22. She was an avid reader who took kindly to bibliotherapy, perusing many books by Albert Ellis on RET and several others on assertiveness. She also listened to selected audiocassettes on related topics. The client received 11 treatment sessions that focused mainly on behavior rehearsal, role playing, and cognitive restructuring. Thereafter, she displayed significant gains in social assertiveness and self-acceptance—improvements that have been maintained to date (some two years later). By most standards, 11 sessions is considered "brief" therapy, though in her case these meetings extended over 20 months. She set the pace, often calling two or three days ahead to cancel appointments. "I still need more time to test the waters," she would say. Was this a manifestation of resistance requiring analysis, or would direct exhortation have been indicated to accelerate progress? In many cases, it may be counterproductive to have clients set the treatment pace, but in this instance, it was deemed appropriate. Sometimes, two or three months would elapse between sessions, but there was evidence that during that time she was not stagnating.

Rather, she was continuing to attenuate avoidance behaviors and in her words, "trying things out in my own good time." She controlled the treatment trajectory (perhaps essential, given her background) and the therapist served mainly as guide, coach, and cheerleader. As Hoyt (1989) points out, if "brief" is taken to mean "no more than necessary," two sessions held six months apart might be considered more brief than three months of treatment entailing one or more sessions per week.

WHAT IS BRIEF THERAPY?

While contemplating this presentation on the subject of brief therapy, we found ourselves in a dilemma. In part, the difficulty arises from the confusion between the public use of the term and its professional meaning. For example, does "brief" refer mainly to temporal truncation, or to a specific methodology, or is it defined by the scope and focus of problems addressed? While clearly the duration is limited (though a three-year, five session per week psychoanalysis is still considered brief by many), are the techniques particularly intensive? Are the goals modest? Is brief therapy better or simply more practical, though suboptimal?

It is clear to at least some observers that brief therapy as an area of specialization would not exist were it not for the dominance of the psychodynamic orientation during the major part of this century. Despite the profusion of therapeutic orientations, in many quarters psychotherapy is still synonymous with psychodynamic therapy. Brief therapy as a specialty seems to have arisen in the psychodynamic context, although history is replete with rapid remissions from all kinds of ministrations. Other popular therapies such as Ericksonian, behavior, and cognitive therapies are brief almost by definition, even if they are not uniformly so in practice. These observations have led us to ask whether the term "brief therapy" is a tautology or an oxymoron. That is, is it redundant to say brief therapy, when therapy should always be as brief as possible, or is it contradictory to use the term when one is dealing with transference, resistance, and layers of unconscious material acquired over a lifetime? Perhaps the situation would have been less murky if psychodynamic or psychoanalytic therapy had been referred to all these years as "protracted therapy" and its more recent developments designated "less protracted" or *briefer* therapy. With few exceptions, psychoanalysis was briefer in Freud's time than in the ensuing decades since his death.

In addition to some of Freud's own cases, the roots of brief psychodynamic therapy may be found in the writings of Ferenczi (1926),

Gutheil (1933), Groddeck (1951), and Alexander (Alexander & French, 1946). For example, Groddeck, who was designated the "wild analyst," lamented the length of analytic treatment, and in a 1927 paper entitled "The Duration of Psychoanalysis" (included in Groddeck, 1951), he described the case of a young woman whose continual vomiting after every meal for a month had led to marked weight loss and inability to work. He reported that " . . . her treatment lasted three-quarters-of-an-hour, and the vomiting has never since recurred. In this treatment I used no other means than psychoanalysis" (p. 90). Groddeck was above all a pragmatist: While enamored of Freudian concepts, he espoused and practiced what worked, regardless of its provenance.

In response to such reports, some psychodynamic theorists, having decried short-term therapies as superficial, inferior, and even dangerous, or else designed for those who are not healthy (integrated) enough to tolerate "real" therapy, modified their product. And with good reasons. Brief dynamic therapy satisfies the growing time and economic constraints imposed by consumers and third-party payers, meets the challenge of literally hundreds of competing approaches, helps boost the decimated enrollment in analytic training institutes, and makes outcome research more meaningful. However, our personal reaction to brief psychodynamic therapy is that it is an attempt to make an archaic model work more efficiently, rather like hitting a nail harder and more rapidly instead of putting it in the right place and using power tools (no psychodynamic allusions intended—or unintended for that matter).

It would be preposterous to suggest that therapy, in the sense of helping the client achieve symptom relief, enhanced well-being, and better functioning, should not be as brief as possible. At the same time, there is no limit to what we can learn and how much we can grow. Whereas some clients would persist at therapy interminably for reasons that serve no constructive purpose, others may continue to evolve into fuller, richer, more actualized individuals over a period of many years. Some clients who are neither pathologically dependent nor financially constrained may have an ongoing relationship with a therapist, as a head of state would consult regularly with a political or economic advisor. The patient makes his/her own decisions, but values the input of someone who is astute, trustworthy, objective, and presumably otherwise rational—a rare combination even in a close friend.

Some long-term therapy is not only inefficient (taking longer than necessary because it was insufficiently focused or precise), but even detrimental because of the reinforcement of pathological self-concepts. One of the greatest advantages of the short-term focus is that if the therapy doesn't work, it will be apparent much sooner.

BREVITY—SOME BEHAVIORAL
AND PSYCHODYNAMIC DIFFERENCES

Behaviorists and psychodynamicists have always had their differences. Most significant perhaps was the vigorous denouncements of behavior therapy when first promulgated (e.g., Lazarus, 1971; Salter, 1949; Wolpe, 1958; Wolpe & Lazarus, 1966). The behavioral orientation has always been relatively brief or short-term (Wilson, 1981), while psychoanalytic clinicians insisted that psychotherapy by its very nature must be protracted (and that brief therapy was therefore superficial). Psychoanalysts pointed to early pathogenic experiences that required cautious and painstaking uncovering; warned against premature interpretations; emphasized the slow and tortuous pathway of regressive urges and transference formation; and mandated a lengthy period of working through for the consolidation of lasting gains. Dire consequences were predicted for those highly motivated, action-oriented patients with circumscribed problems (now considered excellent candidates for short-term therapy), whose complaints extinguished after a brief course of systematic desensitization. We were told that these "transference cures" and "flights into health" reflected the unprecedented naiveté of behavior therapy, whose superficial, mechanistic, symptom-centered methods would herald rapid relapse, or, worse yet, "symptom substitution."

Today, without relinquishing their psychodynamic heritage, the analytically oriented practitioners of brief therapy advocate more limited treatment goals, focus on acute symptoms, educate their clients to expect rapid change, and often accelerate confrontation with psychodynamic interpretations. In doing so, they increasingly use techniques that are more directive and behavioral than exploratory (e.g., Davanloo, 1980; Malan, 1976; Mann & Goldman, 1982; Sifneos, 1979; Strupp & Binder, 1984). Nevertheless, they still remain ignorant of or opposed to behavior therapy per se. Brief, short-term, and time-limited psychodynamic practitioners still lean toward self-exploration and the resolution of intrapersonal conflicts. Even with clients complaining of specific fears, phobias, and compulsions, where the evidence points overwhelmingly to the unequaled success of behavioral methods (Barlow, 1988), brief dynamic therapists prefer to select some "focus" for inward exploration (Lazarus & Messer, 1988). In this regard, to paraphrase an old saying, effective treatment depends far less on the hours you put in, than on what you put into those hours.

But opposition to all forms of short-term therapy is still alive and well. In many quarters it is held that "more is better" (despite the absence of data pointing to the superiority of open-ended or long-term treatment), and the alleged virtues of "deep" excursions into the patient's psychohistory are still touted. Nonetheless, as we have already emphasized, socioeconomic pressures for more efficient methods of psychological treatment cannot be disregarded. Apart from these external restraints, many clinicians and educated consumers are taking the position that even those clients who can well afford to be in therapy year after year are better advised to consider shorter-term, focused, targeted, and goal-oriented methods. One may predict that the 1990s will be an era in which brief therapies will proliferate and therapist accountability will be accentuated.

READINESS FOR CHANGE

Howard, Nance, and Myers (1987) have provided specific tactics for matching optimal therapeutic styles to particular clients at various stages of readiness. In this regard, the concept of *client readiness* is fundamental to the selection of appropriate forms of treatment. Prochaska and DiClemente (1986) emphasize a similar issue by referring to four basic stages of change: precontemplation, contemplation, action, and maintenance. In the terminology of the latter authors, precontemplators are the least likely candidates for brief or short-term therapy. From our standpoint, it is most unfortunate when action-oriented clients in a state of readiness for change consult clinicians who focus on precontemplative intrapersonal conflicts and withhold the action-oriented methods that could effect rapid change.

We also believe that there are three major impediments to the development and clinical implementation of rapidly effective therapies: (1) the lack of a sufficiently broad technical armamentarium—largely a result of factionalism within our profession; (2) ignorance of, or inadequate attention to, the biological aspects of "psychological" problems; and (3) the concept of resistance and its elaboration, particularly the notion that the locus of resistance is within the patient (see Fay & Lazarus, 1982; Lazarus & Fay, 1982).

Our position is that "resistance" does not rest with the patient, but hinges on the methodology of the therapy as well as the skill and personal qualities of the therapist (cf. de Shazer, 1985). It is *our* responsibility to find the keys to the puzzle. Sometimes the simplest interventions are immediately effective with previously unresponsive clients, especially when the therapist's technical repertoire and personal style transcend the confines of narrow theoretical perspectives or the conventional decorous norms of professional conduct. We are referring here to numerous procedures, ranging from strategic reframing, to the sudden reversal of reinforcement contingencies, to an unusual combination of medications.

In our view, major factors that have made brevity possible in psychotherapy are the problem-focused and learning-based approaches, development of the systems perspective, and the evolution of sophisticated and effective techniques for biological assessment and intervention. For example, many careers have been stalled because of stage fright (performance anxiety) unresponsive to months and even years of psychotherapy, when a single dose of a beta-adrenergic blocking drug prior to each performance episode effects marked improvement in a majority of subjects (Brantigan, Brantigan, & Joseph, 1982). Although some may engage in circular argument by questioning whether this is therapy and whether the "real" problem has been addressed, the burden of proof is clearly on them. The failure of many therapists to recognize the relevance of biological inputs and the availability of biological solutions contributes heavily to the failure of both short-term and long-term therapy.

TEMPORAL FACTORS

Part of the preparation for this chapter entailed a simple computer search of the literature on brief therapy. The resultant 50-page printout included hundreds of titles and showed that *brief* is definitely in! It would seem that many therapists have penetrated the "time-barrier" in psychotherapy. But how brief is brief? It seems to range from focused single-session therapy (e.g., Bloom, 1981) to as much as 40 or 50 sessions in some quarters, with a median around 20. Ellis (1989) typically conducts individual rational-emotive therapy on a once-a-week basis for 5 to 50 sessions. For some (e.g., Mann, 1973, Mann & Goldman, 1982; Horowitz et al., 1984), one dozen seems to convey a magical quality. With regard to the time-limited concept propounded particularly by Mann (1973), it would seem axiomatic that it is better to fit the treatment to the patient rather than vice versa! While time-limited therapy undoubtedly serves a purpose for some clients, the idea of a 12-session *policy* seems untenable to us, regardless of the selection criteria. For Wells (1982), more than 15 sessions exceeds the definition of short-term. But for practical purposes, it should be known that many health-maintenance organizations (HMOs) and insurance plans provide for brief treatment of up to 20 sessions.

There are many other temporal considerations. Apart from determining how many sessions a client should undergo, there are questions about how long each meeting should last. The standard 50-minute hour seems to be shrinking, and in keeping with popular books on one-minute managers, perhaps we can soon look forward to the 50-second hour. Goulding and Goulding (1979) seem to opt for 20-minute sessions. Barten (1965) wrote about "the 15-minute hour." Patients seen in understaffed public settings receive anywhere from 5 to 30 minutes. The term "brief contact therapy" with sessions lasting from 10 to 20 minutes was discussed in the 1960s (Dreiblatt & Weatherly, 1965; Koegler & Cannon, 1966). Practitioners experimenting with single-session therapies often extend their meetings to 90 to 120 minutes. Hoyt (1989) asks whether Berenbaum's (1969) single 10-hour marathon session is a form of prolonged brief therapy or a brief prolonged therapy. And some of us have mixed memories about those marathon encounter groups that were so fashionable in the 1960s.

The next important temporal factor is the interval between sessions. For whom might six discrete 10-minute sessions on a single day prove more helpful than one continuous 60-minute session? Who should be seen twice daily, thrice weekly, or at intervals up to several months apart? Therapists who work with children (especially hyperactive ones) have rapidly learned how to adjust treatment time to match attention span. But many other therapists are still disinclined to adjust treatment time to suit the individual needs of their clients. Unfortunately, this factor is probably governed by economic considerations. For example, we court disaster by submitting our usual bill to government agencies unless the face-to-face treatment meets the minimum time mandate. And yet, on occasion, a patient has left midway in a therapy hour with the announcement that he/she has derived exactly what was wanted from the session.

Many writers have stressed that "brief psychotherapy" is not necessarily the same as doing therapy briefly. Others have emphasized that differences exist among the terms brief therapy, time-limited therapy, and short-term therapy. In any event, in brief psychotherapy, time is the critical element, *brevity* is the watchword, and the basic message is "don't waste time but seize the moment" (see Hoyt, 1989).

THE PROBLEM-SOLVING EMPHASIS

The work of de Shazer (1985, 1988) exemplifies many of the slogans and intervention patterns of short-term programs. Perhaps the most important is the emphasis on paying attention to the process of *solution* rather than the origin of problems. De Shazer and his colleagues at the Brief Family Therapy Center in Milwaukee, Wisconsin, also stress the importance of developing an intensely cooperative relationship with clients, while paying limited attention to the details of complaints and focusing instead on what the clients are doing that is good for them. We concur, but in addition, as we shall outline presently, we have developed a systematic method of enumerating and remediating pivotal problems.

A relevant vignette that underscores the advantages of seeking immediate solutions and offering corrective prescriptions concerns an abrasive 36-year-old woman who was distraught over the fact "everybody hates me, my husband wants a divorce, I'm about to lose my job, my parents and only sister aren't talking to me, and my one and only friend has just moved out of state." The client was highly intelligent, vivacious, engaging, and in some ways quite likable, but her interpersonal style was adversarial. "Look here," she said, wagging her finger at the therapist, "you'd better get my husband in here and you damn well tell him that some of the things he does really bug me too." With her permission, information from her previous therapist was obtained after the initial interview. The client had been labeled as "psychotic and dangerous," and the therapist volunteered, "At our last meeting she bit me and that's when I terminated our therapy." When asked about her previous therapist's allegations, the client offered the following explanation: "My husband and I were in session and he was making snide remarks which Dr. N allowed to go on. I got angry, leaned over and punched my husband on his shoulder. Now you need to understand that he is 6'2" and weighs 210 pounds and has a black belt in karate. Well Dr. N jumped up and shouted something about disallowing physical violence, although I am a foot smaller and a hundred pounds lighter and my husband knows very well how to ward off serious attackers. Dr. N grabbed my arm and in so doing, dug her nails into me, so I bit her."

The client was neither psychotic nor dangerous, but she fell into many of the 54 "relationship traps" that Fay (1990) has enumerated, such as criticizing, blaming and self-justifying, making accusations, threatening, being right, using negative emotional language, giving orders, and too freely offering advice without being asked. What at first seemed like a complex if not deep-seated deficit responded rapidly to a corrective focus on the client's unfortunate interpersonal style. She was a fast learner, and after a dozen sessions held at fortnightly intervals, she poignantly stated that she was now "popular"—a term she had never used in reference to herself.

MULTIMODAL THERAPY

One of our major concerns about short-term dynamic therapy is that it is only the exceptional patient who is regarded as appropriate for treatment. For example, Davanloo (1978) selected as suitable for his short-term therapy a mere 23% of 575 individuals who were evaluated.

Several years ago, one of us (AL) participated in a panel discussion with Peter Sifneos. After hearing Sifneos describe his selection criteria for his brand of short-term therapy, Lazarus inquired where such healthy people were to be found.

What is needed, in our opinion, is a pragmatic, systematic, eclectic, parsimonious, and effective approach to all clients. It was partly an aversion to the idea of factionalism in therapy, as well as an attempt to achieve a high degree of efficacy, technical specificity, and durability of results in the treatment of all psychological-psychiatric problems and some social problems, that led to the development and refinement of multimodal therapy (Lazarus, 1976, 1989). Multimodal therapy (MMT) is not a school of therapy. Although it is based on certain assumptions about human beings and the genesis of their problems, it is actually more of a schema for the comprehensive and exhaustive assessment of psychological-psychiatric problems and the selection of specific effective interventions. The multimodal approach looks at human personality in terms of seven interactive modalities expressed in the acronym BASIC I.D. The letters stand for behavior, affect, sensation, imagery, cognition, interpersonal, and biological (for euphony, D = drugs is used as the terminal letter of the acronym). The therapist strives to achieve in the client the enhancement of adaptive elements that are underexpressed and the modification of various maladaptive manifestations in these seven domains. While the multimodal orientation is fundamentally short-term (the average treatment length is between 20 and 30 sessions), the assessment and therapy can be shortened even further (10 to 20 sessions). Unlike the brief psychodynamic therapies, brief multimodal therapy, or what we prefer to call *limited goal therapy*, instead of selecting a circumscribed focus, endeavors to cover several pivotal areas in as short a time period as possible. Our clinical impressions to date suggest that limited goal therapy achieves results that are equal to more extensive treatment procedures. It appears to meet the overriding need for psychotherapeutic methods that are both rapid *and* long-lasting. [See Koss and Butcher's (1986) account of research on brief psychotherapy.]

In MMT with adult outpatients, clients are asked to complete a Multimodal Life History Questionnaire (Lazarus, 1989), in order to identify problems across the BASIC I.D. This allows the therapist to construct a Modality Profile (i.e., a list of problems and proposed treatments across the BASIC I.D.). For example, a 33-year-old woman who sought therapy for "depression and anxiety" was found to have a variety of separate yet interactive problems, which are outlined in Table 1.

TABLE 1
Modality Profile

Modality	Problem	Proposed Treatment
B	"Disorganized/sloppy"	Contingency contracting
	Phobic avoidance	Systematic desensitization
	Leaves things to the last minute	Time management
A	Guilt	Explore antecedents and irrational ideas
	Anxiety related to criticism and rejection	Coping imagery and rational disputation
	Sadness/despondency	Explore faulty thinking and encourage her to seek out positive events
S	Fatigue/lower back pain/tension headaches	Relaxation training/physiotherapy exercises
I	Loneliness images/poor self-image/images of failing	Coping imagery exercises
C	Dichotomous reasoning/too many "shoulds"/over-generalizes	Cognitive restructuring
I.	Nontrusting	Risk taking
	Overly competitive	Cooperation training
	Unassertive	Assertiveness training
	Avoids social gatherings	Social skills training
D.	Uses alprazolam p.r.n.	Monitor to avoid dependency
	Overweight	Weight control methods (e.g., contingency contracting, self-monitoring, support group)
	Insufficient exercise	Physical fitness program

(A thorough medical examination replete with laboratory tests revealed no diagnosable contributing organic pathology.)

Thus, 17 problem clusters were identified for which a corresponding number of specific treatment strategies were recommended. While it is not the goal of MMT to eliminate every problem throughout a client's BASIC I.D. (a perfectionistic ideal!), the usual objective is to mitigate *most* of the entries on a Modality Profile. There is often a "ripple effect," in that specific improvements tend to trigger positive changes in areas that were not specifically addressed. In *Brief MMT*, therapist and client select three to five of the most salient problems that call for remediation. In the foregoing case, three problem clusters were given exclusive attention: (1) unassertiveness, especially concerning fears of criticism and rejection; (2) dichotomous reasoning/too many "shoulds"/overgeneralizes; (3) fatigue/lower back pain/tension headaches. These key problems were the primary focus for about 10 sessions. In essence, she was treated by (1) cognitive therapy and RET (Beck, 1987; Ellis & Dryden, 1987), (2) coping imagery techniques (Lazarus, 1982, 1984: Zilbergeld & Lazarus, 1988), (3) various role-playing or behavior rehearsal techniques, and (4) physiotherapy and relaxation exercises prescribed by a physiatrist). A little more than three months of therapy rendered her a more relaxed individual with far fewer dysfunctional beliefs and with a repertoire of frank and forthright interpersonal behaviors. She rated her presenting complaints (depression and anxiety) as 80% improved. A follow-up after eight months showed that her gains had been maintained and that, at her own initiative she had joined a weight reduction group, lost 18 lbs, and had not used Xanax or any other medication for at least six months.

DISCUSSION

It is by no means unusual for clients who receive multimodal therapy to undergo several brief exposures to therapy. [See Cummings (1977) for a discussion of *serial* short-term therapy.] Clients may elect to work on specific problems at one time and then return to address others at a later juncture. Some have received help in specific areas and then have been referred elsewhere for the "finishing touches." To employ a football analogy, it is important for therapists to feel that they do not have to score touchdowns with each client. One may move the client from the 20-yard line to the 40- or 50-yard line and then pass to someone else who moves him or her another 10 or 20 yards. Most recently, for example, a client who had shown excellent progress seemed to reach a plateau after 16 sessions. While impressive gains were evident vis-à-vis his marriage, work relationships, and new-found capacity for "clear thinking," there was no appreciable diminution of his tension headaches or elevated blood pressure (despite relaxation training), and he was unable to quit smoking. Referral to a biofeedback expert led to rapid relief of his headaches and hypertension despite the fact that on two previous occasions he had not responded to this form of treatment. A colleague who specializes in addictive disorders helped him stop smoking by using an elaborate hypnotic induction coupled with aversive imagery.

This proposed network approach calls for familiarity with the clinical skills of a wide referral base within the professional community, and an appreciation of the value of teamwork. The guiding maxim at all times is: *Who or what is best for this individual?* (cf. Paul, 1967). We see clients whose problems cry out for the inclusion of family members, but whose previous therapy has focused entirely on *intra*personal concerns. We see clients who come from family therapists who are so bogged down at the systems level that individual problems are bypassed. Multimodal therapy provides a framework that brings into focus numerous discrete and interactive problems at both the intrapersonal and interpersonal levels of functioning. There are large numbers of clients for whom traditional methods have been disappointing or ineffective. The expanding spectrum of technically eclectic methods (see Norcross, 1986) vastly enlarges the therapist's capacity to offer something useful and relevant to large numbers of individuals. As already emphasized, the 1990s are likely to witness a far greater professional commitment to providing relevant, practical, and short-term therapy to all segments of the community. This will call for a broadening and redefining of professional roles. A distinct advantage of the multimodal orientation is that it provides a definite framework for rapid, but comprehensive assessment; readily incorporates a diversity of helping disciplines within its purview; is open to input from many professions and professionals (including paraprofessionals); and offers a wide range of practical counseling techniques. Multimodal therapy addresses a crucial point underscored by Barten (1971): "The range of problems which we as psychotherapists encounter is itself so great, and the opportunities for interventive measures so varied, that the hope for a single approach would be specious and indeed undesirable" (p. 4).

REFERENCES

Alexander, F., & French, T. M. (1946). *Psychoanalytic Therapy*. New York: Ronald Press.

Barlow, D. H. (1988). *Anxiety and Its Disorders: The Nature and Treatment of Anxiety and Panic*. New York: Guilford Press.

Barten, H. H. (1965). The 15-minute hour: A brief therapy in a military setting. *American Journal of Psychiatry, 122,* 565–567.

Barten, H. H. (1971). *Brief Therapies.* New York: Behavioral Publications.

Beck, A. T. (1985). Cognitive therapy. In J. K. Zeig (Ed.), *The Evolution of Psychotherapy* (pp. 149–163). New York: Brunner/Mazel.

Berenbaum, H. (1969). Massed time-limit psychotherapy. *Psychotherapy: Theory, Research & Practice, 6,* 54–56.

Bloom, B.L. (1981). Focused single-session therapy: Initial development and evaluation. In S. H. Budman (Ed.), *Forms of Brief Therapy* (pp. 167–218). New York: Guilford Press.

Brantigan, C. O., Brantigan, T. A., & Joseph, N. (1982). Effect of beta-blockade and beta-stimulation on stage fright. *American Journal of Medicine, 72,* 88–94.

Cummings, N. A. (1977). Prolonged (ideal) versus short-term (realistic) psychotherapy. *Professional Psychology, 4,* 491–501.

Davanloo, H. (1978). Evaluation criteria for selection of patients for short-term dynamic psychotherapy. In H. Davanloo (Ed.), *Basic Principles and Techniques in Short-Term Dynamic Psychotherapy.* New York: S. P. Medical & Scientific Books.

Davanloo, H. (1980). A method of short-term dynamic psychotherapy. In H. Davanloo (Ed.), *Short-Term Dynamic Psychotherapy.* New York: Jason Aronson.

de Shazer, S. (1985). *Keys to Solutions in Brief Therapy.* New York: Norton.

de Shazer, S. (1988). *Clues: Investigating Solutions in Brief Therapy.* New York: Norton.

Dreiblatt, I. S., & Weatherly, D. (1965). An evaluation of the efficacy of brief contact therapy with hospitalized psychiatric patients. *Journal of Consulting Psychology, 29,* 513–519.

Ellis, A. (1989). Rational-emotive therapy. In R. J. Corsini and D. Wedding (Eds.), *Current Psychotherapies.* Itasca, IL: Peacock.

Ellis, A., & Dryden, W. (1987). *The Practice of Rational Emotive Therapy.* New York: Springer.

Fay, A. (1990). *PQR: Prescription for a Quality Relationship.* New York: Simon & Schuster.

Fay, A., & Lazarus, A. A. (1982). Psychoanalytic resistance and behavioral non-responsiveness: A dialectical impasse. In P. L. Wachtel (Ed.), *Resistance: Psychodynamic and Behavioral Approaches.* New York: Plenum Press.

Ferenczi, S. (1926). *Further Contributions to the Theory and Technique of Psychoanalysis.* London: Hogarth Press.

Goulding, M., & Goulding, R. (1979). *Changing Lives Through Redecision Therapy.* New York: Grove Press.

Groddeck, G. (1951). *The Unknown Self.* New York: Funk & Wagnalls.

Gutheil, E. (1933). Basic outline of the active analytic technique (Stekel). *Psychoanalytic Review, 20,* 53–72.

Horowitz, M. J., Marmar, C., Krupnick, J., Wilner, N., Kaltreider, N., & Wallerstein, R. (1984). *Personality Styles and Brief Psychotherapy.* New York: Basic Books.

Howard, G. S., Nance, D. W., & Myers, P. (1987). *Adaptive Counseling and Therapy.* San Francisco: Jossey-Bass.

Hoyt, M. F. (1989). On time in brief therapy. In R. Wells & V. Gianetti (Eds.), *Handbook of the Brief Psychotherapies.* New York: Plenum Press.

Koegler, R. R., & Cannon, J. A. (1966). Treatment for the many. In G. J. Wayne & R. R. Koegler (Eds.), *Emergency Psychiatry and Brief Therapy.* Boston: Little, Brown.

Koss, M. P., & Butcher, J. N. (1986). Research on brief psychotherapy. In S. L. Garfield & A. E. Bergin (Eds.), *Handbook of Psychotherapy and Behavior Change.* (pp. 627–670). New York: Wiley.

Lazarus, A. A. (1971). *Behavior Therapy and Beyond.* New York: McGraw-Hill.

Lazarus, A. A. (1976). *Multimodal Behavior Therapy.* New York: Springer.

Lazarus, A. A. (1982). *Personal Enrichment Through Imagery.* New York: BMA Audiocassettes.

Lazarus, A. A. (1984). *In the Mind's Eye.* New York: Guilford Press.

Lazarus, A. A. (1989). *The Practice of Multimodal Therapy* (updated). Baltimore: Johns Hopkins University Press.

Lazarus, A. A., & Fay, A. (1982). Resistance or rationalization? A cognitive-behavioral perspective. In P. L. Wachtel (Ed.), *Resistance: Psychodynamic and Behavioral Approaches.* New York: Plenum Press.

Lazarus, A. A., & Messer, S. B. (1988). Clinical choice points: Behavioral versus psychoanalytic interventions. *Psychotherapy, 25,* 59–70.

Malan, D. H. (1976). *The Frontier of Brief Psychotherapy.* New York: Plenum Press.

Mann, J. (1973). *Time-Limited Psychotherapy.* Cambridge, MA: Harvard University Press.

Mann, J., & Goldman, R. (1982). *A Casebook in Time-Limited Psychotherapy.* New York: McGraw-Hill.

Norcross, J. C. (Ed.) (1986). *Handbook of Eclectic Psychotherapy.* New York: Brunner/Mazel.

Paul, G. L. (1967). Strategy of outcome research in psychotherapy. *Journal of Consulting Psychology, 31,* 109–118.

Prochaska, J. O., & DiClemente, C. C. (1986). The transtheoretical approach. In J. C. Norcross (Ed.), *Handbook of Eclectic Psychotherapy* (pp. 163–200). New York: Brunner/Mazel.

Salter, A. (1949). *Conditioned Reflex Therapy.* New York: Farrar, Straus.

Sifneos, P. (1979). *Short-Term Psychotherapy and Emotional Crisis.* Cambridge, MA: Harvard University Press.

Strunk, W., & White, E. B. (1979). *The Elements of Style* (3rd ed.). New York: Macmillan.

Strupp, H. H., & Binder, J. L. (1984). *Psychotherapy in a New Key: A Guide to Time-Limited Dynamic Psychotherapy.* New York: Basic Books.

Wells, R. A. (1982). *Planned Short-Term Treatment.* New York: Macmillan.

Wilson, G. T. (1981). Behavior therapy as a short-term therapeutic approach. In S. H. Budman (Ed.), *Forms of Brief Therapy.* New York: Guilford Press.

Wolpe, J. (1958). *Psychotherapy by Reciprocal Inhibition.* Stanford, CA: Stanford University Press.

Wolpe, J., & Lazarus, A. A. (1966). *Behavior Therapy Techniques.* New York: Pergamon Press.

Zilbergeld, B., & Lazarus, A. A. (1988). *Mind Power: Getting What You Want Through Mental Training.* New York: Ivy Books.

PART II

Overviews

CHAPTER 4

Therapy Is What You Say It Is
Paul Watzlawick

Toward the end of April 1988, a bizarre incident was reported in the local section of the Italian daily *La Nazione.* A psychotic woman who had been temporarily admitted to the general hospital of the city of Grosseto was to be transferred to a psychiatric clinic in her native Naples. As the Red Cross attendants came to take her to the waiting ambulance, she began to decompensate rapidly. She became abusive and belligerent, began to depersonalize, claiming that she was somebody else, and had to be restrained. About an hour later, on the freeway outside Rome, police intercepted the ambulance and directed it back to Grosseto as it had meanwhile been discovered that the woman in question was not the "real" patient but rather a visitor who had come to the hospital to see a friend who had undergone surgery.

This incident proves again what David Rosenhan (1973) already demonstrated 15 years ago, namely that "to be sane in insane places" (in this case within the frame of an administrative mistake) can create a situation in which any manifestation of sanity becomes further "proof" of insanity.

But if this "epistemological error," as Gregory Bateson (1972) would have called it, can underlie our definition of pathology, could it occur also in the realm of what we call therapy? In other words, is it possible that "therapy" is a name we give to something which, having been given that name, creates a reality of its own?

A hypnotist, highly respected for his skills and clinical successes,

reports that one day he was invited to give a workshop for a group of
doctors in the home of one of them. Upon entering the house he noticed
that, as he put it, "every horizontal surface was filled with flower bou-
quets." The hypnotist had a strong allergy to freshly cut flowers, and
almost immediately the well-known burning sensations made themselves felt in his eyes and nose. He turned to the host and mentioned his
problem and his fear that under these circumstances he would be unable to give his presentation. The latter expressed surprise and asked
him to examine the flowers—which turned out to be artificial. On making this discovery, his allergic reaction subsided almost as quickly as it
had come on (Wilson, 1982).

In 1964, the psychologist Gordon Allport reported the following unusual, but unfortunately not better documented, case:

> In a provincial Austrian hospital, a man lay gravely ill—in fact,
> at death's door. The medical staff had told him frankly that they
> could not diagnose his disease, but that if they knew the diag-
> nosis they could probably cure him. They told him further that
> a famous diagnostician was soon to visit the hospital and that
> perhaps he could spot the trouble.
>
> Within a few days the diagnostician arrived and proceeded
> to make the rounds. Coming to this man's bed, he merely
> glanced at the patient, murmured, "Moribundus," and went
> on.
>
> Some years later, the patient called on the diagnostician and
> said, "I've been wanting to thank you for your diagnosis. They
> told me that if you could diagnose me I'd get well, and so the
> minute you said 'moribundus' I knew I'd recover." (Allport,
> 1964, p. 7)

At the end of a successful brief therapy involving nine sessions, the
client summarizes her view of the change with the words: "The way I
saw the situation, it was a problem. Now I see it differently and it is no
longer a problem."

One more example before I attempt to show the common denominator that I believe underlies this hodge-podge of stories. A man claps his
hands every 20 seconds. When asked the reason for this strange
behavior, he replies: "To chase away the elephants." "Elephants? But
there aren't any around here!" To which the man replies: "See . . . !"

My colleague Fritz Simon (1987) has used this story to point to four
different ways in which therapists, depending on their philosophy of
therapy, might try to help that man:

1. One could prove to that patient that hand clapping does not scare away elephants. This form of "reality therapy" would be technically somewhat difficult, as it would require hiring elephants. Moreover, it would leave the patient without his "protection" and would thus intensify his problem.

2. The therapist could try to get the patient to the point where his *trust* in the therapist is strong enough to believe him that there "really" are no elephants around. This would undoubtedly take a long time and would be complicated by the fact that the therapist really would only be repeating what everybody else has already told the patient, namely, that he is just imagining things.

3. The traditional approach would be to explore the "real" reasons for the patient's absurd fears and to bring about *insight* into the fact that today elephants simply are not the same threat that they seemed to be in his childhood. Again, this would be a lengthy and uncertain process.

4. The patient has a car accident, breaks his wrist, and the hand is put into a cast. He would then have the *corrective emotional experience* that even without being able to clap no elephants will appear. The same corrective emotional experience could be produced by a therapist who would dare to be so "unprofessional" and "unethical" as to grab the patient's hands and thus prevent him from clapping, or—I would add— to get the patient to behave *as if* he were unable to clap his hands.

It may safely be assumed that everyone will consider *one* of these four "techniques" to be the only correct one and consequently reject the other three as being wrong and, therefore, ineffective or even harmful. But what is the origin of this certainty of being right and the rejection of any other technique as being wrong?

Gregory Bateson (1972) published a number of *Metalogues*, by which he meant fictitious conversations with his small daughter. In one of them the daughter asks: "Daddy, what is an instinct?" And Bateson does not give the "correct," "scientific" answer ("an instinct is a complex, genetically transmitted configuration of stimulus-response patterns," or something to that effect), but says: "An instinct, my dear, is an *explanatory principle.*"

The difference between these two definitions is of fundamental importance for my subject. Through the act of giving a *name* ("instinct") the illusion of a "really" existing thing is created, for it is inconceivable to us that there should exist names without the things named by them. But, come to think of it, an instinct is just as "real" as the elephants that have to be scared away by clapping. In other words, once we have created instincts they are part of our reality and we have to do something with (or against) them. In doing so, we are by no means saner than the so-called schizophrenic who eats the menu card rather than the dishes listed on it, complains of the bad taste, and suspects that people are trying to poison him.

The other definition, according to which an instinct is an explanatory principle, avoids this pitfall. It acknowledges that it belongs to the linguistic-semantic domain and identifies itself as a name. It is thus in accordance with Korzybski's (1933) famous tenet: *The name is not the thing; the map is not the territory*. If we disregard this warning, we shall naïvely believe that we are dealing with things, i.e., with properties of the "real" world, and not merely with names. This is tantamount to saying that naming creates what we consider to be properties of a supposedly objective reality, existing independently from us, its explorers. Probably the most monumental example of this, at least in our field, is the DSM-III.

In philosophy, this process of constructing pseudorealities is referred to as *reification:* the "making of things" (from the Latin *res*, thing, and *facere*, to make). Far from being philosophical abstractions, which a practical mind can leave aside in order to forge ahead toward apparently more important goals, we are beginning to realize that they determine— in the most immediate, concrete sense—what can be done in therapy and, in fact, what therapy appears to be all about. If our assumptions *create*, rather than *reflect*, reality, then we are faced with what the philosopher Karl Popper called "self-sealing propositions," i.e., assumptions which, once made, seem to confirm their own truth. Once a nonpsychotic person is *labeled* as being psychotic, then he *is* psychotic, and whatever he now does confirms (recursively) the correctness of the "name" given to him, and the "reality" thus created determines what "must" be done. Once I perceive a room full of freshly cut flowers, I have an allergic reaction; when I perceive them to be artificial, I am all right again. If I do not know Latin and give the word *moribundus* (itself merely a "name") the meaning of a diagnostic term, then there is at least a chance that months later I can thank the great diagnostician for saving my life.

If I subscribe to the explanatory principle that insight into past causes is a precondition for change in the present, and if my client improves, this will be evidence for the correctness of the assumptions regarding the therapeutic importance of insight. If, on the other hand, he does not improve, this makes it clear that my search for the causes of the present condition has not yet been pushed far enough and deep enough into his unconscious. My assumption thus confirms itself—recursively—both through the success as well as the failure of its practical application.

The weirdly recursive, self-sealing nature of such propositions is well expressed in the joke about the great rabbi:

"No one can compare with my rabbi. He not only speaks with
God directly, but, imagine, God speaks directly with him!"
"I don't believe it. Do you have witnesses? If your rabbi says
that, he's not only exaggerating, he's simply lying."
"Really? Here's the best proof: Would God speak with some-
one who lies?"

Therapy, then, is what we say it is, i.e., what names we operate with,
what explanatory principles we use, and what reality we thereby
create.

The reality-changing effect of the so-called corrective emotional experiences, of unexpected events in the life of a person, was already
referred to. The MRI approach to brief therapy is based predominantly
on the introduction of carefully planned "chance" events into the problem situation, of events that give that situation a new and different
meaning—which, of course and of necessity, is simply another name,
another way of seeing the same situation. Hence, the above-mentioned
statement by that client: "The way I saw the situation, it was a problem;
now I see it differently, and it is no longer a problem."

And this is where the main criticism against this form of intervention
is raised: How can a superficial, "cosmetic" change have any lasting effect, if the unconscious cause of the pathology has not been uncovered
and raised into consciousness? But, this objection overlooks the possibility that the view of the unconscious determination of problems is, again,
but one explanatory principle out of many conceivable ones, and not an
objective property of the human mind (which itself is but a *name* and
not a *thing*). Another frequent criticism is that our approach is manipulative, insincere, and dishonest, for the therapist may at times say something that he does not "really" believe. This objection naïvely assumes
that there is "truth" out there, a "real" reality, accessible to human
reason, and whoever sees it other than the way it "really"is, has to be
mad or bad, or both. There can be little doubt that to fancy oneself to be
in possession of truth may be therapeutic for therapists, but not
necessarily also for their clients.

But then what becomes of the concept of *reality adaptation* as a
measure of sanity or insanity? The only possible answer is very uncomfortable for many people, and it is a basic tenet of *radical constructivism:* of the "real" reality (if it exists at all) we can only know what it is
not. This is how Ernest von Glasersfeld, in his "Introduction to Radical
Constructivism" (Glasersfeld, 1984) explains it:

> Knowledge can now be seen as something that the organism
> builds up in the attempt to order the as such amorphous flow of

experience by establishing repeatable experiences and relatively reliable relations between them. The possibilities of constructing such an order are determined and perpetually constrained by the preceding steps in the construction. This
means that the "real" world manifests itself exclusively there
where our constructions break down. But since we can describe and explain these breakdowns only in the very concepts
that we have used to build the falling structures, this process
can never yield a picture of a world which we could hold
responsible for their failure p. 39).

In less abstract terms the same thought may be expressed through the
following analogy:

> A captain who on a dark, stormy night has to sail through an un-
> chartered channel, devoid of beacons and other navigational
> aids, will either wreck his ship on the cliffs or regain the safe,
> open sea beyond the strait. If he loses ship and life, his failure
> proves that the course he steered was not the right one. One
> may say that he discovered what the passage was *not*. If, on the
> other hand, he clears the strait, this success merely
> proves that he literally did not at any point come into collision
> with the (otherwise unknown) shape and nature of the water-
> way; it tells him nothing about how safe or how close to disaster
> he was at any given moment. He passed the strait like a blind
> man. (Watzlawick, 1984, pp. 14–15)

This constructivist view of reality raises more than eyebrows. It appears unscientific, to say the least. But this judgment, too, depends on a
definition, namely, the definition of the purpose of science. If science is
supposed to discover the "real" nature of things, to arrive at objective
truth, then, indeed, the constructivist approach does not qualify as being
scientific. However, modern philosophy of science is no longer concerned with truth, but with the elaboration of effective procedures for a
given purpose. Take the two classic, mutually exclusive views of our
planetary reality, the geocentric and the heliocentric. Neither view is
"true" and the other therefore "false," but the criterion is the *usefulness*
of the one compared to the other. If the earth is seen as the center, then
certain planets (especially Mercury) seem to behave in ways that even
at Galileo Galilei's time were incompatible with what was hypothesized
about the mechanics of planetary motion. If the sun is considered the
center, then these "pathologies" simply disappear. This does not prevent space scientists from returning occasionally to the geocentric

view—not because they suddenly consider this view to be the "true" one after all, but merely because in connection with their enormously complicated calculations underlying the dispatch of space probes to distant planets, it is more practical to consider the earth as being the center.

What does all this mean for our view of what therapy "really" is? If reality is a construct of our minds, if there is no such thing as a "real" objective reality of which sane people (and especially therapists) are more aware than crazy ones, then therapy is what you say it is, i.e., how you define it. But if this be so, then the only useful criterion is the degree to which a given reality construction enables its architect to lead a reasonably problem-free life. Therapy, then, consists in replacing a particular pain-producing view of the world by another one that still is "only" a mental construct, that still does not reflect reality as it "really" is, but that merely fits as the course steered by that metaphorical skipper did fit the unknown strait, or the way a key fits the lock that you want to open, but that you cannot see or "understand." And this view of reality and of existence is by no means a recent discovery. "It is not the things that bother us, but the opinions that we have about them," said Epictetus 18 centuries ago. And long after him, Shakespeare wrote, "There is nothing either good or bad, but thinking makes it so."

REFERENCES

Allport, G. W. (1964). Mental health: A generic attitude. *Journal of Religion and Health, 4*, 7–21.

Bateson, G. (1972). Metalogue: What is an instinct? In G. Bateson (Ed.), *Steps to an Ecology of Mind* (pp. 38–58). New York: Ballantine.

Glaserfeld, E. von (1984). An introduction to radical constructivism. In P. Watzlawick (Ed.), *The Invented Reality*. New York: Norton.

Korzybski, A. (1933). *Science and Sanity*. New York: International Non-Aristotelian Library.

Rosenhan, D. (1984). On being sane in insane places. In P. Watzlawick (Ed.), *The Invented Reality* (pp. 117–144). New York: Norton.

Simon, F. (1987). *Unteschiede, die Unterschiede machen*. Berlin, Heidelberg, New York, Tokyo: Springer.

Watzlawick P. (1984). Introduction. In P. Watzlawick (Ed.), *The Invented Reality*. New York: Norton.

Wilson, D. (1982). Personal communication.

CHAPTER 5

Just Do Good Therapy
Stephen R. Lankton

UNDERSTANDING AND JOINING

Perhaps the greatest problem with therapy is attempting to make it conform to a theory or paradigm. Often, therapy is judged by the language it uses or its conformity to a school (e.g., family therapy, Erickson therapy, cognitive therapy, brief therapy, or whatever). In so doing, therapists and clients become the servants of the model instead of using the model to serve clients and therapists. This paper addresses what I believe makes therapy "good therapy" from three standpoints: 1) the relationship, 2) the therapy practice, and 3) my experience as a client. It is intended to help us maintain perspective and to keep our attention on designing unique treatment for each unique client-system.

As an example of this initial process I want to share an experience which became a personal breakthrough in understanding how to apply Milton Erickson's work in my practice. In 1969 at a crisis intervention center, The Listening Ear, in East Lansing, Michigan, my role included training volunteers in empathy skills and also working with people who were having what were euphemistically called "bad drug trips." The typical action went something like this.

Client: [walking—for lack of better word—into center]
Me: "Hi! Can I help you?"
Client: "Oh, no, man . . . I shouldn't have come here."
Me: "Oh really . . . nah, this is a safe and comfortable place to be."
Client: "Yea, but the walls are moving and the room is getting smaller."

Me: "Oh, I wasn't thinking about that. I was pretty relaxed. Does it seem that way now?"

Client: "Yeah, I can't stand it. I got to get out of here."

Me: "Wait, let me see!" [moving near the head of the client] "Oh, yes, I see what you mean. The walls do seem to be moving. They are moving like, sort of like waves. Yeah, it's like the waves of the ocean, sort of. I love the ocean, don't you?"

Client: "Eh, yeah. I do."

Me: "I think the shadows on the wall make it look like waves rolling in to the beach. That always makes me feel comfortable. I just love sitting in the sun on the beach and watching the waves. Don't you? Do you feel like that, too?"

Client: "Yeah, I really do. It does sort of seem like that."

Me: "Yeah, and the warmth of the room is the sunlight that makes you just relax and watch the waves and dream happy daydreams. Do you know what I mean?"

Client: "Yeah, I do. Yeah, I remember that. Yeah. [long exhale and pause] I'm glad I came in here."

Me: "Yeah, me too. It's nice talking with you. What is your name?"

The subsequent conversation was about the drug that had been taken, and also indicated how much longer I would need to continue this manner of careful communication. Though perhaps somewhat amusing, this example illustrates something of deep significance about understanding and joining, namely, how therapists may, to paraphrase Dr. Erickson (personal communication, 1976), proceed by putting one foot in the client's world and leaving one foot in their own world. After joining in this way, clients are guided or motivated to create an alternate, more desirable reality which contains sufficient resources for coping.

This example does little to illustrate how to further help such a person enjoy life without taking dangerous drugs. Nevertheless, it is an effective beginning. There is no need to stand at a distance and analyze clients. The act of doing so might well produce more bizarre and dangerous results. To create those results and exacerbate the problem further by attributing them to the client, perhaps placing him in a diagnostic niche, could be destructive. Yet, this is exactly what occurs repeatedly in many treatment situations.

In the example, I treat a person-in-relation-to-his-environment. In this regard, the case represents a situation similar to the ones we routinely encounter with individuals and families. A difference is that usually therapy clients have less altered perceptions and less dramatic, but longer-lasting behaviors. Their perceptual distortions are merely harder to spot, since they do not often "leap out" at the therapist. In either case, however, the posture of the therapist needs to be actively engaging, motivating, and guiding. Joining in this way involves temporarily embracing the reality experienced by each client.

Trusting Yourself and Others

I hold certain things to be real, true, and meaningful, and other things to be untrue, unreal, and meaningless. However, I do not need to constantly verify these beliefs. I can consider "reality" from the senses and beliefs of others during therapy. I can believe "as if" something were real, that the walls are moving, and so on. The more I take on "as if real" the beliefs, perceptions, and feelings of others, the more I learn to experience and act in the world as they do.

And, this is where I sometimes place limitations. This empathy is not always pleasant and in some cases it is potentially harmful to my beliefs. That is, I would usually be willing to experience an understanding of the reality of headaches, back pains, depressions, anxieties, and even some hallucinations experienced by others—because I know how to touch on those experiences and move away from them. I can hold onto myself and my beliefs and lead clients and myself elsewhere. But I would not want to *know*, in the experiential sense of the word, how a person desires to do terrible acts of violence, betrayal, or hatred.

Although it does not happen often, there are several types of clients with whom I won't join. For instance, I would not attempt to move my "head and heart" near a murderer and attempt to feel, see, touch, hear, smell, and believe the world from his or her senses. Therefore, I would not attempt therapy with such an individual. Were I to do so, I would be working without the asset of my intuitions; I would hide my intuitive self to keep it safe from the pain of a certain psychological trickery or fate. And, when I hide that intuition, I am looking at clients through a telescope instead of a microscope—doing surgery with a shovel instead of a scalpel. In other words, I can't and won't as effectively work with such a client.

Basically, I will join with and, to some extent, know the world of my clients in most cases. As I join bit by bit, I also suggest, elaborate, and guide the client from the world I experience at the time into a different world. This different world is not mine but one I can simulate as a result of knowing the clients' experiences somewhat. This co-created world is the therapeutic goal for the session, as it can be used to guide clients to novel attitudes, affect, behaviors, and self-perceptions. At the end of the therapy the novel experiences should lead clients to a problem-free world and leave me in mine.

Liking Clients

Liking one's clients is a well-known aspect of therapy, but it bears repeating that if you do not like your clients, you cannot feel "with" them. While this may handicap your work, it will most certainly be observed by clients. Some clients will be more sensitive to social cues and, by this subtle behavior, be provoked into a further rejection of their experience. Defensively, they will become more entangled in the limitations and defenses which produced the problems and brought them to therapy.

It is best, if one does not trust or like a client, to refer him/her elsewhere. (If you find this happens often, refer yourself there too!) What I find I like best about people is their ability and willingness to learn and take joy in learning. Somehow, when I find that a person has a spark of curiosity and a joy in discovering something, anything, I can follow that inspiration and help him/her use it as a part of therapy. Furthermore, the courage to learn, which is demonstrated by the client, is an inspiration to me. This is what I most respect about my clients.

Creating Reality

When clients conceptualize themselves in the world in ways which are self-limiting, one can, with confidence, take the position that the conceptualization held by the client is not true. It may be true for the client but it is not the only truth. And it is important to remember that same dictum when we conceptualize clients' problems: If we conceptualize clients as limited we are mistaken and need to rethink our position.

As an example, I want to relate an incident with my son, Shawn, when he was 15 months old. At that time he could say very little. In fact, it seemed that the only thing he said at that age was " . . . want this!" He came into the kitchen one day as I was putting the groceries away and pointed to the laundry detergent box and said, " . . . want this." I offered the box but he repeated his singular verbalization. To make a long story short, I offered everything on the countertop to him and he continued to request something else. As a good mental health professional would do, I picked him up and asked him to put his finger on what he wanted because I could not quite understand him. He placed his finger on the box of laundry detergent! The box displayed a picture of a magnifying glass and, beneath that, a magnified view of some brown fabric fibers. I thought he must be making a request for a magnifying glass and I made an offer to get him one. He refused it. I even went and got one for him thinking that he merely did not know the word for it. He refused it and pointed and said, " . . . want this."

Now, any reasonable parent would have been inclined to set him down and tell him to go play elsewhere with the instruction "there is nothing here you need." Had I done this, he would have thrown a fit: He was so determined and he would have been frustrated. And if he had thrown a fit, I would have been tempted to say to myself, "He is being a brat." I might have even told my wife, Carol, about the incident when she came home and we would have both "remembered" several other times when he seemed to "have a mind of his own" and thus concluded that, in fact, he was a brat.

What did transpire, however, was quite different. He put his hand on the magnifying glass in the picture. I looked at the "fabric" below it and wondered, "What in the world could this look like to him?" I said, "Do you want a pretzel?" And, he replied, "Yes, Daddy, a prentzel"—saying it incorrectly and thus indicating that he did not know the word. Then he hugged my neck tightly and said, "I love you, daddy." This was not a manipulation to get a pretzel—it was clear that he was getting one. This was a way of saying, "I know you respected my observation enough to stick with me and figure this out and thank you for believing in me." I concluded he was very smart and persistent.

Now the point is this. Is he a brat or is he smart and persistent? Whatever I decided that day, reinforced by Shawn's behavior, and my future perceptions, would have become the "truth." This is what we do with our clients repeatedly for better or worse. We label them and think we have observed reality. We have, along with them, cocreated reality. If we decide that a person is stuck because of his or her marital situation, it becomes a truth we must "cure." If we decide that the person needs medication because of depression, it becomes the truth we must work against. If we decide the person needs a relationship in order to show minimum coping, it becomes the truth. If we decide the person is passive-aggressive, it becomes true. And finally, if we decide our clients have made the best choice they know how to make to cope with the world they perceive, it becomes true. We cocreate the world of choices and limitations with our clients.

Correcting Ineffective Means and Imaginary Ends

What most clients present as a problem is often the result of their attempts to reach ill-conceived goals with in effective problem-solving means. It may be that a man tries to secure a sense of respect by acting jealously, hoping that his wife will eventually cry, apologize, and reiterate that she loves him. Meanwhile, his wife may be hoping that he will admit his tender and weak side and ask her for help, and in so doing make her feel needed. The results will be disastrous. Both are using ineffective means in their attempt to achieve imaginary ends.

Why? Because the man could respect himself and not seek self-respect by means of his wife's external praise, and the woman could realize her own importance rather than artificially gaining importance by seeing herself as worthy because she is needed by her husband. Each wants something from the other in order to complete a missing part of their perceived reality, but they could change the reality so the missing part didn't have to come from outside of themselves. Also, of course, they could each give more attention to the other if the interpersonal requests were more understandable and they were each willing. There is choice.

Therapy must assess the clients' goals and help each person employ the necessary methods (or means) for achieving these goals. If we believe that clients are attempting to achieve something of value with ineffective interpersonal tools, we will be less likely to label frustrating behavior as crazy.

I recently saw a family whose teenaged girl believed herself to be dating "Simon" from the rock group Duran Duran. She was doing this dating via a self-described psychic "channel," who was, in fact, a neighbor girl dressing in a suit coat and speaking with an British accent. (The "channel" was being seen by an HMO therapist. Now it is possible that we could call my client a "teenage schizophrenic" and attempt to "forbid" her to continue this "dating"—this was, by the way, the demand made on the "channel" by the HMO therapist. But I saw her as basically normal and doing an appropriate thing for a teen—learning to date. This was an especially courageous undertaking for her, considering that her father was extremely withdrawn as a result of a neck injury 20 years earlier. He had not had sexual relations with her mother for 12 years. He had made no income for 20 years and showed no affection in the home. He was bitter and quick to provoke hostile rejection from others.

Despite this, these two girls were attempting to do a very normal thing and had only used ineffective means to do this dating. My patient's goal in dating was also slightly skewed or imaginary—that is, it would have been all right to date a regular boy, but she constructed a rock superstar companion to make herself special. Seeing this problem as the use of ineffective means to an imaginary end reduced the attribution of pathology to my clients and propelled me to a treatment direction that was realizable. Working initially with the father and mother, I was able to help him feel pride about himself and guide him to what soon became a process of giving more attention to his daughter. The impact on the daughter's conduct apparently followed, as she was soon receiving phone calls from "real" boys and had a casual date with one within a month's time. But, the actual therapy done is another story and this case is only being used to illustrate the importance of using therapy to help clients correct their use of interpersonal means to desired and realizable ends.

Using the Session to Motivate Clients

The work done in a session might best be seen as motivating clients to relate and experience the world differently. Sometimes the discussions and metaphoric communications in therapy remind clients of past experiences. However, I do not conceive of work done in therapy as getting closure on the past even when clients might be reliving situations concerning their parents. Instead, I understand this therapy to be eliciting a complex and experientially grounded motivation to relate differently in the present. For example, getting angry at a father in imagination during trance might provide a motivation to express anger appropriately toward a husband in the present. That outcome is possible, especially to the extent that therapists are sensitive to helping clients make the events connect.

The same is true for any other elicited behavior, cognition, memory, or fantasy. Optimally utilized, these events produce motivation for action in the present. I consider the metaphorical framework of having clients talk to the children they once were or deal with a parent "as if" in the past, a means for eliciting cognitive, emotional, and behavioral aspects of *motivation*, which must be linked to the extramural life of the present family with assignments and other means.

Helping Clients Diversify Problem-Solving Skills

When clients improve, their families can turn their motivation toward something other than the previously identified symptom. What will have emerged in place of the problems will be hard to predict since, often, the entire balance of the family will have changed. The individuals will begin relating differently. I see this as gaining new problem-solving options.

Perhaps the term "problem-solving options" deserves additional explanation. I see people as involved in an ongoing process, usually outside of their awareness, of adjusting to developmental ecosystemic demands. The tools that are used to meet those demands are the experiences found at several levels of analysis. All the experiences and behaviors we can conceptualize in families are tools that can be used to creatively meet the demands of life. For example, asking for help will sometimes be used to solve problems. Other times, the solving of problems may best be accomplished with divergent abilities such as nurturing a spouse or disaffiliating with and anger.

When clients change, they will relate differently, and then, their symptoms—the anxiety, fears, depression, insomnia, sexual dysfunction, loneliness, drug dependence, domestic violence, and so on—will have a diminished place in their lives. These problems, which often represent ineffective attempts to reach ill-conceived goals, will not be used. Good therapy helps clients solve current problems differently.

Helping Clients Stay Better

In my model it is important to help clients use these tools to stay better. The reinforcement that maintains new experiences and behaviors comes from both internal and external sources. When people reinforce themselves for behavior that is also reinforced by the social system, the behavior becomes stable. There are four factors or levels of needs to consider, and each one can influence any of the others.

1. Developmental and biological growth needs.
2. Expectation and self-monitoring (self-administered positive/ negative reinforcement, self-image).
3. Social sanctions (family and peer).
4. Demands of the larger environment (neighbors, cultural, etc.).

To the exent that there is a match between the needs and sanctions of different levels, there will be creative health. Therefore, it seems that good therapy will be a matter of helping people gain and/or use perceptions, cognitions, feelings, and behaviors that address the developmental biological needs and the ecosystem demands.

Therapy can be conceived of as a way to help clients create change in *each* of these areas *specifically* and accountably. The field of therapy has become sophisticated enough that we can help clients elicit and respond with feelings they have not previously used for problem solving, reshape inappropriate cognitions with useful ones, rehearse changes in their self-concept, solidify new roles, reorganize family structure to support these changes, and so on (Bandura, 1969; Berne, 1966; Ellis, 1971; Goulding & Goulding, 1979; Lankton, 1980; Lazarus, 1976; Lowen, 1975; Madanes, 1987; Meichenbaum, 1977; Moreno, 1972; Perls, 1947, 1973; Wolpe, 1948, 1982; Zeig, 1987). Clients continue to change or stay better by making gains in these areas. The wider array of specific changes that therapy helps clients make in each of these, the better will be the therapy.

DOING THE THERAPY

There are several factors vital to doing good therapy. At one level, the factors I am about to describe are common knowledge. But at another level, they need to be reemphasized because all too often therapists forget to do these things.

Identifying the Problem

I once worked with a couple who said they were concerned with the infrequency of their love making. They didn't need to say more. I had heard how it can be when one has been married for a while. I figured they were not having sexual relations for weeks at a time, and I must have talked to them for 30 minutes assuming this. Finally, I felt a need to get specific and asked them how bad it was. The husband answered: "Three times a day." Since that day I have been extremely sensitive to the need for finding out, specifically, what clients mean about how a complaint is a problem for them.

Getting and Understanding a Contract

After finding out what the presenting complaints are, I do not assume that clients want to change them. The most common problem that I have seen in supervision is that therapists can't tell me concisely what their clients think they are trying to accomplish in therapy. The therapists don't know in which direction to exert energy, and clients grow somewhat impassive about what happens in the session. Under these conditions you can be certain that clients don't think about therapy during the extramural hours and fail to carry out assignments given to them.

In addition to getting a contract for the general treatment goal, find out what clients think they will accomplish if they reach this goal. Don't assume. If the client says she wishes to get away from her mother, ask her, "Why in the world would you want to do that?" If the client says he wants to get rid of his anxiety, don't assume you know why. Don't assume it is desirable to not feel the anxiety. Maybe it is. But ask for a deeper understanding of this goal. Ask, "What do you want to do when you feel less anxiety?" Or, "Do you think you can do everything you do and have less anxiety?" Or, "Why do you think it would be a good idea to have less anxiety?" Ask until you get the client's understanding.

This is equally appropriate when the presenting problem shows emotional pain. When a client cries and says, "I have to separate from my mother," we cannot conclude that we know something about the request. We still must say, "You sure look sad when you think about that and say that you need to separate. Go ahead and take some time to cry if you need to. But tell me what you mean by 'separate' and why in the world you would want to do something like that."

Getting Clients Active

In the last example, my question was, "Why in the world would you want to do that?" Such an inquiry is concerned with why this issue is a *problem* and implies the need to be active. That is, despite the fact that the problem presented by the client is upsetting, why does it constitute sufficient need for therapy? Clients, in answering this real naïve concern that I present, can be expected to devote more energy to the change process right from the start. Initial questioning can be motivating.

This energy is utilized in the therapy as clients become active. I ask clients to do assignments between almost every appointment. I have noticed that even the smallest and seemingly inconsequential performance between sessions amplifies the work done in each session. For instance, having a married couple change the location of five hanging pictures in their home each night for a week turned out to be an extremely meaningful task. The husband, with a rigid "macho" persona, said he thought this was being done to illustrate to him that he ought to be comfortable and even excited about change. His wife, who had been fighting him for her independence, said she felt the assignment illustrated the importance of working *with* her husband instead of against him. In another instance, an unmarried male client who complained about insecurity was given a small Indian Kachina doll that he was to carry with him everywhere he went throughout the week. He returned to my office informing me he realized this meant that, as long as he had his imagination, he could not be insecure! I certainly didn't know that!

In such cases, clients making small changes at home and small changes in relating to the world form the attitude that *they* did the therapy. These clients avoid that dreadful passivity that typically makes therapists feel they should work harder. The motivated client becomes an active client, and the active client helps the therapist make therapy good therapy.

Challenging the Obvious

Once I have expressed my general ignorance about the nature of the problem and begin to understand why *this* person or family wants to change something, I still wonder why they don't just do something different. This common sense position is similar to the joke about the man who says, "Doctor, every time I do this it hurts," and the doctor responds by saying, "Well, don't do that anymore."

I have clients say, "You mean I can just get a divorce?" "You mean I can just pick up and move?" and so on. I have had clients who said they wanted to feel more confident about going to college but then decided that they really didn't want to go to college at all. I have had clients who initially wanted to have less anxiety in their job eventually decide that they didn't want to be in that line of work at all. And there have been clients who wanted to get along better with their spouse but then decided that they did not want to be married after all.

What these situations have in common is that I did not stay with the initial request. Instead, I took the position "I don't understand how this is a problem" and raised questions about the "obvious." And finally, I asked, "Have you considered not doing it at all?" (not going to college, not keeping the jobs, not relocating, not being married).

I do not suggest the change of careers or marriages flippantly. Certainly these things are very serious undertakings. Any client who simply said, "Great idea! I'll do it that way" would find me even more inquisitive than I had initially been. But therapy that is begun when therapists are unclear in their definition of the problem and the motivation of the clients is poorly conceived therapy. I suggest that we inquire about both the problem and the motivation and use the resulting process and content to help clarify and build a productive working relationship.

Using Developmental Assessment Therapeutically

It is important for therapists to assess obvious developmental influences, but they should avoid introducing the obvious developmental needs in such a way that problems are magnified. I recently had a client who complained of anxiety he had about dating. The man, aged 24, was only five feet, two inches tall. I empathized about how hard dating can be. However, I wondered why, since it is a universal problem, he was seeking therapy for it. He said he wanted to marry and have children one day and he seemed to be no closer now than he had been several years ago. I again agreed it could be frustrating but asked what the hurry was, whom he wanted to date, what part of dating behavior seemed connected with his anxiety, what he was anxious about in dating, and so on. I realized that he was not mentioning his relatively short physical height. I was aware that many people consider height an attractive feature in courtship and yet he had not mentioned his lack of height once in his discussion of problems. I wanted, therefore, to explore the topic, but without introducing more anxiety.

In saying something like "I wonder if you are concerned that women prefer a taller man," a therapist runs the risk of reinforcing the client's existing fears. Therefore, they become even more true than they were in his silent imagination. Can't we say the obvious in a constructive way? I could step into his world and begin to unhook myself from being as upset as he seemed to be. In realizing how he was (or I could be) hooked in his dilemma, I began to see how to get unhooked. I said, "You didn't mention when or how you had first discovered your height might be an asset in dating." To this he haltingly replied that he had not really thought of being short as an asset and asked what I meant by the statement, since he thought women usually prefer taller men. He was somewhat fascinated that, while I was "with him," I viewed his height contrary to the popular view. In short, it seemed that the implied suggestion reinforced his hopes about his worth. He began telling me how being 5'2" might, in fact, be an asset.

One of the most obvious aspects of therapy is that clients must adjust to developmental demands. When a family brings a teenager for therapy, I look at the family system to determine its structure. I investigate whether the parents are communicating in a way that will facilitate building a stronger dyad as the girl leaves home. I wonder if their relationship is romantic, sexual, and caring; I assess their ability to ask for and deliver nurturing with each other; and I wonder if interests shared as a couple exist to the extent that they can turn attention away from their children. I examine each individual's experience of pride, joy, and other feelings and discover if the middle-aged couple respect the roles they play. In short, while I assist with the problems centered around the daughter, I also address the obvious experiences and transactions needed by nearly all family members at this developmental phase.

These inquiries should be done, in most cases, without alerting the couple to the fact that they may lack skills they desire. For instance, I once presented a couple with a candle and asked that, for the next week, they go out to dinner and burn the candle as they dined. The assignment was to go out repeatedly until all of the candle was burned, then come back and tell me why they thought they were sent to do this (and how it could be of benefit to their daughter). In this way the obvious growth they wanted and needed to do was therapeutically facilitated without alerting them to the additional problem represented by its absence.

Being Sensitive to Cues

Sometimes therapists place client problems into a "pathology" framework in an effort to "understand" clients and eventually help them feel and cope better. This maneuver puts therapists in the "illusory" position of thinking they know what the "cause" is for the problem and engenders an unfortunate process of "converting" clients to the framework held by therapists. As such, it is a certain way to elicit resistance in those clients who want their uniqueness respected.

Gathering information with subtle, indirect, and even metaphoric maneuvers will prevent this type of "casework" from destroying therapeutic rapport and responsiveness. Therapists who can be alert to nonverbal information indicating the client's feelings and attitudes may not need to resort to perhaps insulting questions like: "How did you feel when your wife left you?" "How did that make you feel when you broke your back?" "What was going through your head when your husband had an affair?" "What did you decide when you dropped out of high school?"

Certainly it is important to get answers to such questions, but the answers are given repeatedly in nonverbal signals from clients. Good therapy is being sensitive to those cues or asking questions that will reveal those cues but not alert the conscious minds of clients to feeling they are guinea pigs or objects of study for our pet theories.

Setting Specific Goals

We have already mentioned contracts, but now I wish to discuss specific goals for each therapy session. If a contract is set to help parents deal with the misconduct of their teenager, our session-by-session contracts ought to deal with specific subsets of this larger goal. For instance, can each parent experience joy at having a child? Can each show his/her joy, sorrow, and pride? Can they ask for help? Can they state their demands coherently and congruently? Can they be comfortable disaffiliating when discipline is called for? Would they like to learn to use any of the above problem-solving behaviors? These are among the many subsets of family experience and behavior necessary for creatively and effectively parenting a teenager.

When we ask ourselves these questions, we must then translate them into goals for each subsequent session. Making specific goals and going one step at a time is the only way in which complex behavior can be learned. This is perfectly analogous to learning to play a musical instrument such as piano. Whether the goal is to play classical or rock music, students must learn to sit, orient toward the keyboard, strike the keys, hold their fingers on the chords, use the pedals, play syntonic notes, change the chords in progressions, and so on. Learning to do this is a relatively methodical process of increasingly difficult tasks built upon the previous learning. This is how good therapy builds with each session toward the complex tasks necessary to fulfill contracts.

FROM THE CLIENTS' STANDPOINT

So far I have mentioned aspects of good therapy. They are not entirely independent of the theoretical approach taken by other therapists. But I want to add to these ideas from an additional vantage point. I want to ask the question "What makes good therapy?" from the standpoint of the client. I can answer this for me and perhaps the answers will stimulate you to discover ideas that fit for you.

I Want an Enchanting Therapist Who Stimulates Pleasant Mental Excitement

Enchantment is a part of all successful therapy. I don't want a boring therapist. I don't want one who dazzles me either. But I want one who challenges me gently and arouses pleasant mental excitement about the change process.

This can be done if the therapist is confident and poised and introduces ambiguity in the session. Assignments ought to be a bit mysterious. Certain pieces of instructions, questions, and advice ought to be somewhat vague so as to be interesting and allow room for my own personal growth. My therapist should use word ambiguity, puns, and some light-hearted humor. I want to know that the therapist is equal to me and worthy of my respect.

I Want a Therapist Who Is Relevant to My Reality

I don't want a therapist who helps me dig around in memories and fantasies of the past. It is the present and the future I struggle with. The good therapist must let me know he or she is interested in the reality of my life now and in the near future.

I Want a Therapist Who Will Not Label Me

I suppose it goes without saying that I want to be a person and not a category. Also, I want to terminate therapy when I wish to do it and not be intimidated into continuing therapy because I might fail to live up to some external criteria, especially criteria that are unstated and apparently hidden from my understanding.

I Want a Therapist with Humanity and Humor

Even though my life is serious to me, I want a therapist who can see the humor in living. I want a therapist who treats me as an equal, intelligent, and important person. I don't want one who is aloof or superior. I don't want one who morosely tries to "analyze" what I say. I actually don't mind if everything I do is analyzed, but I don't want it done with a distancing and condescending quality. The therapist who can help me change while helping me feel fully human is doing good therapy.

THE PARADOXICAL PROBLEM OF DOING GOOD THERAPY

When I began this chapter more than one year ago I had been thinking about how each therapy school wants therapists to adhere to the right and proper tenets of its approach. Therapists of different approaches are criticized for not being family oriented, for not dealing with the deeper problems, for not being elegant, for not attending to the relationship, for intellectualism or the lack of it, and so forth. At the time I was invited to address the Brief Therapy Congress, I thought, "Perhaps I should just make the point that we should just do good therapy."

But now, having made these points, I realize I too have done what I wished not to do. I have made it necessary that you do these "right things" in order to be correct. Paradoxically, I have done what I hoped to encourage therapists to avoid. In an effort to say, "Don't conform to someone else's rules; just do good therapy," I find that I have generated a set of rules. I'm sure that they could be followed to the letter and in such a way the spirit would be totally lost. Perhaps, in summary, what I can best conclude is that each of us ought to understand our own criteria for doing good therapy and follow our own rules—using our own well-developed model and not the model of others.

REFERENCES

Bandura, A. (1969). *Principles of Behavior Modification*. New York: Holt, Rinehart & Winston.
Berne, E. (1966). *Principles of Group Treatment*. New York: Grove Press.

Ellis, A. (1971). *Growth Through Reason*. North Hollywood, CA: Wilshire.

Erickson, M. (1976). Personal communication. Phoenix, AZ.

Goulding, M. & Goulding, R. (1979). *Changing Lives Through Redecision Therapy*. New York: Brunner/Mazel.

Lankton, S. (1980). *Practical Magic: A Translation of Basic Neuro-Linguistic Programming Into Clinical Psychotherapy*. Cupertino, CA: Meta Publications.

Lazarus, A. (1976). *Multimodal Behavior Therapy*. New York: Springer.

Lowen, A. (1975). *Bioenergetics*. New York: Corward, McCann & Geoghegan.

Madanes, C. (1987). *Behind the One-Way Mirror: Advances in the Practice of Strategic Therapy*. San Francisco, CA: Jossey-Bass.

Meichenbaum, D. (1977). *Cognitive-Behavior Modification: An Integrative Approach*. New York: Plenum Press.

Moreno, J. (1972). *Psychodrama: First Volume* (4th ed. with Introductory Notes). New York: Beacon House.

Perls, F. (1947). *Ego Hunger and Aggression*. New York: Vintage Books division of Random House.

Perls, F. (1973). *The Gestalt Approach and Eye Witness to Therapy*. Palo Alto, CA: Science and Behavior Books.

Wolpe, J. (1948). *Psychotherapy by Reciprocal Inhibition*. Palo Alto, CA: Stanford University Press.

Wolpe, J. (1982). *The Practice of Behavior Therapy* (3rd ed.). New York: Pergamon Press.

Zeig, J. (Ed.). (1987). *The Evolution of Psychotherapy*. New York: Brunner/Mazel.

CHAPTER 6

A Grand Unified Theory for Brief Therapy: Putting Problems in Context
William Hudson O'Hanlon

For some years, physicists have been searching for a theory that could reconcile the divergent phenomena that recent observations and experiments have revealed. This elusive comprehensive theory is called the Grand Unified Theory (GUT) or the Theory of Everything (TOE). It is grandiose to claim to have a Grand Unified Theory for brief therapy— I don't have the guts to claim I have a Theory of Everything.

I *am* confident enough, however, to think that there are some common threads that make up the fabric of brief therapy and that I can articulate them here.

HEISENBERG MEETS PYGMALION

Hardening of the Categories

> In the sky there is no distinction of east and west; people create distinctions out of their own minds and then believe them to be true.
>
> —Buddha

Since I started with an analogy from physics, I might as well draw another. A physicist named Werner Heisenberg pointed out some years ago that there is no way that physicists can make precise observations on the subatomic level without disturbing the data they wish to study. This has come to be called the Heisenberg Uncertainty Principle. I'm not the first to make the connection of this principle to the social sciences, but I do think the principle holds true in the therapy field. In therapy, different therapists' observational tools and assessment procedures cannot help but influence the data being observed.

Unfortunately, most therapists have what I call "delusions of certainty" or "hardening of the categories." They are convinced that the observations they make during the assessment process are "real" and objective. They are certain they have discovered *real* problems.

I remember, though, when there were few bulimics and even fewer borderline personalities. Despite my gray hair, I'm not *that* old. These are relatively recent discoveries (or perhaps they should be called "inventities"). I have often told my students that I'm sorry that the therapy field doesn't sell futures in therapy diagnoses like they do in other commodities. Ten years ago I would have bought a few shares of Borderline stock, a couple of thousand shares of Adult Children of Alcoholics, and a little bulimia for a balanced portfolio. These days I'd recommend a hot investment opportunity in Multiple Personality Disorder and Adults Molested as Children. In fact, I'll share with you one surefire way to know when a particular therapeutic stock is about to take off: when it becomes known by its initials. How many of you know what PTSD is? What about ADD? MPD? Just five short years ago, these initials would have been meaningless to most of us.

Language Is a Virus: Linguistic Epidemics

Why can't we diagnose problems without in some way influencing them? Because we live in an atmosphere of language, which steers our thinking, experience, and behavior in certain directions. There are certain to be other psychiatric disorders that are discovered or invented in the future. Why aren't we noticing them now? Because we haven't yet distinguished them in language. We notice things as "things" by distinguishing them in "language land." How many pioneers crossing the plains of America suffered from stress? Probably none. Why? Because stress hadn't yet been invented as a problem for the pioneers. They may have had stress, but they never knew it, so it didn't bother them and they never felt the need to see a counselor about it. The same holds for low self-esteem. Cavemen never worked on their self-esteem, because they didn't have any to work on.

Problems do not exist in a vacuum. They exist only in a context—a linguistic, social, cultural context. They are languaged and interacted and presupposed and metaphored. In therapy, we must acknowledge the therapist as part of the problem context. The therapist helps to create therapeutic problems by the way in which he or she carries on the therapeutic interview and endeavor.

Seeing Is Believing: Pygmalion on the Couch

I maintain that there are no such "things" as therapy problems. I think therapists, for the most part, *give* their clients problems. That is, therapists negotiate problem definitions out of the raw material of clients' concerns by conversing with clients. They either come up with a problem definition that is agreeable to both client and therapist or they try to convince the client that he or she has a problem of the type the therapist says he or she has.

It seems more than a coincidence that when clients have seen Gestalt therapists for more than a few sessions, they usually have Gestalt-type problems and start to use Gestalt-like jargon. Likewise, analytic therapies seem to engender analytic-type problems. Behavior therapists always seem to identify and treat behavioral problems, neurologists usually find neurological problems, and biological psychiatrists almost always discover biochemical imbalances and disorders.

It should be obvious that clients do not usually sort out which theory will work best for them and then seek out that kind of practitioner. They come in complaining about something, concerned about things, and the therapist helps shape those complaints into therapy problems, i.e., some problem that therapy can solve and some problem that this particular therapist with this particular approach knows how to solve.

We advertently or inadvertently influence the descriptions our clients give us of their situations. We do not enter therapy neutrally, finding the "real" problem or problems. We usually only elicit or allow descriptions of problems that fit our theories, that we know how to cope with, make sense of, or solve.

Pygmalion was a sculptor in Greek mythology who created a sculpture of his ideal woman that was so lovely he fell in love with it. The gods were impressed and brought her to life for him. In a similar way, we fall in love with our theories and bring them to life in our clients. I call this "theory countertransference." Robert Rosenthal did some extensive investigation of this phenomenon and called it the Pygmalion Effect (Rosenthal & Jacobson, 1968).

Psychiatrist Jerome Kroll (1988) discussed the political and rather arbitrary nature of psychiatric diagnosis, especially the diagnosis of borderline personality. He writes,

> If we want to describe a horse or a tree, it might be easiest to walk out to a field and point to a horse or a tree. If you want to describe a borderline person, we first have to decide what one is; then, based upon what we have already decided to look for, we could then go out and find one. . . . We tend to reify our concepts, to think we have discovered real entities in nature and real discontinuities between normal and abnormal. (p. xi; p. 3)

So, combining the Uncertainty Principle with the Pygmalion Phenomenon, we come to the idea that there is no way to discover what the "real" problem is in any therapeutic situation. The therapist influences the data and the description in directions that are biased toward his or her theoretical models.

Questionable Realities: Assessment as Intervention

> Questions arise from a point of view—from something that helps to structure what is problematical, what is worth asking, and what constitutes an answer (or progress). It is not that the view determines reality, only what we accept from reality and how we structure it.
>
> Allen Newell

Of course, clients sometimes enter therapy with some clear ideas about what their problems are. During the process of interviewing and assessing clients' situations—talking and interacting with them—we cast doubt on their problem descriptions and offer another or other ones.

On a recent plane ride, I was seated next to a professional woman from the Boston area. When she discovered that I was a psychotherapist, she began discussing her recent experience of entering therapy for the first time in her life. She had sought therapy for some obsessions that had been plaguing her for years. When, at the end of the first session (which took place at the beginning of February), the therapist had warned her that he took his annual vacation in August, she was shocked and amused. Her thought at the time, she said, was that she would be long gone from therapy by that time. Our plane ride took place in July and she reported that she now realized that her problems were much deeper than she had first imagined and could see that the therapist had been wise to warn her of the impending break from therapy, as she was bracing herself to make it on her own for the month. She wondered, by the way, since I did hypnosis, if I could recommend a hypnotherapist in the Boston area to help her get rid of her obsessions. She saw no contradiction in this. She really liked her analyst and planned to continue with him. She just wanted to get rid of her symptoms. She hadn't yet learned that this might be objectionable to her therapist, perhaps viewed as a flight into health, avoidance, or an attempt to find a magical cure.

From what I've read and from my experience, most people stay in therapy, whether it's successful or not, for less than 10 sessions. If that is the case, and if we can negotiate different problem definitions from the raw material clients bring to therapy, then it is incumbent upon us as therapists to choose ways of thinking and talking in therapy that allow for the creation of problems that are solvable. Beyond that, we should be creating problems that are solvable quickly and with only the resources that our clients have available to them.

Most therapists are having conversations with clients that lead to the view that they are suffering from some pathological, psychological, emotional, neurological, or biochemical disorder. These therapists suffer from delusions of certainty when they think they are discovering and identifying real problems.

What I am suggesting is that therapists deliberately have conversations for solutions with clients. Therapy is suffering from an overdose of explanations. By now, perhaps it is becoming clear that no explanation is the only correct one. Probably all of them have some validity; it is their utility that I am discussing here. At best, explanations serve to distract us from our main and direct goal of helping people sort out the difficulties they are expressing. At worst, they become justifications for a lack of results. "It's okay," colleagues say to you, "don't expect much, he's a borderline. Just don't get too many at one time in your practice or you'll burn out."

I've been taking a survey recently in my workshops on how many people have ever cured a borderline personality. I can tell you that the results are rather dismal. A few people have reported cures, however, and I have told them that we should be coming to their workshops because they have found a way of using this made-up diagnosis and helping someone successfully.

Now when I say that borderline personality is an invention, I don't mean to solely pick on that diagnosis: There have been a number of autopsies performed over the past several hundred years and no one has yet reported finding borderline personalities inside people. They have not found any personalities inside people. That is because they do not exist inside people. They exist in language between people. But, so do all the other psychotherapeutic "inventities."

There are many aspects of human behavior and experience, then, that one could focus on in therapy. Where we put our attention and direct our inquiries will inevitably influence the course of treatment and the data that emerge. Since all successful therapy eventually comes around to finding solutions by getting people to do something different or to view things differently, I propose that we all start pursuing these goals more deliberately from the start of therapy. Do not stop at "explanations"; go directly to "solutions."

All theories are not created equal. That is, they may be equally made up, but they have unequal consequences. Choosing certain assumptions and views can create the likelihood of briefer courses of therapy. Other assumptions and views virtually assure longer-term treatment (provided the client stays around to participate). Next, I'll identify some of these views and assumptions, both those that create the likelihood of brief treatment and those that mitigate against it.

NAÏVE LISTENING

Let clients teach you what they are concerned about, what they are seeking, and what does or doesn't work.

Psychotheological Dogma

Most therapists enter therapy with a background of unexamined assumptions that are subtly influencing what they perceive and elicit during therapy interviews. These biases become barriers to actually listening to clients to let them teach you how to resolve their concerns. While there are too many of these biases and assumptions to examine here (see O'Hanlon & Wilk, 1987, and O'Hanlon & Weiner-Davis, 1988, for more detailed discussions), I'll delineate a few examples.

One of the notions that most therapists seem to hold is what I call the idea of *Hidden Information or Conflicts*. This is the idea that there are some hidden, repressed, or other nonobvious items that the therapist has some good clues about and can lead the client to discover or acccept. These ideas are said to be related in some way to the origin or maintenance of the presenting complaint. For example, Jay Haley (1976) and other family therapists have the idea that any problem serves an interpersonal function. Many psychodynamic therapists have the idea that there are some unresolved issues or conflicts from childhood that need to come to consciousness and be "worked through." Cognitive therapists think there are some unrecognized irrational or distorted thinking patterns that create or maintain the problem. I taught a workshop recently with psychologist Jay Efran, who uses George Kelly's Personal Construct Theory in his therapy. He maintains, after an idea of Kelly's, that all symptoms are questions the person is asking. So, of course, as his major orientation to therapy, he searches for the unarticulated questions and helps people articulate them.

Another common idea or tactic in therapy is for therapists to search for the *Universal Pattern*. When a person reports having problems in a particular relationship, the therapist will immediately ask about other relationships to identify a universal relationship pattern. "Do you do this with all women?" Or, "What kind of man was your father?"

Excuse Me, but My Karma Just Ran Over Your Dogma

One of my missions in life is to get therapists to become more aware of the unexamined assumptions that they hold that are influencing their therapy data and results and to be more careful and purposeful in choosing working assumptions. I think it is my karma, as they say in the East.

Milton Erickson's work gives some hints about how to avoid resistance and how to make therapy more brief. Surprisingly, it is very basic. Also surprisingly, most therapists do not use these principles. In essence, Erickson taught that you should listen to your clients without imposing your preconceived psychotherapy theories on them and that you should use as grist for the mill anything they bring to therapy—even things that appear at first glance to be problematic.

Before clients even enter their offices, most therapists already have ideas about the nature of problems and how to resolve them. If your theoretical bias is analytic, you already are certain that people's problems arise from intrapersonal conflicts that derive from childhood experiences. If you are a family therapist, you are certain that the problem arises from or is maintained by family processes or structures. And so on.

Worse than that, before therapy begins, many therapists are already certain of the goals they will have with their clients: Analytic therapists have predecided that clients must have insights and work through conflicts to bring repressed material to consciousness and the like. Family therapists have goals such as reorganizing the family system.

If You Don't Know Where You're Going, You'll Probably End Up Somewhere Else

In the past few years, I have had a few clients enter my office waving brochures they found in my waiting room regarding workshops I was teaching on brief therapy. "What is this brief therapy?" they demand to know. "I've been seeing you for two years!" I tell them that brief therapy isn't for everyone and that they have taught me that their concerns were not to be resolved briefly.

Most concerns that people bring to therapy, however, *can* be resolved briefly. I've done a lot of thinking about this and have noticed that the cases that are brief are almost always those that have clear, identifiable outcomes specified in the early part of therapy.

We should be careful, therefore, to negotiate problem definitions that allow for solutions in a reasonable amount of time. That, in part, is why so few people raise their hands when I ask how many people have cured a borderline personality. It is very difficult, if not impossible, to change someone's personality. Jay Haley (1976) once had a supervisee who told him that the family she was having trouble treating included a mother and daughter who were symbiotically attached to one another. "I'd never let that be the problem" was his advice. And sage advice it was—to stress both that the supervisee could choose different aspects of the situation to highlight in her conception of the problem and that her particular conception wasn't helping to create change in this situation.

WHEN THERAPY STARTS AND WHEN IT SHOULD END

Since I've already said that I think that therapists cocreate problems with clients, I obviously don't think that having a problem is the indication for starting therapy. Many people have difficulties, like our stressed-out pioneers, and never enter therapy. Therapy starts when someone is complaining about something and someone decides that what is being complained about is relevant for therapy. Of course, sometimes someone other than the person who shows up for the session is complaining (as in cases of "involuntary" treatment, such as court-ordered treatment and parents who bring their children to have therapy when the children do not perceive a difficulty).

Therapy can end satisfactorily, then, simply when whoever was complaining about something no longer complains about it. This happens in two ways: one is when what the person was complaining about is no longer perceived as a problem. The other condition for successfully ending therapy is when what the client was complaining about is no longer happening often enough or intensely enough for the person to say it is a problem.

A goal, then, is the magnetic north that can orient the therapist's compass. One of the difficulties in the field of therapy is the inability of our field to define what constitutes successful treatment. Goals should derive mainly from the client's vision of what constitutes success, subject to some negotiation with the client to ensure the achievability of the goal. Measurement of success should come from clients' reports. If clients say that what they were complaining about is no longer a therapeutic issue or if what they were complaining about is no longer happening, then therapy has succeeded.

THE TWO TASKS OF BRIEF THERAPY

Brief therapists have two common tasks. While other therapies may have these elements, brief therapists are just more deliberate in their attempts to accomplish them.

Changing the Viewing

First, we attempt to change clients' views of their "problematic" situation. I put problematic in quotation marks to indicate that even the idea that there is a problem is a view that is open to change and negotiation (O'Hanlon & Wilk, 1987). The situation might be seen as a "challenge" or a "signal for growth" or an "unowned part expressing itself" or an "unavoidable part of life, nothing to be concerned about" as opposed to a "problem." Included in the category of "Changing the Viewing" is altering the client's perception, focus of attention, and frame of reference.

Changing the Doing

In addition to changing the viewing of the "problem" situation, brief therapists try to affect the actions and interactions involved in the situation. The actions include both internal processes and external behavior, what people do inside themselves and what other people can see them do. The interactions include what people do with one another in familiar and other personal and social contexts. This also includes what they say to one another or others about the problem situation.

HOW DO YOU DO IT SO QUICKLY?

Riding the Horse in the Direction He's Going

Some years ago, my father-in-law, who is a therapist, asked me what, in my view, would endure of Erickson's contributions after the Erickson fad and cult passed (I think he was trying to give me an indirect message). I answered without hesitation, "The Utilization Approach." Erickson stressed that therapists should be observing clients' responses and behavior and using this information to tailor treatment for the unique individual. Steve Gilligan (1987) wrote extensively on what he calls "co-operation," which means that instead of the therapist operating on the client, the therapist and client coevolve a working style together that fits with this client and respects all of his or her aspects and expressions. Most therapists make their clients come to their theories and ways of working. If the client doesn't adapt, he or she is resistant or defensive or a poor candidate for therapy.

Erickson, chameleon-like, adapted to the language and response style of his clients. Thus, he was able to rapidly gain rapport and clients' trust. As Werner Erhard (1972) has said, "It's easier to ride the horse in the direction it's going."

Catching Clients Doing Something Right for a Change

For most of its history, therapy has been focused on identifying what is wrong with people and helping them to correct or accept those limitations or pathologies. Erickson's work has a different orientation. One of his cases (cited in Zeig, 1980, pp. 285–287) illustrates this orientation. He treated a woman who was depressed and isolated by having her cultivate African violet plants and give them to the people in her church and social community who were experiencing life transitions such as births, deaths, or engagements. She became known and loved throughout her community as "The African Violet Queen" and was widely mourned at her death. I remember quite vividly when Erickson described that case to me. He noted how he had taken a tour of her house, an old mansion that was dark and dank. The only room in the house with any light and color was the plant nursery, where several African violet plants were growing. Erickson said that once he spotted that patch of life in an otherwise lifeless house, he knew there was a possibility for good results.

Instead of concentrating our efforts on identifying and correcting pathology, we should concentrate on shoring up and amplifying people's resources and strengths. People are more likely to cooperate and change in an environment that supports their strength and resourcefulness, and that offers a view of them as capable, than they are when focused on pathology and problems.

Clients can be more resourceful than we think they can be. I had a client who was frustrated by her husband's avoidance of their marital problems. He was a psychiatrist who complained that he had to listen to complaints and troubles all day long, so when he came home that was the last thing he wanted to deal with. Still, his wife, my client, was dissatisfied and wanted to talk things out. I didn't have any bright ideas, but I told the woman that she was bright and creative and I was certain she would find a way to approach him that would work. I suggested that she approach him in an environment in which he would be likely to listen and respond. She came back the next week to report that she had used my idea and it had worked. She had arranged with his secretary at work to make an appointment with him at his office. When the time came for the appointment, she was waiting in the office waiting room. The secretary played it straight and introduced him to his new patient, so he played along. He invited her into his office and asked her what had brought her to see him. She told him that she was married to a wonderful man whom she loved deeply, but that he wasn't responding to her attempts to deal with some difficulties in their relationship and she couldn't figure out how to get him to respond. She was concerned, she told him, that they were drifting apart, and she didn't want that. He listened and asked her more about the issues and at the end of the session gave her some suggestions for what she might do to get a good response from him. They made another appointment for the next week and continued this for several months on a regular basis. Their relationship remains much improved.

Not Brief, but Effective, Therapy

Dick Fisch (personal communication, 1988) maintains that the issue isn't whether therapy is brief or not, but whether it is effective. Brief therapy can teach us much about how to do effective therapy. I have suggested that recognizing and using the negotiability of the presenting problem is the place to start. Going on to create solvable problems and focusing on changing clients' views and actions, what I called the doing and the viewing of the situation, is the next step. To accomplish this, orienting to what clients are complaining about, and what their goals are, provides a focus for treatment. Rapport and rapid change are facilitated by utilizing clients' beliefs and styles and by focusing on clients' strength and resources.

Now what I have been offering is not only a theory for brief therapy, but one that I think can be used for all therapy. Not all therapy can be brief, but therapy usually can be made more brief by deliberately using the principles outlined herein.

REFERENCES

Erhard, W. (1972). *If God Had Wanted You to Fly, He Would Have Given You Wings OR Up to Your Ass in Aphorisms.* San Francisco: Privately published.

Gilligan, S. (1987). *Therapeutic Trances: The Cooperation Principle in Ericksonian Hypnotherapy.* New York: Brunner/Mazel.

Haley, J. (1976). *Problem-Solving Therapy.* New York: Harper & Row.

Kroll, J. (1988). *The Challenge of the Borderline Patient.* New York: Norton.

O'Hanlon, W. H., & Weiner-Davis, M. (1988). *In Search of Solutions: A New Direction in Psychotherapy.* New York: Norton.

O'Hanlon, B., & Wilk, J. (1987). *Shifting Contexts: The Generation of Effective Psycotherapy.* New York: Guilford Press.

Rosenthal, R., & Jaccobson, L. (1968). *Pygmalion in the Classroom: Teacher Expectation and Pupils' Intellectual Development.* New York: Holt, Rinehart & Winston.

Zeig, J. (Ed.) (1980). *A Teaching Seminar with Milton H. Erickson.* New York: Brunner/Mazel.

CHAPTER 7

What Is It About Brief Therapy That Works?*

Steve de Shazer

The easiest, simplest answer, and perhaps the best one, should come first. Whenever my trainees ask, "What makes brief therapy work?" I tell them simply this: "It is magic. I do not know how clients do it."

Well, all therapy involves some sort of magic. I think we all have unconsciously known this to be true. Where the magician relies on the hand being quicker than the eye, the therapist (particularly an Ericksonian) relies on the mouth being quicker than the ear. Let's be clear: I do not mean to imply in the least that therapy is a trick of some sort, that it is all done with mirrors. But, no matter how scientifically rigorous and philosophically elegant any description of brief therapy is, there is still magic. Like the magician, the brief therapist needs lots of ability and lots of hard work to practice the art and make it effective.

TRADITIONAL CONSTRUCTIONS

Every day I talk to clients and therapists (including trainees, consultees, and referral sources). They all tell me about PROBLEMS (diagnosis) and their CAUSES (etiology). The majority of the time, they paint a horrible picture. Therapists' descriptions suggest that their clients are

---

*As of December, 1988.

infected with massive pathology which has been exacerbated by duration and human weakness. If they are family therapists, then the picture of devastation is frequently enlarged to include the other members of the family and the reified "family system."

Given the bias that problems are rooted in history and pathology, it is little wonder that therapists frequently think therapy needs to be and should be "long term." Given this construction, brief therapy is fundamentally absurd.

Most traditional forms of therapy are based on what seems to be a common-sense point of view about problem solving: Before a problem can be solved (or an illness cured), it is necessary to find out what is wrong. Most forms of therapy share the assumption that a rigorous analysis of the problem leads to understanding it and its underlying causes. That is, what the client presents (i.e., complaints) is ordinarily seen as a symptom or a "deeper" or "real" problem and that "complaints" are the manifestation of the "real" problem. These "causal problems" include, but are not limited to:

1. "incongruent hierarchies,"
2. "covert parental conflicts,"
3. "low self-esteem,"
4. "lack of individuation,"
5. various "traumas,"
6. "deviant communication,"
7. "repressed feelings," and
8. "dirty games."

Frequently, symptoms are seen to have beneficial effects, such as preventing something worse from happening; e.g., anorexia is seen as preventing destruction of the family unit. This "benevolent" assumption leads to the idea that there must be a family problem underlying or creating a situation in which anorexia develops.

Based on the logic of these assumptions, problem maintenance has something to do with:

1. structural difficulties and/or
2. hierarchical difficulties and/or
3. failed attempts at solution and/or
4. intrapsychic difficulties and/or
5. biochemistry and/or
6. systemic homeostasis and/or
7. mislearning.

It is generally assumed that therapy focuses on getting rid of these causes in order to solve the problem (or cure the illness). Thus, the therapeutic objective encompasses breaking up the problem maintenance mechanisms. The structuralists want to change the structure, the systemicists want to alter the homeostatic plateau, the strategists want to change the hierarchy, and so forth.

Clients' constructions, though sometimes related in theme and structure, are relatively benign. I suspect they want to tell therapists the problem's history and their ideas about causation because they think that is what therapists want to hear. They have learned from our Freudian popular culture that therapists think that solving a problem involves "getting at the cause of it." It is little wonder that some are leery about the idea of brief therapy. But since problems are "a pain in the ass" for clients, most often they are willing to suspend their disbelief and give it a try.

A DIFFERENT TRADITION WITH A DIFFERENT CONSTRUCTION

During the past 20 years of doing, studying, thinking about, and observing brief therapy, I have devised about 1,000 different descriptions of how brief therapy works. That is roughly one construction for every 10 cases. Along the way, I have found out that I never know what I think until I see what I write and how I write it. This has allowed me to throw away some of the more obviously stupid answers.

The answers that I thought held up best (the ones that more closely approximated a good answer!) I have used as the material for articles, books, and most recently, expert systems (e.g., de Shazer, 1975, 1978, 1979, 1985). But, just when I have one that I think is the best, the clearest, the most comprehensive and most general, something happens that leads me in another direction. Therefore, today's answer is only for today;[*] tomorrow it might change, or it might not.

For the sake of clarity, "brief therapy," as I use the term, is a tradition akin to, but distinct in some important ways from, both family therapy and Ericksonian hypnotherapy. Some types of so-called "brief therapy" may not fit within this tradition and what I have to say may well not fit for them, but I intend to neither include nor exclude these other "brief therapies" from today's answer.

---

[*]Actually, the answer in this paper is the answer for August 1988 when this was written. My answer could change by the time of the presentation in December 1988. And it may have further changes by the time readers see this.

Mental Research Institute (MRI)

One branch of the tradition of which I am a part evolved from certain facets of Milton Erickson's work which were mixed with general systems theory by John Weakland and his associates at MRI. As a result, they invented a model of brief therapy based on "focused problem resolution" (Weakland, Fisch, Watzlawick, & Bodin, 1974).

Brief Family Therapy Center (BFTC)

Meanwhile, another branch of the tradition evolved that is based on some different aspects of Erickson's work, which, it turned out, serendipitously helped me solve a puzzle I saw within the MRI model, i.e., what to do with poorly formed complaints and poorly formed goals. My associates and I at BFTC blended my earlier work (de Shazer, 1975, 1978, 1979) back into the work of MRI, developing a model of brief therapy based on "focused solution development" (de Shazer, 1985, 1988; de Shazer et al., 1986).

THE TRADITION'S CENTRAL PHILOSOPHY

The magic of brief therapy is only effective when the therapist has ignored a great many red herrings or distractions and instead focused on the clues that he or she and the client have constructed as a sign of successful completion of a task. But, of course, "focusing down" like Sherlock Holmes is not always a simple process and playing Watson or even Lestrade chasing after red herrings is always possible.

Brief therapists have developed some simple guidelines about how to tell the difference between red herrings and clues. These three rules form the basic underlying philosophy of this tradition:

1. *If it ain't broke, don't fix it.* This means that if the client is not actively complaining about it, then it is none of our business. This rule applies no matter how obvious "the problem" is to the therapist and/or society.

2. *Once you know what works, do more of it.* This means that when you and the client find a salient exception to the complaint (i.e., times when the rule "it always happens" is violated), the solution probably lies in making the exception into a new rule (de Shazer, 1985, 1988; de Shazer et al., 1986). Furthermore, when an intervention has prompted movement toward the goal, then the following intervention should be simply "do more of the same."

3. If it doesn't work, don't do it again. Do something different. This means that if you don't know what works, then you at least can know what does not work. What does not work is to be avoided at all costs. Just about anything that is different stands a chance of making a difference.°

TODAY'S EXPLANATION

The underlying law that I have learned to keep in mind when doing or thinking about or studying brief therapy was mandated by a 14th-century philosopher, William of Ockham. It's called Ockham's Razor: What can be done with fewer means is done in vain with many. This has been rephrased in 20th-century terms as "Keep it simple, stupid."

I have long been interested in attempting to produce a clear, concise, and minimal specification of what brief therapy is about and the steps involved in doing it. Some, no doubt, will think that I have, at times, taken this research and theory construction program to its absurd limits. In keeping with this, I will limit my answer to one minor point followed by three major ones. Hopefully, this minimal description will not contribute to making a mystery of brief therapy.

Complaints

The complaints clients bring brief therapists seem to be constructed on a simple premise: whatever it is they are complaining about "always happens." The couple is *always* fighting, the children are *always* misbehaving. Sometimes different words are used to express the same idea: I am crippled; I am depressed; I am an exhibitionist; I am an anorexic; he is an alcoholic; she is a schizophrenic. Regardless, clients have had the bad luck of talking about things in a way that leads them into constructing the complaint as a situation involving a steady state. It is locked into the words they use, i.e., "I am" and/or "It is" and/or "always." Once you hear those words, you expect what follows to fit into the formula, "I am *this*," with "this" being something immutable or unchangeable, such as, "I am a male," or "I am a Swede." As the philosopher Wittgenstein (1958,

---

°There is a point of difference between MRI and BFTC about this. They mistakenly think that the third rule (do something different) is the second and our second rule is the third (Weakland, 1988). What difference this difference makes is up to you. Probably clients do not care.

1968) put it, when we use analogous grammar in different sentences, we (perhaps unconsciously) expect them to have analogous meanings.

Interestingly, you cannot have a problem without first having the idea that a solution is possible. Otherwise, all these complaints would be described as Dorothy L. Sayer's Lord Peter Wimsey puts it: "Life is just one damn thing after another." The "I am" or "it always happens" form of grammar, however, leads clients to the idea that their situations are hopeless and unsolvable: "Our life is a mess because we are always fighting, but we should not be" or "Our life is a mess because the adolescents always do what they want, but they should do as they are told" or "My life is a mess because I am a flasher and that's immoral and illegal."

Clients define their bad luck in this rigid way and, unfortunately, so do many therapists, as evidenced by the standard diagnostic schema. It would seem reasonable that helping clients to change this definition would take a long time. After all, the evidence seems to be in favor of the durability of what is described by these rigid definitions. In fact, given this typical frame, brief therapy appears unreasonable; it should not work. But it does, even though it appears illogical!

Exceptions

Surprisingly, therapists do not even need to know what the problem is in order to solve it as long as they and the clients know what the goal is (de Shazer, 1985). How is this possible? Well, it turns out that clients are mistaken in the depictions of themselves and their situations. For instance, they *say* they are always fighting, but it turns out that when therapists ask in the right way, they will find out that the couple sometimes gets along, that the flasher overcomes the urge to flash, and so forth. Interestingly, exceptions are often "news" to the client as well as to the therapist (de Shazer, 1985, 1988; de Shazer et al., 1986).

For example, at the start of the first session, a couple recently told me that they bickered all the time. As soon as it seemed reasonable, I asked them about any times they were aware of not bickering. By the end of the first session, they had discovered that they really only bickered 60% of the time. This was "news" to them. Their goal was to be bicker-free 81% of the time and their descriptions of life after the goal was met could be seen as a result of increasing the frequency of what they were already doing when they were not bickering. By the third session, each said they were bicker-free 80% of the time; i.e., they had doubled the frequency of their exceptions and, in fact, one could say that being bicker-free was a new rule in their relationship. At no point during any of the three sessions did we discuss bickering, the pattern(s) involved, its possible causes, or its possible meanings. We only talked about what they did when they did not bicker.

Similarly, during another recent first session, a young man started off the hour by depicting himself as a helpless victim of a compulsion to expose himself. As we talked, he discovered that he overcame the urge to flash at least 50% of the time. This ability to sometimes overcome the urge was "news" to him.

It is important to remember that exceptions do not exist out there in the "real world"; they are cooperatively invented or constructed by the therapist and client talking together. Before the therapist and client talk about exceptions, these times are simply seen as "flukes" or differences that do not make a difference. It is the therapist's task to help clients make flukes into differences that make a difference. I am continually surprised by exceptions and frequently I let the client see this. Client stories about times when the complaint is unexpectedly absent frequently "knock my socks off."

As I see it, inventing exceptions pokes holes in the clients' frame ("I am this" or "It always happens") so that they can see through it: The complaint rule is deconstructed so that its immutability is undecidable. The "I am a flasher" rule changes into something else, perhaps: "I sometimes expose myself." The "sometimes" in this sentence is very strong. It is difficult to even unconsciously hear the sentence as analogous to "I am a male." This deconstruction prompts clients to at least begin to doubt their "it always happens" rule. Once doubt is developed, what is really going on becomes undecidable and a new reality can be constructed.

Of course, finding fluke events that can be constructed into exceptions is not always easy and the search for exceptions is not always successful. Then the therapist needs to help the client do something different so that a fluke can develop and be used to deconstruct the complaint. In either case, these exceptions then need to become differences that make a difference to the client, signaling that the problem is solved.

Randomness

Any "randomness" or "spontaneity" or "chance" in the clients' descriptions of their complaints and/or the exceptions is a clue to the therapist that some chance or random element can usefully be structured into the task so that the complaint rule can be deconstructed.

Client descriptions of exceptions are based either on their deliberate behavior or on chance and spontaneity. Of course, when it involves deliberate behavior, then a task suggesting they do more of what works makes sense and is frequently effective. However, when the exception "just happens," then a different approach is called for. I do not really understand how this works, but simply asking the client to daily predict whether or not an exception will occur the following day frequently prompts the client to report an increase in the frequency of exceptions!

For example, at the end of both of the first two sessions with the flasher, I simply asked him to predict, each day, whether he would overcome the urge the flash on the following day. He was then to see if he had been right or wrong and to account for this. He did the task and the frequency of flashing went down. He also discovered more about what he did to overcome the urge. How this works is *really* a mystery.

Goals: The Central Focus of Brief Therapy

"Suppose that one night, while you were sleeping, there was a miracle and the problem was solved. How would you know? What would you be doing the next day that would tell you there had been a miracle? How would other people know without your having told them?" We call this the "miracle question." It is by far the simplest way I have ever developed to help clients state goals in concrete, behavioral terms.

Solution talk (Gingerich, de Shazer, & Weiner-Davis, 1988), or talking about the goal and the steps toward reaching it, seems to be positively related to outcome even in models of therapy that are not solution focused and not intentionally brief (Shields, Sprenkle, & Constantine, 1988).

As I see it, in order for therapy to be brief and effective, both therapist and client need to know where they are going and they need to know how to know when they get there. For me, this is best summed up with the answers to these questions: How will things be after the problem is solved? Once the problem is solved, what will the client be doing that he or she is not doing now? Who will be doing what differently?

Most simply, a picture of "life after successful therapy" can guide the work of both therapist and client. Like Weakland and his team (Weakland et al., 1974), my colleagues and I prefer small, concrete, specific goals; the more behaviorally described the goal, the better. However, this is not always what the client prefers. So we have learned to accept this and to be pleased with a goal as long as the clients are sure they will know somehow that the problem is solved even if they cannot describe

98   BRIEF THERAPY

it to us. In these situations, we might have the client set up a scale with "10" standing for the worst the problem has ever been and "0" standing for the day after the problem is solved. Then, each session we "measure" progress.

Particularly with couples and families, but also with individuals, multiple goals are useful because therapist and client alike then have multiple or optional ways to know the problem is solved. In fact, when there are multiple goals, further talk about which goal will be achieved first can be useful in promoting the clients' expectation of solution.

To a greater or lesser extent, well-formed goals have the following qualities:

1. They are small rather than large.
2. They are salient to the client.
3. They are described in specific, concrete behavioral terms.
4. They are realistically achievable.
5. They are perceived as difficult, involving hard work.
6. They are described as "the start of something," NOT the "end of something."

CONCLUSION

Most simply put, therapy is a conversation between at least two people (minimally one therapist and one client) about reaching the client's goal. When as a result of this conversation clients begin to have doubts about their immutable framing of their troublesome situation, the door to change and solution has been opened. This is the essence of brief therapy.

The MRI approach to this conversation is based on inducing doubt by reframing the problem (Fisch, Weakland, & Segal, 1983; Weakland et al., 1974). They take the same facts the client describes and use them in a different context. This places the client's context ("it always happens") into doubt. Within the new context the problem is no longer a problem and thus a different future becomes possible (success measured by goal achievement). Tasks, as with Erickson (Haley, 1967), are based on using the new frame and the different behavior it calls for, thus prompting goal achievement.

The BFTC approach to this conversation is based on inducing doubt through searching for and most often finding exceptions to the rule "It always happens" (de Shazer, 1988). If it is not always happening, then it is not really a problem after all and thus a different future becomes possible (success measured by goal achievement). Using this approach I bypass even looking for a problem and look directly for any problem-free times. Thus, I "ignore" the problem and work directly on developing the solution. Tasks are based on using the exception to help the client reach the goal.

Obviously, there are other approaches that use different ways to promote doubt, the expectation of solution, and solution. Perhaps I will find another way tomorrow.

REFERENCES

de Shazer, S. (1975). Brief therapy: Two's company. *Family Process, 14*(1), 78–93.

de Shazer, S. (1978). Brief hypnotherapy of two sexual dysfunctions: The crystal ball technique. *American Journal of Clinical Hypnosis, 20*(3), 203–208.

de Shazer, S. (1979). On transforming symptoms: An approach to an Erickson procedure. *American Journal of Clinical Hypnosis, 22*, 17–28.

de Shazer, S. (1985). *Keys to Solution in Brief Therapy*. New York: Norton.

de Shazer, S. (1988). *Clues: Investigating Solutions in Brief Therapy*. New York: W. W. Norton.

de Shazer, S., Berg, I., Lipchik, E., Nunnally, E., Molnar, A., Gingerich, W., & Weiner-Davis, M. (1986). Brief therapy: Focused solution development. *Family Process, 25*, 207–222.

Fisch, R., Weakland, J. H., & Segal, L. (1983). *The Tactics of Change: Doing Therapy Briefly*. San Francisco: Jossey-Bass.

Gingerich, W. J., de Shazer, S., & Weiner-Davis, M. (1988). Constructing change: A research view of interviewing. In E. Lipchik (Ed.), *Interviewing*. Rockville, MD: Aspen.

Haley, J. (Ed.) (1967). *Advanced Techniques of Hypnosis and Therapy: Selected Papers of Milton H. Erickson*. New York: Grune & Stratton.

Shields, C., Sprenkle, D., & Constantine, J. (1988). An analysis of initial interviews of family therapy: The therapeutic interaction coding system (TICS). Unpublished manuscript.

Weakland, J. H. (1988). Personal communication.

Weakland, J. H., Fisch, R., Watzlawick, P., & Bodin, A. (1974). Brief therapy: Focused problem resolution. *Family Process, 13*, 141–168.

Wittgenstein, L. (1958). *The Blue and Brown Books*. New York: Harper. Trans. R. Rhees.

Wittgenstein, L. (1968). *Philosophical Investigations*, rev. 3rd. ed. New York: Macmillan. Trans. G. E. M. Anscombe.

CHAPTER 8

Myths About Brief Therapy; Myths of Brief Therapy
John Weakland

Let me explain my title and clarify what I intend to discuss in this chapter. By "myths about brief therapy" I mean myths held—at least for the most part—by people outside the field, not themselves engaged in practicing brief treatment. Correspondingly, by "myths of brief therapy" I mean myths held by people within the field, engaged in practicing some sort of brief therapy. However, although this is a useful distinction for the purpose of organizing a discussion, it should not be taken as always plain or absolute. It will become clear that there are overlaps across this boundary, especially that myths *about* brief therapy may carry over into the practice of brief therapy, and by doing so strongly influence that practice.

I will not attempt to be comprehensive, either in terms of including all myths currently relevant to brief therapy or in terms of a complete examination of any particular myth. Rather, I will select a few major myths and clarify the messages, explicit and implicit, that seem functionally most important, i.e., most influential in defining an attitude or line of action toward the practice of brief treatment.

THE NATURE OF MYTH

It is first essential to say something about "myths" in general, to make my view and usage of this concept clear. Let me begin with a negative statement, to make plain what I do not mean—that I am departing from perhaps the most common idea of myth. I do not see "myth" as an opposite of "truth," as presenting a fantasy in contrast to describing "reality." Instead, I see myths in general as explanatory schema, as ways of using language to interrelate, order, and make some kind of sense out of some set of observations about nature or life. Both the area of interest and observation and the style and clarity of the language employed in giving some ordered account may vary widely. Yet the basic nature and function of myth making are the same for a primitive tribe's myth of the origin of the world, the scriptures of a world religion, or a scientific theory—even in physics.

To put it bluntly, we cannot state what "truth" or "reality" is, and we will never be able to do so. Many, perhaps most, would view this view with alarm: Where is the firm ground we can stand on? Instead, the greater danger lies in the desperate quest for certainty and the accompanying labeling of myths as truth, or worse, as *the* truth, no matter to what conflicts or impasses this leads. And there is much evidence—from the large scale of history to the small scale of our own work with specific human problems—to support this. This may be one reason why Milton Erickson, though himself a great mythologist—a creator and user of stories and metaphors—was so careful and skeptical about building theory with a capital "T," preferring instead to emphasize the variability of individuals and events and the need to garner specific information on concrete behavior.

On reflection—especially reflection on our own field of problems and treatment—it is rather evident that we do not live by realities, but by *interpretations* of observed events or situations. Even our observations—since we can never attend to everything fully and equally—depend on preconceptions of what is most significant. Even when we evaluate the significance of simple specific behaviors of ourselves and others, interpretation of the meaning of any given behavior may vary widely. One wife may see her husband's frequent late return from work as meaning "He doesn't care for his family," while another sees it as "He cares so much he works extra hard to provide for us." Obviously, interpretation has great consequences for the relationship. And finally, to compound the uncertainty of observation and interpretation, the language we use, not only for interpretation but even for description, necessarily is symbolic and therefore always basically metaphorical.

If one can never have certainty, but only interpretations, what is the point of examining myths in general, and myths concerning brief therapy in particular? The point is this: As humanly constructed interpretive schema (whether constructed deliberately or arising out of social interaction), myths embody and summarize ways of looking at things; they show how people have been accustomed to viewing a certain area of experience. And beyond this, there is the other side of the coin. In another example of Bateson's dictum that every communication is both a report and a command (Ruech & Bateson, 1951, pp. 179-180), any such explanatory schema also proposes how the matter in question *should* be understood and responded to, and this is a directive outlining proper thought and action. Thus, in a fundamental sense myths are like maps; they shape and order our understanding of a given territory and guide our steps in traversing it, or avoiding it, and as ancient geographical maps often warned, "Beyond this point be monsters." Similarly, maps may be judged pragmatically, by their usefulness in helping us get to where we aim to go. In the present case of brief therapy, the territory of concern is that of human problems. The means of travel consists of therapeutic concepts and associated practices, and the goal is effective and efficient (and *therefore* brief) resolution of such problems. On this basis, it is useful to examine some major views concerning brief therapy, so that we may see as plainly as possible the basic views of the territory these myths project, what they propose to lead us toward or away from, and the means of locomotion they recommend.

Two different aspects need to be considered in evaluating and comparing myths as maps. First, there is what in a general sense may be called the content of the myth. This is the major concern of the present necessarily limited examination. The main lines of what the myth says must be summarized as clearly and concisely as possible, to get an overview and not be lost in details. But this is not all. Myths often imply much more than they state explicitly, and since implicit content is usually more general, it is likely to be of great importance in determining broad orientations and the interpretation of more specific details. For maps of psychotherapy, for example, unstated differences in underlying general premises may be critical for understanding differences in approach. Therefore, it is important to make the implicit content of myths explicit, as well as this can be done.

Second, there is what may be called the form of myths of psychotherapy. This includes the breadth of the area covered, the economy of the myth's account of this, its completeness, and its clarity. That is, while attempting to formulate a clear and succinct account of the content of any myth, it is important always to remember that its raw original state also strongly affects its functional usefulness as a map. For example, some myths of psychotherapy are stated in such vague terms that their guidance is ambiguous. Others, while more specific and explicit, are too complex and detailed to follow surely. And especially, where basic premises are left implicit and taken for granted, the voyager may be led in critical directions without recognizing this influence.

MYTHS ABOUT BRIEF THERAPY

Quite naturally and expectably, the most important myths *about* brief therapy—the outside view—come from the proponents of conventional long-term psychodynamic treatment, as the traditionally predominant model of psychotherapy. It is striking, however, that in several important respects these traditional psychodynamic views are quite similar to popular lay views about problems and their resolution, and even to some basic tenets of physiological/biochemical views. There has been so much elaboration, branching, and dispute in a hundred years of myth development about psychotherapy that one easily could get lost in the details, yet it seems possible to discern a few fundamental lines of general significance.

Probably the most important and common characteristic of this viewpoint is that brief therapy—if seen as possible at all—is seen as inherently and drastically *limited* in scope. Two major kinds of limitations, different in kind yet basically related, are posited:

1. Brief therapy is necessarily limited to minor goals or symptomatic treatment, but cannot effect any significant or fundamental change. It is supportive treatment, either as a stopgap or as a second-best measure when real long-term therapy is not available. This may be because either the patient or the helping system is limited in time or money, or the patient is seen as too limited in psychological resources for "real" therapy. The possibility of similar limitation of the professional is seldom considered, though a case can be made that brief therapy requires greater skill than long-term treatment.

2. Brief therapy may be of value in, and should be limited to, minor problems, but "obviously" is inappropriate for major ones. (This ranking or distinction of "major" and "minor" problems again seems to be a matter largely taken for granted as self-evident, rather than being seen as a basic and complex issue needing much thought and clarification.)

It is unclear why such a widespread and powerful view of brief therapy as very limited exists and persists, beyond the obvious fact that for 100 years now a heavy investment in the practice and teaching of this view has been made. Yet two critical underlying premises seem implicit, if seldom explicit. Both lead toward supporting the necessity of long-term treatment, although in a fundamental respect they are different, even opposite conceptions. But this, of course, would not be the first instance of incompatible arguments being used to support the same position.

First, there is perhaps the most basic tenet of conventional psychiatric thinking: If a person behaves in ways that are strange enough and persistent enough to bring him or her under professional psychiatric scrutiny, the cause lies in some significant personal deficit—a pathology—within that individual, and the stranger or more resistant the behavior, the greater or deeper the presumed pathology. At the broadest level, this view is shared by those who see the presumed deficit in experiential terms, in terms of psychological makeup, or in physiological/biochemical terms. Whatever the specific cause ascribed to the presumed deficit, it is plain that in this view, at best there is much work to be done to repair, or compensate for, the deficit. This is a possible, and certainly a popular, interpretation of strange and unusual behavior, but it is not the only possible interpretation, or even the only one advocated in the course of human history.

The other line of thinking is more humanistic, even implicitly verging on an interactional view, but no less pessimistic about any possible brief resolution of problems involving human behavior. This is the view—and here again the professional and the layman stand on similar ground—that human life and behavior are inherently and necessarily complex. The obvious corollary is that if someone is behaving in strange and self-defeating ways, it will take a lot of time, thought, and effort to understand such behavior, and probably much more to alter it—if this is possible at all.

Perhaps this is so. But before accepting this as a given and thus accepting only major coping or remedial measures as relevant to human problems, two possible alternative views should be recognized:

First, there is the possibility that we humans make complex problems out of originally rather simple, if difficult, situations. Although we habitually assume that serious problems must have correspondingly large and weighty causes, this is not necessarily so, for at least two reasons. First, what is a large or serious problem is not a given or an absolute, but again a matter of our interpretation, the same also holds for "complexity" itself. In parts of sub-Saharan Africa, for example, syphilis is so common that it is not considered a "problem," only a fact of normal life. Second, now that we have some understanding of cybernetics, it is increasingly apparent that through positive feedback, repetitive error in handling a difficulty—"more of the same"— can readily and rapidly lead to the escalation of an originally minor and simple difficulty into a major problem (Watzlawick, et al., 1974). And this problem may appear different from the original difficulty not only in *scope* (quantitatively) but also in *shape* (qualitatively).

Another, alternative view is that the complexity we discern is, at least in large part, an interpretive illusion. Such an illusion can occur as a consequence of our failure to gather or attend to data that would simplify the picture; or of habits of interpreting the data we have in terms of complexity rather than seeking simpler (and perhaps more useful, if apparently less profound) interpretations; or both. An analogy makes this point clearer: In almost any good detective story, the mystery involved appears both complex and obscure, until at the end the detective reveals the true clarity and simplicity of the matter. Perhaps this analogy seems too trivial and unrealistic, even though much of the literature basic in establishing the psychodynamic approach, including especially the work of Freud himself, approaches the mysteries of "mental illness" and its treatment much like a problem of crime detection.

If this example still seems inadequate or inappropriate, however, consider the case of the organization and dynamics of planetary movements. As long as the Ptolemaic view of an earth-centered universe was held, the more the data that were gathered, the more complex was the explanation necessary to make some order and sense of them. But once people shifted to a Copernican viewpoint, taking the sun as central rather than the earth, the apparent complexity became relatively quite simple.

While it is not a necessary part of the present argument, it is certainly possible to suggest that there are plausible reasons why we might become involved in making or interpreting things as more complex than necessary. To mention just two: This saves us from rethinking accepted premises, which is always a difficult and painful task; and if human problems are seen as complex, everyone involved is, to a corresponding extent, absolved from responsibility for resolving them.

MYTHS OF BRIEF THERAPY

Brief therapy, in any modern form, is a quite recent development. Moreover, its adherents tend to be clinicians, more concerned with practical results than with theory. For both these reasons, the mythology of brief therapy is relatively scanty up to the present; however, we can at least examine what exists.

Since brief therapy is the "new kid on the block," probably there is already more mythology about brief therapy deriving from psychodynamic sources than from those who have moved toward brief treatment as a basically new approach to treatment. The latter may have some advantages in relative freedom from limiting preconceptions, but the former certainly have the advantage of numbers, prestige, and weight of tradition. The guiding myth of brief psychodynamic therapy may be characterized quite simply and briefly as "less of the same." That is, although practice may involve more activity and intensity, the basic

views involved in this approach to brief treatment seem essentially the
same as those described earlier for conventional long-term therapy: a
postulate of brief treatment as basically limited in scope, evidenced by
selectivity as to patients accepted for treatment, and based on similar
underlying premises about pathology and the complexity of human
problems. Much of this is neatly summarized in Gustafson's (1986) book
The Complex Secret of Brief Psychotherapy; indeed, the title alone offers
much of the essence of this myth. This is not to say that the development
of this approach to brief treatment is not an important step forward. It is;
yet it also seems clearly a step constrained and limited by unquestioning
acceptance of the most basic features of the prior conventional assumptions.

Alternative visions of, and approaches to, brief therapy instead are
based, more or less explicitly, on an interactional view of human problems rather than an individual-pathology view. These approaches
largely derive from family therapy, as the primary locus and exponent of
a basically interactional view of behavior.

Probably the most extreme view is the one that, I think, can with
reasonable fairness be categorized as a strictly technical or procedural
view: "Don't confuse me with theory; let's just get clear what interventions a therapist should make, in what situations, in order to solve interactional problems." Although such a characterization often seems intended as a caricature or a putdown of brief treatment, there is
potentially more to it than this. Beyond those eager but naïve therapists
who at workshops demand, "Give me a paradox for this case situation,"
there are experienced and serious therapists whose focus is mainly on
techniques for promoting change. To a significant extent, this again was
true of Milton Erickson himself. Although neglect of general principles
and a guiding framework may have accompanying limitations or draw-
backs, the corresponding freedom from limiting presuppositions as to
how things "really are" may also keep open the door to finding useful
new practices, which may eventually give rise to useful new conceptions
of problems and their resolution. Sometimes theoretical ideas lead to
useful innovations in practice, but often it goes the other way.

An intermediate position is taken by some brief therapists, including
Haley, Madanes, Papp, and Silverstein, whose basic views are closely
related to mainstream myths of family therapy, but who attempt to work
briefly by active, and often creative, techniques of intervention. One
could, perhaps, see them as the family therapy analogs of the psychodynamic brief therapists, and a similar question arises: How much
may these therapists, again unwittingly, be constrained by their unquestioning acceptance of certain premises of conventional family therapy,
for example, that a symptom must have an important function, or that a

specific problem must reflect an underlying pathology in the family system?

Finally, another myth is that to make progress toward doing therapy briefly, effectively, and over the widest possible range of problems, we must make a fresh start: in effect, to construct a new myth, a new view of problems and their resolution that is minimally constrained by past myths. On this view, both practice and thought basically should be exploratory. I see the work of my colleagues and myself at the Brief Therapy Center of MRI (Fisch et al., 1982; Watzlawick et al., 1974; Weakland et al., 1974) and that of Steve de Shazer and his colleagues in Milwaukee (de Shazer, 1985, 1988)—among others—as exemplifying this view. Of course, no view or myth is perfect and without its accompanying difficulties or defects. To take this sort of view, in any field and especially in a clinically related one, means that one knowingly risks criticism and subjects both oneself and one's clients to certain chances in the present, in the hope of improving matters in both the immediate and more distant future. Clearly, and especially in the present social and professional climate, a more conservative approach is the safer course to follow.

REFERENCES

de Shazer, S. (1985). *Keys to Solution in Brief Therapy*. New York: Norton.

de Shazer, S. (1988). *Clues: Investigating Solutions in Brief Therapy*. New York: Norton.

Fisch, R., Weakland, J. H., & Segal, L. (1982). *The Tactics of Change*. San Francisco: Jossey-Bass.

Gustafson, J. P. (1986). *The Complex Secret of Brief Psychotherapy*. New York: Norton.

Ruesch, J., & Bateson, G. (1951). *Communication: The Social Matrix of Psychiatry*. New York: Norton.

Watzlawick, P., Weakland, J. H., & Fisch, R. (1974). *Change: Principles of Problem Formation and Problem Resolution*. New York: Norton.

Weakland, J. H., Fisch, R., Watzlawick, P., & Bodin, A. M. (1974). Brief therapy: Focused problem resolution. *Family Process, 13*, 141–168.

PART III

Family Therapy

CHAPTER 9

The Therapeutic Debate
Peggy Papp

I will describe a method of working that was developed in the brief therapy project of the Ackerman Family Institute called "the therapeutic debate." We found the debate to be a powerful tool in working with couples, families, and individuals, particularly in situations in which the therapist felt "stuck."

The brief therapy project was founded by Olga Silverstein and me some years ago to experiment with strategic and paradoxical interventions with families who had a symptomatic child. A consultation team was an integral part of our therapy and we used it in many different ways. Initially the team was used primarily for consultation and to send messages commenting on the relationship between the therapist and family. Later we developed a therapeutic triangle by having the team disgree with the therapist over some issue of change. In this triangle, the therapist generally supported the family's resources and pointed a direction for change, while the team presented all the individual and systemic transactions taking place in the family that might prevent change.

For example, the therapist might enter the session and say, "The team believes I'm being overly optimistic in trying to get Jessica and Father to stop fighting, because they think Jessica is fighting Mother's battle for her and that Mother is afraid to fight her own battles with Father because he gets depressed and withdraws whenever she tries. So they think for the time being Jessica must remain the only fighter in the family.

The therapist is hoping for a recoil, which is what happened in this case. The mother said, "That's ridiculous. What kind of a team do you

111

have that would propose such an idea? Why should Jessica have to solve the problem between my husband and me?" After Mother asked this crucial question, the therapist joined the family against the team by saying, "I don't believe she needs to. I think you are perfectly capable of bringing up whatever issues you need to bring up with your husband and that he is perfectly capable of dealing with them." The focus of therapy is no longer Jessica's rebellious behavior but who is fighting whose battle for whom and why.

At a later stage in the development of the project, we decided to bring the team out from behind the one-way mirror into the session and hold the debate in front of the family. This allowed the therapist and team to elaborate on their ideas and also allowed the family to actively join in the debate. At the time we decided to do this the team was composed of three therapists and we took three different positions around change. One therapist, taking the stability position, maintained that no one person in the family could act unilaterally because all were controlled by their system and that this system was more powerful than any person within it. The other two therapists disagreed, maintaining that the individuals were more powerful than the system and could act unilaterally. The two therapists taking the latter position presented different possibilities for change. The juxtaposition of these different perspectives facilitated the family's own ideas and decision-making process.

The debate changed both the context and the content of the therapy. It removed the family from center stage and placed them in the position of an audience listening to their own drama. It temporarily took the problem away from them and held up a mirror that reflected their own dilemmas. This mirror changed their perception of the problem.

The family generally listened intensely and gradually became involved in the debate, taking sides, agreeing and disagreeing with the therapists and among themselves. In the process they were compelled to constantly reexamine previously held beliefs and behavior.

It was important that the three therapists all agreed on one hypothesis around which to take different positions. The hypothesis defined the central theme in the family and the way in which the symptom was connected with it.

I will now provide an example of how the debate worked with a holocaust family around the theme of separation:

CASE ONE

The presenting problem was described by the family as an undiagnosable illness in their 19-year-old daughter, Sarah. For the past seven years she had had a strange malady which continued to incapacitate her, until finally she refused to work or go to school. She was afraid to leave the house and stayed in bed all day complaining of stomachaches, depression, and an inability to breathe. She often cried and screamed for hours on end, during which time everything in the family revolved around her. She dropped out of a work study program in college after the first semester and had not been out of the home alone for the past year.

At home Mother waited on her hand and foot and came running whenever she manifested a symptom. Father was jealous of Mother's intense involvement and felt abandoned by his wife.

The historical background of the family emerged from routine questioning regarding each parent's family of origin: Mother had been separated from her parents at the age of eight during World War II when all the children in her native village were sent to Israel. Although other members of her family perished, her parents survived the concentration camp, and after the war she was reunited with them in Israel. They all lived together and Mother was very close to her parents.

Father also was separated from his parents during the war and sent to Israel, where he met his wife. After they were married, the couple lived with the maternal grandparents. After several years, Father finally persuaded his wife to come to the United States, where his own parents had settled after the war. Although she agreed to come, we suspected that deep down she never forgave her husband for tearing her away from her family a second time. Her parents were heart-broken at her departure and the maternal grandmother fell into a deep depression from which she never recovered. Mother stated, "When I left my parents I took everything away from them. I've never stopped thinking about them." Mother had never returned to Israel, claiming it was financially impossible. She had tried many times to persuade her parents to visit her but they claimed they were too old and too sick. They kept urging Mother to come to Israel. None of these events were ever discussed in the family.

We hypothesized that these past separations were connected with Sarah's inability to separate from her family and that her symptoms were a way of preventing any more painful separations in the present or future. The three therapists took three different positions around the theme of separation which represented the present, past, and future.

One therapist, supporting the present arrangement in the family, argued that Sarah's symptoms were a way of making sure that no one in the family ever separated because Sarah believed the family could not tolerate any more separations in light of their past experiences. She had chosen symptoms that kept her mother from abandoning her father and returning home to her parents in Israel. They also prevented Mother from abandoning Sarah by keeping her constantly involved with her, and they prevented Sarah from leaving home and abandoning her parents because they could never leave an "ill" daughter. This therapist predicted that Sarah would continue to keep her family together forever as she had been doing.

The other two therapists disagreed that the family could not overcome their fear of separation, which was normal under the circumstances. Each offered a different solution, one related to the past and the other to the future. The second therapist maintained that nothing could change in the family until the past had been dealt with and Mother had made peace with her parents. The first order of the day was for Mother to return to Israel and visit her parents. Father should help her find a way to raise the money for airfare and should urge her to go. This therapist explained to Father that Mother had been grieving ever since she left Israel and it was difficult for her to be a wife and let go of her own daughter as long as she felt she was a bad daughter to her own parents. He was told this would give him a way of redeeming himself in Mother's eyes for what she had never forgiven him for—taking her away from her parents.

The therapist arguing for the status quo maintained that Mother would never be able to follow through on this suggestion because it would mean she would have to do something she had never done before, namely, put her own interest above everyone else's in the family. And, even if she did manage to make a decision in her own best interest, her daughter would surely create some kind of a crisis to prevent her from going so she could remain safely at home for Father.

The third therapist, the advocate for the future, interrupted a lively exchange between these two therapists to disagree with both of them. This therapist took the position that regardless of what decisions the parents chose to make about the past, the future belonged to Sarah and she must get on with her life. It didn't matter what the parents did or didn't do; it was up to Sarah to declare her independence. This therapist argued that it was not the parents' job to let their children go. Parents were expected to hold on to their children with all their might. It was up to the children to fight to go free. That was part of growing up.

Turning to Sarah, the therapist explored her interests and learned she had been hoping to study medicine and become a doctor. The therapist entered into a discussion with her as to what would be required to accomplish this.

The different positions taken by the therapists separated the generations and gave the message to the family that they need not be tied together forever with unpaid debts.

Mother's initial reaction was that it would be impossible for her to visit her parents because they couldn't afford it and she couldn't leave her ill daughter. Father agreed with his wife that it would be impossible. Sarah, who until this point had remained almost comatose, suddenly came vigorously alive. She rose up in her chair with a horrified look and exclaimed, "I will never let my mother go. I will stop her!" adding with a determined look, "And believe me I know how!"

The status quo therapist congratulated her for continuing to protect her father regardless of the cost to herself, at which point the second therapist challenged Father and urged him not to let his daughter deter him, emphasizing that he must be stronger than his daughter. The status quo therapist maintained this was impossible because Sarah had more effective weapons than her father and she had had more practice using them. Sarah agreed with this and began enumerating all the different ways in which she would use her symptoms to prevent Mother from going. The parents were stunned at the revelation that this mysterious illness Sarah had suffered with for seven years was under her control.

The debate continued along these lines for the next several sessions, with each therapist fitting whatever new information that emerged into his or her particular frame of reference.

Mother began the fourth session by announcing she had decided to go to Israel and Father had agreed to raise the money to send her. The two change therapists congratulated them on their decision, but the status quo therapist remained pessismistic and predicted Sarah would find a way of stopping her. Actually, it was not Sarah who ended up having a crisis; it was Father who fell off a ladder two days before Mother was to leave and broke his ankle. However, Mother decided to go anyway and left Sarah to take care of Father. Since Father's leg was in a cast, she had no alternative. They reported they got to know each other for the first time and much of the tension between them disappeared.

Mother returned a month later after an emotional reunion with her parents to say she had persuaded them to come to this country for a visit. Within a few weeks of Mother's returning, Sarah decided to go back to school and got a job so she could work her way through college. She is now in her first year of premed.

This is one example of how the debate changed the family's perception of the problem from an undiagnosable and incurable illness in the daughter to the family's collective fear of separation.

There are a great variety of ways the debate can be used, and it doesn't always require three therapists. It can be equally effective with two working as a cotherapy team. One therapist can remain on the other side of the one-way mirror and enter the session at unexpected moments, or both therapists can conduct the session together and provide different perspectives as critical issues arise. One of the most propitious times for the therapist to take different positions is when one person makes a significant change. While one therapist is supporting the change, the other one can anticipate all the individual and systemic ramifications of it.

CASE TWO

In the following example the cotherapists decided to express differing points of view when the wife suddenly took a giant step forward. For as long as they had been married, the wife had worked two jobs to allow her husband, who was an aspiring opera singer, to pursue his career. The problem was that he only pursued it half-heartedly and the wife constantly pressured him to pursue it more vigorously. She wanted him to send out resumes, call agents, go to auditions, follow up on contacts, and so on. The husband admitted he should be doing all these things but resented his wife's pressure and resisted it by doing less and less.

In exploring their family backgrounds it was discovered that the wife had accommodated to everyone all her life and had ended up feeling deprived and resentful. The husband described himself as having been stubborn and rebellious all his life and spoke rather proudly of his ability to defy authority.

After this session, the wife was determined she was no longer going to accommodate her husband. The female therapist discussed with her how she intended to carry out her resolve. In exploring this it was discovered that the husband had a rather large inheritance tucked away in a savings account. Neither had ever considered dipping into this. The female therapist suggested the wife earn half of the income and let the husband be responsible for the other half.

The male therapist said she would never be able to do this because her way of getting love was to accommodate to others. This was a lifelong pattern and if she stopped accommodating she would no longer feel needed. Therefore, the husband should continue to do what he was doing as this gave his wife a reason to continue to accommodate. The male therapist then defined the husband's stubbornness as having protected him all his life and given him his sense of identity. If he were to give it up, he might lose feelings of independence and autonomy that were vital to him, and therefore he should remain stubborn.

In the four-way debate that followed, essential questions were raised such as, "Could the wife find other ways of feeling needed without accommodating? What would happen to the husband if she stopped? Was it possible for the husband to establish a sense of independence and autonomy without rebelling against his wife? What would happen to the wife if he became responsible?"

One might well ask at this point, "Why the debate? Why can't these same questions be raised by a single therapist?" Certainly that is a viable option. The main advantage of the debate is the added dimension of distance and perspective that is created as the family members move back and forth between being an audience and participants in their own drama.

Shortly after the above session the wife quit one of her jobs, started yoga lessons, and spent more time with the children. The husband obtained a part-time job teaching singing lessons in order to pay his half of the family expenses.

In our follow-up study a year later the couple singled out the debate as having been particularly useful. The wife stated, "It was helpful that you two disagreed. We had to try and decide which of you was right, and in thinking about it we came up with our own answers. The husband stated, "If you had told me I had to change my way of doing things, I would have said, 'Well, I'm not going to change it.' My religion was resisting authority. But you said that served me well and I thought, wow, he sees that, he understands me. He gave me permission to hold onto myself. A person is much more willing to give something up when they think it belongs to them—when they have a right to it." The husband explained, far better than most therapists ever could, the power of respecting and going with a person's defenses.

THE THERAPEUTIC DEBATE IN SOLO PRACTICE

Since most therapists work alone, it is important to discuss ways of using the debate as a single therapist. There are many different ways of doing this. One way is for the therapist to split his/her own opinion and carry on a debate with him/herself, asking the family for help in resolving it. The dialogue might go something like this, "You know I've been trying so hard to establish more intimacy between the two of you but now I suddenly realize that in order for that to happen you would each have to give up something that seems more important to you than intimacy. You would each have to forgive each other for what you consider to be unforgivable crimes. You, Mary, would have to forgive John for neglecting your mother, and you, John, would have to forgive Mary for not looking out for your children. You have erected a scales of justice between you which you keep balanced by neither forgiving the other.

"Now, on the one hand, my judgment tells me it would be too risky to upset that balance and we should leave it alone. On the other hand, it leaves you both feeling isolated and lonely and nothing could be worse than that. Or could it? Is it worth taking a chance? Help me out on this." The couple is invited to take sides in the therapist's internal debate.

Another way a single therapist can use the principles of the debate is by holding regular consultations between sessions with either a real or imaginary colleague who sends back provocative messages questioning the direction of the therapy.

A more fanciful way of dramatizing the dilemma of change is to cast it into the form of a fantasy or dream. The therapist constructs a fantasy that portrays the consequences of change in metaphorical pictures. For example, recently I was working with a couple who had one crisis after another and constantly triangulated everything and everyone into the relationship, including animals, relatives, friends, neighbors, employers, and alcohol. After a number of such crises, I said to the couple, "You know I had a dream about you. I dreamt the three of us were in this huge room together. You two were at the opposite sides of the room and I was at one end. You couldn't reach each other because there was this huge pile of debris between the two of you and it was swirling round and round. There were dogs and cats, and your mother and her mother, and your boss, and the landlord, and your friends and the neighbors, and bills and whiskey bottles—and the two of you couldn't even see each other.

"I had a huge broom and I was trying to sweep all the debris out the door. And I swept and I swept and I swept until it was all cleared away. And when I finished I turned around and expected you to rush into each other's arms and instead you just stood and looked at each other kind of scared and then you both turned and walked out the door.

"I don't know what to make of that dream. Do you have any idea what it means?" After a long pause the husband said, "Yes, I know what it means. It means we related through the problems rather than to each other." I replied, "Oh, is that what it means? Well, what do you think we should do? My colleague thinks I should give up and terminate therapy. She says you will never change; you will just go on repeating these patterns over and over again. I don't know. What do you think would happen if you were alone in that room together without the debris?"

This was the turning point in the therapy. From then on, whenever they diverted their problems through someone or something outside their relationship, I began to wonder if my "colleague" were not right. Her presence became an invisible part of the therapy.

If the team is composed of a male and female, they can divide along gender lines, with the woman therapist presenting a feminine point of view and the male therapist a masculine point of view. In cases of a generational conflict, the older therapist can support the parents while the younger therapist speaks for the children. Sometimes it is more effective to cross gender and generation lines. When Olga Silverstein and her daughter, Laura, work together, they have found it more effective to criss-cross generations, with Olga voicing the children's concerns and Laura supporting the parents.

SUMMARY

The therapeutic debate is a way of reflecting back to couples, families, or individuals their particular dilemmas around change in such a way that they become involved in resolving them. The juxtaposition of the different perspectives offered by the debate stimulates new ideas and facilitates the decision-making process.

CHAPTER 10

How to Utilize
a Therapist's Bias
Gianfranco Cecchin

I will tell you the story of our training in Milan. In the beginning there was The Expert. The therapist had to train him/herself to observe the system in a correct manner, that is, the systemic manner, which was an arbitrary choice, the choice of looking at the family with the cybernetic epistemology we learned through the work of Bateson (1972). This epistemology consists of the following principles: Everything we see is seen as a world of messages and information. Everything a person does or says is a message to somebody. If nobody listens, there is no message. Therefore, if there is a message there must be a listener.

We had to train ourselves to see the family system as a network of complicated messages and responses in which the message becomes response and the response becomes message. So-called "lineal" explanations became insufficient to describe the family in such a manner. We needed a different way of observing and a different way of describing things. The cause-effect explanation, which was so useful in most situations, had to be discarded. We began to avoid the verb "to be" in our descriptions and substitute appear, show, seem, exhibit, pretend, communicate, and so forth. This could be done because our descriptions were elaborated in the team discussions and we could check on each other's use of words. The result was that we could not define people with a diagnosis that included words like "depressed," "angry," "maternal," "narcissistic," or even "healthy." People existed only "in relation." We began to see only interconnected activities.

We also began to describe what we called "games." Naturally, games have rules, so we began to see or make up "the rules of the system." Every person is playing a part in the game. So we don't have "a passive husband," but a husband who is playing the part of a passive husband in relation to an assertive wife, or rather a woman who is playing the part of an assertive wife.

Slowly we began to change our focus of attention. Instead of looking for causes, we began looking for patterns and for circular causality. The result was that we could not blame anyone any longer. Everyone was both victim and actor in the game.

The motivation of the therapist had to change, from curiosity about etiology to curiosity about patterns. The therapist had to become, so to speak, neutral. This takes time, so we created the following exercise: After seeing a family for a while, the therapy team meets and tries to explain what is happening. Each of us would try to explain the game or story by blaming one member of the family as being the cause of everything. One of us would blame the father, the other would blame the mother, and so on. By blaming everyone, we began to see the different actors being equally responsible and victim at the same time.

However, we ran into trouble almost immediately. To be neutral and curious is difficult, and soon the supervisor began to scold the therapist for not being neutral and curious: "You don't like this father or this daughter and you are fascinated by facts and not by patterns." We were repeating the blaming behavior we tried to change in relation to the family with our students. We became lineal again.

To come out of the impasse we had to make a change in our behavior as supervisors. (When we are in trouble, the trick is always the same: Go from content to pattern!) Instead of scolding the therapist for not being circular or curious or neutral, we began to observe the behavior of the therapist, whatever it was, as a response to the family, and therefore as a useful instrument for understanding family dynamics.

This became clear one day when an observing team noticed that the therapeutic team was copying the pattern of the family. The parents in the family were fighting about everything and the children were always trying to create a compromise. In the team, the same thing happened. The two older members of the team, male and female, started to fight about ideas and the two younger members tried hard to help them compromise. What was strange was that when the team was told about their behavior, they changed immediately and could use spontaneously what happened among themselves as part of an intervention with the family with whom they were working.

As a result of this, we began to observe the response of the team or the

therapist. We could see that the therapist or team was not only responding by imitating the patterns of the client, but more frequently was responding in a personal way. Every person has a peculiar way of responding to aggression, depression, abuse, being victimized, seduction, and so
forth. Basically, the therapist responds with his or her own style, way of
seeing things, and "biases."

The question for the observing team was: How can we use this
peculiar response in the therapeutic process? Because we have only
biases or prejudices, we cannot see the world except through our own
lenses, which have been constructed through years of interactional experience with others. If we are flexible, we keep confronting our ideas
with others; if we are rigid, we fight to defend our ideas against different
opinions. The observing team can make use of both characteristics. For
example, if a therapist reacts with moral indignation, he or she could be
helped by the team to say to the patient something like: I am upset by
your behavior. How many people do you know who react in this way?
Am I the only one? How do you react to this reaction? When did you
first notice this reaction? How many people in your family react in
this manner?

Another example is a therapist who reacts with compassion and a
strong desire to help. He or she could be helped to say: I am sure I can
help you, and I have a strong desire to do so. Suppose I give in to my feeling. How long do you think our relation could last? Or: If I succeed in my
attempt, who will be happier, you or me at the end?

Another example: You look so helpless, that I feel I must take control
over your life. So I am going to take control over your life for a period of
time. I will ask my supervisor and, of course, you for permission to follow
my wish.

Another helpful therapeutic reaction is: I have this idea that the
parents are not taking care of the children properly. My need is to give
the parents some instruction even if my team thinks it is useless.

Again: We are cotherapists, and at the end of every session we begin
to disagree about what is going on. Could you help us? You have some
experience about fighting for years without destroying the relationship.
How did you do it?

This is a way of playing the drama of the family in the team. Again, this
is an example of the therapist changing the level of the conversation. Instead of talking about the fight itself, the therapist talks about how to survive in the fight. In doing so, he or she takes responsibility for his/her
reactions. Probably this is a better way to define what I call "neutrality."

When we are stuck with objectivity without quotation marks, we
necessarily think that what we see is independent of our observing. Our

way of observing becomes underutilized. Instead, if we continuously reflect on the biases of the patient, we create a dynamic interaction which goes beyond the problem of neutrality or social control.

This way of working is different from the method of the Ericksonian therapists who train themselves in the ability to influence patients' emotions (e.g., Lankton & Lankton, 1983). I, instead, assume that emotions and thinking are closely connected and when therapists reflect on their own reactions, which are made up of emotions and thoughts. They are not manipulative in this manner, they are simply and consciously avoiding interactions that produce symmetrical escalation with the client. They consciously utilize contradictions by exaggerating them, bring forth paradoxes compelling the system to come out of them, and offer at least two points of view about anything that is coming out to show that there are different options. Such a therapist is not strategic because he or she does not plan actions with the purpose of changing the power organization or the equilibrium of forces. The therapist is utilizing his or her own responses (physical, emotional, intellectual) to engage the client in a conversation with the purpose of rediscovering or creating reality based on a new language, a reality with a future and new options.

REFERENCES

Bateson, G. (1972). *Steps to an Ecology of Mind*. New York: Ballantine.

Boscolo, L., Cecchin, G., Hoffman, L., & Penn, P. (1987). *Milan Systemic Family Therapy*. New York: Basic Books.

Cecchin, G. (1987). Hypothesizing, circularity, and neutrality revisited: An invitation to curiosity. *Family Process, 26*, 405–413.

Lankton, S. R., & Lankton, C. (1983). *The Answer Within: A Clinical Framework for Ericksonian Hypnotherapy*. New York: Brunner/Mazel.

Selvini Palazzoli, M., Boscolo, L., Cecchin, G., & Prata, G. (1978). *Paradox and Counterparadox*. New York: Jason Aronson.

CHAPTER 11

Clinical Road Maps
for Prescribing Rituals
Joel S. Bergman

This chapter describes some of the clinical road maps I have been using to do brief therapy. The idea seems overwhelming for several reasons: First, it is difficult to transfer successfully right-hemispher maps into left-hemispher language. The fear is that the very act of thinking about them may detract from the experience.

A second fear is based on the well-known disparity between what therapists say they are doing and what they are actually doing. Another disparity involves what therapists are not writing about, but what they are actually doing that makes treatment successful.

Having stated these concerns, I also acknowledge that I am stuck with the scientific side of me which believes strongly that therapy has a procedure, a sequencing, a puzzle to be solved, and a logic. And, although some of it is quite emotional, spiritual, and personal, it is far from magical or unknowable; some of it can be communicated to others.

For me, brief systemic psychotherapy in its highest form is an art form. And as an art form, it requires a certain balance of thought, feeling, and technique. Any excess of one over the others will distract from its poetry and perhaps its effectiveness. So without further procrastination or self-protecting precautions, let me try to share some thoughts on the clinical road maps I have been quietly drawing somewhere in the back of my mind while doing brief therapy. I have named the three maps "affect," "language," and "resistance" respectively.

AFFECT MAP

The map I use when beginning therapy is an affect map. I start with this map because it's the one I generally use in life. You have to know about the predominant feelings going on in you, as well as in the people around you. This helps you focus on where you are and what you are going to do. It's one of my more primary life maps, and I know quite well where it comes from and how it developed.

When I say I use an affect map, it does not mean that I ask people what they are feeling. Rather, while I am gathering information about the presenting symptom, learning how the family is organized around the symptom, and thinking about how the occurrence of the symptom is related to any possible shifts in a three-generational family system, I am listening closely to the feelings aroused or expressed by the patient or family. The affect will highlight or underscore certain information. It will signal how such information is more related to the presenting problem than is information presented without this accompanying affect. One of the tricks in doing therapy is knowing what's important and what's not important. The family's feelings, aroused or expressed in the session, punctuate what's important, and direct clinicians toward asking additional questions in this affect-laden area.

There is also a sub-affect map to this larger affect map. This submap tells me whether or not the feelings being expressed in the session seem primary. I contrast primary feelings to secondary feelings (what I call Yiddish Theater or melodramatic feelings) where affect is exaggerated. Also included as secondary feelings would be hysterical feelings, as well as reactions such as self-pity, as when one feels badly about feeling badly. If my submap indicates that these expressed feelings are not primary, I am inclined to give the information accompanying such feelings less importance.

This affective submap is "powered" by the right hemisphere and is also based on disparities between verbal and nonverbal communications. When there is considerable disparity between these two forms of communication, I am inclined to take what I am hearing differently than when the affect "coming down" seems primary, with little disparity between verbal and nonverbal modes.

The right hemisphere is simultaneously picking up nonverbal information on many different channels which the left hemisphere knows less about because it processes information differently. When feelings are not primary, I pick up overtones and other nonverbal signals that tell me something is not right. I respect these signals and treat the information I am gathering as different than when the signals are congruent. Incongruent signals are the same ones a person gets when being sold a bill of goods or when being lied to.

So my first map, which determines the value of incoming information related to the presenting symptom, has to do with whether the information is accompanied by what I call primary affect.

For example, I have difficulty using it with patients or families who come in with substance abuse problems. Since alcohol or drugs often mask the affect or dissociate the primary affect from the problem or information related to the problem, treating these patients is much more difficult, since it keeps me from using this primary map.

Sometimes, when it is difficult to detect the affect needed to highlight the incoming information, I may provoke the patient or family to produce the affect. This is tricky, because the provocation is done to highlight and generate important clinical information, and not to frighten a family out of treatment. Provocation should be used with caution.

LANGUAGE MAP

A second map, also a right-hemisphere map, entails remembering the family or patient's language. By language, I am referring to Milton Erickson's use of the word "language," that is, listening to the way in which the patient conceptualizes his or her world, and also problem(s) (Haley, 1967). Using this map requires getting under the skin of patients and learning how they organize and conceptualize their world. This map is drawn by me while the drama in the session unfolds.

My language map is important for two reasons: first, to understand or appreciate the patient's world view; and second, to then use that language to ask a patient at the end of the session to do something. When you use the patient's own language to ask them to do a task, you increase the chance that they will understand why you are asking them to do it. This understanding will, in turn, increase chances that a therapeutic prescription will be acted upon.

When doing brief systemic therapy, you have a better chance of being successful when a patient acts on a particular prescription. While you can learn important information when someone doesn't do a task, you get more change out of people when they follow your instructions and *act* differently.

RESISTANCE MAP

As much as some of my purist systemic colleagues wince at the word "resistance," I still use it because I find it helpful. While gathering information about a presenting symptom and the context in which a symptom occurs, one also must keep track of how much anxiety, discomfort, or pain is associated with change or with the elimination of a symptom. More often than not, nonverbal cues best indicate how frightened, rigid, or oppositional the patient, family, or system is to therapeutic change, or to the suggestion of change. The way one frames information-gathering questions will not only provide content information about a family system, but will also help elicit the family's affect associated with these answers. This begins the determination by the therapist of how difficult it will be to change behavior in a family system.

As previously mentioned, I use provocation to generate an affect map when affect is not available by asking provocative questions. This has two purposes: one, to get clinical information about how a family is organized around a symptom, and two, to get affective information about how resistant a system will be to change. Here are examples of provocative questions: "What will the danger in this family be once your anorectic daughter begins to start eating again? What will be the danger to this family once Johnny stops drinking or hallucinating? Who, your mother or your father, will secretly be a little unhappy, once your marriage starts working again? Who among your siblings will be the next drug addict once Johnny stops protecting your parents with his drug abuse?" The family's emotional response to such questions begins the process of drawing a resistance map.

Part of this resistance map will plot anxiety, another term some of my systemic colleagues don't like much. How upset the family or patient is during the session will determine, in part, how much opportunity there will be for change. When the anxiety level is high, or of crisis magnitude, then resistance usually is low, and there is more opportunity for change. When there is little or no anxiety involved, then resistance will often be high and change thus less likely to take place.

Sometimes both anxiety and resistance are high. When this occurs, resistance is not necessarily determined by anxiety in the session (or lack thereof), but more by an impressive history of prior treatment failures. In such situations more therapeutic leverage will be needed. Here the treatment is tricky, and outside help may be needed in the form of a cotherapist or a team behind a one-way mirror. In such cases the therapist can deal with the anxiety and the prospect of change while the team gives a totally contradictory message and prescribes the resistance or the homeostasis operating in the family system.

GATHERING SYSTEMIC INFORMATION AROUND THE PRESENTING PROBLEM

Most presenting problems have to do with separation. When a couple comes in for treatment, they are unhappy because while they are legally married, they can't "get married" emotionally, partly because each partner is still more married to the family of origin than to the partner (Bowen, 1978). When an individual patient comes in depressed and lonely, I wonder, "To whom is this individual still married in his/her family of origin?" Once this is determined, the separation work between the patient and the family of origin can begin.

Symptoms also may be related to making the necessary transition from one developmental stage to the next. Sometimes these developmental transitions are related to separation issues. Sometimes they are not. For example, a son who is struggling to act like an adult is stuck in his attempts to separate from his mother; a wife is stuck because she is giving up too much of her sense of self in her marriage; someone is lonely because he can't make himself available to be with a partner; a young woman is anorectic because she can't leave home; or a young man is psychotic because he can't leave home.

Since I see most symptoms as having to do with separation, I believe the task of the clinician is to find out how a patient is stuck, and from whom he or she is struggling to separate. The therapy then powerfully focuses on helping this person separate. Separation is constructive for the patient as well as for the person(s) from whom he or she is separating.

Symptoms can be seen as metaphors. When you look closely at a symptom metaphorically, it often has to do with keeping someone from getting closer to someone else. As long as a symptom maintains some distance from another person, it also maintains closeness and loyalty to someone in the family of origin. To reduce or eliminate the symptom will, for example, increase closeness in the couple and, as a consequence, produce more separation from the family of origin. The increased distance from the family of origin enables a different kind of relationship to evolve with that family.

To summarize, an affective language and resistance maps are developed or constructed. The clinician finds out what the presenting symptom is; how the symptom is related to developmental transitions; how the symptom is related to separation; and from whom the separation will be. From all of this information, therapists generate a clinical hypothesis as to why and how a particular symptom is related to an interpersonal system, one which is usually undergoing some developmental transition. Once a clinical hypothesis is developed, we can start thinking about therapeutic change.

PRESCRIBING RITUALS

When you are prescribing an action, rather than a feeling or a thought, and that action is performed in some interpersonal context in which you think a symptom is embedded, that action forces the interpersonal context to change quickly. And when the clinical hypothesis is correct, the prescribed action begins to change the interpersonal context that created and sustains a symptom (Watzlawick, Weakland, & Fisch, 1974). To prescribe a new action is powerful because it produces change so quickly. It's also important to the patient, since it initiates a sense of hopefulness and ends the demoralization cycle that has taken place because of the patient's history of prior treatment failure. When a therapist gives a patient a ritual, inherent in this task is a message that there are possible solutions and that everything is not hopeless.

Prescribing powerful rituals requires creativity and depends on the therapist's personal style. For me it means using as much humor, absurdity, and playfulness as I can (Bergman, 1985). This communicates to the patient, "Let's have some fun and play here while we are helping you get out of this serious business."

I am also saying other things with humor and playfulness. I am saying that life is basically absurd. I am saying that sometimes the problem is not so much your problem as it is your seriousness about your problem. When I laugh with a patient about a problem, I also signal to the patient that there is a solution.

Using humor in treatment is also a powerful way of reframing a problem. Sometimes humor reframes a painful symptom into a more positive situation. And when a symptom has a new positive affect associated with it, it takes on a different meaning. Changing the affect associated with a symptom from negative to positive also reduces secondary negative reactions such as self-pity and demoralization, which after a while if unchecked may take on a life of their own.

Humor also provides the patient with some emotional distance from the presenting problem. And, with some distance and less negative affect associated with the problem, there is more opportunity for change.

Using humor to reframe a symptom also gives me the opportunity and freedom to prescribe a symptom at absurd levels to the point where the symptom begins to lose its original meaningfulness to the patient. Positive reframing takes some of the seriousness and negativity out of the symptom and provides the therapist with more opportunity and freedom to use a larger variety of therapeutic interventions.

I will briefly present two cases to illustrate some of the things mentioned above:

CASE ONE

I once had a young man come into treatment obsessed over his girlfriend's calves, which he thought were too fat.

The task at the end of this consultation was as follows: I told this young man that he indeed had a problem and that he really was not ready to deal with his problem at this particular time. The solution had to wait until he was ready to hear it. I then told him that he had basically two choices: He was either to join Overeaters Anonymous or work part time in a woman's shoe store; and that once he did one of these two things for a while, he could come back to see me.

About a year later he called and asked whether he could come in with the woman with "fat calves." The crisis now was not focused on fat calves but on the possibility of breaking up with this young woman, who recently decided that she was moving back to Philadelphia from New York. On one hand, he couldn't be with her; but on the other, he didn't want her to leave New York. So, the problem was now relational and no longer anatomical.

The couple came in, and the woman turned out to be a delightful and beautiful 22-year-old, with perfect calves from my perspective. The patient's presenting problem was that the woman did everything he wanted her to do and showed no resistance to what he wanted. This made him distrustful about how "real" her deference and compliance were.

I ended the session by telling this young man that if he loved and wanted this woman, he was to do whatever he had to do to keep her in New York. I further noted that if he did this, his current concern over her being so compliant and needing to please him would certainly change by itself over the next 10 years.

The tone or coloring of prescribed rituals will come from the therapist as well as from theory. The more one does brief therapy, the more one uses one's own strengths and style, and the more the coloring of the ritual will reflect qualities that the therapist brings to the treatment. Another thing to keep in mind when prescribing rituals is to keep the therapeutic moves simple and small. Therapists must work to ensure that they are not bringing more complexity into the treatment than is necessary. One reason for keeping the individual moves small is to ensure initial success for the patient as well as for the therapist. It is important to keep in mind that a major reason patients begin treatment is because they are somewhat demoralized over prior failures to solve problems. Patients also have lost some perspective along the way. Often, they see their problem magnified and are no longer able to see the difficulty within a larger framework.

Keeping things small and in perspective reminds me of an unusual case I was involved with a few years ago:

CASE TWO

The patient was a 35-year-old artist, who was talented, accomplished, and well known in his field. His presenting problem was his terror over his live-in girlfriend finding out that he was a cross-dresser. Sometimes, when she was not home, he would go to a hidden box of clothes, take out some women's clothes, and dress himself in these clothes. Then he would tie himself up into a chair, very tightly, and become sexually aroused by this ordeal. He was terrified of his girlfriend walking into the bedroom, where he performed this ritual, and finding out what he was doing.

My initial advice to this artist regarding his terror of being discovered was that he should lock his bedroom door whenever he was "doing his thing." He looked delighted over this advice. My second suggestion was that if and when the girlfriend asked him what he was doing behind the locked door, he was to casually say that "he was tied up for the moment, and would be out shortly." My patient and I then laughed together.

A few sessions later, I learned that this patient had an intrusive mother. She was totally focused on, and concerned about his entire internal and external existence as a child. He was her life, and as long as that was the case, he had no identity of his own. In my mind, the cross-dressing, or more important his secret about the cross-dressing, was a metaphor for his small sense of self, or for an identity separate and distinct from his mother's incessant intrusions.

The cross-dressing served a similar function when he got involved with his girlfriend. Later on in the therapy, I was able to coach him to be more overtly himself in his girlfriend's presence so he would not have to be so secretive. This involved coaching him to speak up more for himself so he could be less tuned into pleasing her and less reactive to her unhappiness. This enabled him to develop experiences of being more tuned into himself, which he missed and postponed as a child as a result of being so tuned into his mother's unhappiness.

As it turned out, later in the treatment, I learned that the girlfriend also was a cross-dresser! The couple eventually got married. His mother did not attend the wedding ceremony. And there were indeed *two* ceremonies. One was the conventional one with the bride wearing the gown and the bridegroom wearing the tuxedo. The second ceremony was more private and involved my patient wearing the gown and the girlfriend the tuxedo.

This case illustrates a few things. The conflict was first reframed with humor, giving this patient the message that all was not so tragic and that a solution was at hand. In addition, the initial interventions were kept small and simple, with the therapist maintaining a perspective on things, particularly when that perspective had been lost by the patient.

Also, in a brief therapy model, you stay with where the client is and work backward. There was no reason to wait in the treatment until I figured out why he was cross-dressing to help him with his problem. I found that out later. And I found it out later because I stayed focused on the presenting problem, which was that if his secret was revealed, his girlfriend would leave him. After his panic over being found out was reduced, he and I had more freedom and therefore more access to the information about what led up to his problem.

WHY AND HOW RITUALS WORK

Prescribing a ritual has many purposes, one of which is to change the ongoing game that sustains a particular symptom. Since symptoms can be seen as evolving out of interpersonal contexts one must understand the interpersonal game that leads to symptom onset. The symptomatic game then has to be replaced with a new game, a "therapeutic game."

Prescribing a therapeutic ritual begins the process of replacing a family game with a therapeutic game because the very process of the therapist prescribing a ritual adds the therapist and thereby changes the context. By joining the patient or the family and prescribing a ritual, the therapist changes the interpersonal context.

Now there are rituals and there are rituals. Some rituals, when presented in the presence of all of the major players in the old game, may be comprehensive enough to change the structure of the family sufficiently so the old game becomes a self-sustaining new game, which no longer requires the presence of a symptom. These are the most powerful rituals, requiring all or most of the major players, and are based on an accurate understanding about why and how the old game produces and sustains a symptom (Palazzoli, Cirillo, Selvini, & Sorrentino, 1989). These rituals may be sufficient for changing the family structure and sometimes constitute the entire therapy needed.

Other rituals may be sufficient for breaking up an old game without necessarily immediately replacing it with a new game or structure that is self-sustaining. Here, additional rituals or nonritual therapeutic work may be needed to help the family develop a new structure.

Now, as we well know, often in therapy, all the major players are not available. When this occurs, therapists must work with the players who are willing to play. This too can be therapeutic, because when the therapist is working with an individual, this new context is a smaller game, a scrimmage directed toward changing the individual's behavior within the larger game, namely, the family. This works too, although less quickly and less powerfully than when one has all the major players in treatment.

One reason family therapy is powerful is that when all of the major players are in treatment, the therapist is able to change the old game faster. It's not by chance that change occurs more readily in this order: treating families, treating couples, and lastly treating individuals. The difference between these treatments has to do with the inclusion of the major players who are participating in a family game.

Rituals are also action-oriented. By encouraging a patient to do a ritual and act differently in the interpersonal context that sustains a symptom, one can produce positive change quickly. Once the patient sees the positive effect of these new behaviors, these positive consequences end the demoralization cycle, encourage the patient in continuing to act differently, and increase the patient's willingness to try additional new behaviors. The momentum for change has begun, and this momentum provides the patient with more opportunity to take new risks and try new behaviors.

There are probably many other legitimate explanations for why rituals work, the scope of which is too great to include in this chapter. I suspect that as I continue to prescribe rituals in my clinical practice, and continue to think about why and how they work, some of these clinical maps for prescribing rituals will become clearer and more refined.

REFERENCES

Bergman, J. S. (1985). *Fishing for Barracuda: Pragmatics of Brief Systemic Therapy*. New York: Norton.

Bowen, M. (1978). *Family Therapy in Clinical Practice*. New York: Aronson.

Haley, J. (1967). *Advanced Techniques of Hypnosis and Therapy: Selected Papers of Milton H. Erickson.* New York: Grune & Stratton.

Palazzoli, M. Selvini, Cirillo, S., Selvini, M., & Sorrentino, A. (1989). *Family Games: General Model of Psychotic Processes in the Family.* New York: Norton.

Watzlawick, P., Weakland, J., & Fisch, R. (1974). *Change: Principles of Problem Formation and Problem Resolution.* New York: Norton.

CHAPTER 12

A Model of Integrating Individual and Family Therapy: The Contract Is the Key
Ruth McClendon
and Leslie B. Kadis

Redecision family therapy is a brief therapy model that integrates interpersonal and intrapsychic approaches to therapeutic work with families and individuals. Through weaving systems and individual dynamics redecision family therapy seeks: (1) to reconcile the conflict of personal autonomy versus the authority and power of the family system; (2) to reconcile the conflict of individual creativity versus the expression of family tradition; and (3) to reconcile the conflict of personal freedom versus togetherness. Redecision family therapy addresses the ongoing, continuous, dynamic interaction of the family and the individuals who make up the family.

The key to this model and to integrating the individual into family therapy is the therapeutic contract, the explicit agreement between the therapist and the individuals who make up the family unit. Contracts center therapy by creating the boundaries that remind each person of his or her obligations and objectives. They bring two disparate units, the family and the professional, together under the same umbrella and provide them with a common purpose while focusing attention and problem-solving abilities. By attending to one area of the family's functioning, other areas of family life are implicitly defined as areas of strength which then can be utilized on behalf of therapy. The clear contractual focus shifts the family into the problem-solving mode, outlines and supports their strengths, tests their abilities to find solutions, and teaches them how to carry out these new solutions.

McClendon (1977) first described the redecision family therapy model for integrating individual and systems therapy. The approach was further developed by McClendon and Kadis (1983), who stated:

> ... current behavior (in the form of interactional patterns) and personal history (in the form of early decisions) operate in a reciprocal relationship. We work first on one aspect and then the other, but dealing with both is essential to family therapy. (p. 307)

Around the same time Gurman (1981), in commenting on previous work of his own, noted:

> ... the most salient and fundamental exchanges in marriage involve the reciprocal exchange, over time, of behaviors that confirm each partner's projections and maintain relatively consistent self-perception. (p. 130)

This shift from a systemic to what we call an integrative paradigm is presently rippling through the field of family therapy. It is particularly apparent in a paper recently published by Andolfi and Angelo (1988), who, in revising some of their earlier positions, noted:

> ... it follows that the individual members are not completely determined by the system, but that they actively contribute to determining the system's characteristics and equilibriums .... This leads us to hypothesize a circular movement of exchange between a family structure and an individual structure which are hierarchically superimposed and whose contents influence each other reciprocally. (p. 239)

While individual behavior and, by extension, clinical symptoms may be a manifestation of various aspects of the system, the system also may be the outward manifestation of the negotiations of the various individuals to maintain constancy in their self-perceptions. In keeping with the principle of circular causality, it seems more likely that the individual and the system exist in a state of dynamic equilibrium and there is an ongoing negotiation in the process to simultaneously maintain the integrity of the larger units and the smaller subunits, of which the individual is only one.

General systems theory (GST) holds that every unit is made up of smaller units and that the larger unit is more than the sum of its parts (Miller, 1969). Family systems theory is a special application of GST that focuses entirely on the larger unit and says that any significant change in the family unit will necessarily result in change in the individual. While this may be so, it misses an important point: The family is made up of individuals and each person brings his or her own personal history to the party, perceives and interprets events in the context of his or her own personal history, makes decisions about him/herself and the world, and finally, acts on the basis of this personalized processing. Unless individuals can find a way to bring changes in the family system into line with their internal processing and their early decisions, they will either resist or become a casualty of the change. In one of the earliest outcome studies in the family therapy literature, Bader (1976) found that when individual family members made redecisions in the context of family therapy, change was more likely and also more likely to be sustained over time.

What is good for the whole family or for part of the family may not be good for each individual in the family. For example, research on children in divorced families shows that while divorce may be the best answer for the couple or for the family, children suffer differentially (Wallerstein, 1985). Younger children seem to have problems (e.g., depression) that manifest soon after the divorce, while older children have more enduring problems that surface later (e.g., they become disenchanted with marriage and modify their lives accordingly) (Wallerstein, 1985). Other research investigating the aftercare of hospitalized schizophrenics has revealed a similar finding. Specifically, Leff and Vaughn (1985) found that in families with a schizophrenic member, reactivation of the disease process correlated more closely with the way the family spoke to the schizophrenic than it did with other aspects of family life. Communication, however hostile or demanding, did not seem to affect healthy family members in the same way it did the schizophrenics.

These studies suggest that it may not be enough to focus on the system without attending to the individuals who comprise the system. They also suggest that it is important to focus on the interface between the individual and the system. What makes sense as a systemic change may sometimes cause debilitating individual pain. For example, in one family engaged in a business together, the son and heir apparent was advised by a consultant to leave the business because of the severe conflict with his father. This move replicated earlier systemic patterns and contributed to the father's depression. The son was free to develop his own business and sense of himself.

With this background in mind, let's take a first look at two different cases we will follow:

Janet A. is a bright, outgoing 15-year-old girl who entered therapy with her foster parents. Janet was referred by the school psychologist because of excessive school cuts, not working up to her abilities, episodic drinking, and angry outbursts with peers and teachers.

This is Janet's 10th foster home and her 22nd and 23rd parenting figures. Her current "family" consists of Mark and Joan, a dual professional couple involved in the medical and mental health fields. Mark has two adult children from a former marriage. Joan has no biological children. Janet is a ward of the court and had previously lived with Mark and Joan for 22 months. Janet had previously left Mark and Joan's to live with a half-sister and, when that didn't work out, had spent some time "on the run." This time, Janet has been with Mark and Joan for three months.

Janet is the youngest of five children, each of whom was conceived by a different father. Her mother was not married to her father and she has no recollection of him, not even his name. Janet has been in some type of public care since she was four. At that time, she was taken from her biological mother after being shot and raped by one of her mother's "friends." She was placed in an orphanage-type setting in Denver, Colorado. Even though she came from a rather large family, none of her biological relatives was willing to provide a home for her. Their comment was, "She's a bad seed just like her mother."

During her early years in public custody, Janet's mother had access to her and would frequently disappear with her for weeks at a time. Janet would arrive back at the foster home badly bruised, reeking of alcohol, and essentially alone since her mother had left her on the lawn or down the street. Not only did her mother's visits affect her physically, they also had severe effects on her emotionally. Janet's moods and behavior have been described as ranging from sweet, loving, obedient, and submissive to angry, raging, mean, and manipulative.

Janet had been adopted at the age of nine years. She began the fourth grade with a new family and in a new school. Unfortunately, after three and one-half years she was removed from her adoptive home by Child Protective Services and again placed in public custody. It was at this time that Janet first joined Mark and Joan in their home.

The case of Janet A. is presented as an example of an environmentally and emotionally handicapped child. Her personal history had nothing to do with Mark and Joan and yet she developed a similar pattern of relationships as she was integrated into her new family, thus demonstrating the importance of the individual in creating the patterns of the family.

Susan B. is a 47-year-old married woman referred after her 14th conviction for shoplifting. Susan served time following previous convictions and was currently facing the possibility of being "put away" for an extended period. In the past Susan received extensive individual therapy. This time her astute lawyer realized that the individual therapy had been unsuccessful and referred her for marital therapy.

When first seen, Bill and Susan had been married for 18 years and had two children who were in college and doing well. There were many important strains in their lives but money was not an issue, and never had been. Upon examination, Susan's early life and personal history revealed no unusual or traumatic events. In fact, Susan could be said to have come from a "normal, middle class, white American family." Susan was the second of three children and was raised in the Midwest by both parents. She had completed two years of college and had been successfully employed before marriage.

The atmosphere in the consulting room when Bill and Susan were there could best be described as somewhere between chaos and pandemonium. Susan was vocal and explosive, but also vague and inconsistent. She had no apparent insight about the cause of her shoplifting or the antecedents of her behavior. Moreover, she was not able to focus on her actions for more than one sentence before she would be off on a tangent complaining about her husband. It was as if her own actions were completely alien to her and, as such, she dismissed them. She complained that Bill "is always on my case." She thought he was critical, jealous, and untrustworthy with respect to the family finances. Bill's response to the outbursts was to look down and inward. One had the feeling that if Bill could physically disappear, he would. He, too, had little insight into his wife's behavior. In fact, he knew so little about it that it wasn't until a week before she was due in court that he learned that she had been arrested six months previously.

Bill and Susan are presented to demonstrate how the circular movement of exchange between individuals actively contributes to and binds the psychological and emotional baggage carried by each of us from childhood. They are an example of how the pervasiveness and chronicity of the current family dynamics affect the individual's present-day functioning.

REDECISION FAMILY THERAPY

When we work with the individual and the family we are working from the specific frame of reference of redecision therapy (Goulding and Goulding, 1978) and its special application to family systems therapy. We have described this previously (McClendon & Kadis, 1983) as redecision family therapy and will review it here. In the redecision family therapy framework, children of all ages are seen as being engaged in an active process of adapting to their environment to guarantee, at the very least, their survival. The adaptations they make are based on their own needs, neurobiological givens, and personal experience to date. With time and repeated experience the same adaptations begin to coalesce to form a pattern and children can be seen to act "as if" they had made a formal decision. These early decisions influence perceptions as well as behaviors and are one of the roots of personality style.

Since decisions are made at such an early age, they carry with them the affective force of survival and are repeated and continually reinforced into adulthood. Children perceive the world through the lenses of their early decisions and interpret current events based on these perceptions, which in turn validates their perceptions as well as their way of perceiving. Early decisions, usually operating outside of awareness, are frequently carried into adult life and influence, along with developmental markers and current circumstances, every aspect of life, from choice of career, to choice of mate, to style of parenting.

Since these early decisions represent the individual's best attempts to manage his or her feelings in any current situation, it is essential to identify those that contribute to the family's reaction to stress and to the presenting problem. Once recognized, the early decisions can be reframed so that family members will better understand and empathize with each other. Identifying an early decision alerts us to the importance it has for the individual and the tenacity with which he or she will hold on to a particular position.

In our view, the family is the product of the interplay between the individuals who are living out their early decisions or what Berne (1961) called scripts. Said differently, families are conceptualized as groups of individuals in which each person, no matter how big or small, stars in his or her own life production while simultaneously playing a part in the cast of each other's productions. In this interlocking of life plans each person then reinforces each other's accommodations. Since the system and the individuals are dynamically interwoven, lasting change may be achieved only by changing both the individual and the family system.

Redecision family therapy, as mentioned, is a three-stage model combining systemic and individual therapeutic approaches. The overall goals of redecision family therapy are (1) to initiate change with family members so that their conversations and behaviors with each other change in directions that they prefer, (2) to initiate change in family members' internal sense of themselves, and (3) to help family members resolve the particular presenting problem.

Stage One is a systems stage focusing on symptom or problem resolution through structural and process changes that lead to emancipation of the individual. Stage One examines and then interrupts the ongoing, continuous patterns of the family that negatively affect problem-solving behavior, positive coping skills, task mastery, social competence, and intimacy.

Stage Two is the redecision, or intrapsychic, stage focusing on the transformation of personal structures. This involves helping individuals confront their past (early decisions) so that they may gain confidence in mastering the present and deciding on the future. Redecisions are cognitive and affective reinterpretations of one's sense of self. The focal point for redecisions is derived from the individual's process and participation with other family members.

Stage Three, or reintegration, is a focus on the prevention of future individual and systemic disablement. Here, careful attention is paid to describing and teaching effective and healthy ways to function within the family and to facilitate self-enhancement.

CONTRACTS

As mentioned earlier, the key to integrating the individual into family therapy is the therapeutic contract, the explicit agreement between the therapist and the individuals who make up the family unit. A contract establishes a boundary that defines the working environment, defines the work to be done, sets limits on expectations, and prescribes behaviors. With a contract as a point of reference, distraction or interpersonal maneuvering become obvious and can be explored or handled therapeutically. Group dynamics such as fight-flight, dependency, or authority conflicts stand out in stark relief (Bion, 1959; Gadlin, 1985). Since much of what goes on in a group can be seen as a manifestation of boundary regulation (Kissen, 1981), the way the family manages distance and closeness can be observed and incorporated into the therapy when appropriate.

In spite of their importance, contracts have received little direct attention in the family literature. Behavior therapists are most explicit in the way they use contracts. They focus on specific behaviors that the family wants to change and offer specific strategies aimed at changing those behaviors. In our view behavioral contracts are too constricting in that they frequently accept the family's definition of the problem without addressing the forces that maintain nonproductive behavior. Structural therapists make an important conceptual leap. They relate dysfunctional behavior to the structure of the family and formulate contracts aimed toward changing the structure of the family as a way of relieving the symptoms or eliminating the unwanted behaviors. In a similar vein, strategic therapists attempt to integrate the family's view of the problem with their (the professional's) view of the family's problem-solving strategies. The purpose is to alleviate the symptoms through devising a contract and a strategy for changing the way the family solves the problem. Another approach, and the one closest to ours, is the multilevel contract seen in the work of the Milan school. In this approach, the family, at some point, is given a statement that explains the symptom in a way the family can understand, states it in positive terms, and addresses each person's view of the family and the problem. Furthermore, their statement, or formulation, brings each person's individual struggle under the umbrella of helping the family.

In our frame of reference, a contract includes four elements: (1) a clear delineation of the major complaint, (2) a systemic appreciation of the family as a whole, (3) a way of integrating each family member's unique history, world view, and early decisions into the picture, and (4) a positive and understandable framework. Such a contract provides the structure that permits individual and family systems dynamics to be included in the same therapeutic process.

The Major Complaint

Several things must occur in the "getting ready" or assessment phase before the contract is framed. The first step, getting agreement among family members on what the problem is, has been written about extensively (Haley, 1971; Weakland et al., 1974). Frequently family members disagree about the main problem, and even more frequently family members and referral sources disagree about the problem. This may be due to different ways of seeing life in general, different values, or defensive processes that protect people from either knowing or communicating their experience. It is not surprising that families who can't agree on what the problem is have great difficulty solving it.

Even when the problem is obvious, as in the case of someone

hallucinating or behaving violently, reaching formal agreement may be hampered because family members are reluctant to speak up. This may be due to fear of retaliation, fear of hurting someone else's feelings, or a need to maintain the family's boundaries by keeping personal things about the family private. Whatever the case, the first step in contract formation is getting agreement on what the main problem is, to identify that issue which brings the family and professional together.

Evaluate the System

The second step in the process of contract formation is to evaluate the system. It seems to make little difference which formal system of evaluation is used, provided it is congruent with the family's values and its ability to understand itself. In fact, some evidence suggests that different approaches work best for different families and different therapists work better with some approaches than with others (Karasu, 1986).

We prefer to identify the repetitive pattern or patterns that interfere with the family's ability to go beyond a certain point. We believe that these patterns represent regressions in the group dynamics that occur when a family is under stress. To accomplish this end we might, for example, introduce stress by bringing up a charged issue and observing what happens. Perhaps there will be evasions or distractions, or perhaps someone will display feelings that divert the family's attention. When any of these responses recur, we infer that we have seen some aspect of the family's preferred "operating under stress" mode and can begin to relate the problem to this broader pattern, namely, the system. We conclude that there is a reciprocal relationship between the problem itself, the family's inability to resolve the problem on its own, and the recurrent patterns. For example, a family may agree too quickly on the nature of the problem. This could represent a pattern of covering up differences, which makes it difficult for family members to express themselves and, in turn, not uncommonly leads to the development of symptoms. The contract in this situation would include the problem definition, a plan to interrupt the pattern of covering up differences, and an understanding of how each family member's early decision contributes to maintaining the pattern.

Identify Early Decisions

Because each family member reacts in a characteristic way, the third step in the contracting process is to consider the individuals and their own preferred "operating under stress" mode. The key to identifying the presence of an early decision in the current environment is through the observations of either idiosyncratic responses to particular situations or regressions under stress. To locate early decisions we watch each person's posture and demeanor and we listen to voice tone and choice of words in each area of activity and interaction with current family members. We discover the imprint of early decisions through the repetitive behaviors and absolute beliefs. When a husband yells at his wife and we watch her eyes glaze over, we wonder where she "went," what archaic experience she was responding to, and how that archaic experience may have interfered with her reactions to her husband. We similarly wonder about the husband's early decisions, how they may be the driving force behind his current anger.

While the parents are the "architects" of the family, the children nonetheless have their own experiences and make their own early decisions which color their perceptions, determine the way they interpret the current events, validate their internal beliefs, and ultimately guide their actions. The literature on suicide in young children attests to the importance of the decision-making process (Pfeffer & Trad, 1988). Assessing the child's method of operating under stress mode or early decision is necessary, and after redecisions are made by parents and the system is changed, it is then safe enough for children to redecide.

Frame the Contract

At this point, we have made explicit an agreement about the problem, or at least an agreement about which of the problems the family will work on first. We have arrived at an understanding of how the family, as a unit, reacts to stress, and how that reaction limits their ability to solve the problem. We have identified early decisions, or how each person in the family reacts to the environment of the family under stress. With these three elements in focus we are now ready to frame the contract.

The contract, as we have just described, is a complex concept. It can be a specific instrument, a therapeutic strategy, a specific intervention, or even a description of a process between the therapist and the family. In practice we arrive at a contract by a series of approximations which are similar to the process Penn (1982) called "hypothesizing." When we discuss each approximation with the family, we are using the contract as we would any intervention. Usually we arrive at the contract after several sessions, discuss it with the family to monitor how they receive it and gauge the degree of acceptance at each of the system's levels. We describe how we believe the presenting problem relates to the recurrent pattern and how each person, child or adult, in their desire to make things work best for himself or herself and for the family, contributes to the maintenance of the pattern. Through this process, the pattern itself is implicitly labeled maladaptive while each person's efforts are considered understandable, but not necessarily helpful to themselves and to others. Moreover, each person's behavior is understood in the context of his or her early decisions. This allows for distancing from the emotional quagmire of the interpersonal "force field."

To illustrate, let us now return to Janet A. and to Susan B. and her husband, Bill.

The initial contracting with Janet occurred over several sessions. The presenting problem of Janet's behavior within the school context and her aggressive, sometimes mean and defiant behavior within the family was easily agreed upon by Janet, Mark, and Joan. The overall systems contract was framed with respect to how difficult it is for Janet to make an attachment to a family even though this is what she wants most in her life. Her contract was to learn safe and constructive ways to belong. It was acknowledged that the degree of mistrust ran deep because of Janet's past and that Janet, Mark, and Joan would each need to find gentle ways of protecting themselves in this new family relationship as well as working out appropriate ways of getting close.

Janet has trouble with engagement. She sets up fights that provide intensity but promote disengagement. A behavioral contract that supported the overall contract was therefore devised. This contract, which defined specific consequences for Janet's drinking, drug, school truancy, and staying out all night behaviors, was agreed upon, written, and signed.

On the individual level, Janet's contract was to believe in herself as a good and worthwhile person who deserved to be alive and get good things. This formulation was needed to directly counter the belief that she was born "a bad seed like her mother" and had no chance of overcoming her bad beginnings.

In the second case, Bill and Susan were seen as enmeshed, relatively undifferentiated, and, as a result, not willing to accept adult responsibilities. Within several sessions, Bill and Susan had agreed that their mutual dependency prevented them from noticing, commenting on, and correcting problems. The contract that both Bill and Susan agreed to was to become more self-reliant, self-assured, and independent so that they could develop more functional and mature ways of helping each other. Susan recognized and agreed that as much as she loved and cared for Bill, her way of helping him, by becoming a little girl and shoplifting so that he could focus on her and not have to deal with his internal stress, was not working.

Susan quickly figured out that when she regressed, she effectively stopped thinking. She formulated her own contract to "grow up" and honor herself as a competent, responsible, and gracious woman. It was clear to her that when she did this, she would no longer act out by shoplifting. Bill recognized the serious flaws in his way of managing stress and his life in general and saw, for the first time, his own failure to notice anything or anyone outside himself, including his wife. His personal difficulties, along with his attempts to manage them, were seen as a result of his belief that he was basically a bumbling, incompetent idiot. Bill's contract was to open his eyes and discover who he really was rather than to blindly go on believing what his father and brothers had told him when he was growing up.

AFTER CONTRACTS

Contracting is an important part of the therapy work itself. Sometimes the clarity, boundary definition, or new focus derived from the contracting process is all that is needed. When more is needed, the rest of the therapy work proceeds from the contract. Systems interventions may be direct, paradoxical, strategic, structural, dynamic, or educational; all serve the purpose of reinforcing the boundaries delineated in the contract as well as supporting the new patterns of interacting that replace those defined as maladaptive. Individual redecision work identifies and reinforces the individual as unique and special and helps each person maintain his or her separateness in the face of emotionally laden family transactions. This separateness is itself an essential element of problem solving that transcends any particular problem. Developing the ability to keep oneself from the knee-jerk reactions that characterize repetitive family patterns is a reinforcing experience which, while sometimes threatening at first, is usually experienced as relieving.

Stage One

As therapists in Stage One, we are confrontive and challenging of the family's repetitive patterns or constant attitude that confines the individual in the historical and rigid trap of his or her early decisions. Our goal is to intervene in a creative and supportive way so that the individuals are emancipated from the dysfunctional system and therefore available to make changes in their view of themselves and others.

With Janet, Mark, and Joan the dominant systemic interventions had to do with interfering in the pattern of disengagement. Janet, in her inability to make an attachment and her fear about trusting and being close to anyone, would regularly act out in a way that resulted in Mark's first deciding that he didn't care what happened next because he had had "enough of the meanness and disregard from Janet." Next Joan would defend Janet. Then Janet would attack Joan, and Joan would counterattack with the sense that she no longer cared either. The result of this was that Janet was constantly setting herself up to be kicked by her foster parents or her "rejecting family" and Mark and Joan would be disagreeing about how to handle Janet. The therapist interfered with this pattern by pointing out Janet's "kick me" game; helping Mark and Joan to respond in a way that expressed their hurt rather than their anger; and helping Mark and Joan with a commitment not to become divided by Janet. As Mark and Joan began to respond differently to Janet's setup, it freed Janet to take responsibility and look at her own hurt as well as how she kept driving to prove that she was the bad seed she believed she was. When Janet was no longer able to shift the focus to the "bad people" whom she pictured as abusing her, she was free to begin to deal with some of her own intense pain.

When in the room with Bill and Susan, one could feel the tenseness. Susan was loud and frantic. Bill's response to Susan's outbursts, whether they were directed toward him or related to some other matter, was to look down and away. It looked as if he tried to literally "go away" and not see or notice anything. It was this manner of Bill's emotional disappearance and his not seeing or knowing that repeated itself over and over and seemed to signal both his and Susan's regressions to early decisions. Direct ways of interrupting this pattern were taken, and at one time Susan was asked to sit in a chair on the other side of the room facing away from Bill. Such interventions to disrupt the enmeshment between Bill and Susan made it possible to follow up on the regression with Bill. It was only at this time that Bill revealed his long history of repeated personal failure, compulsive gambling, barely manageable anxiety, and associated symptoms and behaviors. Furthermore, he talked about impulsive and antisocial behavior that predated his marriage. Bill's self-disclosure was followed by a noticeable reduction in Susan's volatility and exposed a frightened side of her that had a little-girl quality.

Stage Two

Once the individual decisions have been defined and included in the contract, the individual work itself can be done in the family setting, peer settings (marital, sibling, male/female), or individually. The principal element with respect to integrating the individual work with the family work is the awareness of the impact of each person's early decisions on the family and on other family members. It is, therefore, necessary to identify each individual's early decisions. However, to accomplish family change it is not essential to help each person through to redecision. It is only necessary to identify those people in the family who are central to the family's functioning, and to work through their early decisions to redecision.

The process of redeciding begins when an individual reexperiences his or her thinking, feeling, and being of an earlier time. This process continues as the person metaphorically becomes the child that he or she was and is guided (1) to the discovery of his or her own unique early decision and (2) to the formulation of a redecision or new and updated perception of himself or herself, others, and the world. Drawing on abilities acquired by the evolution of adult (or more grown up) perceptions and resources, people were helped to recognize the value and significance of their early decision and then to develop a new conclusion about themselves and others. The redecision occurs when one is able to incorporate updated and current information into the early model of self and the world. Through the redecision process, the individual takes a step to free himself or herself to feel and behave differently in current life.

The individual or redecision work with Janet involved her confronting, both in reality and symbolically, the members of her biological family who had been so rejecting of her and had defined her as being bad. Janet redecided that the conditions of her conception and birth were not within her control and that she was not the cause of her biological mother's disablement. Janet learned that she must change her behavior and that even when she behaves in a mean and rejecting way she is not a "bad seed" or a bad person. She received (1) permission to accept herself and to feel kind and caring toward herself, (2) permission to belong in a family, and (3) permission to be successful in her own life.

Susan's early decision was that she was an unimportant person. She had decided to stay a little girl until her parents recognized and validated her and to do anything to get them to do this. In her redecision work Susan (1) gave up waiting for her parents, (2) decided that she herself would judge the kind of person that she was, (3) decided that she was important to herself, and (4) decided to behave only in ways that honored herself.

Bill recognized for the first time how his unwillingness and inability to notice anyone outside of himself created problems for his wife and certainly for himself. He redecided that he could be competent and recognize others at the same time. His redecision came through recognizing the dependent relationship with his mother as she referred to him as the "savior" and treated him as if no one else in the world existed or mattered. This relationship had countered his father and brothers, who made fun of him.

Stage Three

Reintegration work comes after redecisions are made. We help ground or anchor the individual in the present and with current family members. We have conversations about how things will be different now and how each family member can support the others. We also make explicit how each family member can interfere. We involve the family in a process of prediction and, therefore, a process of prevention.

In this stage we help the family to concretize systemic and individual changes that have been initiated. We do this through an educational approach focusing on the elements of healthy family functioning. We talk about healthy family structure and the essentials of successful problem solving and communication. We provide exercises for the family to do in the office and home assignments to do on their own time and in their own living arrangement. In this way we help guide families in practicing behaviors that support healthy family functioning. We help families create an environment that encourages and supports the individuals' new sense of themselves.

CONCLUSION

Redecision family therapy is a brief therapy model based in the belief that contracts are the supportive structure that allows for the integration of individual and systemic principles. It stresses the dignity of people and their ability to change. As a treatment approach it brings action, vitality, and humor to the process. It focuses on symptoms, emphasizes the positive, utilizes what the client brings to the therapeutic situation, and is an approach tailored uniquely to each family and individual.

At this time Janet remains in the home with Mark and Joan. She talks about someday going to college and is attending school regularly. She is making her best efforts to be herself and to be different than her rough beginnings. Janet is getting ready to go to her first formal dance. Her date is a boy who actually likes her rather than beats her.

The instances of Susan's impulsive acting out have quieted. She continues with her efforts to know and be herself and is now working outside of Bill's office as well as developing her own friends and some separate social activities. She is not in jail.

REFERENCES

Andolfi, M., & Angelo, C. (1988). Toward constructing the therapeutic system. *Journal of Marital and Family Therapy, 14,* 237–247.

Bader, E. (1976). *Redecision in family therapy: A study of change in an intensive family therapy workshop.* Dissertation Abstracts: Ann Arbor, MI, University No. 7625064.

Berne, E. (1961). *Transactional Analysis in Psychotherapy.* New York: Grove Press.

Bion, W. R. (1959). *Experience in Groups.* New York: Basic Books.

Gadlin, W. (1985). Psychiatric consultation to the medical ward: A group analytic and general systems theory point of view. *International Journal of Group Psychotherapy, 35,* 263–278.

Goulding, R.L., & Goulding, M. (1978). *Changing Lives through Redecision Therapy* (2nd ed.). New York: Brunner/Mazel.

Gurman, A. (1981). Integrative marital therapy: Toward the development of an interpersonal approach. In S. H. Budman (Ed.). *Forms of Brief Therapy.* New York: Guilford Press.

Haley, J. (Ed.) (1971). *Changing Families.* New York: Grune & Stratton.

Karasu, T. B. (1986). The specificity vs. nonspecificity dilemma: Toward identifying change agents. *American Journal of Psychiatry, 143,* 687–695.

Kissen, M. (1981). Exploring general systems processes in group settings. *Psychotherapy: Theory, Research and Practice, 18,* 424–430.

Leff, J., & Vaughn, C. (1985). *Expressed Emotion in Families.* New York: Guilford Press.

McClendon, R. (1977). My mother drives a pickup truck. In G. Barnes (Ed.), *TA after Eric Berne: Recent Advances in Transactional Analysis.* New York: Harpers College Press.

McClendon, R., & Kadis, L. (1983). *Chocolate Pudding and Other Approaches to Intensive Multiple Family Therapy.* Palo Alto, CA: Science and Behavior Books.

Miller, J. G. (1969). Living systems, basic concepts. In Gray, W., Duhl, F. J., & Rizzo, N. D. (Eds.), *General Systems Theory and Psychiatry.* Boston: Little, Brown.

Penn, P. (1982). Circular questioning. *Family Process, 21,* 267–280.

Pfeffer, C. R., & Trad, P. V. (1988). Sadness and suicidal tendencies in preschool children. *Journal of Development and Behavioral Pediatrics, 9,* 86–88.

Wallerstein, J. S. (1985). Children of divorce: Preliminary report of a ten year follow-up of older children and adolescents. *Journal of the American Academy of Child Psychiatry, 24,* 545–553.

Weakland, J. H., Fisch, R., Watzlawick, P., & Bodin, A. M. (1974). Brief therapy: Focused problem resolution. *Family Process, 13,* 141–168.

CHAPTER 13

Family Myths and Reality: Ericksonian Approaches to Family of Origin
Betty Alice Erickson Elliott

Each of us has a family of origin. Each of us carries at least some of the rules, burdens, memories, images, and roles learned from our families. Each of us is faced with the challenges of leaving behind hurtful issues, reconciling today with the memories of yesterday, and bringing forward the good we obtained from our family. Sometimes this task seems insurmountable, and a person enters therapy with urgent pleas such as, "Help me to accept who I am and how my parents treated me," "I want to understand and forgive my parents," and perhaps saddest of all: "I want to raise my children better than I was raised and I can't seem to let go of my past."

Resolution of these issues is difficult for many reasons. Not only are memories faulty, but people change. Episodes which were once so important and which left a lasting mark have faded and are seen by more adult and cognitive eyes as insignificant. Yet we all know that the remembered past is carried with us and that events have a lasting influence.

Insight and understanding usually are not enough to change these issues. A client can realize intellectually that his or her parents meant no harm. But the limitations, burdens, and maladaptive behaviors of the parents impacted just as deliberate mistreatment would have impacted.

There is difficulty in putting away the hurts and injustices done even when realizing that these injuries were unintentional. Each of us, however, must come to grips with the idea and the reality that childhood and the past is gone. It never can be factually altered.

There is not a great deal in the literature detailing Milton Erickson's methods in dealing with people struggling with family of origin issues per se. One of the few references is Erickson and Rossi's (1989) discussion of Erickson's "February Man" technique in which they describe how Erickson added to the life experience of a patient through hypnosis by enriching her memories. These hypnotically implanted "memories" became a part of the person so that she could draw upon "them" in present living. It is a rewarding experience to study *The February Man* (Erickson & Rossi, 1989; see also Haley, 1973, and Erickson, 1980 for more information on this case).

I believe that many of the principles of Ericksonian psychotherapy are essential for effective therapy. I am in the fortunate, though perhaps biased, position of being Erickson's daughter. I am the first of his children whom he used as a demonstration subject in hypnosis for both his patients and his students, so I have been lucky enough to have seen and experienced his methods in that more formal setting as well as in my home. I have almost finished my doctorate in counseling and I have been taught all sorts of theoretical frameworks. But as I have observed other counselors and supervisors, I have become even more convinced that the most powerful tools and interventions are those found in an Ericksonian approach.

Erickson was adamantly atheoretical and believed strongly in the uniqueness of each individual. There are some ideas, however, that are common to a great deal of his "Uncommon Therapy" (Haley, 1973). Bill O'Hanlon (1985) listed these frameworks noting that virtually all of them, from Haley to Rossi to the Lanktons, include the ideas of (1) entering and then using the client's world and behaviors as a basis for change, (2) a future orientation, and (3) the use of symbolic and metaphorical communications. In each framework, the therapist is willing to take responsibility for initiating change while allowing the clients the productive self-sufficiency to change themselves. Further, Erickson was flexible and creative. He was firmly grounded in reality and found humor and pleasure in everyday life. I believe that each of these basic orientations is important to the practice of effective Ericksonian psychotherapy. To illustrate how they can be applied in the treatment of family of origin issues, I will describe four relevant cases:

CASE 1: CHARLENE

Charlene was 35, a divorced mother of an eight-year-old daughter and a full-time college senior preparing to be an elementary teacher. Her college tuition was being financed by scholarships, loans, and grants as well as a small monthly stipend from her parents. Charlene paid rent to live in the home of her younger sister and her husband and their 10-year-old daughter. She had been in various types of therapy for several years. Her presenting complaints focused first on her recent divorce, then on chronic feelings of depression, and finally on a need to resolve family of origin issues.

Charlene claimed her parents always had liked her younger sister best. Whatever Charlene did was not good enough. Her failed marriage and present living circumstances were a constant reminder of her inferiority to her sister. Charlene felt that she had lost a competitive battle, and she experienced great sadness and depression as a result. She had asked her parents directly about her childhood and confronted her mother with the belief that her lack of self-esteem, failed marriage, and depression stemmed directly from lack of good parenting. Her parents were stunned and hurt and wanted to make amends. Charlene was willing to accept their financial help for her school tuition as partial reparation.

Charlene still strongly believed, however, that the pattern of favoritism was continuing. Everyone in the family thought the sister's 10-year-old was much smarter than Charlene's eight-year-old and the two girls were treated accordingly. Both Charlene's sister and niece had beautiful glossy hair and received frequent compliments on its beauty. Both Charlene and her daughter had thin frizzy hair and Charlene felt resentful that they were never complimented on their hair. This was but one item on an unending list of areas in which Charlene felt she and her daughter were slighted. For all I know, they really were.

Charlene came to me with the stated goal of learning to accept her dreary life better. As we talked, it became clear that her style of parenting was similar to the parenting she believed she had received. I told Charlene I understood her life was dreary, that she wanted to overcome this, and that there were a number of unresolved issues from her growing-up years. I told her that I knew she loved her daughter dearly, and because the girl was already eight, there weren't a lot of years left for Charlene to be effective in teaching her daughter to be wise, wonderful, and happy. Charlene agreed that this was an important goal, especially as her sister's child was already seen as superior. We agreed that each session would be spent half on Charlene's distress and half on ways to help her daughter learn to be wise, wonderful, and happy.

Charlene was an excellent hypnotic subject. Her hobby of painting pictures was used as a basis for creating images of her life. In a trance, she would paint a mental picture of her sad and dreary life describing its contents to me. Each image gave material for a slight alteration. For example, she saw her woes and tribulations in a big burlap sack on her back. She had rocks and sandy gravel and pointed boulders digging into her as she trudged along a seemingly endless path. When she concentrated on the burlap sack, she could examine the weave. She discovered that burlap has a coarse weave, that gravel and sand can leak out of a coarse weave, and that pointed boulders can rub holes and then even more could leak out.

Once she saw her depression as horrible little creatures nipping and snapping at her heels as she ran down a road. Interestingly, she saw the road as covered with gravel and rocks and pointed boulders through which she had to maneuver as she attempted to dodge the little monsters yapping at her ankles. I helped her note that the nasty creatures were so short that they had trouble running around the rocks and boulders; thus, she could easily outdistance them. I didn't point out to her that her own unhappiness was helping her get away from her depression.

We dealt with the parenting of her daughter on a much more direct basis. Charlene rarely had fun with the girl, so her first homework assignment was to go to the library and find a book of riddles to ask her daughter. As she was going to be an elementary school teacher, I knew she would select an appropriate book. She was told to ask riddles of her daughter until they both laughed three times. She did not want to do this; she felt it was a silly assignment. I agreed and told her to think of just how silly it was to read to her daughter in order to laugh with her. Furthermore, I was limited because currently I did not have an eight-year-old daughter so I could only think up silly assignments.

When she returned, she told me she had done the silly assignment and even enjoyed it. She had decided, however, that this was not the way to teach her daughter to be wise and wonderful. So she was going to think up an assignment by herself and was not going to tell me anything about it until it was complete. I was reluctant but she convinced me. The next week, Charlene reported she was working on it and refused again to give even a hint. The next time, she told me she had helped her daughter with a lemonade stand and all the neighbors had been pleased to buy lemonade from her daughter. Her daughter even had the idea of including entertainment: for an extra nickel, she would tell a riddle.

They had made more than $5.00 and bought some clothes for the girl's Barbie doll. I thought that such actions were pretty "wise and wonderful" and even had an element of the daughter learning to be a good mother to her doll. I resisted the temptation to point this out to Charlene though—therapy one-step-removed, as Zeig (1985) calls it, can be more effective than direct approaches.

Charlene continued to think up good interventions for her daughter. Sometimes she needed help. I was best at thinking up the ones aimed solely at having fun, but they were always silly and Charlene hated to do them.

As therapy progressed, Charlene's unhappiness changed. She used to picture herself backed into a corner, she told me, flailing and stabbing with a big butcher knife at all who approached. Now she saw herself in the kitchen chopping food with that same knife—a nice, warm place and a nurturing and motherly activity. Charlene also told me that she saw herself as covered with hundreds and hundreds of bandages. If she lifted up the corner of a bandage, though, she could see that she was healing but realized it was too soon to remove the bandages. I felt Charlene was clearly instructing me and thereby taking full responsibility for her own therapy.

In one of the final sessions, she saw herself as if in a black-and-white movie. She had a "cloak of confidence" wrapped around her—something we had developed in a trance. (It had been suggested that whenever she felt inadequate or incompetent or scared, especially during her student teaching, she could take a deep breath and wrap that cloak of confidence around her and present that appearance to the world.) In her present image, Charlene was walking down a dark and dreary pathway in a forest. The wind was blowing her cloak of confidence behind her. The billows of the cloak were frightening away the nipping, yapping creatures of depression who were still lurking among the rocks, waiting for a chance to leap at her. I told her to take that picture home with her and weave it into a bedtime story. She and her daughter were a family unit and, as such, could help and support each other. She was to ask her daughter, without giving information inappropriate to an eight-year-old, how to make that story happier.

When she returned, she reported that her daughter had listened and told her that if the lady picked up a bird's feather from the forest path, the bright colors of the feather would make the lady feel better. Charlene and her daughter then made the story together. The lady picked up the feather and then another and another and wove them into the cloak, which became so bright and colorful that the monsters were chased away.

That, indeed, is a magic story with a magic ending. But both Charlene and her daughter liked it. As Charlene learned to parent her daughter productively, she learned to parent herself and provide for herself the nurturing and care she believed she had missed. Charlene's past was unchangeable but her future, and more important, the future of her daughter were not. Charlene provided all the components for a snowballing effect. As she parented better, she took more joy in her child and received positive reinforcement both from her daughter and from her own pleasure in the interactions. With more joy in her life, she became less depressed and sad and was able to create more happiness for herself and her daughter. As they both blossomed, she was increasingly able to find strength and security within herself. As she changed her childhood parenting through parenting her daughter, she was able to reconcile her feelings of anger and sadness and inadequacy about her own childhood.

CASE 2: JERRY

Jerry was a 37-year-old man who had enormous anger and resentment toward his father. He felt he had been physically abused, although he could recall only one childhood event which may or may not have been abusive. He claimed his father had promised to put him through law school and, for some unknown reason, did not. Jerry said he had never been loved, appreciated, or even accepted. His three siblings had similar childhoods but he had been the scapegoat. So while they were able to forgive and forget, he was not able to do that.

His presenting problem was that he obsessed over the injustices his father had done to him. Whatever happened was blamed on his father. When he went off his diet, it was his father's fault for not teaching him proper self-discipline. If he couldn't afford something, it was a direct result of not attending law school (which would have made him a rich and successful attorney). Every time life did not run smoothly, every time he had to wait too long at a red light or forgot to set his alarm, it was somehow because of what his father had or had not done in rearing him. Jerry obsessed about his father and his mistreatment by him for four to five hours every day.

Jerry's situation was complicated by his writing and then mailing letters to his parents and siblings. In them, he detailed all the real and imaginary wrongs done to him and attacked his parents mercilessly. Consequently, his family cut off contact with him. He then attempted to reestablish contact by sending what he called "understanding" letters in which he explained that he understood his father had been such a bad parent because the father's mother had raised him so poorly. In this view, everyone's problems really stemmed from the long-dead grandmother. Needless to say, these letters did not mend any fences.

My first approach was to listen attentively as Jerry described in endless detail all the misery he had endured. It became obvious that he was an intelligent man who prided himself on being rational and reasonable. I told him I had a definite response to all the information he had given but I was hesitant to tell him because I did not want to add to his burden of hurt. I reiterated that I really wanted to tell him, but I felt sincerely that it might be too much for him and we might have to build up to it slowly. Naturally, he insisted that he was extremely strong and could take anything I could hand out. Indeed, he would welcome it. This structured double-bind was only partly a therapeutic maneuver. I genuinely believed that what I had to say would be strong, direct, and threatening. I also felt it essential to say it at the outset in order to set the direction of therapy.

Zeig (1980) pointed out in *A Teaching Seminar with Milton H. Erickson* that anecdotes can be both nonthreatening and engaging. They foster independence by requiring the client to make sense of the message and they ensure that the listener cannot use habitual means of defense and control. They also model flexibility and bypass normal resistance to change. Therefore, I used a story with Jerry.

I told Jerry that in my personal life I have a tendency to be a martyr. Make no mistake, I added, I like to be a martyr. I earn it and then enjoy it. But this is rather irritating to those around me. My oldest son, David, has evolved an effective means of handling this. When I finish my tale of woe, he looks at me and, with friendliness and humor, screws his hands into fists, rubs his eyes with an exaggerated circular motion, and says, "Waah," as though he is a crying baby. I demonstrated. Jerry asked if this provoked anger in me. Of course not, I replied. David was bringing me back to reality in a nice way. He never did this when I had a genuine problem or hurt. When he said, "Waah," I knew I was trying to be a martyr, which I really don't want to be, and the sight of 25-year-old David scrubbing at his eyes and saying "Waah" always made me laugh.

There was a long pause before he asked me if I was saying "Waah" to him. Because he had accepted my first message, I felt he would accept the next without being threatened, especially since it was being given with genuine warmth and concern. I told him I was also saying to him, "*So what.*" He was 37 years old and *so what* if his father didn't put him through law school. *So what* if his father had not bought him a coveted pair of shoes when he was in the sixth grade a quarter of a century ago. *So what.* Each time I said, "So what," I used the same gentle tone I had used for the "Waah."

The next week Jerry told me he wanted to stop obsessing about his father. Understanding the difficulty of breaking a habit pattern of over 15 years' duration, he indicated he would be pleased, initially, if he obsessed only two hours a day. I told him I could help him stop his obsessing but he would have to do exactly what I told him to do. Personally, I did not think he was ready even to shorten the time he was spending obsessing. He was to return the next week, ready to convince me that he really did want to stop at least a part of his obsessing. Then I would tell him my plan, which would, I assured him, guarantee a stop to the obsessing *if* he followed it to the letter. He returned with a list of carefully thought-out reasons why he wanted to stop obsessing and said he was ready to follow my plan to the letter.

I told him he was to purchase two notebooks. He was to keep a small one in his pocket so he could keep accurate track of the time spent obsessing each day. If he spent more than two hours, he was to figure out exactly how many additional minutes were involved. Each additional 10 minutes counted as one unit; in other words, he could obsess for the agreed-upon two hours and a "free" nine minutes each day before the plan would kick into action.

For each unit over the two hours he was to write in the larger notebook one wrong his father had done. On the next page he was to write the opposite of that wrong. For example, if he wrote, "My father did not send me to law school," he could write, "My father supported me all through grade school, high school and four years of college." The flip of the instance of physical abuse—"My father picked me up by the heels and whipped my butt"—could be something like "There were many times when my father became furious with me and may have wanted to hit me but controlled his temper." "My father never listened to me" could be turned into "My father helped me with my homework many times." Each wrong and each of the opposites was to be a true memory or happening.

When there were 25 of these wrongs and opposites, Jerry was to bring the notebook to me for review. We would go over the entries together. If each of the 25 opposites was a positive and true statement, Jerry was to head the page "Dear Father" and then write, "These are some of the things I have been thinking about." Then he was to sign the letter "Your son, Jerry."

Jerry responded by announcing he would not add "Love" to the letter. I assured him I did not want him to write anything he did not feel was true and at this time he could not say truthfully that he felt love for his father. I took his list of reasons to stop obsessing and used it as scratch paper to figure out how many hours he could obsess over his stated desire of two hours a day before he would actually have to send the positive letter to his father. Twenty-five units of 10 minutes each is more than four hours; he had four extra hours of "free" obsessing over and above his desired two hours a day. As his intent was to reduce the number of hours a day he spent obsessing, perhaps we should reduce the number of minutes to make a unit. Besides, I reminded him, he had agreed to follow my instructions to the letter.

Hooked into his rational and intellectual side and with his list of reasons in front of him, Jerry had no option but agreement. However, he told me, he would never write his father a positive letter. I interpreted this, without telling him, as an indication that he would quickly control his obsessive thinking.

During the next few weeks Jerry was able to reduce his obsessing to 45 minutes a day. It was interesting that several times he would obsess to the stated limit and then nine minutes more. But he was always able to control his thoughts before he had to write the flip of one of his obsessive thoughts. Next, keeping track of the time became too much trouble. Days would go by without a single entry in his little notebook. Jerry had decided, on his own, that a passing thought did not count—if it took longer to write the thought than to think it, he would not list that thought. I agreed that occasional fleeting thoughts were hardly worth the trouble. Therapy terminated at this point. I still see Jerry now and then where he works and he indicates things are going well.

Jerry has not resolved all his anger toward his family, and his family of origin issues are not settled. However, for the first time in many years, he is not limited by spending hours in obsessive thought. He also has heard and understood that a 37-year-old man who is still complaining that his father won't send him to law school is acting inappropriately. He has been forced to consider, on one level at least, that his father did some good and caring parenting.

Erickson believed strongly in the value of practice. Jerry is now practicing more productive behaviors. Perhaps in the future Jerry might want to deal with some of his anger. But perhaps also, that anger and distance serve a useful purpose at this time in his life. He told me early in our sessions that one of the reasons he had put himself through a graduate program was to "show" his father that he didn't need law school to be a success. For Jerry to quit obsessing was to open new vistas for him and he needed time to reassess and regroup.

CASE 3: SALLY

The next two cases deal with adult victims of sexual abuse. Hypnosis and metaphors were used with both women. The first was a 22-year-old referred to me by another therapist. Sally had been abused by her father for almost four years. When she was 12, her mother had returned home unexpectedly from work one night and discovered the abuse. She immediately divorced the father. Sally blamed herself completely for the dissolution of her parents' marriage. She believed she had been a willing participant in the incest and had "ruined" her mother's chances for financial security and companionship in her old age. Sally was unable even to contemplate leaving her mother and establishing her own life as her mother earnestly had urged her to do.

Sally had asked her referring therapist to use hypnosis to help her relive her abusive experiences. She believed she would then realize she had not been to blame and this knowledge would free her from her responsibility. When the therapist obliged, Sally had seen herself, not surprisingly, as a willing participant.

Sally was an excellent, if wary, hypnotic subject. We spent quite some time just exploring the trance state. She learned how to induce self-hypnosis and how to use a trance for relaxation and for controlling headaches. When I felt she had redefined hypnosis as a useful tool, I began working with her on redefining her role in the abuse so she also might open the door to redefining her relationship with her mother.

As she listened in a trance, I talked about my childhood and the childhoods of my children. In this removed and nonthreatening way, I could access the common memories that we all have. I talked to her about teaching my children how to crack an egg. That is actually a difficult task. It must be aimed exactly right, hit just hard enough but not so hard as to crush the shell. If the shell was damaged, repair work of fishing out the unwanted bits and pieces of shell had to be done in order to use the good parts. This was a metaphor for what we were going to do as well as a common memory with which she could identify.

I talked about a time when my oldest brother Bert forgot to pick me up from kindergarten. To this day, he vividly remembers how upset and worried he was when he realized that he had forgotten me. I remember it differently. I had the whole playground to myself and there were no big kids to take the swings away from me. When Bert came, he let me sit in the more comfortable basket on his bike instead of balancing on the crossbar as I usually had to do.

Then I talked about when I once forgot to pick up my children from the movies. They were delighted to stand around out front and mingle with the bigger kids and couldn't understand why I was upset and apologetic.

Sally told me, after she came out of her trance, that she had remembered her mother had left her at a birthday party once. Sally was not only the last guest to go home, but she got to stay and eat dinner with the host family. She had been an adult before she realized why her mother had been so embarrassed and apologized so profusely when she finally arrived.

The message delivered and understood was that a child must be taken care of. A submessage was that children interpret things far differently than adults. We continued in this vein for several sessions. Remember the first time you made Jello? Who would guess that if you mixed a powder and water into a Kool-Aid-like liquid, you really got Jello? Things sure aren't when they seem—especially to a child's eyes.

With Sally in a trance, I talked about the first meal my son Michael prepared. When he was about eight, he fixed dinner for the family—homemade vegetable soup (with his favorite meat as the base) and toasted sandwiches. He worked for hours chopping potatoes, carrots, and onions. He even toasted the bread ahead of time. Then he triumphantly served the meal: bologna sandwiches on cold toast and hot bologna soup! Michael thought it was a great meal and crunched his toast and bologna sandwiches and ate his hot bologna soup. He is an adult now and an excellent cook; but he is still defensive over that meal and claims it was very tasty. He had so much of himself invested in what occurred that, to this day, it's hard for him to see it differently.

We talked about other food both in and out of trances. We both like pizza. The worst thing about it, we agreed, is the way it can burn your mouth. The cheese on top is cool but the tomato sauce inside is still hot. It's so hard to protect kids from that—they can feel it with their hands and it feels cool. They can't believe that under the surface is something that will harm them.

I noted how even adults make mistakes sometimes. I've had my microwave oven for years but I still occasionally burn myself with the hot food in a cooler dish. Sally told me how she once attempted to thaw frozen margarine. The outside shell was still frozen while the inside was melted. She cut into it and the hot melted margarine squirted out and burned her hand. We laughed over our mistakes. Here we were sophisticated adults, and we still didn't realize that sometimes things aren't what they seem.

It's obvious what information was being given and hypnotically processed. The stories I told her were mixed with other stories and casual conversation, and it was clear Sally was making sense of her past. She began talking about moving into her own apartment and planning dinner for her mother there. She also decided that if she asked her mother to pick out curtains, her mother would feel included in Sally's new life. Sally explained to me more than once that her mother had excellent taste and could cover windows beautifully. Since her mother had that talent, Sally had decided to take advantage of it. I decided not to comment on the symbolism I saw in this. Sally was dealing with her issues in her own and now productive way.

Eventually we discussed her abuse. Sally was still angry, but the focus of her anger had changed. She now believed her father had taken advantage of her. At this point in time, Sally wanted to stay angry at him. She had been angry at herself too long to put this anger away "too quickly." The words "too quickly" indicated, of course, that eventually she would put it away.

CASE 4: CONNIE

The last case is that of a 36-year-old woman who also had been sexually abused by her father. Connie had sought therapy for these issues before and felt she had been successful in dealing with most of them. However, she still felt a deep anger at her mother for not taking better care of her. Logically, she had resolved this anger. She believed sincerely that her mother had been and was, to this day, completely unaware of the abuse, which had begun when Connie was eight. The abuse continued until she was 12, when she returned home from summer camp and told her father that if he didn't leave her alone, she would tell her mother. The father complied and the abuse was never mentioned again. He died when Connie was 27.

Connie explained that her one unresolved issue was her anger toward her mother. She had no desire to confront her mother with something she believed to be illogical and, besides, her mother was almost 70 and in poor health. She would do anything I asked except confront her mother.

I assured her that I didn't believe it necessary to confront a frail, 70-year-old lady with an issue like this. The first thing I wanted Connie to do was to describe her anger fully and exactly to me. I was pretty sure the emotion she was calling anger was based on feelings of powerlessness and helplessness, but I wanted to hear from her exactly how she experienced it. I have found that intellectual clients, like Connie, can describe emotions clearly. They may not be able to feel or change them, but they can describe them in the most extraordinary way.

The only other thing I would ask her to do was to go into a formal hypnotic trance and then listen to me talk to her about many things. She didn't have to understand everything I was going to say but she did have to be in a deep trance and listen openly and carefully while I talked.

She had offered to do anything and I had asked only those two things. So she worked hard at doing both. She described her anger as helplessness and total powerlessness. She was "a feather in the wind" with no control over herself. She felt like a bit of fluff that could be stepped on or swept up and thrown away or just ignored. She had no control and no ability to take care of herself. In the sessions she was defining her feelings clearly, she also worked on learning to go into a trance. She learned quickly and was an excellent subject.·

While she was in a deep trance, I talked about different behaviors and practices in the world. Did she know that some people use geese as watchdogs? Geese are territorial and honk loudly at intruders. I talked about the farmers in France who use gaggles of geese in their fields. Not only do the geese eat unwanted weeds, but they chase away animals that eat the valuable crops. What a surprise an intruder would have if he happened upon a gaggle of geese protecting their territory!

After she had time to picture and absorb the idea of geese serving as watchdogs, I talked about swans. Swans are really fierce birds—large and strong. One blow from a swan's wing can break a man's arm or leg. Swans are courageous too. They will attack a threatening intruder and can injure him severely.

Then I asked her if she had ever seen a baby goose, a gosling. They are fuzzy and yellow, little and cute and sweet, just like youngsters always are. Even eagles start out as fuzzy little balls of fluff, tiny and helpless. Next I asked her if she had ever seen a cygnet. I deliberately chose the unfamiliar word for baby swan, knowing she would listen even more carefully as she figured out the meaning. I have never seen one, I noted, but I bet they are tiny and helpless just like all young beings are. I am sure they are vulnerable and sweet and cute and need to be cared for and cherished—fuzzy little bundles of trusting sweetness who have yet to grow up to be the fierce adult swan.

Then I asked her if she ever read stories as a child. A good story to read is the one about the baby swan who grows up to be a big beautiful bird, white and lovely, graceful and strong. It is by Hans Christian Andersen. I carefully did not say the name "The Ugly Duckling," believing it would be more impactful if she named it herself. I made sure she knew which story I meant and told her the little swan had a lot of things happen before it was able to realize what it really was.

I reinforced to Connie that she didn't need to remember on a conscious level everything about which we had talked. As Erickson frequently pointed out, sometimes it's more helpful to leave things in the unconscious where they can be of more use.

I saw Connie only a few more times. She felt better each time and began to realize she could leave her sense of anger and helplessness behind her in the past. She wasn't sure why she was feeling this way and attributed the changes to maturity and, perhaps, to the benefits of talking it over. We never discussed the session in which Connie heard the stories about birds. She never brought it up and I assumed that it stayed in her unconscious where it could really help her. She did make a point of telling me, however, that she had given her mother a bird feeder for her apartment window and that they both enjoyed watching the birds.

SUMMARY

The four cases I have described differ from the usual interventions designed for family of origin issues. However, with an Ericksonian approach, small changes can have a snowballing effect. New perceptions and behaviors are reinforced by the new context created by a small change. This, in turn, creates other changes in perceptions and behaviors to create new environments. In this regard, anecdotes and metaphors are extraordinarily powerful tools (see Zeig, 1980).

While each of these four clients may still have unresolved issues about their families of origin, they are now more competent to deal productively with these feelings and beliefs. Haley (1987) points out that the goal of therapy is to get people out of therapy. The clients I have described are now out of therapy, involved in practicing new behaviors and beliefs in order to create a more satisfying experience of life. Perhaps they will decide, at some point, that there are other issues they want to explore in therapy. But perhaps not. Perhaps their new perceptions will lead to further changes that are just right for them.

REFERENCES

Erickson, M. H. (1980). *The Collected Papers of Milton H. Erickson on Hypnosis*, edited by Ernest L. Rossi. New York: Irvington Publishers.
Erickson, M. H., & Rossi, E. L. (1989). *The February Man: Evolving Consciousness and Identity in Hypnotherapy*. New York: Brunner/Mazel.
Haley, J. (1973). *Uncommon Therapy*. New York: Norton.
Haley, J. (1987). *Problem Solving Therapy*. San Francisco: Jossey-Bass.

O'Hanlon, B. (1985). A study guide of frameworks of Milton Erickson's hypnosis and therapy. In: J. K. Zeig (Ed.), *Ericksonian Psychotherapy*, Volume 1. New York: Brunner/Mazel.

Zeig, J. K. (Ed.) (1980). *A Teaching Seminar with Milton H. Erickson*. New York: Brunner/Mazel.

Zeig, J. K. (1985). *Experiencing Erickson*. New York: Brunner/Mazel.

PART IV

The Temporal Factor
in Brief Therapy

CHAPTER 14

Brief Intermittent Psychotherapy Throughout the Life Cycle

Nicholas Cummings

There is a need in our society for someone to replace the old-fashioned general practitioner who was not too proud to make house calls, who took time to listen and to know all of the family, and who truly manifested a dedicated caring. Cummings and VandenBos, when they published their "General Practice of Psychology" in 1979, saw this person as being the psychologist. Also, these authors set the parameters of brief, intermittent psychotherapy throughout the life cycle and gave an illustrative case spanning many years to demonstrate the efficacy and efficiency of their model. The delineation of the model was expanded in subsequent publications (Cummings, 1986, 1988).

Most illness is caused by the faulty ways in which we live: how we "stress-out," smoke, drink, pollute, eat, do not sleep, resort to drugs, and eschew exercise. The psychologist, functioning as a psychological family practitioner, has the goal of not only helping the patient resolve emotional distress, but helping the patient avoid illness (both physical and emotional) by altering life-style. In founding American Biodyne, a mental health maintenance organization (MHMO) now in eight states and serving more than one million people, I chose the word *Biodyne* which comes from two Greek words meaning "life change."

PRINCIPLES OF BRIEF INTERMITTENT PSYCHOTHERAPY

The Developmental View

The underlying reason why brief, intermittent psychotherapy works is because of what Freud alluded to as the "repetition compulsion," which I can restate in a somewhat different perspective: The first response to the first trauma in life often becomes the prototype of subsequent response to later life traumas. Thus, the person's attempt to solve the crisis is predictable from one trauma to another.

This is a developmental view. Patients continue to grow beyond the actual course of therapy, which serves as a yeast for years to come. There also are developmental crises in life—entering school, adulthood, marriage, parenthood, divorce and separation, middle and old age, and death. During these crisis points, individuals will repeat the original response to the first trauma or stress in childhood. This may be depression, phobia, hysteria, and so forth. It may be somaticization ("Mommy, my tummy hurts too much to go to school and take my spelling test"). Once established, this prototype will be repeated during the life cycle in response to new threats. For example, in the histories of alcoholics or drug addicts, it has been noted that the childhood response to stress was to seek sugar or carbohydrates—the quick fix.

One need not remain in therapy seeking the ultimate cure from all future anxiety, for anxiety is a normal accompaniment of living. Therapy can be conceived as brief, intermittent episodes to meet recurring crises throughout the life cycle. The psychologist remains the unifying thread, for he or she remembers the patient and cares. Each trauma occurring after the initial therapy requires relatively few additional sessions, no matter how severe the crisis. Our patients have learned "life change" and are restored to health quickly. We now have data on thousands of patients from more than 30 years of experience. It is an effective, gratifying way to practice for both patients and practitioners.

Targeted, Focused Interventions

The model that's going to do the job efficiently is going to be the model that blends many schools of psychology and psychotherapy into one. When many of us received our training, the Freudians didn't talk to the neo-Freudians, and no one talked to the Jungians. The Adlerians and Rankians were around somewhere. Leaders of the various schools said that these schools of psychotherapy could never meld. Psychologists in intensive group practice are going to have to get over the concept of the ideal therapist, that there is one person who can do all things for all people (Cummings & VandenBos, 1979). Psychologists are going to have to go back to school and learn brief, targeted psychotherapy. The parameters of brief therapy are different from those of long-term therapy. Brief therapy does not mean less therapy; it means more efficient therapy. And what is meant by efficient therapy is *targeted therapy.*

Every patient who walks into a therapist's office receives the type of therapy the psychotherapist has to offer. If the therapist is a Freudian analyst, he or she often does not attend to specific complaints of the patient—alcoholism, marital problems, or job problems: That patient is going to get the couch. If the therapist is a Jungian analyst, the patient is going to paint pictures. If the therapist is a behaviorist, the patient is going to get desensitization. It's not surprising that this is done, but what is surprising is that it works. It really works. We help our patients. But the problem is we help them with many more sessions than might be needed. When treatment programs are targeted for specific conditions, the patient responds more readily, more efficiently. It is not necessary to limit psychotherapy to 10 sessions, or 20 sessions, or to mandate a 50% coinsurance. The patient looks up and says, "Gee, you know this is great. My problem is solved." Given effective interventions, the patient knows when therapy is completed even before the therapist does.

At Biodyne we use more than 60 targeted therapies (Cummings, 1983). One might well ask, would you go to a physician who treated everybody who came in the door with penicillin, whether one person had a broken leg from skiing or another had pneumonia? Of course you wouldn't. Fifty years ago physicians practiced in that manner. They had five favorite medications; if one didn't work, they gave the next one. If that one didn't work, they gave the third, and so on until they exhausted their repertoire of medications. At that time the list of the pharmacopoeia of the United States was contained in one volume. Now the volumes containing that list would stretch clear across a large room. Physicians have literally thousands of specific treatments for specific conditions. It is time we all began to understand that we have far more specific treatment approaches in psychology than most practicing psychologists ever dream of because we are stuck in the rut of doing what we were initially trained to do regardless of the patient's condition.

Giving up the Concept of "Cure"

Therapists have to give up the concept of cure (Cummings & VandenBos, 1979). That concept has held back psychotherapy more than any other concept. George Albee (1977) has been chiding us for decades for practicing in the house of medicine. We're finally extricating ourselves from that house, but we still use medicine's concept of cure. And so, psychologists keep patients in treatment until they are sure that every recess of the unconscious has been analyzed as to its conflicts, because both patient and therapist get only one chance. If three years from now the patient has another problem, the psychologist hasn't done the job correctly. This is absolute, sheer nonsense. The only time all of us are going to be free of anxiety is when we're six feet under and there are gravestones over us.

At Biodyne we employ what we call "brief intermittent psychotherapy throughout the life cycle" (Cummings, 1983). This means that when a patient comes in with a problem, the psychologist takes the problem seriously but not necessarily at face value and he or she treats that problem. When that problem is resolved, the psychologist interrupts treatment. Now, I didn't say "terminates." I said "interrupt" because in this model the psychological practitioner is seen as behaving like the old-fashioned family doctor. The patient goes to the doctor because he or she has the flu. With treatment, the patient recovers from the flu and stops going to the doctor. The patient does not keep seeing the doctor to keep from catching the flu again. Two years later, the patient may come back with a broken leg. The patient doesn't stay in treatment to prevent something else from happening, and the physician is not deemed to have failed because the patient now has a broken leg. Psychotherapy is the only area of health where both patients and therapists traditionally get only one chance. I have been doing brief intermittent psychotherapy for so long that I have seen not only children and grandchildren of my patients, but I've also recently seen two great-grandchildren.

Not long ago, I saw an 11-year old and I said to him, "Of all the psychotherapists in San Francisco, why did you choose me to come to with your school problem?" He said, "You're legendary in our home. You saw my great-grandfather, and when it was time for me to see somebody, I said to Dad, 'Can I go see Nick Cummings?' My father said, 'Of course.' I said, 'How do I find him?' And he gave me your number and I called you." Two weeks later I saw the boy's older brother.

Interruption, Not Termination

One of the therapist's problems in doing brief therapy is that the therapist often has separation anxiety. There's a tremendous turnover of patients because you're terminating constantly, and as a therapist you're often depressed because of separation anxiety. Haley (1978) suggests that many psychotherapists gravitate to long-term therapy because the constant separation anxiety imposed by brief therapy is too painful, especially if there has been early bereavement or rejection in the therapist's own history.

In the Biodyne model we don't terminate. Rather, therapy is interrupted. After almost 30 years of experience, given therapists trained in the model, 85% of the patients who come opt for brief therapy. They enter treatment under this model, use it, and come back when they have the need. In tracking patients for 10, 20, or 25 years, our research has shown that it takes less time in psychotherapy overall than it would if we kept a patient in therapy twice a week for a year or a year and a half or even eight months. The experience of thousands of cases demonstrates this fact (Cummings, 1977).

In brief, intermittent psychotherapy throughout the life cycle, you can free yourself from the concepts of the ideal therapist, where each of us has to be all things to all people. You can free yourself from the concept of cure, and you can free yourself from the bother of termination.

Parameters of Brief, Intermittent Psychotherapy

What are some of the parameters of "brief intermittent psychotherapy throughout the life cycle"? Space permits a brief discussion of only a few of them (Cf. Cummings, 1983).

1. *Hit the ground running* (Budman & Gurman, 1988). The first session must be therapeutic. The concept that you must devote the first session to taking a history is nonsense. Now, it's important to know some of the patient's history, but you know, I haven't learned all of the history of some of my patients until they've come back five or six years later. One must know the salient history, particularly the earliest, and consequently the recurrent manner in which the patient has met crisis or psychological trauma. I concentrate on the following items:

2. *Perform an operational diagnosis.* An operational diagnosis is different from some vague DSM-III (American Psychiatric Association, 1980) psychiatric diagnosis that labels a person. The operational diagnosis asks one thing, "Why is the patient here today instead of last week or last month, last year, or next year?" When you answer that, you know what the patient is here for. The operational diagnosis is absolutely necessary to set a treatment plan, and it is best that it be done in the first session. If you don't get it in the first session, try in the second session, but do not stop trying to solve the issue of the operational diagnosis until you have an answer.

Examples of appropriate operational diagnoses abound. If the psychotherapist concludes that the patient is here because he is an alcoholic, that is not an operational diagnosis because the patient has been alcoholic for many years. If the therapist learns the patient's boss cautioned the patient he must get help or be fired the next time he misses work on a Monday, this is the basis for the operational diagnosis. Similarly, a wife may have been anorgasmic throughout her marriage, but she comes in now because she learns her husband is having an affair and the marriage is threatened. Frequently patients present themselves because their attitudes and behavior have created situations that are intolerable. They want the situation rectified without the therapist tampering with the problem that created the situation in the first place. Proper assessment of the operational diagnosis and the discerning of the patient's implicit contract are critical to formulating a successful treatment plan.

3. *Replace the implicit contract with a therapeutic contract.* Every patient makes an implicit contract with the therapist in the first session, every time. In 99% of the cases the therapist misses the implicit contract and concludes erroneously that patient and therapist are both working toward change in the patient. Fritz Perls (personal communication, September 1972) cautioned us that patients do not come for treatment or for change in themselves. They come to us "to make it all better," presumably without much effort on their part.

As Paul Watzlawick (personal communication, May 1979) pointed out, if the patient gives the therapeutic contract and the therapist doesn't hear it, then because the patient wants to be a good patient, he or she goes along with what the therapist says the contract is. And then a wrestling match occurs between patient and therapist that the therapist often erroneously labels resistance. Now there is such a thing as resistance. But I find that 80% of what most therapists term resistance is nothing more than a therapist's failure to recognize a patient's goals in treatment. For example, if a single middle-aged woman comes into the office of a male therapist and says, "Doctor, I'm glad you have this comfortable chair because I'm going to be here awhile," and the therapist doesn't respond to that, the therapist has just made a contract for long-term therapy. Even worse, the therapist has unwittingly agreed to be this patient's weekly date in her otherwise dateless life. In short, he has agreed to be nontherapeutic. If the patient says, "I want to come in here and save my marriage, but whatever I do, I'm going to end up getting divorced," the therapist has just made a contract for that patient to divorce. And if the therapist breaks his or her neck over the next two years trying to save that marriage, he or she is going to wonder, "What's happening?" The therapist does not realize that the patient's implicit contract was to be able to say, after the divorce, "I did everything to save my marriage, even going into psychotherapy." Space does not permit the hundreds of such examples. Listen for the therapeutic contract.

After you discern the patient's therapeutic contract, talk about it. It is more than appropriate to refuse treatment if the patient insists on a new therapeutic contract, but most patients, once their implicit contract is verbalized and discussed extensively, will opt for a legitimate therapeutic goal. Still, the therapist must use his third ear and all of his or her therapeutic acumen to make certain the patient is not merely mouthing what the psychotherapist wants to hear. Then say, "Now that our goals are clarified, I would like to add the following to that contract: I will never abandon you as long as you need me. In return for that, I want you to join me in a partnership to make me obsolete as soon as possible." Don't just allow perfunctory answers. Discuss it, and eventually the patient will agree to this amended contract. Demonstrate that you, as the therapist, mean what you say. You have now set the stage for the patient to take responsibility for his or her own treatment and life change.

4. *Do something novel in the first session.* This isn't easy, but find something novel, something unexpected, to do the first session. This will cut through the expectations of the "trained" patient and will create instead an expectation that problems are to be immediately addressed. For some patients the experience that someone is really listening is novel, but psychotherapists rely on this far too much. Most of our patients today are character disorders and even borderline personalities who are jaded and covertly cynical. Doing something novel most often means doing the unexpected. It catapults the patient into treatment in spite of his or her resistance.

5. *Give homework in the first session and every therapy session thereafter.* It isn't possible to have some cookbook full of homework that you just arbitrarily assign. Tailor the homework to be meaningful for that patient's goals and the therapeutic contract. The patient will realize, "Hey, this guy isn't kidding. I'm responsible for my own therapy."

6. *If you take steps 1 through 5, you'll find that there is no such thing as a therapeutic dropout.* Patients know when to discontinue treatment better than therapists. It is time to interrupt treatment, with a discussion with the patient inviting him or her to resume treatment whenever problems arise that would require help.

I was trained in analysis, and I did long-term therapy. In my career, I remember when I had so honed my craft as a psychotherapist that by the appropriate interpretation I could prevent any patient from terminating. And then I went through six weeks of some of the most soul-wrenching self-examinations I've ever experienced because I asked myself, "Am I doing this for the benefit of my patients or for the benefit of Nick Cummings?" I finally concluded that I was doing it for the benefit of Nick Cummings, and I stopped.

CASE EXAMPLE: "AMAZING GRACE"

The case example of a patient our center called "Amazing Grace" illustrates the principles presented: hit the ground running, perform an operational diagnosis, elicit the implicit contract, help the patient assume the first step in self-responsibility, and do something novel.

Patients come in expecting things from us, and Grace was no exception. Before our clients come in they usually have some idea of who we are and what we do. Grace was referred to me by a colleague who had been seeing her for three years and he said he couldn't handle her anymore. His hostility was so great he disqualified himself from treating Grace, who was a "schizoholic." He warned me that Grace would come in drunk one session. She would urinate in his chair the next session and, finally, would do some semblance of therapeutic work the third. The sessions alternated among those three behaviors but he would never know whether the current session would be the urination session. To ward off the consequences of this in his office, before Grace came in he always put a rubber sheet over the therapy chair, the kind used in a baby's crib. He also told me that all attempts to stop this symptom resulted in Grace's falling to the floor, stopping breathing, becoming cyanotic, and turning blue, at which point he would have to call the paramedics to come in and resuscitate her, literally saving her life.

At this point I had to assume certain educated risks. I became an authority on cyanosis during the next couple of weeks before I saw Grace. Before Grace came in she had spent the time becoming an authority on me. She had cleverly pumped her previous therapist about what kind of a person I was, and in order to justify his sending her to me he told her, "I'm a very, very easygoing, kind man. But, Nick Cummings is tough; he's a tough s.o.b." So Grace came in anticipating my behavior. True to her expectations, I said, "Grace, the first time you urinate in my chair that ends our therapeutic relationship." Now why did I do this? This is one example where it would be deleterious to continue treating a patient under the circumstances of allowing her to urinate in my chair, because that would permit a contract where she can behave in the most regressed antitherapeutic fashion, while I impotently expect change from a position of extreme opposition. People do not change from a position of opposition. So I said, "Grace, the first time you urinate in my chair, that's the end of your therapy." She looked at me and without saying a word she cleared her throat and spat on my carpet. I handed her a box of tissues and I said, "Grace, clean it up." She replied, "You didn't tell me I couldn't spit on your carpet." I said, "Grace, I don't intend to tell you a lot of things that I know your mother taught you not to do. I'm not going to tell you when you leave my office that you shouldn't squat in the middle of the boulevard that's in front of my office and urinate. I'm not going to tell you a lot of things you already know. But I am telling you that kind of behavior is out." She stared at me without a word for about three or four minutes, fell to the floor, stopped breathing, and began to turn blue, which is a symptom of cyanosis. Instead of calling the paramedics I did what I was prepared to do and I had planned to do; I started fumbling in my desk for my camera. I discovered, much to my dismay, that my camera was empty. I started fumbling for film, all the while saying: "Grace, keep that up, it's fantastic, we're going to make medical history with this. I've got to take pictures of this." I completely unraveled the first roll of film before I got it into the camera; I reached for another roll of film, all the while pleading, "Grace, keep this up, please Grace." Every once in a while Grace would open one eye and stare up at me in total disbelief.

Finally, when I got the camera loaded and I began to take pictures, my flash didn't work, so I started fumbling with the flash. Before I could get the flash attached and functional with a new battery, Grace was back in her chair saying, "Oh, you!" I saw Grace four times.

Grace was known as a woman who often appeared in emergency rooms of hospitals in San Francisco, falling to the floor in the waiting room and becoming cyanotic. After our fourth session, I got her permission to give my name and telephone number to each hospital emergency room in San Francisco. She agreed to that. So, when Grace would appear in the middle of the night at an emergency room, I would be called. I went to the emergency room only one time. As I came down the hall, I could hear her gasping as she turned blue. I called out, "All right, Grace, get up," and I heard, "Oh, Dr. Cummings." By the time I got to the waiting room from the hallway, she would be sitting up in her chair and the blueness would be leaving her face. After the first time I went to the emergency room, I was able to arrange to talk to her on the phone. The emergency room intern, who by the time I called was baffled by this weird case, would be instructed to merely hold the telephone up to Grace's ear. I would yell over the phone, "All right, Grace, up," and I would hear Grace say, "Oh, you!" as she got up. The even more baffled intern would come on the phone and say, "What did you do?"

I'm happy to say that within three weeks Grace stopped her symptom.

This is an example of a situation where the primary patient may be the physician. In this case, the primary patient was the psychiatrist who referred Grace, and secondarily, the emergency room staff who had to deal with her "cyanosis." Her previous therapist retired right after he referred Grace to me, probably either in a state of exhaustion or from the pungent smell of stale urine in his office. I don't know which. But he was obviously the patient in this case, and I was able to take Grace off his hands and also help Grace in the process. By the time Grace and I terminated after the 18th session, Grace had gone from looking like a bag lady to a self-respecting human being. She started to groom herself; she stopped drinking. She was still schizophrenic, but she was no longer a schizoholic who had to go through life getting attention by becoming cyanotic or urinating in therapists' chairs.

Following this experience we developed what we call the Patient's Bill of Rights:

> A patient has an inalienable right to relief from pain, anxiety, and depression in the shortest time possible and with the least intrusive intervention.

This means that every psychotherapist has an obligation to so hone his or her craft that the patient need not spend months or years in treatment to experience relief from pain, anxiety, or depression. If this can be effected in brief rather than long-term therapy, the patient has that right. And if the relief from such distress can be performed on an outpatient basis rather than in a mental health hospital, do it: It is preferable to spare the patient and the family the dislocation and lifelong stigma that inevitably follows such hospitalization. Most psychiatrists and many psychologists fail to recognize that mental health hospitalization is never a benign event. It affects the patient's subsequent life pervasively: one's driver's license, the ability to become bonded, eligibility for life insurance or certain occupations, and the likelihood of running for public office, to name only a few.

There are patients who will be treated throughout the life cycle who will experience sudden episodes of acute psychosis. It is easy to hospitalize such patients and essentially wash one's hands of them. We have seen thousands of such patients episodically two or even three times a day for several days in order to successfully avert hospitalization and its lifelong consequences. This is hard work and involves extending one's office to the home, the street, or the workplace. It is also rewarding, because patients do respond to intensive, targeted outpatient intervention.

CASE EXAMPLE

At this point, I will return to the concept of intermittent brief psychotherapy and illustrate some of the techniques used by citing a case that spanned two decades. In 1967, I was confronted with a young man of 28 whom we shall call Kevin. He was in my waiting room without an appointment, suffering severe withdrawal from drugs. He was quite "strung out." When I finished with my preceding client and first saw him in the waiting room, he looked wild. Along with the withdrawal I wondered how schizophrenic Kevin was. I had no prior knowledge of him, no history.

I learned in the first session that Kevin had been born in Indianapolis, had gone to Purdue University and had been graduated an elementary school teacher. On the Wednesday of his first week of teaching, on his first job, he "freaked out," ran out of the classroom, and without going home, he got on the automobile beltway that surrounds Indianapolis and hitchhiked to San Francisco with just what he had on his back. Home was really his parent's home. He came to San Francisco with what he had in his pocket. The first week there he was introduced into drugs. For the next three years Kevin's feet did not touch the ground. Kevin became what I call a cafeteria addict; one who will take anything that is put before him or her, be high all the time, all the while claiming, "See, I'm not addicted to anything." You don't know what to expect on withdrawal in a cafeteria addict. In the detoxification of heroin, barbiturates, alcohol, or Valium one knows what the course is and can plan on appropriate intervention. But with the cafeteria addict, withdrawal is a crapshoot.

I also found out that at Purdue Kevin was an isolated young man. He never had a date. His social life consisted of weekends when he would go back to his parent's home in Indianapolis, then he would go to skid row, and with a couple of bottles of cheap wine he would get the alcoholics there on skid row intoxicated. He would get intoxicated with them, and he would perform fellatio on these derelicts. This young man, for all intents and purposes, would have to be called either schizophrenic or certainly borderline ambulatory schizophrenic.

It was apparent that Kevin did not want to come off drugs. What he wanted me to do was to make him feel better. He was startled when I refused to see him for a second appointment, and when he asked me why, I said, "Kevin, I treat drug addiction. In order to treat your drug addiction, I would have to get a commitment from you that you would be clean for six months because it takes me that long before I can sort out everything that is involved in your drug addiction. You're not really prepared to do that; therefore, you would be wasting your time, and I would be wasting my time. There are other patients who would want to see me who might want to clean up and work harder." At this point Kevin became desperate. I told him, "I cannot see you because I don't think you're serious." He then spent about 10 minutes telling me how serious he was. He said, "I will do anything if you will give me help." Finally, I said, "Well Kevin, I'm very skeptical, but I'll tell you what I'm willing to do. If you can go for 72 hours without any drugs, I will give you a second appointment. That will prove to me I'm wrong."

Now there isn't an addict on earth who can't go 72 hours without drugs. It's been done many times, so I wasn't asking the impossible. Kevin agreed to do this and was surprised that I wasn't going to hospitalize him for the detoxification. Next, he was surprised that I would not make another appointment with him for 72 hours. He questioned this. I replied, "The reason I won't give you an appointment is that I don't think that you can do this. If you stay off drugs for the 72 hours, I'll be surprised. Then, you can call me, and I'll see you then, right away." Kevin did call very proudly on the 70th hour. I said, "Kevin, I'm sorry I can't give you an appointment. You've got two more hours to go." He raged, "What do you mean two more hours? I've gone now three days!" I said, "Kevin, your 72 hours are up at 3:30 this afternoon. You call me in two hours and then, if you're still clean, I'll give you an appointment. I know people like you who do drugs after getting an appointment before the 72 hours. I believe you called me two hours early because you don't think you're going to make the last two hours." He said, "What makes you think so?" "Well Kevin, have you ever waited all day to go to the bathroom because you're too busy and you keep about your work and after several hours you decide to go to the bathroom and you don't think you're going to make the last 10 feet? That's where you are. Our bargain, our agreement, our contract is that you will be 72 hours clean before you call me to make an appointment." Kevin said, "You're the craziest doctor I've ever talked to" and he slammed the phone down. Two hours later, to the minute, he called. I gave Kevin an appointment at my dinner hour. He came in, and at that second appointment I began to prepare him to enter my addiction program, which is a group program of 20 sessions. This required six sessions before he entered the group.

While brief therapy may be anywhere from 1 to 20 sessions, it doesn't mean the sessions should be spaced at once a week. There are patients whom I will see in brief therapy daily for four consecutive days. I have seen the same client twice in one day. I have seen the same client every other month. Spacing is important. So brief therapy does not mean 15 sessions, once a week. I saw Kevin three days after our first session. Kevin also earned his way into my drug therapy program. That was in 1967. Kevin graduated from that therapy program and continued to be clean. He had also gone back to work. The first job he obtained was relief work at the post office. In that era, at Christmas time, if you could breathe, you could get a job at the post office. In cases where there is a copayment or fee (and this is not the procedure at Biodyne, since it is a capitated system), we demand that everybody who comes into treatment pay for his or her therapy out of what we call real money. There is real money, and there's "mother's milk." An example of mother's milk is getting a stipend from home because the family doesn't want you at home because you would embarrass them.

You cannot pay for your therapy with remittance money. Patients are given four sessions to get a real job and pay with real money. Another kind of mother's milk is money from drug dealing or money from prostitution. We do not accept that kind of money. Often I see people free for the first four sessions until they can pay me with real money. Kevin was such a case. His first job was doing relief work in a post office. His next job was driving a cab. His third job, which he got before he finished the drug treatment program, was as an eligibility intake worker in the county hospital. Remember, Kevin was a college graduate.

In 1968, Kevin came to see me again. During the intervening year Kevin had married, and his wife, Carol, was pregnant. Kevin told me he could never be a father. I'd helped him a great deal, but a man like him could never be a father. His self-image was too low to allow him to think of himself as a father to his forthcoming child. We talked about this. Kevin's self-esteem had risen enough so that he was able to get married. Apparently, up to that day, he was having a happy marriage. I had four sessions with Kevin, and he learned to feel comfortable about the impending birth.

I did not see Kevin during 1969. In 1970 he not only was the proud father of a two-year-old son, but he and Carol were buying their first house. Carol was also pregnant again. He had to borrow money from his father-in-law, whom he hated, as a down payment for the house. I saw Kevin three times in 1970, helping him raise his self-esteem to the point where he bought the house. He also settled his antagonism toward his father-in-law, and they became good friends during the next two or three years.

In 1971 Kevin came in for one session over a marital problem he had with Carol. He was harboring a lot of anger toward Carol, which he was expressing through premature ejaculation. The symptom cleared. A couple of months later, also in 1971, as a result of my session with him regarding his premature ejaculation, Kevin called to state that he and Carol wanted to go into couple therapy. I referred him to one of my colleagues at Biodyne, who saw Carol and Kevin for six sessions in couple therapy. During the couple therapy, Kevin resolved his overidentification with his first son. Kevin was sure that his first son was going to turn out to be a "creep" like himself.

In 1972, Kevin came in anxious over the fact that he was about to take a civil service examination for probation officer. He had been hired under temporary aegis as a probation officer for the county and had finished the six months' probation. If he didn't pass the civil service examination, he would lose his job. Kevin and I decided in that session that he would enter biofeedback training. He had 12 sessions of biofeedback training and easily passed the civil service examination. He became a permanent probation officer for the county.

In 1973, I did not see Kevin at all. Rather, Carol came in and saw a colleague of mine for four sessions. I haven't any idea of what Carol and her therapist talked about.

In 1974, Kevin and Carol bought their first duplex. Kevin came in for five sessions as he was uptight about buying their first rental property. He asked, "Am I really good enough to be a landlord?" They did buy that duplex, the first of the four duplexes that they now own.

In 1975, Kevin came in to see me in a homosexual panic. I opened the door, finding him in my office waiting room. He was content to stay there, shaking, for about three and one-half hours until I was able to see him upon the completion of my scheduled appointments. He told me the following story. One of his apartments was rented to a large, tall, handsome black man toward whom Kevin became sexually attracted. One day Kevin was there to collect the rent. There was some aborted fondling under the pretext that he was going to have a sexual experience with this man and waive the rent. But Kevin plunged into a homosexual panic and before he did anything else, he jumped in the car and drove to my office and ensconced himself in my waiting room. I saw him in five more sessions in which Kevin resolved his homosexual panic.

I didn't see Kevin again until 1977. When I asked what was the problem that brought him in, he said, "Nothing, I just came in for a check up." We talked for a session. I said, "Fine; call me when you need me." In 1978 Kevin came in to boast that he was the father of a baby girl. He didn't come in to get my permission to become a father this time. Rather, he came in to boast that after two sons it was wonderful to have a baby girl.

In 1979, I saw Kevin's older son, who was having a school problem. We had three sessions. I also saw the younger son twice, and I saw Kevin three times.

I did not see Kevin at all in 1980. In 1981 I saw him three times about his being promoted to supervisor in the probation office. He didn't want to become a supervisor because he had become, in the estimate of his employers, the number one probation officer in the county. He was assigned all of the interesting cases. Kevin said, "I don't want to become a paper pusher sitting at a desk; I want to do real field work." I told Kevin he had to make his decision. At the end of our three sessions, he decided to become a supervisor.

I did not see Kevin in 1982. In 1983 Kevin came in for two sessions. He was offered a top federal Department of Justice job. He didn't know whether he wanted to take it. I said, "Kevin, again it's your decision to make." Kevin accepted that assignment, and he's enjoying it.

I did not see Kevin again until 1987. He came in for one session, as he did again in 1988. Both of his sons have graduated from high school and have gone on to college.

Kevin and his family were seen over 20 years, during which there were individual sessions with Kevin, his wife, and their two sons. There was also drug therapy, couple therapy, biofeedback training, and emergency sessions. In over 20 years there was a total of 93 sessions. I have often wondered if I had seen Kevin in continuous long-term psychotherapy for five years, would the outcome have been better? It certainly would have involved more than 93 sessions. But would this have produced the kind of contented and happy marital, occupational, and life adjustment that Kevin made with this brief, intermittent psychotherapy throughout 22 years of his life cycle? I know that I shall see Kevin again. I don't know when and I don't know why. I also know that I shall see Carol. If the family is like the other families I have worked with the past 25 or 30 years, I know that one day I will see not only Kevin's children but his grandchildren.

This case illustrates the model that I would put forth to you and which I call brief intermittent psychotherapy throughout the life cycle, or the general practice of psychology, or, if you will, the psychotherapist as a psychological family practitioner.

REFERENCES

Albee, G. W. (1977). Does including psychotherapy in health insurance represent a subsidy of the rich from the poor? *American Psychologist, 32,* 719–721.

American Psychiatric Association (1980). *Diagnostic and Statistical Manual of Mental Disorders* (Third Edition). Washington, DC. APA.

Budman, S. H. & Gurman, A. S. (1988). *The Theory and Practice of Brief Therapy.* New York: Gulford Press.

Cummings, N. A. (1977). Prolonged (ideal) versus short-term (realistic) psy-
    chotherapy. *Professional Psychology, 8* (4), 491–501.
Cummings, N. A. (1983). *Biodyne Training Manual.* San Francisco: American
    Biodyne Inc.
Cummings, N. A. (1986). The dismantling of our health system: Strategies for the
    survival of psychological practice. *American Psychologist, 41* (4), 426–431.
Cummings, N. A. (1988). The emergence of the mental health complex:
    Adaptive and maladaptive responses. *Professional Psychology: Research and
    Practice, 19* (3), 323–335.
Cummings, N. A., and VandenBos, G. R. (1979). The general practice of psy-
    chology. *Professional Psychology, 10,* 430–440.
Haley, J. (1978). *Problem Solving Therapy.* New York: Harper & Row.

CHAPTER 15

Brief Therapy Tactics in Longer-Term Psychotherapies
Michael D. Yapko

Every day that my mail is delivered, I am inundated with brochures promising opportunities to learn "new and improved" approaches to psychotherapy. Now, I don't know who does the grocery shopping in your household, but I do about half of it in mine. Products that are well known to me since my childhood are now ostentatiously labeled "new and improved." But, are they really? Personally, I am rarely aware of any substantive differences between the "new and improved" version and the "old and however-good-it-was-before" version. So, I wonder about "new and improved" as a marketing strategy in the Eighties for everything from laundry detergent to mental health services. While labeling something "new and improved" may have appeal to the consumer, it also may be a less than truthful claim.

As a provider of training opportunities who mails brochures essentially describing "new and improved" approaches to hypnosis and psychotherapy, and as a consumer of others' trainings, I am especially interested in knowing who my fellow practitioners of brief therapy approaches are. This Congress focuses on that interest and I believe that this focus has some profound implications for the direction that the field of psychotherapy will ultimately take. Unlike other therapy meetings, the focal point is *not* on a single therapy modality, nor is it on a specific clinical disorder or patient population. Rather, this Congress brings together divergent views on the "new and improved" ways to do therapy, all of which subscribe to the notion that effective therapy can be done briefly.

Why the focus on brevity? Why is the construct of "time" becoming so significant a variable in conducting psychotherapy? Does this focal point promise to offer "new and improved" therapy, or is it a myopic view of the nature of psychotherapy? In this chapter, I share perspectives I have about the role of time in some aspects of experience, with special consideration of its role as a pivot point in psychotherapy. Specifically, I am interested in how a particular therapist's own relationship to time affects his or her choice of therapeutic frameworks for conducting clinical practice.

SOCIALIZATION AND TEMPORAL ORIENTATION

The evolution of psychotherapy takes place in a larger social milieu which invariably impacts the course of its developmental path. Similarly, the evolution of an individual psychotherapist occurs in the larger context of a culture of which he or she is a part. "Socialization" is the term generally applied to the conscious and unconscious learnings people develop as they assimilate into the existing culture. Socialization is a universal process, and its power is evident in the way human beings are so readily absorbed into shared, but arbitrary realities.

One specific aspect of socialization concerns the possible frameworks one might develop for relating to the ongoing experience of "time." I use the term "temporal orientation" to describe one's most usual and predictable pattern for relating to experiences ranging from past to present to future (Yapko, 1988). To a large extent, temporal orientation and the life experiences derived from it are shaped by the socialization process. Temporal orientation emerges in the form of predictable patterns for relating to ongoing experiences unfolding over time.

Let me be specific about the effect of socialization on temporal orientation in relation to our shared interest in brief therapy methods. I will use myself as an example, but you may apply the ideas to your own experience in a suitable way.

I grew up in this country in the Sixties, and I am a product of that culture. I am not just a product of a particular set of biological parents and family of origin. Certainly my family's patterns influenced me greatly, but so did the rest of the culture in which I developed. As a product of the Sixties, I had some of my most significant developmental experiences in an environment that stressed the questioning of authorities, the breaking away from seemingly purposeless or arbitrary protocol, experimenting with drug-induced states in order to explore the limits of consciousness, and the increasing desirability of immediate gratifications that rapidly advancing technological and social changes permitted. My generation grew up on television—in large doses measured in hours per day. Studies have shown that today's average American watches approximately 30 hours of television per week—an average of over *four hours per day* (Medrich, Roizen, Rubin, & Buckley, 1982). I am not by any means the first to question the consequences for such large time expenditures in front of the television. In fact, many social scientists have commented on the primary role of television in forming distorted perceptions in regular viewers. I and many others grew up with constant images of major problems being solved in an hour or less, with just a few commercial breaks. What impact has this had on me? Is it a significant factor in my interest in brief methods of psychotherapy? Is it a coincidence that so many of my close colleagues are about the same age as me? What about therapists of *all* ages who have developed a value for the immediacy of experience?

During the Sixties, when the country was in an uproar over a number of important issues, people my age simply could not resist wanting to rapidly change the world. Getting out of Vietnam could have been achieved on Monday, rebuilding the ghettos seemed like a good idea for Tuesday, Wednesday would be the day to clean up the polluted environment, Thursday would provide a chance to ensure the election of a favored politician, and Friday would be a little slower—dealing with any miscellaneous problems needing equally focused, rapid problem-solving energy. Of course, having the weekend off to "party" was considered mandatory. What an era to grow up in! So great was the ability to *under*estimate the complexity of the problems we faced that most eventually evolved an "If you can't beat them, join them" mentality to complete the transition from the idealism of youth to the occasional cynicism that seems to inevitably follow.

And then came the recent surge of interest in brief therapy—a game of *Therapeutic Name That Tune* where each practitioner gets to say "I can name that cure (tune) in three sessions (notes)." The emphasis on therapy being done briefly is an interesting phenomenon from this socialization angle because the metaphor of the generation gap between parents and children that seemed epidemic in the Sixties seems so apt an example. Are brief therapists of whatever age the hippie tradition busters of the therapy establishment? Living amid social forces that suggest immediate gratification as the ideal to strive for whenever possible, the long-term effects of our choices sometimes seem either invisible or so distant as to be irrelevant to a current course of action. The immediacy with which most of us have come to live surfaces in many ways. For example: How is your savings account? Are you saving in an organized and consistent way for your retirement? What are your charge card balances (buy now—pay later!)? These are trite, but true monetary examples of life-styles built around a present temporal orientation.* Of course, to be healthy one must have some orientation to each of the three spheres of time—past, present, and future—but the issue here is which temporal orientation tends to dominate one's experience and life direction.

I grew up around "speed" and "power." Images from the other side of the world were beamed into my living room instantaneously, airplanes could fly me to the other side of the country while I slept for a few hours, computers could do my math for me, and credit cards could get me what I otherwise couldn't afford with just a signature. (I now have a rapid, well-practiced signature!) With so strong a socialized value for solving major problems quickly, is it a coincidence that brief therapy is so appealing to me? In what ways does the viewpoint of someone *not* of my generation or culture differ from my own? Imagine someone who is socialized in an environment that strongly encourages a sense of maintaining past traditions simply for tradition's sake. The dominant frame of reference is a past temporal orientation, with the present and future considered to be merely extensions of the past.

Progress occurs slowly, permitting ample time for all to adjust comfortably to changes that must be slow enough to absorb. Include strong injunctions in the socialization decrees to never question authority or violate tradition, and you have the makings for a slow-moving, sometimes nearly stagnant condition. (Consider most academic institutions' heavy emphasis on the "old classics" of psychology and the glaring omission in training programs of recent innovative methods of brief therapy.) Tradition doubtlessly has a value, but so does innovation. The past is valuable, but the future is what pulls all of us forward in our lives.

TEMPORAL ORIENTATION AND THERAPEUTIC STYLE

What leads one therapist to choose a lengthy, past-oriented approach to treatment, while another focuses on present and future-oriented brief intervention methods? Why is one individual preoccupied with developing insight into historical antecedents to the client's current

---

*Editors' note: Erickson discussed the "now" orientation of urban-reared people in *A Teaching Seminar with Milton Erickson*, J. Zeig (Ed.), New York, Brunner/Mazel, 1980.

symptomatic problems, whereas another all but ignores history while doing therapy even in the first few minutes of the initial interview? Do such choices reflect the needs of the client, or are they simply an extension of the therapist's personality dynamics existing independently of the client's presentation?

These are difficult questions to answer. On one hand, insights about the past provide continuity. Continuity within oneself is generally a more functional way to go through life than is dissociation of parts of oneself. On the other hand, is such "psychological archaeology" necessary when each hour of digging is both painful and a potential source of delay to more rapid progress?

The issue of a past, present, or future temporal orientation is a critical one in therapy that has not been fully explored in the literature. In the same way that one can discuss how a therapist's dominant temporal orientation influences his or her choice of a particular therapy approach, one can also discuss the role of temporal orientation in the client's symptom structure. For example, in *When Living Hurts: Directives for Treating Depression* (Yapko, 1988), I discussed the role of a dominant past temporal orientation in the maintenance of depression. For a therapist to not recognize this pattern in a depressed client, and simply proceed with his or her usual past-oriented historical and insight-oriented methods, is probably a major reason such therapies take a long time and allow unnecessary ongoing suffering before eventual symptom relief. [Of course, many depressions are self-limiting anyway: If one does *nothing*, they are likely to eventually go away. (Davison & Neale, 1986). In such cases, was it the therapy that worked? Or did it delay progress?]

Generally, an a priori selective emphasis on any temporal orientation to the exclusion of others does not seem beneficial for therapy. Such a therapist bias may absorb a client into a therapy structure regardless of his or her dominant temporal orientation. For example, consider the increasingly widespread movement known as Adult Children of Alcoholics (ACA). Here is a therapy perspective that is rooted in a developmental and historical explanation of current difficulties for those who accept the ACA label. How the label may affect a given individual does not seem to be well considered, nor does its stabilizing effect and building of a negative identity seem adequately addressed. During the past few years, I have seen numerous clinically depressed clients who have identified themselves as ACA's to me as an explanation of their current difficulties. In ACA support groups in which they participated regularly, they had seemingly limitless opportunities to examine, scrutinize, analyze, and ultimately immerse themselves in the pain of their respective pasts. However, such focus on a past temporal dimension can reinforce these clients' inability to move forward with their lives. Ultimately, I had to make it a condition of treatment for some depressed clients to suspend participation in the ACA meetings in order to engage in future-oriented work that built more immediate and realistic problem-solving skills. Rather than immerse the person in seemingly endless past episodes of pain, with depressed clients the opposite is generally necessary (Yapko, 1988). Without a consideration for the role of temporal orientation in the client's problems, the therapist can unwittingly project his or her temporal framework onto the client to the client's detriment. Thus, it becomes the responsibility of the therapist to set aside a personal temporal framework in order to deal effectively with this component of the client's presenting problem(s). For example, if a client is depressed and past-oriented, and the therapist favors past-oriented historical/developmental methods, it is the therapist's responsibility to recognize that such an approach may be antitherapeutic in this case, and therefore a different approach is warranted.

THE LONG OR SHORT OF IT

Addressing the relationship between temporal orientation and the duration of treatment, it may be valuable to examine how it is influenced by the particular therapy approach one practices. For example, the directive therapy that I practice (which includes hypnosis, task assignments, and other goal-oriented methods) requires a detailed future orientation in order to produce beneficial results. If the goal is vague, and/or the steps toward the goal are poorly defined, then therapy is unlikely to produce successful results. Similarly, if one does not have a well-developed future orientation as a generalized cognitive component, then the dominant present or past temporal orientation will be likely to lead to a lack of clarity in formulating goals and clearly identifying the steps necessary to reach them. Therapy simply does not progress in such circumstances.

As one who regularly conducts trainings in clinical hypnosis and brief therapy methods, I am aware that not all therapists can easily practice such a future-oriented approach. For some, the apparent lack of emphasis on history seems troubling, especially when the past is greatly valued by the therapist. For others, their global thinking style precludes recognition of specific detailed component patterns of a client's problem; they "can only see the forest, and not the trees." For others, the goal is clear, but previous clinical training may have led them to focus on irrelevant dimensions of client experience, thereby making it difficult to formulate clear steps in the right direction. For example, some therapists take literally the notion that to be effective they must match the client's breathing rate, eye blink rate, voice tone, and other such peripheral characteristics (Bandler & Grinder, 1979). Paying an inordinate amount of attention to such cues may distract one from attending to more important factors.

Deeper understanding of the problem's dynamics and structure as well as the ability to impart to the client the elements of empathy and hopefulness far outweigh in potency such lesser factors as matching eye blinks. In general, the therapist's personal qualities will dictate the degree of attraction to whatever methods are being taught.

Clearly, then, brief therapy methods are not suited to all therapists. Likewise, such methods are not suited to all clients. What determines whether a client will benefit from brief therapy interventions? I suggest that a principal factor is his or her primary temporal orientation, evident in general life-style as well as in the presenting problem(s). Another factor is the individual's general value regarding "change." Is the client more invested in maintaining tradition or in seeking change? A third factor is the client's belief system about what constitutes a complete therapeutic experience. For some, it is an intense, enduring relationship permitting exploration; for others, it is merely the acquisition of specific information from a knowledgeable consultant.

The point, simply stated, is that one way to create a better fit between therapy approaches and the clients who seek them is to develop an awareness for the client's patterns and then tailor the therapy to them, at least at the outset of treatment. Later, perhaps, such patterns may be made the target of treatment, but initially the entryway into the clients' inner world is through their frame of reference. Milton Erickson's emphasis on accepting and utilizing the client's reality as the framework for treatment is a cornerstone not only to Ericksonian approaches, but of other approaches that also emphasize the patterning of experience without an emphasis on interpreting the (projected) "meaning" of those patterns (Zeig, 1987).

THE LONG AND SHORT OF IT

For many, brief therapy assumptions and techniques seem incompatible with long-term therapies. Overly simplistic contrasts paint a picture of brief therapy as solution-oriented, long-term therapy as problem-oriented; brief therapy as symptomatic and superficial, long-term therapy as dynamic and deep; brief therapy as goal-oriented, long-term therapy as process-oriented; and, brief therapy as (negatively) manipulative, long-term therapy as benevolent. Such reductionistic caricatures of *either* model are too simplistic to be true. For example, Smith, Glass, and Miller (1980) performed an analysis of nearly 500 therapy result studies, calculating nearly 1,800 effect sizes, and found that in general, different theoretical orientations or different intervention methodologies produce neither different degrees nor different types of improvement. Such outcome studies provide convincing evidence that both short-term and long-term therapies are effective. Does brief make for better? This is a value question, with no correct answer other than an individual one that is made in an *educated* way by the client. In this view, educating the client as to the viability of short-term approaches or the lack thereof for his or her particular problem(s) or personal needs is a basic responsibility of the therapist. Having the flexibility to work in either a brief or long-term style as the client's needs dictate is another basic responsibility of the therapist. Separating one's preferred way of relating to clients in favor of relating according to what will work best for a given client is perhaps the best evidence of such flexibility.

Integrating short-term strategies into longer-term approaches does not indicate an internal inconsistency within the therapy. In fact, it appears to be a more realistic framework for conducting longer-term therapies. Some problems can only be addressed in longer-term therapies because of their chronicity, pervasiveness, or structure. Actively using brief therapy methods within the structure of longer-term therapies permits a client to define and achieve specific desired outcomes while reinforcing the possibility and even the inevitability of change. Furthermore, employing such methods at specific choice points in the therapy provides concrete benchmarks for overall progress. Ambiguity about the helpfulness of a therapy after lengthy treatment is virtually never desirable.

As a known practitioner of briefer, more outcome-oriented approaches, I have observed an interesting phenomenon in recent years. Clients are being referred to me for brief interventions for specific problems by their therapists who are conducting, in the therapist's (and sometimes even the client's) views, the "real" therapy, i.e., the deeper, more psychodynamically oriented work. When I ask the referring therapist about the rationale for the referral and why he or she chooses not to address the client's specific concerns within the ongoing treatment, I am offered a variety of reasons. These have included a fear of "contaminating the transference relationship" by being directive; a concern that "the client will become too short-sighted" by focusing on specific issues; a concern that if his or her attempts to change specific symptoms are unsuccessful (or only partially successful), it will undermine the value of the entire therapy; and so forth. In essence, these are examples of therapists who have restricted the development of their therapy skills to a long-term framework where the time factor provides a safety net for the lack of specific results obtained in treating well-defined problems.

The flip side of this is the problem mentioned earlier—underestimating the complexity of a problem and using too brief or simple a therapy approach without the appropriate indications. Brief therapy methods, because of the recency of their development, have not yet been well defined enough such that there are explicit and well-understood indications and contraindications for their use. I see two consequences of this in participants during the therapy trainings I conduct: One is a tendency to become more technique-oriented despite the absence of clear indications and contraindications (How many therapists can be specific in answering this question: When should you *not* use a symptom prescription strategy?) The other is a difficulty in sequencing stages of treatment and recognizing how short-term strategies may fit into a longer-term framework. Often I am asked, "How do you keep therapy going after the first few sessions when nothing particularly dramatic happens? What do you talk about after the problems have been described and you've already shared your views?" The underlying assumption of those who ask such questions is that therapy should be a rapid process with dramatic results if it is being conducted properly. The insecurity of every therapist is evident in the anxiety felt when secretly entertaining the question "Am I being as effective and skilled as I should be?" Consider, for example, the influence of the Neurolinguistic Programming (NLP) model in the brief therapy marketplace. With the promise of dramatic and rapid cures, and the troublesome lack of data to support such claims, NLP has promoted the idea that it is not client resistance, but therapist ineffectiveness, that delays or prevents treatment success (Bandler & Grinder, 1979). The effect is double-edged: While such a view encourages more diversity of approaches to treatment, it also promotes higher levels of stress and guilt in carrying out an already stressful job (Yapko, 1984). Most relevant here, though, is that such a framework precludes developing an appreciation for and skill in conducting longer-term therapies when such therapies are indicated.

CONCLUSION

Focusing on the temporal dimension as a primary feature of one's therapeutic practice raises some important issues. I have encouraged the reader to consider the presence of a dominant temporal orientation that, in part, regulates experience in patterned ways. I described the role of socialization in shaping perceptions related to time. In discussing the therapist's internal frame of reference for relating to the construct of time, I suggested that therapists often choose an approach to therapy that corresponds to their own personal frame of reference rather than the client's frame of reference or the structure of the client's problem. If brief therapy methods are teaching us anything, it is the need to dissociate our own patterns from the experience of the client to the greatest extent possible—in other words, join the client's frame of reference rather than expecting him or her to come to ours.

Ultimately, a goal of therapy is to have as wide an array of therapeutic tools as needed in order to effectively address the problems presented to us. Outcome studies of therapy's effectiveness consistently show us that most therapies are about equal in efficacy. What, then, determines "new and improved" for our profession? Is brief better? The question is much like asking which is the best car to drive—best for what? For speed? For safety? For durability? This Congress has promoted an awareness of choice—that therapy does not have to be lengthy, nor "should" it necessarily be brief. What we strive for is making sure that no one is doing lengthy, costly therapy that could be done as well briefly; likewise, we also want to make sure that no one is underestimating a problem's complexity and doing the client the disservice of a temporary "patchup" job that is delaying or preventing more substantial interventions.

Overcoming the proponents' prejudices that brief therapy is better or the opponents' prejudices that brief therapy is superficial is something we desperately need to do if all the members of our profession are ever to be comfortable with the expanded recognition of the value of both shorter-and longer-term approaches. I'd like to see us overcome these prejudices *immediately*.

REFERENCES

Bandler, R., & Grinder, J. (1979). *Frogs into Princes*. Moab, Utah: Real People Press.

Comstock, G., Chaffee, S., Katzmen, N., McCombs, M., & Roberts, D. (1978). *Television and Human Behavior*. New York: Columbia University Press.

Davison, G., & Neale, J. (1986). *Abnormal Psychology* (4th ed.). New York: Wiley.

Haley, J. (1987). Therapy—A new phenomenon. In J. Zeig (Ed.), *The Evolution of Psychotherapy* (pp. 17–28). New York: Brunner/Mazel.

Lynn, S., & Garske, J. (1985). *Contemporary Psychotherapies: Models and Methods*. Columbus, Ohio: Charles E. Merrill.

Medrich, E. A., Roizen, J. A., Rubin, V., & Buckley, S. (1982). *The Serious Business of Growing Up*. Berkeley, CA: University of California Press.

Smith, M., Glass, G., & Miller, T. (1980). *The Benefits of Psychotherapy.* Baltimore, MD: Johns Hopkins University Press.

Yapko, M. (1984). Implications of the Ericksonian and Neurolinguistic Programming approaches for responsibility of therapeutic outcomes. *American Journal of Clinical Hypnosis, 27* (2), 137–143.

Yapko, M. (1988). *When Living Hurts: Directives for Treating Depression.* New York: Brunner/Mazel.

Yapko, M. (1989). Disturbances of temporal orientation as a feature of depression. In M. Yapko (Ed.), *Brief Therapy Approaches to Treating Anxiety and Depression.* New York: Brunner/Mazel.

Zeig, J. (1987). Introduction: The evolution of psychotherapy—Fundamental issues. In J. Zeig (Ed.), *The Evolution of Psychotherapy* (pp. XV-XXVI). New York: Brunner/Mazel.

CHAPTER 16

How Long Should Brief Therapy Be?
Herbert S. Lustig

I earn my living by being a healer with the spoken word. I do this in my offices by paying full attention to what is happening *now* with the patient, and by simultaneously *focusing* all of my efforts on achieving the greatest amount of constructive *change* that can occur *comfortably* for the patient during the therapy session. The tools necessary for the work I do are a vast reservoir of technical skills, a limitless source of delightful creativity, a warm regard for all the people in the room, a keen observational mechanism for perceiving the ephemeral and subtle changes that occur within those people, and a mind that becomes perfectly clear as soon as the session begins. Since I carry these tools with me all of the time, there is nothing that I have to do in preparation for encountering a situation that requires my clinical services. For me, it is the easiest job in the world: nothing to read, nothing to write, nothing to do except be there and available, sitting comfortably in a chair.

My orientation as a clinician is experiential, strategic, and behavioral. I believe that change for anyone, whether patient or therapist, occurs in a state of consciousness that is different from the one in which the dysfunction typically is expressed. For this reason, I first attempt to discover the parameters of the patient's symptomatic state and then to guide the person into a more comfortable state of consciousness, where healing and change and peace can occur.

When I teach, as I am now, I prefer that members of the audience experience an altered state of consciousness similar to the therapeutic ones that are created in my offices. As I began thinking about this chapter several months ago, I thought about the great disparity that would exist among the experiences of the people who would be exposed to it: those who sit on uncomfortable chairs in a meeting room while listening to a version of this chapter being delivered versus those who leisurely listen to an audiotape of the presentation versus those who read a printed and more formal version of the chapter in the published proceedings of the Congress. I realized that people in the audience would be denied the opportunity to experience the altered state of consciousness that people whom I teach usually enjoy. That realization disturbed me.

When working clinically, I usually guide the attention of people's sense organs and minds towards a pleasant and captivating stimulus, which is provided for them by my body, voice, and words. Here, however, the degree of intimacy that occurs in my offices is difficult to achieve, because of the physical distance that separates us. Bodily comfort also is difficult to achieve here, because of the stiff chairs that are being used. In order to provide the members of this audience with a silent and fascinating focus for their eyes, while allowing their ears and minds to take in all the meanings of my words, and their muscles to feel especially relaxed, I have asked Katrina Grinn from Denmark, half the duo of "Grinn & Bear-it," to join me and to offer you the opportunity to feast upon her beauty, dexterity, and agility. So please be my guests, and enjoy her juggling and magic! And, if your attention must be diverted from the words that are being produced now by my voice, please let the cause of distraction be a lovely and quiet one that is outside of your control. (Katrina begins her juggling routine.)

ELEMENTS OF BRIEF THERAPY

What is therapy, and what is so special about its permutation called brief therapy? One similarity among the various therapies is that they all have, to some degree, an experiential element. That is (a juggled item noisily falls to the floor), we *drop* from one state of consciousness into another, one in which we are functional and symptom-free. An additional similarity is that the various therapies ask people to behave differently during therapy, to feel differently, to think differently. With some therapies, entire systems of people are asked to interact among themselves differently.

Therapy is also goal-directed. People who come for therapy want to achieve some particular outcome, which usually involves a constructive change in how they feel, think, or relate to others. Brief therapy, because of its limited duration, must be more precise in defining exactly what its goal is. Because of those same time constraints, brief therapists must pledge to their patients that they will steadfastly pursue the agreed clinical goal, despite their patients' natural efforts to divert the process. And good brief therapy, after having accomplished the clinical goal quickly, must also perpetuate it with equal swiftness.

Whereas regular therapy, with its seemingly limitless time frame, sometimes allows patients to assume passive roles, brief therapy requires the vigorous participation of the patients. This renders them different from the outset of the therapeutic process. Although long-term therapy may be ideologically rigorous or eclectic in its orientation and vague in its goals, brief therapy is pragmatic in its clinical methodology and focused in its goals. This stimulates the brief therapist to think and act differently than the long-term therapist from the outset of the therapy.

THE POWER OF WORDS

There are many skills that therapists acquire during their education that provide opportunities to refine their clinical techniques. These skills involve not only use of the spoken word, but also control of vocal apparatus; not only reading of the communications from other people's bodies, but therapists' control of their own body language. These skills also include being able to precisely define a therapeutic goal and to resolutely focus on that goal during the entire course of treatment. And they involve being creative and economical in devising clinical strategies, so that patients rapidly achieve comfortable and effective changes in their functioning.

Many years ago during my psychiatry residency at The Johns Hopkins Hospital, I participated in a series of experiential group relations training programs that were sponsored by the Washington School of Psychiatry and were based on clinical research performed by Wilfred R. Bion at the Tavistock Clinic and Institute in England. The culmination of these training programs in America was a one-week residential conference at Mt. Holyoke College. The culmination of these same "Tavistock" training programs in England was a two-week residential conference at Leicester University.

During my residency, I attended many of the local programs in Baltimore and also the one-week conference at Mt. Holyoke. After my first year of child psychiatry fellowship at the Philadelphia Child

Guidance Clinic, I went to England to participate in the Leicester residential conference. By then, I had become quite familiar with the "Tavistock" model of group relations, including the kinds of exercises that were routinely used at these conferences. The Leicester conference was divided into two one-week segments. The first week consisted of exercises with which I was already acquainted. The second week, however, was more interesting. A training activity was to be conducted during which the entire conference membership would meet initially in one large room and then organize itself into smaller groups that would meet in smaller rooms. The training purpose of the activity was for these smaller groups to have the experience of conducting some sort of negotiations among themselves. The faculty for the conference would also function as a group during this activity, either by "consulting" to the other groups or by negotiating with them.

I thought it would be interesting to find out what would happen if something unusual were to occur during this large group exercise. Before it actually began, I assembled some people whom I had met at the conference. I suggested that we form our own little group whose purpose would be to kidnap the director of the conference faculty. This was at a time when kidnappings were receiving a great deal of exposure in the media. In preparation for the large group exercise, I had explored the building where the training activity was to be held. I discovered that on the first floor was a small room with a door leading to a private patio, at whose rear was a shed that contained a washing machine and a clothes drying machine. I also discovered that if the washer and the dryer were both operating simultaneously, the sounds of loud human voices were almost completely muffled. This meant that we might be able to kidnap the director, take him through the front door of the room, whisk him through the patio door to the shed, hide in the shed while the machines roared, and discover how the conference membership and leadership responded to his disappearance. It took several private meetings during the initial stages of the large group exercise for the people in my group to conclude that the kidnapping might be a useful learning experience *if* the conference director were not physically harmed in any way.

To test our agenda on a smaller scale, we invited a faculty member to our room, ostensibly to consult with us about the "dynamics" that were occurring within our group. When the consultant entered the room, he closed the door and stood facing us expectantly. Everyone in the group was seated far from him, and no physical obstacles were interposed between the faculty member and the door through which he had just entered.

As the group's spokesperson, I said to the consultant, "This group has been formed to conduct an experiment to find out what would happen if a member of the faculty were kidnapped. Please consider yourself kidnapped." No one moved, no one spoke. The consultant turned pale, began perspiring profusely, and stated rapidly, loudly, and repetitively that the group was violating the rules of the exercise and that we would be reported immediately.

No one moved, no one else spoke. I told him, whenever there was a pause in his avalanche of words, "Consider yourself kidnapped." Nobody was within 10 feet of him. His back was to the door. Three feet of space *that he controlled* were all that separated him from the door. Yet for an entire hour, this educated and trained person was frozen to the floor, while his gaze repeatedly swept the members of the group—all of whom were equally motionless. Even though the faculty person had complete freedom to quickly turn and exit the room, he did nothing to extricate himself from this dilemma of words except continually rant.

At the conclusion of the scheduled time period for that day's large group exercise, I stood up and said, "Well, the exercise is over for the day. It's time to leave." Then the members of the group slowly walked through the door, and the consultant filed out with them, somewhat flabbergasted by what had happened. The group never did proceed further with its kidnapping agenda. We were too stunned by what we had experienced that afternoon, and we spent the rest of the exercise recovering from its aftershocks. We all learned that day in Leicester how incredibly powerful words can be, how literally people sometimes interpret them, and how important it is to carefully and deliberately use them in the processes of healing and communication.

THE POWER OF NONVERBAL COMMUNICATION

Nonverbal communication has that same potential. On the trip from Philadelphia to this Congress, I took a flight from St. Louis to San Francisco. Sitting across the aisle from me were a woman and a toddler. The little girl had blond hair and blue eyes, and she wore a cute pink outfit over her diapers. She had four top teeth and two bottom teeth, but she didn't use spoken words for communication. The woman was doing an excellent job of keeping her daughter entertained and amused, while allowing the girl sufficient freedom to play within the confines of the row in which they were sitting.

Their meals had been served to them well before mine, so that by the time I received my food, they had already completed theirs. After I had begun eating, the girl became irritable and started to cry. The mother stood, picked up her daughter, moved to the aisle, and began patting the girl and rocking her back and forth. The woman, I presumed, thought it was naptime for the girl, since it had just been mealtime. (They usually follow each other closely.) The girl quieted down and began to fall asleep in her mother's arms. I commented to myself, "Good job, Mom, good job!" The mother gently put her daughter down on the seat. Instantly, the crying and irritable behavior erupted again. Mother picked up the girl, patted her, rocked her, and cooed to her, and the child snuggled against her mother and fell asleep again. The mother continued to rock the girl to ensure that, this time, she would stay asleep. Tenderly, the mother placed her child down on the soft cloth. But as soon as the girl was down, she was awake and irritable again.

"Maybe it's not naptime, this time," I theorized. The mother must have thought similarly, because she allowed the girl to play again.

The child busied herself in noisily rejecting every plaything her mother offered for amusement. Suddenly, the girl reached toward her baby bottle, which was in mother's diaper bag. The woman took the bottle from the bag, removed its cap, and gave it to her daughter. The toddler responded by promptly throwing the bottle onto the floor.

"Let's try again," I thought in the woman's stead, as she picked up the bottle, talked to the child sweetly, handed the bottle to the girl, and waited. The girl took the bottle and, once more, threw it to the floor.

"No, she doesn't want the bottle," I surmised. Mom slowly and quietly put the cap back on the bottle, returned the bottle to the diaper bag and placed the bag near her daughter. The child immediately reached for the bottle cap, took it off, and began examining it carefully and curiously, as if it were an object with which she wanted to play but for which she couldn't figure out a game.

I like children. The only time I don't like being around them is when I want some quiet or privacy. This was one of those occasions. I wanted quiet. So I began thinking, "What can I do to help this little girl play, yet still allow me to have some relative silence?" As I was eating, I realized that I would not be needing my empty plastic coffee cup, which was still clean. Without saying a word, because no words had been exchanged between the aisles, I reached across with the coffee cup, so that my movement entered the mother's peripheral vision, and proffered the cup to her. She took it and said, "Oh, thank you!"

I assumed that the woman would give the coffee cup to her daughter and that the girl would play with it. The mother, however, knowing her daughter better than I, held the cup with one hand, silently took the baby bottle from the diaper bag, squirted some juice from the baby bottle into the cup, handed the cup to her daughter, and watched as her daughter began drinking confidently from it. While the child was imbibing her juice, she looked at me sheepishly from behind the cup. I gave her a wide-eyed appreciative look and smiled. That's how we became friends. Thereafter, every time that the girl drank from the cup, she would peek from behind it, and I would look at her and smile. She would then remove the cup from her lips proudly and smile back.

The few squirts of juice from the baby bottle that the mother put into the cup were being quickly swallowed by the child. Finally, the woman took the nipple off the bottle and just poured the liquid into the cup, half filling it. After several repetitions of this procedure, the girl had drunk most of the bottle's contents.

When the child had satisfied her thirst, she began "reading" silently from a magazine and quietly playing peek-a-boo with me from behind it. After a short while, the girl seemed to lose interest in playing peek-a-boo, because she began having a conversation with me that did not involve words. She started babbling to me loudly, but in a friendly way. To my ears, however, it was noise. I didn't want to offend this child, since she had become an enjoyable playmate for me, but I did want her to become quiet. So I gave her the same expression of delight that I had used when we were playing peek-a-boo, but I put my index finger over my mouth. And the girl became quiet.

Hoping that my request for silence had been only temporary, the child began another raucous conversation with me several minutes later. Again, I gave her a look of wide-eyed pleasure and put my index finger over my mouth. Again, she instantly became quiet. For the remainder of the flight, we occasionally played peek-a-boo or she "read" her magazine. Sometimes, she displayed a particularly interesting page to me. She even took a long nap. And no words were ever spoken by me to her during the entire trip. At the end of the flight, I asked the woman how old her daughter was; she was 18 months old.

It was enlightening for me to experience on that airplane just how powerful and precise nonverbal communication with persons of any age can be and to appreciate some of the qualities of the information that can be exchanged by two people without using spoken words.

CASE EXAMPLES

Katrina, we're ready for the finale. (Katrina climbs upon a tall unicycle, balances herself carefully, and resumes juggling)

As mental health practitioners conducting brief therapy, it is important that we choose carefully the therapeutic tasks that we ask our patients to perform. Many years ago, a boy was brought to my office by his physician father and his psychotherapist mother. The expensive Oriental carpets in their home were found to have wet spots on them, attributable neither to the pets nor to household accidents. The father's hospital laboratory determined that the wet spots contained only human urine. The parents and the boy all disclaimed responsibility, but the parents assumed that the son was the culprit. Naturally, the parents were concerned about the psychological implications of this display of aberrant behavior, and they were equally concerned about the financial losses they were incurring.

After obtaining additional backgroup information from the trio, I turned to the boy and asked nonchalantly, "How far can you pee?" He replied, "I don't know." I was incredulous! He was about eight years old, so I continued, "You mean you don't know how far you can pee? Boys much younger than you know exactly how far they can pee—and with good aim, too!" I told him that it was very important that he determine precisely the distance that he could pee. I suggested, therefore, that he go into the bathroom, get into the bathtub, stand far back from the bathtub drain, pee toward the drain, and find out how far his urine stream traveled. "You can learn to pee accurately later," I added. His father was to assist him in this endeavor by measuring the distance peed, which the boy was then to record in a notebook. They were to do this regularly, I instructed, because the distance peed would probably increase.

In one week, the boy had graduated from the drain in the bathtub to the drain in the basement floor, and he proudly told me that he was able to pee a distance of seven feet. I was impressed, I told him, because the farthest I had ever peed when I was a boy was about six feet—and that was with a really full bladder. The wet spots, I was informed by the parents, had vanished.

Soiled carpets were not a problem in that household again. I never did find out whether the boy actually had peed on the Oriental carpets and, if he had, why he might have done so. It just was never discussed in my office. The parents announced, one week later, that they would be living apart. An amicable divorce followed, without the need for therapy, and all the family's members resumed satisfying lives.

I recently taught a workshop about the psychotherapy of sexual abuse trauma. My coteacher was a former client whose distress about her sexual abuse I had first treated in December 1984. Two-and one-half years had elapsed between her first and second therapy sessions with me, during which time she visited a variety of health and mental health professionals to assist her in the process of her self-healing. Her third visit with me occurred the day after the second session, at which time we both agreed that her recovery was then complete.

One of the instructive elements in this woman's story was the fact that her psychotherapy with me occurred at "pivotal points" in her recovery process, and that she did not require continuous or regular treatment sessions with me in order for it to be successful. If a person experiencing emotional distress has sufficient resources in the community and has the necessary personal courage and capabilities, much of the "work" of psychotherapy can be done or directed by that same person. In these circumstances, the therapist merely provides intermittent and irregular assistance at times that the patient considers "pivotal" to the process. Besides being "brief" in the number of clinical visits, as this woman's story attests, therapy can also be "brief" in the duration of treatment, as the tale of wet spots illustrates.

CONCLUSION

So, how long should brief therapy be? The obvious answer is "As long as it takes." Even that glib estimate depends, of course, on the technical skills of the therapist, the rate of change that the patient is comfortable experiencing, and the functional altered state of consciousness that the therapist has guided the patient to achieve.

The treatment duration that I set as the standard for my own clinical work is 45 minutes, the length of a typical appointment in my offices. Actually, I prefer that the therapy be shorter than 45 minutes, so that I can use the remaining time to enjoy the people who are visiting me. I don't always achieve that standard, but I certainly do refine my skills in the attempt.

How can therapy be done in one session? Well, if we are really careful with the wording and delivery of the questions we ask and alert to all the nuances of the information we receive during the initial consultation, we will be able to identify many of the rules governing the patient's dysfunctional behavior fairly quickly. (Katrina accelerates her rate of juggling) Then we can invent an intervention that might work, implement it rapidly, modify it swiftly, and implant it promptly into the patient's behavioral repertoire. Even if the patient does choose to return for a few more visits, the sessions will be merely for the purpose of fine-tuning the original intervention—so that the patient can personalize the therapy, and ultimately, own the altered state of consciousness that created the beneficial life changes.

REFERENCES

Allen, C., with Lustig, H. S. (1986). *Tea with Demons.* New York: Ballantine Books.

Bion, W. R. (1961). *Experiences in Groups.* London: Tavistock.
Bion, W. R. (1962). *Learning from Experience.* London: Heinemann.
Lustig, H. S. (1983). *A Primer of Ericksonian Psychotherapy* (videotape). New York: Irvington.

CHAPTER 17

The Myth of Termination in Brief Therapy: Or, It Ain't Over Till It's Over

Simon Budman

Over the years, mental health clinicians, theoreticians, and supervisors have perpetuated the unfortunate myth that the patient who is really "cured" by psychotherapy terminates after an effective course of treatment never to return (except perhaps to present the therapist with a potted plant and to thank him or her for all of the invaluable assistance received). Since a truly useful course of psychotherapy is viewed as having a prophylactic (i.e., preventive) effect, the patient who returns for additional treatment is a walking indictment of a therapy's (or a therapist's) deficits.

This view of treatment, although probably more pervasive and overt among analytically oriented psychotherapists, is true for clinicians of most theoretical persuasions. Furthermore, since brief therapy may have relatively clear temporal constraints (e.g., 12 sessions), practitioners of a given approach may be tempted to proclaim that their method is not only faster than others, but better. The simplest, "common sense" way for the brief therapy developer to indicate that his or her treatment is "better" is to state that patients treated by this method are more likely to be completely cured and not to return. Lest the reader assume that my view is exaggerated, I offer the following quote from a prominent short-term therapist about his approach: "[A]t the time of termination there is definite evidence of the *total resolution* of the patient's core neurosis" (Davanloo, 1980, p. 70, italics added). Davanloo's statement, which is not unlike the implicit or explicit view of many brief therapy developers, carries with it the implication of complete cure and of the finality of termination. After all, once one's core neuroses have been "totally resolved," what else is there to do?

Presumably, the view that psychotherapy can be "curative" in the present, preventive in the future, and therefore terminable derives, in part, from Freud's early optimism regarding the beneficial qualities of psychoanalysis (Roazen, 1971). Furthermore, Freud's view of the analyst as a surgeon, of sorts (rather than a minister, priest, accountant, etc.), added to the cure-oriented position.

The behaviorists (much later) also contributed to this stance. This occurred because early behavior therapy began with a strong emphasis on the treatment of symptoms. Once the patient's symptoms were resolved, he or she left therapy. For the patient to have to return meant that his or her symptoms had again appeared and that he or she had "relapsed." Once more, return for therapy was seen as a type of "failure" with pejorative implications for the therapy, therapist, and patient.

In this chapter, I elaborate on the currently accepted views of termination and then offer evidence that this model represents an inaccurate perspective, totally unrelated to the reality experienced by most patients concluding a course of treatment. Finally, I pose an alternative view of termination and present some clinical case materials that exemplify this perspective.

THE "IDEAL" TERMINATION

Firestein (1978), in his review of termination from the psychoanalytic perspective, presents the following description as the ideal state for the terminating patient in analytic treatment:

> A typical characterization would indicate approximately the following: Symptoms have been traced to their genetic conflicts, in the course of which the infantile neurosis has been identified, as the infantile amnesia was undone ("insight"). It is hoped all symptoms have been eliminated, mitigated, or made tolerable. Object relations, freed of transference distortions, have improved, along with the level of psychosexual functioning, the latter attaining "full genitality." Penis envy and castration anxiety have been mastered. The ego is strengthened by virtue of diminishing anachronistic countercathectic for-

mations. The ability to distinguish between fantasy and reality
has been sharpened. Acting out has been eliminated. The
capacity to tolerate some measure of anxiety and to reduce
other unpleasant affects to signal quantities has been improved. The ability to tolerate delay of gratification is increased, and along with it there is a shift from autoplastic to
alloplastic conflict solutions. Sublimations have been strengthened, and the capacity to experience pleasure without guilt or
other notable inhibiting factors has improved. Working ability,
under which so many aspects of ego function, libidinal and
aggressive drive gratification are subsumed, has improved. (pp.
226–227)

In the above, it is hoped that the terminating patient is in a nearly perfect state of mind. Further, any discussion of future therapeutic contact
is discouraged. Indeed, for Ticho (1972), an analytically oriented writer,
even the act of reassuring the patient that future treatment with the
therapist may be possible should be viewed with suspicion. After all, if
the patient were really ready for termination, the therapist would not
feel compelled to provide such reassurance and the patient would not
need it.

This same absolute view of termination is maintained by many leading
brief therapists (Davanloo, 1978a,b; Mann, 1973; Sifneos, 1972). Mann
and Goldman (1982), as an example, strongly warn against informing
the patient that the short-term therapy will include a one-year follow-
up:

At no time during the treatment does the therapist make any
mention of a follow-up interview. It is incumbent on the
therapist to make certain that the separation phase of treatment is *unequivocal;* anything less will suggest to the patient
that the separation is not genuine, that more time will be available. (p. 13, italics added)

Much of this focus on termination is due to the fact that some
therapists see the termination process as an ideal opportunity for the
patient to "finally" work out (or "work through") some of the painful
losses he or she has experienced over the course of his or her life. For
these clinicians termination is also a chance for the patient to attain a
better ending for treatment than has been achieved at the ending of
other key relationships. Thus, the termination process and its apparent
finality is critical. In this regard, Mann (1973) explains:

It is absolutely incumbent upon the therapist to deal directly with the reaction to termination in all its painful aspects and affects if he expects to help the patient come to some vividly affective understanding of the now inappropriate nature of his early unconscious conflict. More than that, active and appropriate management of the termination will allow the patient to internalize the therapist as a replacement or substitute for the earlier ambivalent object. *This time the internalization will be more positive (never totally so), less anger laden and less guilt laden, thereby making separation a genuine maturational event.* Since anger, rage, guilt, and their accompaniments of frustration and fear are the potent factors that prevent positive internalization and mature separation, it is these that must not be overlooked in this phase of the time-limited therapy. (p. 36, italics in original)

The view held by many clinicians is that termination of therapy is not only a total and final process, but a process of enormous pain and turmoil for the patient (Edelson, 1963; Fox, Nelson, & Bolan, 1969; Gould, 1978). In fact, some writers have even likened termination to the process of dying (cf. Mikkelson & Gutheil, 1979). Through this intense pain and intensity, the termination of treatment is viewed as a great opportunity for the clinician to help the patient "once and for all" deal with prior losses.

THE "REALITY" OF TERMINATION

In actuality, a mythology has developed around the termination process which is not supported by the facts. The above-described ideal of intense and absolute termination may reflect what occurs in perhaps a small minority of treatment cases. However, for most therapy clients the reality of how treatment ends is considerably different.

Of all the individuals who visited outpatient mental health settings in this country in 1980, nearly 70% came for six or fewer visits (Taube, Goldman, Burns, & Kessler, 1988). The modal number of visits was only one! Thus, in the majority of incidences of psychotherapy, termination is probably never addressed as a topic at all. It is highly unlikely that termination is a key topic in the first few visits (which are as many as most people ever have in a given episode of treatment).

Additionally, there is evidence that even when patients come for many more visits, termination is not the intense emotional process suggested in the literature. Marx and Gelso (1987) explored this issue in an interesting study of client reactions to termination. They found, in a setting where the average number of visits was 10 (with some patients having as many as 51 hours of therapy), that patients uniformly had a surprisingly positive and nontraumatic reaction to the end of treatment with a notable lack of intense fear, anger, or emotionality.

Another important piece of evidence that contradicts the "ideal" termination model is that patients do not simply end therapy never to return. It appears that many patients return for multiple episodes of treatment at different times over the course of their lives. Patterson, Levene, and Breger (1977) studied patients in time-limited psychodynamic or behavioral therapy and found nearly 60% returned for more treatment within a year of their previous termination. Furthermore, 60% of the patients in this study had received prior mental health treatment before the project began. Kovacs, Rush, Beck, and Hollon (1981), in a study comparing cognitive behavior therapy and antidepressant medication, found that about 50% of the patients in their study, regardless of the therapy they received, had additional treatment after the project ended. Weissman and her colleagues (1981) compared pharmacotherapy and interpersonal brief therapy for depression and found that only about a third of the patients treated received no additional therapy in the year following their supposed treatment terminations. In an interesting project investigating the nature of brief, intermittent therapy within an HMO setting, Siddall, Haffey, and Feinman (1988) found that more than one-quarter of the patients seeking care within a four-month period had had previous psychotherapeutic contact at the health maintenance organization being studied. Of these returning "help seekers," 26% were asking for help with the same problem, while 51% requested assistance for a new problem. Nearly 80% of the returning patients had found their prior therapy helpful.

The reader should not assume that returning for additional therapy is a phenomenon limited to those in brief treatments. In surveying graduates of the William Alanson White Institute, Goldensohn (1977) found that 55% had additional therapy after completing a lengthy psychoanalysis. Hartlaub, Martin, and Rhine (1986) surveyed psychoanalytic institute graduates in Denver and found that even among "successfully analyzed" patients more than 60% returned for additional treatment. Additionally, Grunebaum (1983) and Henry, Sims, and Spray (1971) found that psychotherapists themselves tended to have many courses of therapy over their lifetimes. The number of times they received treatment was unrelated to how good or how poor they perceived the outcomes of their earlier therapies to be. Indeed, Grunebaum found that the best predictor of how many therapies a therapist had had was the age of the clinician (the older, the more therapies!).

In regard to this issue of repeated courses of therapy in brief and long-term treatment, an experience I had several years ago is instructive: While doing a consultation in Boston, I was asked to see a difficult out-patient, and to advise his therapist about appropriate treatment. Before ever seeing the patient, I sensed something familiar in just hearing him described. I wondered if I had previously treated the patient or super-vised his care. After I met him, I quickly ascertained how I knew him. He was a man whom I had seen presented on videotape at a large national conference by one of the country's foremost short-term thera-pists. He was viewed by this clinician as an example of an extremely dif-ficult patient who had been "cured" in brief therapy. When I asked the patient whether he had in fact seen Dr. Y, he was quite enthusiastic and pleased as he discussed that treatment. He reported having an excellent experience with Dr. Y. Shortly after that therapy ended he sought group therapy with another therapist, and then after a break, he entered couples therapy. He had then waited some time before seeing another clinician for individual treatment. At the time that I met him he was seeking therapy in regard to some difficulties his child was having.

Dr. Y was certainly remembered with great fondness by the patient. However, while the brief therapist viewed himself as having completed a definitive treatment with the client, the client viewed things quite dif-ferently. From his perspective, Dr. Y was one of a large number of clinicians from whom he had received help over the course of his life. The patient neither viewed himself as having been cured by that treat-ment, nor did he believe that therapy to have been in any way definitive for him.

The weight of the evidence appears to indicate that the idealized pro-cess is considerably different than the reality of termination. Patients in their actual behaviors generally do not conform to the "cure" model of how therapy ends. They are in many cases pleased to stop therapy. Perhaps this is because regardless of what they are told by their clini-cian, they realize that they can always get more help as needed. And this they most certainly do. As discussed previously, in many reports, well over half of the patients seen in long- or short-term therapy seek ad-ditional mental health care within one year of their "termination." Patients appear to learn to use psychotherapy as an option when they are feeling upset over various problematic issues in their lives. It may be that for some, once the barriers to mental health care have been broken by having contact with a clinician, their future sense of comfort about using mental health services is greatly enhanced. Therefore, the greatest likelihood is that if the client were again confronted with difficult circumstances, he or she would seek out additional psychological treatment.

AN ALTERNATIVE VIEW OF TERMINATION

Two of the major underlying reasons that the absolute cure ("you-will-never-ever-need-therapy-again") model of termination does not represent reality are the issues of adult development and of chance events over the course of one's lifetime. Although for many years psychoanalytic thinkers assumed that an individual's emotional and characterological destiny was fixed in childhood, recently this position has been challenged by those taking an adult developmental perspective. The adult developmentalists such as Erik Erikson (1963), Gilligan (1982), Gould (1978), and Vaillant (1977) assume that one's personality continues to grow and develop through different stages over the course of one's life. At various points in life, a person is faced with challenges or difficulties for which earlier stages may be only partial preparation. For example, the hard-driving, successful businesswoman who is able to achieve outstanding work success meets a man with whom she becomes close and marries. This woman, although a high achiever in all aspects of her life, may feel totally overwhelmed and unprepared for the challenges of motherhood. Indeed, some of her prior developmental successes may not have tapped into the issues, problems, and concerns that are raised as she tries to deal with an irrational, needy, demanding six-week-old infant.

The most important point to be made in regard to this issue of adult development over the life course is that people are not static, unchanging entities. Life is an ongoing process of changing, aging, growing, and dying. As we get older we all must deal with changes in ourselves and in those around us. Children are born and grow up. Friendships and love relationships are made and broken. Parents and friends age and die, as do we all.

Another factor which is denied by those who would seek to finally treat, cure, and terminate with their patients is the issue of chance in one's life. Although a position which has been taken by some therapists in the past (and which is still adhered to by many) is that "one makes one's own luck," it seems to me more likely that some people are, through little fault or action of their own, plagued by either good or bad luck. In this regard, an interesting pair of articles were recently juxtaposed in the *Boston Globe*. One article (Kranish, 1988, August 21) was about then Senator Dan Quayle, who had just been selected by George

Bush as his Republican vice-presidential running mate. The other article (Jacobs & Ribadeneira, 1988, August 21) was about a young woman named Mary Beth Lenane, who a week earlier had been brutally attacked, for the fourth time, in a small variety store she owned in the Dorchester neighborhood of Boston. The article on Quayle, based on interviews with friends, colleagues, teachers, and classmates, painted a picture of an unintelligent, unindustrious, disconnected man, who by dint of his father's pressures and huge family wealth and influence careened from one fortunate circumstance to the next. At age 41, to the shock and dismay of many of those who knew him, he was running for the second highest office in the country.

Quayle's extraordinary good fortune stood in sharp contrast to Ms. Lenane's bad luck. A high-school graduate, from a lower-middle-class family, Ms. Lenane always had wanted a business of her own. From age 14 she had worked part time and saved money in order to achieve her goal. Finally, at 20 years of age she had saved enough money to buy a small variety store in her neighborhood. Within weeks of purchasing this store she was robbed for the first time. In the ensuing months she was again robbed, then sexually assaulted, robbed again, then kidnapped, beaten, and threatened with death if she testified against her attackers. It appears unlikely that either Quayle or Lenane "made their own luck." Rather, through a variety of circumstances based neither on character nor on intent, these people found themselves the "victims" of either good (Quayle) or bad (Lenane) fortune.

A CASE EXAMPLE

A far more realistic perspective on termination than the "cure" model is to view psychotherapy as a resource that the patient may use and return to at many points over the life cycle (Budman & Gurman, 1988). Such a model is not only more likely to accurately reflect the ways in which patients actually use therapy, but it also does not unnecessarily extend a given course of treatment in an attempt to finally resolve a patient's neuroses. By leaving the door open to future treatment, the brief therapist does not make the patient feel that returning for more therapy is an indication of failure. Further, the patient can be encouraged to see his or her work on self-improvement and change as a lifelong process, rather than as something one does, completes, and gets over with.

To illustrate brief therapy during the course of a long-term relationship I will briefly describe my work with a patient I call Dennis. I have worked with Dennis intermittently for over 12 years and expect to have occasional contact with him for many more. The excerpt below comes from my book with Alan Gurman, *Theory and Practice of Brief Therapy* (1988):

> At the time of his initial evaluation, Dennis was having frequent anxiety attacks and was becoming increasingly agoraphobic. He could only drive in a limited area of the city without being overwhelmed by his terror. He also found himself unable to enter a subway, elevator, or airplane. Thus, his professional and recreational activities were becoming increasingly constricted.
>
> Dennis also had extensive social deficits. He had had only one girlfriend in his life (for 3 weeks) and had never had a male friend for any extended period of time. To complete the picture, he hated his dreary and tedious job as a bank teller. His most extensive social contacts were with his eight younger siblings and his parents, all of whom lived in the area. However, even in his family, he felt lonely and depressed. His parents were initially described as "hard-working, generous, and strict people." Dennis' characterization of them changed quite dramatically over the course of the therapy.
>
> The first area of focus for Dennis and his therapist was upon his agoraphobia and anxiety. Over a series of six individual sessions, it was clarified that his anxieties had become much more severe during a period of 3 months prior to his initial visit with the therapist. That month, July, represented the second anniversary of the brutal rape and near-murder of his youngest sister, Nicole. During this crisis Dennis' parents had been completely unable to cope and to help Nicole deal with the trauma. Instead, they put great pressure on Dennis to deal with the police, lawyers, counselors, and so on. At the same time, they were harshly critical of and dissatisfied with the things he would do to be helpful. It became clear to Dennis after several individual therapy visits that although his agoraphobia was "real" and not contrived, its severity prevented him from being able to travel to his parents' home—a trip that would have required him to drive or take public transportation.
>
> Following the individual therapy, Dennis was treated as part of a time-limited 15-session psychotherapy group for young adults. It was felt that this would be beneficial regarding some of his social (developmental dysynchrony) problems.
>
> As it turned out, much of the focus in the group for Dennis was on his sister's rape. In talking about this trauma and his

parents' reactions to it and to him, Dennis became far clearer about his feelings. Many of the group members were incredulous that his parents would be so attacking and belittling, when it was they who had abrogated their responsibilities toward their daughter. For Dennis, who had always tried to be the "perfect son" and never would be overtly critical of his parents, these reactions were eye-opening. By the end of the group Dennis was doing much better symptomatically, and was beginning to express a sense of hurt and anger regarding his parents' harsh treatment of him.

At the completion of the group, all of the members were asked to take several months to consolidate their gains before getting more treatment. Dennis did this and recontacted the therapist after about 6 months. He was now traveling freely by car and train, but still was frightened of traveling by airplane. He had begun to be more direct with his parents and had had several confrontations with them about their dealings with him. Dennis had profited a great deal from his group experience and wished to be in another short-term young adult group. This time, he wanted to "learn more about relating better to women." In his second short-term interactive group, Dennis was able to begin to be more open and interactive with men and women. He could be a caring and supportive person and was therefore very positively regarded by the other members. Also while in this group, Dennis made plans for getting some additional training in a new line of work.

A little more than a year after this second group ended, Dennis was seen individually once again for about 4–5 months. This time the treatment focused upon the difficulties he had been having with his girlfriend, Bette. She was beginning to pressure Dennis to get engaged and to move in together. He did not wish to do so at the time. Bette was determined that the marriage would be "now or never." They therefore separated, got back together, and separated again. Dennis came in shortly after the second separation. During this course of treatment Dennis also discussed his continued problems with his parents. He wished to get closer to and perhaps marry Bette, but at the same time "could not imagine" being with someone and having a relationship "the way my parents have a relationship." Dennis' fears about getting too close to Bette were examined in light of his family origin.

Over the next several years, Dennis was not seen. He then

called at one point to say that he and Bette were back together and thinking seriously about marriage. He came in with Bette to talk about issues in their relationship. After about 3 months of couples treatment, Dennis and Bette decided to move in together.

A short while later, Bette received an offer for an outstanding job in another city. She and Dennis decided that they would get married the following spring and that he would join her at that point in that city. Dennis had done very well in his new field, and was reluctant to leave an outstanding job situation. However, his relationship with his parents had continued to deteriorate, and he was not altogether unhappy with the thought of moving. In the next course of treatment, which lasted about 6 months, Dennis tried to prepare himself to go to the new city and mourned his increasing alienation from his parents.

About 3 months after he had moved and married, Dennis called the therapist prior to coming back to town for a business trip. His fears of driving had returned, and he wished to deal with this problem "very quickly," since it had begun to impede his work (which required extensive travel). Dennis was seen in a two and one-half hour visit directed toward the hypnotic/behavioral treatment of his symptom. The stimuli for his panic were elicited. Once these were specified, a variety of posthypnotic suggestions were given to him. Also, a hypnotic relaxation tape was made for Dennis' home use. When Dennis called back later in the week, he was much calmer and was getting over his driving problem.

Dennis has continued to visit the therapist about once a year. Altogether, he has been seen for relatively few visits over a period of 10 years. He has developed an extremely successful career and marriage. At this point he has one child. There remains a major rift between him and his parents, which may be unchangeable. His psychotherapy has been very beneficial to him; it is not possible to determine whether he would have done better or worse in long-term, open-ended treatment. As it is, however, his outcome to date has been most favorable, and has been achieved in a highly cost-and-time-effective manner. (Budman & Gurman, 1988, pp. 292–294)

CONCLUSION

It is only the most arrogant of therapists who would assume that as clinicians we can definitively and prophylactically "cure" our patients. Therefore, the assumption should be made that patients can and do return for more therapy at different points in their lives and that returning in this way is unrelated to the quality of the original therapy or its benefits to the patient. We should view the therapeutic process as a lifelong process and view ourselves as change agents over the course of people's lives. It is most unlikely that until our deaths, the termination of therapy is ever absolute, or that our "cures" are ever definitive. Sophocles (ca. 429 B.C./1949) may have said it best when he wrote in *Oedipus the King:* "Look upon that last day always. Count no mortal happy till he has passed the final limit of his life secure from pain."

REFERENCES

Budman, S. H. & Gurman, A. S. (1988) *Theory and Practice of Brief Therapy.* New York: Guilford Press.

Davanloo, H. (1978a). *Basic Principles and Techniques in Short-Term Dynamic Psychotherapy.* New York: Spectrum.

Davanloo, H. (1978b). Evaluation criteria for selection of patients for short-term dynamic psychotherapy: A metapsychological approach. In H. Davanloo (Ed.), *Basic Principles and Techniques of Short-Term Dynamic Psychotherapy* (pp. 9–34). New York: Spectrum.

Davanloo, H. (1980). A method of short-term dynamic psychotherapy. In H. Davanloo (Ed.), *Short-Term Dynamic Psychotherapy* (pp. 43–71). New York: Jason Aronson.

Edelson, M. (1963). *The Termination of Intensive Psychotherapy.* Springfield, IL: Charles C Thomas.

Erikson, E. H. (1963). *Childhood and Society.* New York: Norton.

Firestein, S. K. (1978). *Termination in Psychoanalysis.* New York: International Universities Press.

Fox, E. F., Nelson, M. A., & Bolan, W. M. (1969). The termination process: A neglected dimension in social work. *Social Work, 14,* 53–63.

Gilligan, C. (1982). *In a Different Voice.* Cambridge, MA: Harvard University Press.

Goldensohn, S. S. (1977). Graduate evaluation of psychoanalytic training. *Journal of the American Academy of Psychoanalysis, 5,* 51–64.

Gould, R. L. (1978). *Transformations.* New York: Simon & Schuster.

Grunebaum, H. (1983). A study of therapists' choice of a therapist. *American Journal of Psychiatry, 140,* 1336–1339.

Hartlaub, G. H., Martin, G. L., & Rhine, M. W. (1986). Recontact with the analyst following termination: A survey of seventy-one cases. *Journal of the American Psychoanalytic Association, 34,* 895–910.

Henry, W. E., Sims, J. H., & Spray, S. L. (1971). *The Fifth Profession.* San Francisco: Jossey-Bass.

Jacobs, S., & Ribadeneira, D. (1988, August 21). Victim and accused—Same neighborhood, different worlds. *The Boston Globe,* pp. 1, 32.

Kovacs, M., Rush, A. J., Beck, A. J., & Hollon, S. (1981). Depressed outpatients treated with cognitive therapy or pharmacotherapy. *Archives of General Psychiatry, 38,* 33–39.

Kranish, P. (1988, August 21). Dan Quayle: A life of contrasts. *The Boston Globe,* pp. 1, 24.

Mann, J. (1973). *Time-Limited Psychotherapy.* Cambridge, MA: Harvard University Press.

Mann, J., & Goldman, R. (1982). *A Casebook in Time-Limited Psychotherapy.* New York: McGraw-Hill.

Marx, J. A., & Gelso, C. J. (1987). Termination of individual counseling in a university counseling center. *Journal of Counseling Psychology, 34,* 3–9.

Mikkelson, E. J., & Gutheil, T. G. (1979). Stages of termination: Uses of the death metaphor. *Psychiatric Quarterly, 51,* 15–27.

Patterson, V., Levene, H., & Breger, L. (1977). A one year follow-up study of two forms of brief psychotherapy. *American Journal of Psychotherapy, 31,* 76–82.

Roazen, P. (1971). *Freud and His Followers.* New York: New American Library.

Siddall, L. B., Haffey, N. A., & Feinman, J. A. (1988). Intermittent brief therapy in an HMO setting. *American Journal of Psychotherapy, 62,* 96–106.

Sifneos, P. (1972). *Short-Term Psychotherapy and Emotional Crisis.* Cambridge, MA: Harvard University Press.

Sophocles (1949). *Oedipus the King* (D. Greene, Trans.). In C. A. Robinson (Ed.), *Anthology of Greek Drama,* first series (pp. 55–100). New York: Holt, Rinehart & Winston. (Original work published ca. 429 B.C.)

Taube, C. A., Goldman, H. H., Burns, B. J., Kessler, L. G. (1988). High users of outpatient mental health services, I: Definition and characteristics. *American Journal of Psychiatry, 145,* 19–28.

Ticho, E. (1972). Termination of psychoanalysis: Treatment goals, life goals. *Psychoanalytic Quarterly, 41,* 315–333.

Vaillant, G. (1977). *Addaptation to Life.* Boston: Little, Brown.

Weissman, M. M., Klerman, G. L., Prusoff, B. A., Sholomskas, D., & Padian, N. (1981). Depressed outpatients: Results one year after treatment with drugs and/or interpersonal psychotherapy. *Archives of General Psychiatry, 36,* 51–55.

PART V

Techniques of Brief Therapy

CHAPTER 18

Seeding
Jeffrey K. Zeig

PREFACE

I will begin by asking you to participate in a learning experiment. Carefully study the following paired associates; e.g., "warm—cold." Later I will test you: If you are presented the word "warm," the correct answer, of course, will be "cold." Here is the list of five paired associates:

1) Red—Green
2) Baby—Cries
3) Light—Name°
4) ro bin—bird

5) Apple—Glasses
6) Picture—Frame
7) Ocean—*Moon*
8) Surf—Paper

INTRODUCTION

Milton Erickson discovered numerous creative methods to promote therapeutic change in his hypnotic/strategic approach to psychotherapy. Two of his most famous techniques were the interspersal method (Erickson, 1966) and the confusion technique (Erickson, 1964). These innovations were among his greatest technical con-

The author is grateful to Brent Geary and Giuseppe Ducci for reviewing this manuscript and for discussions that led to ideas incorporated into the final draft.

tributions to hypnosis and psychotherapy. Another technical advance was his use of "seeding." Although seeding was a common part of Erickson's hypnosis, psychotherapy, and teaching, this little-understood method has yet to be more fully elaborated. There are no papers or chapters on seeding. No references to the technique are found in Erickson's collected papers (Rossi, 1980) or in the books coauthored with Rossi (Erickson & Rossi, 1979, 1981; Erickson, Rossi, & Rossi, 1976).

The purpose of this chapter is to present and develop the concept of seeding as an integral part of the process of Ericksonian psychotherapy. Seeding did not originate there, however; its analogs are used in literature, social psychology, and experimental psychology. Suggestions and examples are provided so that practitioners from all clinical disciplines can include this technique in their therapeutic armamentarium.

WHAT IS SEEDING?

Seeding can be defined as activating an intended target by presenting an earlier hint. Subsequent responsive behavior is primed by alluding to a goal well in advance (Zeig, 1985a, 1988). By preceding the eventual presentation of a future intervention with a cue, the target (a directive, interpretation, hypnotic trance, etc.) becomes additionally energized. It then is more readily and effectively elicited. Seeding establishes a constructive set from which a future goal can be elicited.

Here is a simple example of seeding: If a therapist knows in advance that he will offer a hypnotized patient a suggestion to slow down his eating, the therapist might simply cue this idea by appreciably slowing down his rhythm of his own speech—perhaps even prior to the hypnotic induction. Also, the therapist can emphasize during an early phase of trance work that one of the real pleasures of hypnosis is the experience of *spontaneously slowing down rhythms of movement.* These seeded ideas will be subsequently developed. More complex examples of seeding will be presented later.

THE HISTORY OF SEEDING

Jay Haley first introduced the idea of seeding in 1973 in *Uncommon Therapy.* He pointed out that:

> In his hypnotic inductions, Erickson likes to "seed" or establish certain ideas and later build upon them. He will emphasize certain ideas in the beginning of the interchange, so that later

if he wants to achieve a certain response, he has already laid the groundwork for that response. Similarly, with families, Erickson will introduce or emphasize certain ideas at the information gathering stage. Later he can build upon those ideas and situations as appropriate. (p. 34)

Zeig (1985b) noted that seeding was one of Erickson's most important and least understood techniques and provided examples of how seeding could facilitate amnesia. Zeig (1985b) emphasized how Erickson was acutely attuned to the *process* of intervening: "He would not just present an intervention, but would seed the idea well in advance" (p. 333). This use of indirection could elicit a responsive set and build response potential by gradually energizing sufficient associations to the intended intervention so that it would be acted upon once it was offered. Therapy, as Erickson conceived it, was often a process of using indirect techniques to guide associations and build enough positive associations to "drive" constructive behavior (Zeig, 1985c). Zeig (1985b) added, "The importance of this type of priming cannot be overemphasized. Erickson would not only seed specific interventions, he also would seed his stories before presenting them" (p. 333). Additional references to seeding can be found in Zeig (1980, p. 11; 1985a, pp. 38–39; 1987, p. 401; 1988, pp. 366–367).

Steven J. Sherman (1988), a noted social psychologist, described the concept of *priming*, the term experimental psychologists use for "seeding." He indicated that "priming refers to the activation or change in accessibility of a concept by an earlier presentation of the same or closely-related concept" (p. 65). Sherman reviewed some of the experimental literature and concluded, "The extent of priming effects is remarkably comprehensive and general. Seeding concepts and ideas can alter what subjects later think about, how they interpret events and how they act. . . . The possible uses of priming techniques for altering clients' thoughts and behaviors have only begun to be appreciated. Understanding both the techniques for priming concepts, as well as the likely consequences of priming, should be of great value to psychotherapists" (pp. 66–67).

Seeding is a technique that often is effected on the level of preconscious associations. Via an earlier indirect presentation, an association to a target concept is elicited and strengthened. Accessibility of the seeded concept is thereby altered. When the previously implied idea, emotion, or behavior is presented more directly, there is enhanced activation. The arousal provided by seeding can be conscious and dramatic or subtle, working on a level of building preconscious associations. This diagramed timeline of therapy illustrates the process of seeding:

SEED   TARGET INTERVENTION

The initial "seed," which is analogous and/or alludes to the subsequent target intervention, is presented indirectly. During the time between seeding and intervention, the patient is stimulated into an unconscious search around the idea (or category of ideas) alluded to by the seeded concept. Thus, psychotherapy is woven into a process of moving in directed steps.

PREHYPNOTIC SUGGESTIONS

Seeding can be an integral part of the process of effective psychotherapy. In his initial formulation, Haley (1973) emphasized how therapeutic seeding of ideas ensures continuity: "Something new is introduced but always within a framework that connects it with what was previously done" (p. 34). In outlining the stages of Erickson's utilization approach, Zeig (1985a) described the process of psychotherapy, indicating that interventions should be properly timed and *seeded*. This methodology was described as SIFT—an acronym standing for (Seed and move in Small Steps), Intervene, and Follow-Through. Target Interventions should be seeded and "braided" together in small steps. "By the time Erickson's main intervention was presented, it was one small step in the chain of steps to which the patient had already agreed" (p. 38).

Sherman (1988) also emphasized that seeding was part of the therapeutic process. "Setting clients up for things to come implies that Erickson was always looking forward and planning ahead.... [He] predicated his current behaviors on the basis of what he knew was coming" (p. 67).

In the process of seeding, therapists naturally practice strategic therapy, a form described by Jay Haley (1973) as any therapy in which the therapist is actively involved in determining a specific outcome and individualizing an approach for each problem. By definition, whenever therapists seed an intervention, they are being strategic because they are planning ahead to increase effectiveness.

Seeding also can be conceived of in a slightly different way: It can be considered a *"prehypnotic suggestion."* (The concept of "prehypnotic suggestion" is used at the Erickson Foundation's training clinic, The Milton H. Erickson Center for Hypnosis and Psychotherapy, and was introduced by two of our clinicians, William Cabianca and Brent Geary.) Prehypnotic suggestions refer to the class of maneuvers that enhance the acceptance of subsequent directives and injunctions. Because the way in which directives are "packaged" often determines the extent to which the patient accepts them, as part of our training model at the Erickson Center, we teach the concept of "bonding the client with the intervention." Prehypnotic suggestions allow future directives to be placed in a "fertilized bed" where they can be better accepted. Prehypnotic techniques include using patient values; speaking the patient's experiential language; pacing (meeting the patient at the patient's frame of reference); moving in small strategic steps; the use of therapeutic drama; and the confusion technique (Erickson, 1964). Seeding is one of the most important types of prehypnotic suggestion.

It may seem that prehypnotic suggestions are not worth the effort, yet we have found that, paradoxically, the additional time devoted to prehypnotic maneuvers makes therapy briefer because these maneuvers decrease patient resistance. The words of a popular song echo this philosophy, "You get there faster by taking it slow."

Seeding is also worth the trouble because, by its very nature, it can elicit drama. When the target intervention is offered, there is increased drama—and arousal—as the previously seeded associations "coalesce." When patients suddenly realize the relevance of the indirectly seeded precursors, the target is energized.

This dynamic tension helps to make the therapy into a Significant Emotional Event (SEE). Building on the work of Massey (1979), Yapko (1985) has elaborated on how psychotherapy can be "viewed as the artificial or deliberate creation of a SEE in order to alter the patient's value system in a more adaptive direction" (p. 266). Building on this position, I would define psychotherapy as the creator of a SEE, the imperative of which is "By living this (dramatic) experience, therapeutic change will happen."

Drama is, of course, an important part of literature, and a concept similar to seeding is often a part of good literature.

SEEDING IN LITERATURE

In an earlier work (Zeig, 1985a), I pointed out that "Erickson challenged his students to develop an ability to predict behavior and to use predictions diagnostically as well as therapeutically" (p. 81). I remember the time Erickson (personal communication, 1974) instructed me to read the first page of the novel *Nightmare Alley*, by William Gresham (1946), and then tell him what was said on the last page. This was an attempt to help me understand how behavior is unconsciously patterned. I didn't understand the point of the exercise when I read the first page, but after I'd read the entire novel, I realized Gresham had seeded the ending in the beginning. This literary technique is called *foreshadowing* (cf. Zeig, 1988). Examples of foreshadowing can be found throughout literature, in theater, in movies, on television, and even in music, where a musical theme can be alluded to early in the piece and subsequently developed. I think it was the Russian playwright Chekhov who said, "If there is a gun on the mantle in the first act, somebody will get shot by the third act!"

Take, for example, the movie version of *Wizard of Oz*. In the initial scene, the martinet, Miss Gulch, tries to hurt Dorothy's dog, Toto. When she subsequently confiscates Toto, Dorothy calls her "You wicked old witch." And, in Oz, Miss Gulch is in fact depicted as a witch.

In the beginning of the movie, we also are introduced to the three farm hands, Auntie Em, and the Professor. The Bumbling Huck tells Dorothy, "You aren't using your head about Miss Gulch. Don't you have any brains? Your head isn't made of straw." Of course, in Dorothy's subsequent fantasy, Huck is portrayed as the straw man.

The reactive Zeke, who eventually is seen as the timid lion, says when we are first introduced to him, "[Miss Gulch] ain't nothing to be afraid of. Have a little courage, that's all. Walk up to her and spit in her eye." He is very bold when Miss Gulch is *not* there.

The emotional Hickory, who eventually becomes the cataleptic tin man, tells Dorothy, "Some day they will erect a statue to me."

The "Wizard of Oz" is initially presented as Professor Marvel, a good-hearted, but incompetent and grandiose huckster, a presentation that is structurally similar to the Wizard in Dorothy's fantasy.

Dorothy's fantasy also is "seeded" by Auntie Em, who explains, "Find a place where you won't get into trouble." This starts Dorothy thinking about her special place over the rainbow.

Obviously, the author and script writers went to considerable lengths to foreshadow their story. Their efforts were rewarded by enhanced dramatic and emotional impact.

An analog of foreshadowing has been extensively researched in experimental psychology, where it is known as *priming* or *cueing.* Next, I present a brief, but comprehensive, review of the experimental literature in priming.

PRIMING IN EXPERIMENTAL AND SOCIAL PSYCHOLOGY

In experimental psychology, priming is used to study models of memory and learning (Collins & Loftus, 1975; Ratcliff & McKoon, 1988; Richardson-Klavehn & Bjork, 1988) and social influence (e.g., Higgins, Rholes, & Jones, 1975). For example, priming is used to research a "spreading-activation" theory of memory. Collins and Loftus (1975) indicate that when a concept is primed, activation tags are spread by tracing an expanding set of links in the network of memory. When another concept is subsequently presented, it makes contact with one of the tags left earlier to make an intersection.

Priming is defined by Ratcliff and McKoon (1978) as the "facilitation of the response to one test item by a preceding item" (p. 403). It has been used to understand and advance theoretical formulations of learning and memory (Ratcliff & McKoon, 1988). Yet, none of the literature that I surveyed attempted to make a bridge and suggest practical applications of priming in psychotherapy or any other field.

However, research in priming has guided developments in several areas relevant to psychotherapy. For example, it led Schacter (1987) to differentiate between implicit and explicit memory. It is implicit memory that is directly related to seeding. According to Schacter (1987), "Implicit memory is revealed when previous experiences facilitate performance on a task that does not require conscious or intentional recollection of those experiences" (p. 501). Research on implicit memory has been concerned with the phenomenon of direct or repetitional priming, described by Schacter as "facilitation in the processing of a stimulus as a function of a recent encounter with the *same* stimulus" (p. 506, italics added).

Richardson-Klavehn and Bjork (1988) summarized three distinct types of priming described in the experimental psychology literature: *direct or repetition priming,* in which prior exposure to test stimuli generally increases accuracy and/or decreases latency of response; *associative or semantic priming,* where there is a decrease in time to make a decision about lexical matters (such as whether or not a string of letters forms a word) consequent upon presenting associatively or semantically related words prior to the test stimulus; and *indirect priming,* which is "any change in performance resulting from the presentation of information related in some way (associatively, semantically, graphemically, phonemically, or morphologically) to test stimuli" (p. 479).

Priming is a relatively new idea in experimental psychology, though the concept is not as modern as one may think. For example, prior to the turn of the century, Korsakoff (reported in Schacter, 1987) studied amnesia and described how brain-damaged patients retained "weak" memory traces that could unconsciously affect behavior. However, these traces were not "strong" enough to enter conscious memory.

In experimental psychology, priming has been used extensively to study multiple areas of human behavior. To develop the idea of priming and perhaps stimulate thinking among clinicians as to the applicability of this technique, I will provide examples of how priming is investigated experimentally in ten different areas of human functioning, and I will provide a brief summary of representative experiments:

1. *Speed of Lexical Decisions.* In an experiment conducted by Tweedy, Lapinski, and Schvaneveldt (1977, reported in Ratcliff & McKoon, 1981) regarding facilitated lexical decisions, a series of letters were presented to test subjects, and they were asked to indicate whether those letters formed an actual word. Decision time was faster when priming was used. For example, the word "nurse" was recognized as a word faster when it was preceded or primed by a semantically related word such as "doctor."

2. *Item Recognition.* An experiment was conducted in which the subject learned a list of paired associates. Subsequently, another list of individual words was presented and subjects were asked, "Was this word in the list of paired associates you just learned?" Results indicated that if a test word was immediately preceded by its paired associate, reaction time was faster than when it was preceded by some other word from the study list (McKoon & Ratcliff, 1978). Similarly, priming subjects with a particular word enhances their later ability to identify that word when it is exposed for short durations on a tachistocope, regardless of whether or not subjects recognize the word as one presented earlier (Jacoby & Dallas, 1981, reported in Druckman & Swets, 1988).

3. *Change In Later Interpretation.* Eich (1984) conducted a study in which critical pairs of words, such as "taxi—FARE" and "movie—REEL" were presented on an unattended auditory channel in such a way that subjects could not consciously recognize that such a word pair occurred in the experiment. Subsequently, it was demonstrated that

spelling of the homophone was biased toward a less frequent interpretation. For example, when FARE was primed, it was spelled more frequently in relationship to FAIR.

Having described those effects in the abstract, let me digress to enlist your participation in the previously mentioned learning experiment. Take a piece of paper and write your answer to four questions:

1. Name a Girl's na me.°
2. Name a laundry *Detergent.*
3. Name a bi rd.
4. Pick a number from "one to ten."

Now compare what you wrote down with the list of paired associates presented at the beginning of the chapter. Did you name the laundry detergent, the name, the bird, or the number that I had seeded? What were the seeded concepts? How were they seeded? All of the seeded ideas were not merely presented. They also were "marked out" with paraverbal technique. I will return to these ideas later.

4. *Accessibility of a Concept.* A study by Nisbett and Wilson (1977) was performed in which subjects were required to memorize a list of word pairs, some of which were meant to prime a later experiment. For example, subjects who memorized the word pair "Ocean—moon," were more likely to give the target "Tide" when later asked to "name a laundry detergent" than were subjects not previously exposed to the word pair. This semantic cueing doubled the frequency of the target response from 10% to 20%. Interestingly, when debriefed, subjects adamantly denied the fact that cueing influenced subsequent behavior. Actually, this effect seems to be derived from response to indirect suggestion rather than priming. However, it is included in the priming literature because it makes the target more accessible.

5. *Influenced Preference.* Nisbett and Wilson (1977) also described a study in which subjects were asked to listen to tone sequences. A dichotic listening procedure was used in which tones were presented to an unattended auditory channel while subjects tracked a human voice on the attended channel. Subsequently, subjects were presented with both familiar (previously heard) and new tone sequences. Subjects were unable to tell whether or not they previously heard the tone sequences. However, they showed distinct preferences for the tone stimuli to which they were previously exposed on the unattended channel. Typically, sequences that are familiar are judged as more preferable than novel tone sequences.

6. *Problem Solving.* An experiment was conducted in 1931 in which two cords were suspended from the ceiling of a room that contained numerous objects such as tools and extension cords. Subjects were asked to solve the problem of tying the two ends of the cords, even though the cords were far enough apart to make it impossible to simply hold one cord and reach the other. There were a number of easy solutions, such as tying the extension cord to one of the ceiling cords. After each solution, the subjects were told to find a different way to solve the problem. One of the possible solutions was more difficult and remained undiscovered by many subjects. When the subjects were stumped, the experimenter, who had been "aimlessly" wandering through the room, casually put one of the cords in motion. Within less than a minute, the subjects picked up a weighted object, tied it to one of the suspended cords, and used it as a pendulum to solve the problem. When the subjects were asked how they came to the idea of the pendulum, they denied that the experimenter's cue was a factor. (Reported in Nisbett & Wilson, 1977.)

7. *Attitude Formation.* Priming can be used to influence subsequent attitudes. An experiment was conducted in which there was minimal exposure to adjective-noun pairs (e.g., *old—tree*). When subjects were later queried about their attitude to the noun (e.g., Is a tree *big* or *old*?), they tended to choose the adjective that had been previously primed (reported in Schacter, 1987, p. 506).

8. *Impression Formation.* Higgins, Rholes, and Jones (1975) showed that covert exposure to terms that could be descriptive of personality (e.g., "reckless," "persistent") influenced subsequent judgment. Before reading a description of a person, subjects were unobtrusively presented positive or negative trait terms that were either applicable or inapplicable to that description. Prior exposure to applicable trait terms influenced subjects' evaluations of the described stimulus person. Interestingly, there was a greater delayed effect than immediate effect. Perhaps it took time for the primed concept to develop its full impact.

9. *Social Behavior.* Even social behavior can be influenced by priming. In a study by Wilson and Capitman (1982), male subjects read either a story describing a boy-meets-girl encounter or a control story. Those who read the boy-meets-girl story subsequently behaved in a friendlier manner toward a female confederate than those who read the control story. That is, they looked at the confederate more, smiled more, talked more, and leaned forward more. The study concluded that although primed scripts had a powerful effect on behavior, they seemed to be temporally limited: Even a short delay (four minutes) between reading the story and meeting the confederate led to a significantly lower amount of "friendly" behavior.

In another experiment on commitment, homeowners were asked to sign a petition about keeping California beautiful. Two weeks later, these same people were asked to place a large sign saying "Drive Carefully" on their front lawns. The degree of consent was higher for the group who signed the petition. It was as if these people had established a set of civic commitments. Once this set was seeded, it was more accessible (reported in Cialdini, 1985).

10. *Moral Thought.* In an experiment by La Rue and Olejnick (1980), subjects were primed with reasoning tasks. For example, one group was given verbal tasks that were considered to represent the stage of "formal operations": They were given series problems, such as "Phyllis is happier than Martha; Martha is happier than Ruth. Which of the three women is the saddest?" Another group was given tasks considered to represent "concrete operations": They were required to solve addition and subtraction problems. No specific cognitive exercises were provided for the control group. Subsequently, subjects completed an objective test of moral development, and a significant effect was found: Students primed with formal operational thinking scored significantly higher than either the control group or the group that was primed with concrete operations.

WHAT CAN WE LEARN FROM SOCIAL PSYCHOLOGY AND HOW CAN CLINICIANS USE PRIMING IN WAYS THAT DIFFER FROM EXPERIMENTAL METHODS?

Priming has been used to study models of memory and learning and theories of social influence. Experiments have shown that priming works, that it affects subsequent behavior and perception. Now therapists should search for ways to use priming/seeding to help solve human problems. In the clinical setting, indirect priming will be used more than repetition or semantic priming. However, direct seeding also can be used. For example, a therapist can have the patient visualize aspects of intended changes as a method of establishing a set of accessibility.

Clinical seeding will probably work better when the therapist thinks in terms of categories instead of qualities. An experiment by Collins and Loftus (1975) provides clarification. For example, "apple" was primed more effectively by the prior presentation of the concept "fruit" than it was by priming with the letter "A" or the adjective "red." Therefore, it might work better in treatment to seed with a category. For example, seeding a therapeutic task might be facilitated by earlier indirect discussions of "following through with homework in school" or "practicing for athletic competition" rather than a more direct reference to the word "task" as a prior cue.

Clinicians also can use seeding in ways that differ from experimental priming. The constraints of the experimental situation are such that most priming is done with presentation of neutral primes. This is necessary in order to determine the nature of the effect. In the clinical situation, standardization is not a genuine concern, and we can individualize our approach. The concepts that we seed can be idiosyncratic and derived from the patient's experiential language. For example, a patient described her pain as "sharp." In the next session, when I induced hypnosis, during the induction I seeded (and reframed) the concept of "sharp" by alluding to the idea of a *sharper perception* of certain sensations, such as warmth and comfort. Subsequent therapeutic posthypnotic suggestions were built on the idea of how sharper perceptions could be used to modify pain.

For added effect the seeded idea can be tailored to unique aspects of the individual patient. For example, with a quiet patient, one could seed using understatement. For a bold person, the seeded idea could be overemphasized by using a louder voice.

It is a great advantage that in the clinical situation there are many appropriate ways to "mark out" the seeded idea. Clinicians are not limited to one form of presentation, and we needn't use exposure that is completely unobtrusive or subliminal. We can incorporate into therapy the methods of overemphasis, underemphasis, distraction, stuttering, unusual gestures, and so on. In clinical situations, we want to attend to the process and not merely a static effect. Priming is not an isolated event, though in experimental situations it is often studied as such. Seeding happens as part of a rapidly ongoing interactional process. Clinicians are not readily able to study isolated and segmented aspects of behavior. In clinical situations, we can progressively build seeded ideas and even use multiple seeds, for different concepts, as indicated in the following diagrams:

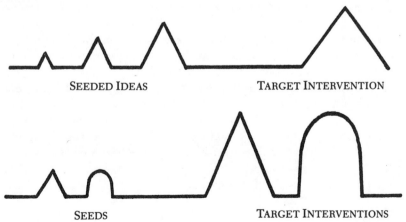

SEEDED IDEAS   TARGET INTERVENTION

SEEDS   TARGET INTERVENTIONS

Let's examine the four answers you provided to the "learning experiment." Did you write "Robin" as the name of the girl and/or the bird? Did you name "Tide" as the laundry detergent? Did you pick the number "five" or "eight"?

These target concepts were seeded on the first page of the chapter. The names were marked out with unnecessary punctuation, the addition of a space between the letters of the word, and the use of italics. These forms were used as a conditioned way to "bring back" the previously seeded associations. (The concept of "surf" also was used to seed the target idea of "Tide" because of its similarity.) The numbers "five" and "eight" could stand out because of the "jarring" inaccuracy on the first page of the chapter when I indicated I would present five pairs and actually offered eight.

In verbal presentation additional paraverbal markers could be used. In the oral presentation of this chapter at the actual Congress, I marked out the target concepts by using understatement, overstatement, an unusual gesture, and a cough. Results of this field experiment were extraordinary; most attendees responded with the previously seeded concepts.

Now then, how can seeding be used to provide maximum therapeutic effect? It is the thesis of this chapter that *any important therapeutic intervention is best presented when there has been prior seeding.* This is true whether a therapist wants to alter problematic behavior; offer an interpretation; change the hierarchy; prescribe medication; offer hypnotic suggestions; access motivation; seed ideas from one session to the next; or achieve a host of other therapeutic goals.

With those possibilities in mind, let us turn to Ericksonian therapy. Seeding was used extensively by Erickson, and it can be used in hypnosis and strategic therapy.

SEEDING IN ERICKSONIAN THERAPY

Seeding is a logical outgrowth of the "utilization" approach championed by Erickson. The utilization method alerts the practitioner to the fact that anything that patients bring with them—including the social system, personal values, resistances, and even symptoms—can be harnessed to serve the goals of the psychotherapy. A corollary to the utilization principle is that "whatever the patient does to be a patient, the therapist can do constructively to be a therapist" (cf. Zeig, 1987, p. 396). For example, if patients are confusing in order to be patients, therapists can use confusion constructively. If the patient speaks schizophrenic language to create distance, the therapist can use schizophrenic language to create closeness (Zeig, 1987).

This is also the case with seeding. Patients commonly seed ideas for their therapists; therefore, therapists can seed ideas for their patients—both as a matter of courtesy, and particularly in order to increase the effectiveness of future interventions.

How Do Patients Seed Things for Their Therapist?

Take, for example, the patient who is eventually going to cry. Even before the patient's eyes mist, there may be an unconscious gesture that hints at the behavior to follow. For instance, the patient might point an index finger toward one eye using an unusual gesture (Zeig, 1988). Actually, nonverbal behaviors frequently are precursors ("seeds") of subsequent verbal behavior. If a patient is going to talk about "going around in circles," his nonverbal behavior of making a circular gesture usually occurs in advance of the verbal report.

Patients commonly seed even complex constructs for the therapist. A patient who is concerned about an unwanted pregnancy may come into the consulting room and make a casual comment about children or look at a picture of children that happens to be present. Recently a patient began a session by asking about the "feminine" side of her husband. Only later, when she was able to admit a worry about the possibility that her son was gay, did I realize how nicely she had seeded something for me. A more alert therapist might have read her clues sooner. Milton Erickson would have; his literature is replete with examples of how he attended to "seeded" behavior by his patients. For example, Erickson said that if he were sitting in the back of a car, he could tell in advance in what direction the driver would eventually turn by observing that the driver made small preparatory movements in that direction (Zeig, 1985a).

Seeding can be used to improve therapeutic impact with both formal and informal hypnotherapy.

SEEDING IN STRATEGIC THERAPY

Strategic techniques are methods that Erickson referred to as "naturalistic," i.e., hypnotherapy without the necessity of inducing a formal trance. The therapist has a target intervention, which might be a symbolic assignment, a task, symptom prescription, reframing, or a pattern-disruption technique. Therapists can maximize patient cooperation by use of prehypnotic suggestions, such as motivating the patient, using the patient's experiential language, distraction methods, and confusion. The therapist also can use seeding.

Let us take the case of a weight-control patient. The therapist wants to elicit from the patient more control over eating, and he/she knows that direct suggestion is notoriously ineffective. Telling an obese patient, "Decrease your calorie intake" is tantamount to telling a depressed patient, "Cheer up!" However, the essential message to get across to an obese patient is obvious: "Eat less!"

Seeding can be beneficial in these cases. An example of seeding occurred in my work with a morbidly obese man who was losing weight slowly in response to hypnotic methods. During one particular session, he excitedly described going out with a woman who interested him. Let's call her Violet. Clearly, Violet would be another good reason for this man to lose weight. Remembering Erickson's predilection for utilization, I struck upon an intervention and I decided to seed it. I presented the intervention in six discrete steps, using drama along the way. The first step entailed seeding.

1. I engaged the man in a discussion about naming things. I talked with him about how people name their cars or their boats. I discussed how people even name tools (sic), such as guns.

2. I quickly distracted and discussed the concept of dissociation, which was unfamiliar to the patient. We discussed how dissociation is common when driving a car: One really doesn't think about the direction of movement of the steering wheel, the amount of pressure that is applied to the brakes, and so on. These actions "just happen."

3. Again, I distracted—this time to a discussion of how a baby is fed, and how it must seem like magic that the food "just appears" in his/her mouth.

4. I discussed the case of a couple in therapy. I explained that one of the difficulties with the wife was that she felt undervalued and unappreciated. One facet of the therapy was allowing her to recognize that her husband had only "rudimentary" ability to appreciate things. For example, on Sunday mornings her husband often played the flute. When she saw him playing the flute, she could recognize how appreciative he was of the music and the appreciative way in which he held the implement (sic) that he used to create music.

5. Quickly shifting from the previous discussion, I asked the patient if he could come up with a name for his hand. He was surprised by the request and balked at the task. Then I asked him what name I would want him to use for his hand. It delighted him that he could name his hand "Violet."

6. I took a pen and marked the letter "V" on his right hand. I held up my fingers, in the shape of a V, and explained to him that each time he sat down and ate, it could seem to him that a dissociated hand named Violet was holding the "tools" and "implements" that were feeding him.

(I also wanted to associate him to the idea that his hand could be used for victory rather than serving to victimize him, hence the "V" for victory sign.)

This intervention is only one part of a complex treatment plan through which the patient has lost significant amounts of weight. The emphasis is on creating a SEE and using seeding to increase dramatic impact. As I used seeding, I also proceeded in small steps, using a naturalistic form of posthypnotic suggestion.

Note that the main intervention was not merely presented: A fertilized bed was established and, subsequently, the main intervention was "implanted" within it. This maximized possibilities that things will take root (i.e., that constructive actions would be elected). Also, this type of intervention does not require the patient to be consciously aware. In fact, there is a form of amnesia that often occurs around such suggestions. (See Zeig, 1985b, for additional information on the therapeutic use of amnesia.)

Main interventions, such as the one above, frequently can be seeded. However, microscopic elements of the therapy also can be seeded.

SEEDING IN ERICKSONIAN HYPNOSIS

I do not think it is hyperbole to say Erickson used seeding almost every time he employed formal trance. There are many ways to effect seeding as part of hypnotherapy. One can seed macrodynamic elements such as the major intervention, and one can seed microdynamic elements— small goals that build toward the major intervention. Let's look at seeding microdynamic elements first:

A therapist could decide that an arm levitation would serve as a good microdynamic "convincer" technique, ratifying the development of a trance state. Prior to suggesting the levitation, the therapist could touch the patient's hand very lightly, thereby seeding the concept of lightness to be elaborated through subsequent suggestions (cf. Zeig, 1988).

It is one way among many. Erickson seeded macro- and microscopic interventions during hypnosis by the use of nonverbal techniques, extraverbal methods, symbols, key words, and so on. He seeded future ideas in the very first statement of his induction. He even seeded by using anecdotes. Let's take the idea of arm levitation and look at additional ideas for seeding that target behavior.

One could tell a series of stories, all of which have the theme of a dissociated movement of the arm. For example, the therapist could tell a story about raising one's hand in a classroom, about harvesting fruit from a tree, about scratching one's head, and so on. These stories cue the target behavior of arm levitation, which could subsequently be suggested either directly or indirectly.

One could use truisms, perhaps by pacing ongoing behavior (Erickson et al., 1976). For example, in eliciting arm levitation, the therapist could use a series of truisms, all of which seed by implication the target behavior of arm movement.

> Your hand is resting on your lap, now.
> You can still feel the texture of the cloth of your slacks.
> You can't notice all of the movement sensations in your hand.

As the therapist seeds future suggestions, he/she builds toward the desired goal in small steps. A central idea behind "seeding" is to build therapeutic momentum by starting slowly and then picking up steam en route to a goal.

A therapist can even seed reorientation from trance by using truisms. Again, this is a matter of courtesy as well as effectiveness. For example, prior to directing a patient, "Take one or two or three deep breaths, and reorient completely," I might offer a series of truisms:

> You can *alert* yourself to the capacity of your body to guide you.
> You can *reorient* yourself to the way in which your conscious mind can be more interested in things.
> You can *awaken* within yourself certain sensations in your mind and in your body.

Subsequently, the actual directive to reorient can be presented; e.g., "Take one, or two or three deep breaths . . . ."

There is an additional point regarding seeding in formal hypnotic induction. It is a global macrodynamic technique, not merely a microdynamic method of priming future goals. Structurally, seeding happens as part of the very process of induction. It can be maintained, therefore, that induction seeds therapy: In induction, one builds responsiveness, especially to indirect suggestions (Zeig, 1988). In therapy, one harnesses the responsiveness developed during induction. In this sense, responsive behavior is directly seeded in induction and built upon in the therapy immediately subsequent to the induction.

Erickson was ingenious in his use of seeding, and his techniques were often quite complex, as the following examples illustrate.

CASE EXAMPLE 1

The Milton H. Erickson Foundation distributes a videotape, *Symbolic Hypnotherapy*, in which Erickson conducts hypnosis with a woman name Lee during two consecutive sessions. Actually, these two sessions were part of more comprehensive work with Lee over a two-week period, in which she worked with Erickson on an almost daily basis. Video recordings of these sessions can be found in the Archives of The Milton H. Erickson Foundation.

During a particular session, Erickson unexpectedly asked Lee, "If there were a blond woman sitting across from you, you wouldn't have any reason to be jealous, would you?" Lee, nonplussed by Erickson's apparent non sequitur, shrugged her shoulders and replied, "No." Erickson then continued the trance work.

I saw a tape of Erickson working with Lee a week later. During these sessions, Erickson brought in a blond woman and did mutual hypnosis to demonstrate the mental mechanisms of a deep-trance subject (Zeig, 1988).

This type of foresight shows how much faith Erickson had in the process of seeding. He wanted to elicit a conciliatory mood in Lee, and he seeded it well in advance.

CASE EXAMPLE 2

In *A Teaching Seminar with Milton H. Erickson,* (Zeig, 1980, pp. 84–96), Erickson conducted hypnosis with a psychology student I called Sally. Sally arrived for the session 20 minutes late. Erickson immediately asked her to sit in a seat beside him and commented that she did not need to cross her legs, a symbolic intervention meant to take charge of the interaction and promote "openness." His next intervention was to ask her if she knew a particular nursery rhyme, "A Dillar, a Dollar, a Ten-O'Clock Scholar." This unexpected inquiry was an indirect comment on her lateness. (The next line of the rhyme is "What makes you come so soon? You used to come at 10 o'clock, but now you come at noon.")

The directive was not only an indirect confrontation; it also was seeding. After a few more technical suggestions, including the judicious use of confusion, Erickson began an induction in which he made an abortive attempt at arm levitation. Then he used a hypnotic phenomenon as a fixation device. What hypnotic phenomenon did he use? Age regression, of course! Regression was seeded earlier in the interaction. By introducing a nursey rhyme early in the contact with Sally, he primed responsiveness in the targeted direction.

It was as if Erickson decided during this initial interaction that he was going to conduct hypnosis with Sally. Then he decided that regression was going to be used. If he was going to use regression, he would seed it in advance with the rhyme. Note that this is a fail-safe technique. There is nothing to resist and little chance of failure. If the subject does not respond to the seeded concept, it will merely be treated as an irrelevancy.

CASE EXAMPLE 3

In his later years, Erickson induced hypnosis by eliciting his patient's absorption in a memory of learning to write the letters of the alphabet. This was called the early-learning-set induction (Erickson & Rossi, 1979). Often Erickson seeded hypnotic phenomena within the induction of hypnosis. As he talked about learning to write the letters of the alphabet, and related themes, he also alluded to dissociation, time distortion, hypermnesia, and amnesia. Subsequently, he built upon these previously cued concepts. (Hypnotic phenomena commonly are used as resources to solve a problem. For example, time distortion can be a tool with pain problems: It can be used to decrease the duration of discomfort and/or increase the duration of comfort. Amnesia also can be a resource. Patients proficient at amnesia can hypnotically forget aspects of their pain.)

As part of the patterns in the early-learning-set induction, Erickson might have indicated, "You have had much experience in forgetting things that would seem upon ordinary thinking to be unforgettable. For example, you are introduced to somebody and you reply, 'I am very pleased to meet you, Mr. Jones,' and two seconds later you are thinking to yourself, 'What on earth is his name?' You have forgotten just as fast as you hear it. In other words, you can do all the things I will ask of you" (Erickson, 1973, p. 68). The naïve patient did not realize consciously that Erickson was seeding amnesia and that he would build on this cue later in the therapy.

CASE EXAMPLE 4

A group of therapists came to Erickson specifically for therapy rather than merely to attend a teaching seminar. Each member of the group brought a specific problem to Erickson, and Erickson provided hypnotic and strategic treatment. The first hour of the first day concerned a man ("Jim") and his wife ("Jane"). Jim requested help from Erickson for a problem in reading and writing. He explained that he became tense when he read and wrote. Erickson asked Jim to what extent he (Erickson) had worked with Jim before. Jim had come to Erickson twice previously—once for help in stopping smoking and again for couples counseling just before he and Jane were married.

Erickson quickly established a hypnotic induction with Jim, who proved to be a quite responsive subject. The induction was the aforementioned early learning set. On superficial analysis, it was peculiar that Erickson chose this induction. Jim had been in to see Erickson twice before; certainly he heard this induction previously. However, a deeper analysis indicates that Erickson had an additional design. He didn't render the induction in his usual way. Although he started out talking about the difficulty children have in learning to write letters, he then diverged, saying ". . . the same thing with numbers. Is the 6 an upside down 9—a 9 an upside down 6? Which way do the legs of the number 3 go? Is the 3 a letter "m" standing on one end?"

This allusion has strong sexual connotations. In most cultures, the number 69 is considered sexually suggestive, and talking about three legs can lead a man to think about his own sexuality.

It is not immediately clear at first why Erickson made this sexual reference. Did he pick up on a sexual problem, or was sexuality itself a metaphor for potency? At any rate, Erickson seemed to alert Jim on a covert level (remember that there were other people present when Erickson was conducting the session) that Erickson would be working on intimate aspects of Jim's life, in addition to helping him with the presenting problem.

The idea that Erickson worked with a patient on multiple levels was well understood. Part of the unstated contract of being with Erickson was that he would work intimately with students, helping them to bring out undeveloped physiological and psychological potentials.

In subsequent hypnotic work, Erickson helped Jim establish the hypnotic phenomenon of dissociation. Jim easily accessed the state of being "a bodiless mind." This reference experience was precisely the state Jim needed to solve his problem of excess tension in reading and writing. Erickson used indirect techniques to help Jim develop the resource state of dissociation and use it as a way of solving the presenting problem. After working with Jim for about 30 minutes, Erickson turned to Jane and said, "And Jane, go way back, way way back. Maybe to the time that you had pigtails, and saw something funny. Slowly, gradually, way back then, you will open your eyes and tell me what funny thing you are seeing; open them very slowly."

This was a hypnotic suggestion for age regression; however, no induction of hypnosis was first offered. Jane had closed her eyes when Erickson was working with her husband. Erickson took that as an invitation to work with her hypnotically. However, it was difficult to imagine that Jane would respond to a complex age-regression instruction when no induction or intermediate steps were developed.

As it turned out, Jane did not respond fully to either the suggestion of opening her eyes slowly or experiencing age regression. She alluded to achieving a partial hypermnesia, a partial revivification of a memory, but not one that was relived. She explained that she saw herself as a child and noticed the pigtails and the part in her hair.

Erickson continued to work with Jane. He asked her to revivify a memory of how she looked as a child, to become absorbed in that memory and then relive it with Erickson. She was to close her eyes and have the regression. Again, he asked her to open her eyes slowly. For the second time, Jane did *not* open her eyes slowly and reported only a partial revivification.

Erickson tried for a third time with Jane. He asked her to have an age regression *and* the additional phenomenon of a negative hallucination. Again, she was asked to open her eyes slowly. Jane did not open her eyes slowly. Neither did she fully achieve the effects that Erickson tried to elicit. Erickson was not to be denied: He tried a fourth time, using mostly direct suggestions. Jane did not achieve the suggested age regression, but she did open her eyes gradually. At this point, Erickson stopped the hypnosis with Jane. He looked down to the floor and related the following story:

> One bitterly cold day in Wisconsin, on a Saturday, I was in high school. My father drove a condensary milk route. He gathered up the milk at various farms and took them to the condensary *nine* [my italics] miles away. He took the entire forenoon to pick up the milk and deliver it at the condensary.
>
> He had made arrangements in Juno to stable the horses and give them a chance to eat and rest while he made arrangements to eat his lunch in the warm kitchen of a resident of Juno.
>
> On that particular day, the weather was zero. I made the trip. I stabled the horses, fed and boarded them. I went into the house, knocked at the door, identified myself, went into the kitchen.

While I was taking off my overcoat and galoshes, a girl about *six* [my italics] years old came in, walked around me, eyed me carefully from head to foot—walked around me about *three* [my italics] times. Then she turned to her mother and said, "Who is that strange man?"

Up to that moment, I knew I was a farm boy, just a 16-year-old farm boy. When that girl asked her mother, "Who is that strange man?" I felt my boyhood slide off my shoulders, and the glorious weight of manhood descend upon my shoulders. Never again was I a boy. I felt like a man. I thought like a man. I behaved like a man. I *felt* [Erickson's emphasis] like a man.

That little statement by that little girl, "Who is this strange man?" produced a lasting effect. Because every little boy wants to become a man desperately. Every little boy wants to feel his manhood comfortably. He wants to know that he has the strength of a man to do this, to do *that* [Erickson's emphasis], and to feel good while doing it.

[To Jim] Close your eyes and really understand that story.

[To Jane] And every little girl wants to be a woman some time; so close your eyes and recall vividly all of your feelings, all of your surroundings when you are convinced that you are a woman. By some little thing no more important than a little girl saying something to a boy and changing him into a man immediately.

The woman was named Virginia; she had a sister named Della. I never knew the little girl's name.

I was standing in the kitchen facing East. Virginia, the girl's mother, was a few steps to my right. The little girl was in front of me about three feet away, asking her mother, "Who is this strange man?" Her hair was blonde. It was in *pigtails* [my italics].

This was a remarkable intervention. It was a sensitive story about a girl empowering a boy, and it was a bridge to create some good feelings between Jim and Jane. Note that Erickson did not merely tell the story to the couple. He prepared this anecdote carefully. He worked with Jim, who was quite responsive to hypnosis, and helped to elicit even more therapeutic responsiveness. He seeded the numbers "3, 6, and 9," and brought them back when he talked about the male protagonist in the story. In this way, Jim could use "his" numbers to identify more fully with the protagonist.

Erickson worked with Jane, who was characterized by more internal locus of control and was less responsive to hypnosis. Erickson gave her a task to accomplish, namely regression, which she refused. He also asked her to open her eyes slowly. On the fourth try, when Jane responded to the latter suggestion and opened her eyes slowly, it was as if Erickson assumed that some of her "resistance" had been discharged. She had said "No" to Erickson enough times; now she could be more open to his ideas.

Earlier, Erickson had unobtrusively seeded the idea of pigtails, an idea to which we knew he would return later. There was no reason to mention the concept of pigtails except seeding. The idea of pigtails would be brought back in the story and used to help Jane identify with the female protagonist. The numbers were Jim's cue, the pigtails were Jane's.

It was as if when Erickson began the induction with Jim, he had already decided that he would tell the anecdote about fully becoming a man. Then he seeded concepts, built responsiveness, and discharged resistance. Only when the bed was fertile did he "plant" the target story.

This is a superficial analysis of a quite complex therapy; there are many additional facets to this session. A more detailed analysis will be published in a future paper. However, it gives some indication of the extent to which Erickson would go to seed ideas.

OTHER USES OF SEEDING

Erickson also used seeding in his teaching; he did not only use seeding in his strategic therapy and formal hypnosis. For example, in *A Teaching Seminar with Milton H. Erickson* (Zeig, 1980), Erickson lectures to students about human sexual development. He initiates the didactic material with a vignette about his father planting oats in which he makes a veiled reference to sex by indicating that some people plant "wild oats" earlier than others. Only after seeding his intended topic, does he present the lecture about sexuality.

It is not surprising that Erickson used seeding within his lectures. There was structural similarity between his hypnosis, therapy, and teaching because Erickson's intent was similar when he was inducing trance, promoting therapy, or lecturing, namely, his goal was to dramatically elicit inherent strengths (Zeig, 1985a).

I also have used analogs of seeding personally. When I write a paper, I seed a target concept in my mind that is the intended topic of the paper. Because of the effect of the seed, I more easily notice usable examples of the topic in my work and daily life. Also, it seems to me that the seeding is effective in helping me to generate creative ideas about the subject of my paper.

PROVISO

Seeding alerts therapists to the potential effects of innuendo at shaping a patient's construction of reality and subsequent behavior. Therefore, therapists should be careful about what they present to clients and how they offer it. Erickson often admonished his students that patients—especially those in hypnosis—were responsive to minimal cues from their therapists. Therefore, Erickson was quite deliberate about his choice of words and behavior and the potential implications of each. The point is that seeding can have both positive and negative effects. For example, after a widely publicized suicide, commercial airline crashes increased by 1,000 percent; automobile fatalities increased and suicide rates rose for months (Reported in Cialdini, 1985). One explanation for this effect is that via priming the concept of suicide (be it deliberate, accidental, and/or accidentally on purpose) becomes more accessible.

CONCLUSIONS

It is recommended that therapists of every therapeutic orientation augment their approach by seeding. This is true for psychoanalytic interpretations or confrontations or for the use of psychotropic medicine. Any target subsequent intervention can be enhanced by prior seeding.

This requires the therapist to develop a strategic mentality. The therapist needs to think, "What do I want to elicit? What do I want to communicate?" Such a strategic orientation is certain to make therapy more effective and briefer.

POSTSCRIPT

In *The Wizard of Oz,* Dorothy is advised to find the Wizard by following the yellow brick road. She looks up at her mentor imploringly and asks, "But how do I start?" The reply is quickly forthcoming, "It's always best to start at the beginning." Remember that the next time you greet your patient at the door.

REFERENCES

Cialdini, R. B. (1985). *Influence: Science and Practice.* Illinois: Scott, Foresman and Company.

Collins, A. M., & Loftus, E. F. (1975). A spreading-activation theory of semantic processing. *Psychological Review, 83*(6), 407–428.

Druckman, D., & Swets, J A. (Eds.) (1988). *Enhancing Human Performance.* Washington, DC: National Academy Press.

Eich, E. (1984). Memory for unattended events: Remembering with and without awareness. *Memory & Cognition, 12*(2), 105–111.

Erickson, M. H. (1964). The confusion technique in hypnosis. *American Journal of Clinical Hypnosis, 6,* 183–207.

Erickson, M. H. (1966). The interspersal hypnotic technique for symptom correction and pain control. *American Journal of Clinical Hypnosis, 8,* 198–209.

Erickson, M. H. (1973). An induction technique. In *A Syllabus on Hypnosis and a Handbook of Therapeutic Suggestions* (Special issue) (pp. 68–69). Des Plaines, IL: American Society of Clinical Hypnosis.

Erickson, M. H., & Rossi, E. L. (1979). *Hypnotherapy, Exploratory Casebook.* New York: Irvington.

Erickson, M. H. & Rossi, E. L. (1981). *Experiencing Hypnosis: Therapeutic Approaches to Altered States.* New York: Irvington.

Erickson, M. H., Rossi, E. L., & Rossi, S. I. (1976). *Hypnotic Realities.* New York: Irvington.

Gresham, W. L. (1946). *Nightmare Alley.* New York: Rinehart.

Haley, J. (1973). *Uncommon Therapy: The Psychiatric Techniques of Milton H. Erickson, M.D.* New York: Norton.

Higgins, E. T., Rholes, W. S., & Jones, C. R. (1975). Category accessibility and impression formation. *Journal of Experimental Social Psychology, 13,* 141–154.

La Rue, A., & Olejnick, A. B. (1980). Cognitive "priming" of principled moral thought. *Personality and Social Psychology Bulletin, 6*(3), 413–416.

Massey, M. (1979). *The People Puzzle: Understanding Yourself and Others.* Reston, VA: Reston Publishing.

Nisbett, R. E., & Wilson, Timothy De Camp (1977). Telling more than we can know: Verbal reports on mental processes. *Psychological Review, 84*(3), 231–259.

Ratcliff, R., & McKoon, G. (1978). Priming in item recognition: Evidence for the prepositional structure of sentences. *Journal of Verbal Learning and Verbal Behavior, 17,* 403-417.

Ratcliff, R., & McKoon, G. (1981). Automatic and strategic priming in recognition. *Journal of Verbal Learning and Verbal Behavior, 20,* 204–215.

Ratcliff, R., & McKoon, G. (1988). A retrieval theory of priming in memory. *Psychological Review, 95*(3), 385–408.

Richardson-Klavehn, A., & Bjork, R. A. (1988). Measures of memory. *Annual Reviews of Psychology, 39,* 475–543.

Rossi, E. L. (Ed.) (1980). *The Collected Papers of Milton H. Erickson, M.D., Vol. I–IV.* New York: Irvington.

Schacter, D. L. (1987). Implicit memory: History and current status. *Journal of Experimental Psychology: Learning, Memory, and Cognition, 13*(3), 501–518.

Sherman, S. J. (1988). Ericksonian psychotherapy and social psychology. In Jeffrey K. Zeig & Stephen R. Lankton (Eds.), *Developing Ericksonian Therapy: State of the Art* (pp. 59–90). New York: Brunner/Mazel.

Wilson, T. D., & Capitman, J. A. (1982). Effects of script availability and social behavior. *Personality and Social Psychology Bulletin, 8,* 11–20.

Yapko, M. D. (1985). The Erickson hook: Values in Ericksonian approaches. In Jeffrey K. Zeig (Ed.), *Ericksonian Psychotherapy, Vol. I, Structures* (pp. 266–281). New York: Brunner/Mazel.

Zeig, J. K. (Ed.) (1980). *A Teaching Seminar with Milton H. Erickson.* New York: Brunner/Mazel.

Zeig, J. K. (1985a). *Experiencing Erickson. An Introduction to His Work.* New York: Brunner/Mazel.

Zeig, J. K. (1985b). The clinical use of amnesia: Ericksonian methods. In Jeffrey K. Zeig (Ed.), *Ericksonian Psychotherapy, Vol. I, Structures* (pp. 317–337). New York: Brunner/Mazel.

Zeig, J. K. (1985c). Ethical issues in hypnosis: Informal consent and training standards. In Jeffrey K. Zeig (Ed.), *Ericksonian Psychotherapy, Vol. I, Structures* (pp. 459–473). New York: Brunner/Mazel.

Zeig, J. K. (1987). Therapeutic patterns of Ericksonian influence communication. In Jeffrey K. Zeig (Ed.), *Evolution of Psychotherapy* (pp. 392–406). New York: Brunner/Mazel.

Zeig, J. K. (1988). An Ericksonian phenomenological approach to therapeutic hypnotic induction and symptom utilization. In Jeffrey K. Zeig and Stephen R. Lankton (Eds.), *Developing Ericksonian Therapy: State of the Art* (pp. 353–375). New York: Brunner/Mazel.

CHAPTER 19

Metaphor: A Myth with a Method
Kay F. Thompson

We want the creative faculty to imagine that which we know.
—Shelley, *A Defense of Poetry*

Imagination lets us make the experience of trance real. And in doing so, therapy is enhanced through creative metaphor. Talking a myth is a method to let the truth be learned by appearing to not teach.

The use of trance in therapy, and metaphor as an accelerator of trance, facilitates brief therapy (and for that matter, any kind of therapy). But using metaphor is not as simple as it may sound. It requires acknowledging the many factors influencing words and mandates an ability to weave or create a myth appropriate for the individual patient's needs at the specific moment in time and therapy in which the intervention occurs. When this is done successfully, the myth assumes a reality for that individual at that point in time and makes that reality available to facilitate both trance and therapy. Understanding how metaphor facilitates therapy requires a distinction between theories of therapy and the specific techniques employed to expedite the chosen method of therapy.

Theories explain behavior within a specific context, but methods or facilitators can be seen as multiple paths to one end—the (normal) functioning of the individual involved. Thus, facilitators can be used across therapeutic approaches. In general, therapists now agree that even radically different theories of therapy share methods that cross boundaries between theoretical disciplines. For example, metaphor and myth, like hypnosis, can be used in multiple approaches. Fortunately, such mixing is far more acceptable today than it was when Milton Erickson began his work, when the strictures of the field practically required one to declare oneself a specific type of therapist and to use the approach and methods sanctioned by that approach. Erickson's method was unusual for that period in that he combined and utilized all types of psychotherapeutic and hypnotic interventions in his therapy; he didn't feel bound by rules to stay within any one parameter. Perhaps that was one reason people had so much trouble with his therapy—they wanted to make it a theory. For Erickson, however, hypnosis was an adjunct to any type of therapy that was appropriate for the patient; it was not intended as a theory in and of itself.

Erickson's approach also was unorthodox in that he did not restrict himself to one type of therapy any more than he restricted himself to one way of approaching a problem. He always looked for a novel way for the individual to recognize his own capabilities for change, and he would do almost anything to effectuate that change. His goal was to help the patient; any approach, theory, or therapy that achieved that goal was both permissible and welcome. This use of multiple approaches and theories, novel and misunderstood during much of Erickson's life, is now more clearly understood and accepted.

Because of this relaxing of the strict "one-theory" approach to treatment, Erickson's use of metaphor became an issue to practitioners newly interested in broadening their own foundation of knowledge about the use and possible impact of other theories and therapies.

Myth, and the multiple metaphors through which it is developed, facilitates trance, and thus therapy, by combining the layers of meaning inherent in words and metaphors with a story that allows the message to be a significant communication for the patient at the level at which it is needed. Ironically, the use of metaphor increases the power of the therapist by allowing him or her to be less precise in assigning meaning to the myth and thus freeing the patient to choose the most useful interpretation. The ambiguity and possibility of choice allow the patient to relate to what is needed by him rather than struggling to accept or reject an imposed framework.

Because of their pliability, myth and metaphor can help circumvent a problem endemic to therapeutic situations—the tendency of both therapist and patient to concentrate on building frameworks rather than addressing specific problems. Frameworks tempt and trap both therapists and patients. The therapist tends toward framework building in order to use the bits and pieces garnered from the patient to build a whole picture and decipher its meaning. In doing so, conversely he often will be tempted to force the pieces into a framework, either preconceived or newly constructed for the occasion, and thus impose a preconceived structure on the problem.

The client has a similar and closely related tendency. Because he is entering a new situation, he may be inclined to listen more than speak. He may thus accept the therapist's framework or combine his own bits and pieces with those supplied by the therapist to build a framework of his own. This seems to be natural and necessary, but concentrating on the framework may interfere with listening and hearing because one may be listening for building blocks rather than dealing with the problem at hand. As a result, the client may latch onto an offered framework as a convenient, though not necessarily helpful, answer. When this occurs, neither the therapist nor the patient is well served. Instead each should be assembling a new framework, or at least keeping an open mind for modifications in the existing framework.

The practitioner is under an especially strong obligation to avoid ready-made frameworks because he may be seen as the authority figure. Additionally, he may have less to gain from a new framework and thus have less incentive for the hard work of constructing one. In contrast, the client has more to both gain and lose because he is entering a novel situation. He probably sees his current position as a unique and poorly understood problem that requires definition and resolution. The practitioner may look at the same situation and see a problem he has encountered in many previous forms. The client then has more personal motivation and a stronger need to understand the situation as unique rather than common. The therapist, in contrast, must recognize the common elements of a situation clearly enough to choose an appropriate approach and simultaneously allow the client to see the individual aspects of the problem while avoiding the tendency to fit the situation into a preconceived mold. Learning to teach the clients to sense changes in belief and behavior that will improve their functioning need not stress the common structure of the problem.

It may help if therapists can think of themselves as automobile mechanics and clients as cars brought in for repairs. Mechanics listen to the car and then fine-tune it, not taking anything away, but working with and modifying what is there—perhaps using different lubricants for different speeds, reducing the discords, or removing the grating of metal on metal. Accepting this analogy forces therapists to take only what is there and stimulate it to greater potential—smoother running, longer life expectancy—rather than trying to create a new and better model. We adjust the existing model, helping it to run at its full potential. We

also can teach the owner how to remove rust and put in softer up-
holstery. Sometimes we must even teach the owner of the car how to
drive.

But with all of our maintenance, it is still the client who ultimately will
drive the car and determine the desired destination. The mechanic may
make alternate routes available and be present to offer directions and
maps, to suggest a change of route when necessary, and to maintain and
repair the equipment. He does not, however, choose the destination or
drive the car, although he may go along for the ride.

As with all trips, some will be short and others quite long, but always it
is the destination that must be kept in mind. A trip may cover a lot of
territory (or therapy) in a brief, but concentrated time. As I use the term
"brief," I rely on both senses of the word: first, the reference to a shortened or curtailed period of time, and second, the sense of being concise
and involving only the most pertinent facts and line of argument, as in a
brief presented in a court of law.

Brief is a matter of perspective and depends on the people, the problem, the circumstances, the readiness, and the need. It also depends on
the therapist, who must be willing to be concise and incisive but also
compassionate and respectful. In addition, brevity can be expedited by
the use of metaphor, which facilitates the speed with which the patient
can respond. I categorize "brief" as three to six appointments, but
generally these appointments are longer than an hour, and so some people might count them as more than one session. Although the period of
treatment is brief, I expect the results to endure.

Most of the patients I typically see are referred principally for physical pain control. In the process of teaching them hypnosis and subsequent pain control, many nonphysical contributing factors become evident, and the teaching varies widely regarding the apparently common
factor of pain. If I believed the patient's initial characterization of the
problem, dealing with the pain itself would be all I would try to do. But
then neither trance nor therapy would be effective, and hypnosis probably would be blamed. Actually, the failure would arise from the fact that
I was not dealing with the entire problem of which the pain is a symptom
rather than a cause.

To achieve a therapeutic relationship with the kinds of innovative interventions I intend, I must first initiate trust between me and the
patient. After an initial interview with the individual, we investigate the
involvement of tension in the pain, and the patient institutes some self-
control to reduce tension. At this point, the patient must begin to perceive the relationship between the tension and the pain, but he must
also, and perhaps more important, accept my belief that he can change

and control *both* pain and tension. This positive view of potential must permeate the positions the therapist proposes.

This positive view is communicated verbally and nonverbally. Language involves more than the way we communicate IN words. We have sign language, body language, tone of language, touch, nonverbal communication. Trust, rapport, and expectancy are the ingredients on which trance learning is based, and they are much easier to communicate if one relies on more than just the spoken word. At the same time, the spoken word has great power and flexibility, and its multiple dimensions should be understood and utilized.

Words, like metaphors, are more than simple referents to objects, ideas, or relationships. For each of us, any word, or group of words, carries a web of associations based on the contexts in which the words were learned. As children, we listened to and tried to make sense of the sound we heard because somehow we knew the people speaking the words understood something we did not yet know. Initially, language develops AFTER understanding and becomes a way of labeling, referring to, and accessing experience. How did we learn to talk? By practice. We knew what the words MEANT long before we knew what the words WERE, or how to say them. We could, for example, crawl on the floor long before we knew it was named "floor" or that the motion we enjoyed was called crawling. In a similar way, we knew the warmth and comfort of our mother's arms long before we knew the word "love." Only gradually did the connection between THINGS and WORDS become significant. Our curiosity to be admitted to that world of understanding through spoken communication drove us to learn the words for the images they inspire. And for that reason, communication through word play comes even before storytelling. It sets the stage, the background in which the performance will take place. Tapping into the ENDLESS energy and curiosity for learning that we had as children, but which becomes submerged or stifled as we grow, is an unending well of potential to be well.

How does word play serve as an instrument of therapy? One of the first things it does is provide the opportunity for safely exploring the relationship between the therapist and the client. It affords a means of learning to communicate trust and individual differences to the patient, the opportunity to test, to play, to discover that creative behavior is encouraged in this environment even though it may be absent elsewhere. All of these strengthen the desired change in learning set. Then, too, looking at "words" differently lets one look at the possible difference in meanings, for which the words are only symbols.

The ambiguity and possibilities for personal interpretation make words a difficult medium to control, but perhaps control is not necessary to the degree one might think. Perhaps, for example, what may appear to be the "wrong" word, metaphor, or story for a given situation may be accepted by the client, using his own definition and referents, as entirely proper and helpful. There is always the danger, of course, of the reverse happening, and we must guard against the devastating potential of words that can be interpreted as being negative.

To some extent, we have an ally in this battle: There is the tendency—recognizable in the child's chant "Sticks and stones may break my bones, but words will never harm me"—for the individual to assume an armor of self-protection. A further ally is the tendency of the individual in trance to recapture the child's ability to say the truth as it is perceived even when this truth is ignored by adults who dismiss it rather than listening to what is being said. In trance, both the protectionistic and truth-telling tendencies are enhanced, and the therapist must learn to tolerate and build on both. In particular, the therapist must resist the common adult tendency to dismiss bold truths which may be hurtful or just too plainly stated to feel comfortable.

As therapists, we must, in effect, travel along part of the journey we expect our patients to take and learn to recapture the magic and truth of words. As children we, like our patients, learned that we had to understand our strong and often negative feelings and harness them. It was permissible to HAVE them until we gave them a word; then we had to learn not to demonstrate them. And so we learned to suppress and repress the words, and eventually even the feelings that went with them. And we are still so afraid of the feelings that we cannot address them or deal with the conflict that this creates inside. Our deepest longings and needs and conflicts are so powerful that we respond to them with childlike emotions. To deal with those emotions requires using words that have true meaning, possibly many meanings. And so we must be careful in our choices, because words trigger emotions by way of memories.

Word play and metaphor can trigger both emotions and memories while avoiding the overly rigid one-on-one correspondence that strengthens negative responses. Riddles, nursery rhymes, puzzles, tongue twisters, charades, all can add to the intrigue of learning sets. Tapping into these learning sets by using familiar themes can lead to unconscious solving of other puzzles, using the puzzles presented at that time to do so. Another important type of word play that can be utilized with trance learning is "fill in the blanks" perpetuated at a later age when we take tests in school. We also can scramble letters to make words or develop codes, and that can be important in the secrecy of trance, as a means of keeping unconscious thoughts from the therapist or from ourselves. In all these forms, word play can teach through demonstrating that one word can have more than one meaning. This lets us open our minds to a whole new word world of possible changes. Then, too, we learn that feelings can have more than one description attached to them. Anxiety, for example, may be seen as anticipation, and this type of relatively simple redefinition can sometimes change attitudes and subsequent behavior.

Words are a playful way to build in the therapist the kind of trust that we had in adults when we were children. Words also are useful ploys to distract the client from the fact that the words are also the induction and the utilization. "Pay close attention to the words used" means pay close attention to the symbolism in the words. We want the patient to do this subconsciously, but we must attend to the multiple possibilities on a more conscious level. We can, for example, work with words that appeal by sound, words that sound alike, words that repeat parts of the whole and so demand attention and descrimination, words that distinguish parts of a pattern, words that play games and thereby confuse the meanings and allow the "right" meanings to emerge, because words evoke constellations of meaning and experience. Those who study language use terms such as "antonyms" and "homonyms" for words that stimulate childlike curiosity and playfulness in the patient.

But word play does not end when we move beyond induction to another phase—storytelling or metaphor. We must continue to be alert to signals in words, and to listen for and provide multilevel messages. We incorporate the initial elements of word play to continue preparation for, and involvement in, change. Words are NOT just words; they are symbols for experience, and we must be respectful of that experienced message.

We can combine types of word play by using words that carry a meaningful message for the client's experience, such as: Inhibitions are tied up in "nots." And often we make many things naughty, because they are knotty, and not just plain "nots." And we do not know about the things we "no" until it is too late to go back and pick up the pieces of the ribbon that got tied into the knots we did not know how to unknot. But you can pick at even the most painful knot and retie it into a beautiful bow that will bow to the need to know that it was once a knot, but know it is not a knot now.

As we move from words to metaphors, we take along the capacity for hearing the meaning in the words. Why metaphors? Because they tap or access both childhood behaviors for learning and also memory skills from the period before the memories have been imprinted with negative associations. In addition, metaphors contain encapsulated myths themselves and prepare the way for more complex and fascinating stories and myths.

What are myths, anyway? They are stories rooted in the most ancient beliefs of people, stories that tell of high ideals and healing truths. Myths hold an almost sacred place in the cultural evolution of mankind. They capture cultural beliefs in a communication of understanding that holds wondrous solutions. They are evolutions in themselves and thus can involve an individual in self-evolution.

Fairy tales are closely related to myths and might be considered the myths of childhood used to teach social relationships, yearnings, and values. The listening child does not seek a reason or a motivation for the story but just listens openly, with curiosity and wonder. The child does not wonder why a particular story was the one chosen at a given moment, or whether or not it has an application or a moral. The child simply listens attentively from the beginning through to the nice, neat, satisfying ending. Going back to the ideals of childhood, and the attitudes of learning instilled then, and still in us, is a most effective way to teach change by accessing long-stifled traits of curiosity, WONDER, openness, and trust and thus expand the facts of a given experience. When such childlike listening can be recaptured through trance and metaphor, magical transformations can occur. A paragraph from a client illustrates:

> In each of us lies sleeping beauty, wasted potential, dying dreams. We sleep and live in dormant twilight never knowing what it means to live, to love the bits of heaven that we can unearth deep in our hearts; not recognizing that our salvation is ever present in those parts we have disowned, denied, forgotten. The thorns of fear thwart feint attempt. The prince is courage, the kiss believing and then with these our life begins.

Since a metaphor is initially a myth, it is practically possible to propose a parable particularly appropriate for the parts of the person you perceive as needing to listen. We must meet the mind of the patient to determine motivation and then incorporate the method for accessing the skills necessary for change. It isn't necessary, however, to develop a new story for every client. Probably it would be impossible to do so. But one should develop a repertoire of stories, which can be applied to many situations, and then vary the story to fit the idiosyncrasies of each situation. Developing of metaphors thus requires careful listening to the individual.

Erickson was fond of talking about the experiential life of his patients. He was also extremely knowledgeable in his ability to "go to where the patient is." His broad-based experience is not easy to acquire, and most practitioners do not anticipate having to overcome the personal health problems that gave Erickson so much knowledge about body movement, but we do need a variety of experiences so that we can relate as closely as possible to the situation of the patient. The skill of understanding and telling stories is convenient, but one must be able to listen to the story one tells in relation to the client. One must also be able to shift directions smoothly when the client takes a different tack. Flexible modification is mandatory.

The fundamental idea behind the use of metaphor is to allow the client to recognize that he has options. Stories can be remembrances, projections, pure fantasy. They can be based on things the individual likes or doesn't like, or they can be merely a simple statement. They can affect physiological and psychological domains; they can affect health and emotion and well-being. They can be used as induction techniques and as fundamental components of therapy.

It is useful to bear in mind that induction is a metaphor and that an indirect induction technique provides the opportunity for the metaphor to be effective on multiple levels. If one doesn't need to know one is in trance, then the story can appeal to both the conscious mind, which hears only a story, and the unconscious mind, which hears meaning at a deeper level. The involvement thus can be a symbol of magic for the client who experiences something that he did not control or make happen. Participating in this process can sometimes allow the patient to submit problems that he has been unable to control to the application of that same magic. Something *can* happen: And that recognition alone can make the difference.

What are some examples of my brief short and brief long metaphors? One of my favorite devices is very brief and goes by the name of "Yes, but. . ." This simple technique of redefinition allows the client to acknowledge the surface facts of a particular experience, but also to recognize how to alter those facts with new information that was not originally available (or not assimilable). We are, in effect, asking the client to expand old memories with new information, and assume a new way of looking at an old concept to elicit changes in thoughts, language, and eventually behavior.

Metaphors need not be long and involved. They can be a word or phrase that taps into the memory bank of the mind, just as a single tap into a maple tree brings forth a slow, steady drip of liquid. But then it is necessary for the liquid to be boiled slowly, to distill it down to the essence of what we know as maple syrup. Thoughts are like that, too. And frequently we forget that we do not get good maple syrup production if we have not had a cold and snowy winter. Forgetting things brings other things closer in the past. Forgetting the hard winter makes it easier to remember the wonder of maple syrup.

The introduction of storytelling can also be a means of distracting the patient from the experience of pain. To tap into the child part of each of us, using words and meanings to play with, is a convenient way of accessing basic understandings. Children like to learn through puzzles. A child can be curious, can be wondrous about the way of things. A child can look at things with newness and excitement for the learning involved. A child can thrill about arriving at some new bit of information and wonder how it will fit with other bits of information. A child can laugh and can play, or be hurt and cry, but in both cases still be learning. So using myth and metaphor to look at things from different dissociated perspectives can let one see other options, other ways of looking.

To be effective, however, the story must be matched to the individual. An individual who can accept the idea that mountainous stress contributes to his pain, for example, also may accept hearing that learning to climb both literal and figurative mountains requires necessary safeguards for such a risky but exhilarating task: a knowledge of the territory; sufficient warm clothing for changes in the weather; food for the day's climb and extra food in case of inclement weather; ropes for tricky climbing areas; hammers, pitons, and carabiners for help in difficult pitches; and being roped to someone who can serve as a guide, someone who knows the route and the weather, and the best way to conquer that mountain and achieve the summit. All of the word images are accurate for literal mountain climbing but can easily by expanded to refer to ANY mountain, a physical or a psychological one.

And yet, another individual may not perceive the undercurrents of life as contributing to the pain experience. In this case, it may suffice to simply tell a relaxing tale for the patient to listen to when practicing the relaxation exercises connected with learning pain control. The method in this metaphor is to offer the unconscious the knowledge it needs without the conscious need to understand. In this flow of conversation, it might be pleasant to go sailing on a body of water that offers differing currents, tides, and winds, and permits the master of the sailing vessel to learn to navigate by practicing until the vagaries of wind and water are handled—almost automatically resulting in a straight and relatively smooth course. This type of storytelling does not demand anything of the client on the surface, but all the information is available to the unconscious and ready to be used to help the individual chart the future course through the storms and the calms, the undertow and the waves.

And so the method behind all this "myth-ery" mystery is, in a very complex way, to simply teach the patient how to change by tapping into the unconscious potential he had before words and before language. Myth uses words, language, and forgotten memory skills to encourage learning by listening to a model and then exploiting hidden resources. Myths take one back to a time before problems were extant and tap into the wondrous curiosity for learning that is present but generally forgotten. Myth has the capacity to permit a different look at things, first by changing the patient's view of the past, and then by allowing new learning to be generalized to present and future experiences. When the patient returns to the present and combines his current maturity with his newly recovered abilities, he has the potential to see and understand anew. Myth thus provides a method, through metaphor, to manage to make therapy more brief.

CHAPTER 20

Concretizing of Symptoms and Their Manipulation

Sidney Rosen

I was first impressed with the possibility of treating symptoms as concrete realities after reading about Erickson's 1966 treatment (Erickson, 1980a) of a woman who was bedeviled with hallucinations of naked men who flew around after her. Erickson told her that she could leave her naked men in his closet and return regularly to ensure that they were still there. As a result, she was free of hallucinations and was able to work and conduct a relatively normal life. When she moved to another state, he had her mail her hallucinations to him and he kept the envelopes, knowing that she would come back some day to see them. His contact with her continued for more than 25 years. Because Erickson had treated the hallucinations as real objects, they could be locked in a closet and shipped in an envelope. They could, in other words, be manipulated. I have applied this same principle with many patients who were not psychotic but who were suffering from extreme anxiety, pain, or depression. I have found it especially effective with patients who, in deep trance states, get in touch with material which their conscious mind is not yet able to tolerate and which consequently causes them significant discomfort. These are patients who would call between sessions complaining that they felt "unreal" or fearing that they might lose their minds. Suggestions of amnesia for the disturbing material often are helpful, but in some cases these are not enough. In a trance state I suggest to them that they leave their symptom or the material that is emerging *here,* in my office. I tell them that we will work on their deep troubling problems here, in my office. During the week, between sessions, they are to live their life, as comfortably as possible, "not needing to think about these things."

The process of concretizing and manipulating symptoms stems partly from Erickson's (1980b) observation that hypnotized subjects often respond literally. A more recent study by McCue and McCue (1988) found that this tendency toward literalism may be dependent on the way that suggestions are presented. Thus, Erickson's subjects may have responded literally because he expected them to do so. (We know that hypnotized subjects are often eager to do what they sense the hypnotist expects.) In any case, hypnotized subjects do show the capacity, whether due to trance characteristics or demand characteristics, to think and respond "concretely," in a way characteristic of some schizophrenics and many brain-damaged patients. For example, when a hypnotized subject is asked, "What do you feel?" he or she may respond with, "the wool of my trousers." In these situations literalness and concreteness seem to be practically synonymous.

It is, of course, possible to give suggestions in ways to ensure that they are likely to be taken literally and so that images are concretized. We may start by suggesting to the patient that he simply "imagine" a color or form that is connected with a symptom or quality of a symptom. Then we may gradually lead the patient to the perception that the form *is* the symptom or the quality, or that the quality (strength, anxiety, etc.) is embedded in that form. The concretizing is encouraged by having the patient focus on details, perhaps even specifiying each of the senses— sight, hearing, smell, and touch.

Whether or not concretizing is an automatic aspect of imaging in hypnosis or whether it is simply easier to concretize in a trance, this tendency can be utilized in treatment. After we have concretized the symptom, we can change its size, shape, color, location, function, motility, and so on. In short, we can manipulate it. For example, a patient with a headache could be directed to see it, concretely, as a red ball and might then image the ball as rolling down a hill, far away from his or her aching head. We could suggest that the pain, embedded in the ball, could be disposed of in this way. Remarkably, the patient often will be relieved of the headache.

PHYSICAL OBJECTS THAT EMBODY CONCRETIZED QUALITIES AND FORCES

As with other phenomena that we observe with hypnosis, the tendency to concretize occurs naturally in many other areas of human activity, especially in the promotion of healing and the search for wisdom and security. For example, individuals throughout the ages have sought security and magical protection by touching objects such as touch-stones, rabbits' feet, and wood. For some people these objects actually embody the comfort, safety, protection, or good luch they seek. The animal symbols in Shinto religion, the symbols of Kaballa in Judaism, and the symbols used by "witch doctors" and shamans also can be seen as ex-amples of concretizing. They offer a wide range of modalities for tap-ping into the unconscious and for accessing and changing symptoms and resources. Stevens and Stevens (1988) have noted how shamans operate on the belief that:

> all elements have their source in the spirit world and therefore are infused with spirits that can be contacted for any number of purposes.
> . . .each form [of air] may be called upon for its unique con-tribution of knowledge. Light breezes, whirlwinds, and cold winds, . . . Each form has a special store of wisdom that may be garnered by forming a relationship with it. By acknowledging the wind and talking to it, shamans gain in wisdom, power, and mastery because they know what the wind knows. . . . (p. 82)

In concretizing symptoms it is useful to remember that some in-dividuals may prefer to use mental imagery while others may prefer ac-tual physical representations. Perhaps there is a parallel with the use of religious objects, including paintings and sculptures of deities. Many years ago, in Kyoto, I talked with a leader of the Shin Buddhist group, which, I believe, is the largest Buddhist group, in Japan. I commented on my observation that Shin, like Catholicism in the West, seemed to utilize statues and religious objects more than other religions. His response was, "Some people can feel closeness and love by simply thinking of their beloved. Others feel it better by looking at a picture." Perhaps the religions that utilize real external objects of worship have the largest numbers of followers because they offer the opportunity for both ways of relating to the deity or worshipped one—both through abstractions and through concretizing.

SYMBOLIZING AND CONCRETIZING

Is concretizing the same as symbolizing? I believe that they are both part of the same process and that the difference between them may be mainly one of degree. A country, for example, can be symbolized in the form of a flag. Thereafter, the display of that flag may evoke patriotic feelings whereas desecration of the flag-symbol may evoke rage. But if a flag desecrator or a patriot were to believe that destruction of a flag was the same as actually damaging the country or threatening its existence, he or she would be concretizing that symbol. Similarly, an emotion can be symbolized by being put into words. But then the word "joy" is not, itself, joy. It does not even contain a substance that could be experienced as "joy." The map is not the territory (Korsybski, 1933). However, if a person can experience the word itself as containing the quality of joy, then that emotion has been concretized—in the form of that word.

Once I had a patient who tended to concretize even without a hypnotic induction. She felt devastated when she was rejected by a man in whom she was interested. I asked her to close her eyes and tell me what she saw and how she felt. She saw the word "LOVE," broken in two, with the letters "VE" having separated from the "LO" and fallen down. She felt sad, heavy, hopeless. I suggested that she repair the word—raise the "VE" and stick the letters to the beginning of the word. She did this and reported that she felt content, happy, and light. Thus, the concretizing process by which the patient represented loss was used to effect positive changes.

In a related application I once witnessed Erickson therapeutically move a student/patient from symbolizing to concretizing (Rossi, 1978). The patient, an ex-nun ("Sara"), was first hypnotically reoriented to a road beside a river she had previously described in detail. Erickson then suggested that Sara "walk about 50 yards down the wash and look back to see what you've left behind you." When Sara saw some shoes, Erickson had her play with that image for a while, asking her if the shoes were moving. At first she said that they were not; then she said, laughingly, that they were dancing. After making certain that she could clearly visualize this, he again repeated his suggestion, but in a different form: "Now walk down the wash about 70 feet, and you will have left behind you something very important to you. . . and look back and tell me what you've left behind you."

At first Sara responded that she thought she had left her fear behind. She said, "The thing that comes to my mind is my fear and what I see is outer clothing. I guess it's like that's symbolic. And my wish is that that would be so." So far she was symbolizing, not concretizing.

She went on, observing, "I see a pile." When asked to elaborate, she described the contents of the clothing pile, which included some underwear. As she described these intimate details, we observers got the definite feeling that she could see, feel, and perhaps even smell the clothing. The clothing appeared concrete, real. At this point she had moved toward what I call "concretizing."

Erickson then evoked the help of Dora, another ex-nun who was present, to help Sara remove some of her clothing from the pile. This action is what I refer to as the "manipulation of the concretized symbol."

Similar strategies can be used with patients suffering from symptom complexes such as depression, phobias, pain, and anxiety. Such patients often describe concrete aspects of their suffering. For example, a depressed person will feel a heavy weight on his or her back or chains around his or her chest. A patient with extreme anxiety may feel "tied up in knots" or a knotting in the abdomen. The therapist does not need to work toward the creation of new concrete images, but can simply have the patient see or feel the chains being cast off or the knots being untied, cut, or displaced to the outside.

When the concretizing of symptoms does not occur spontaneously, the therapist can help to develop some concrete forms in which to embody them. This can be done most directly by having the patient focus on the symptom. For example, the therapist might suggest the following: "As you are concentrating on your pain, can you note the shape of it? Does it have a color? Does it move, or is it still? Hot or cold? What image comes to you as you are doing this?"

Patients sometimes come up with surprising, idiosyncratic images: dancing bananas, weeping rocks, and so on. Depression may be concretized as smoke or as a weight; anxiety may be concretized as flashing colored lights, or electricity, or as a buzzing noise.

Symptoms also can be concretized in the form of written descriptions, in imagination or in actuality. The descriptions then can be disposed of by being launched in a rocket or balloon, buried or burned. Or they can be revised. The sentence "I am helpless," for example, can be changed to "I am competent." Simple as this sounds, this mental manipulation of word symbols while in a trance often can be effective.

Another strategy is to find colors that represent the symptoms. The colors, which may or may not be connected with an object, can be altered. The red of pain or anxiety may be faded as one looks at a field of red tulips, so that in the distance the tulips appear pink and finally white. It is remarkable how often this simple approach will lead to immediate relief of a headache or the ending of a panic attack.

CONCRETIZING OF RESOURCES

Just as a phobic situation or word may trigger panic, a positive association, connected with a concrete object, may trigger healthy, comforting responses. Everyday examples include the practice of touching something, as in the already mentioned superstition of knocking wood. In some cases this will evoke a feeling of reassurance (or "real-assurance," the assurance that one is real). In fact, touching some concrete or "real" object can be especially helpful with patients who are disturbed by panic-evoking feelings of unreality. These patients can, for example, literally and figuratively "get in touch" with themselves by touching one hand against the other. In other words, one's own body can be felt and utilized as a concrete resource.

Natural omnipresent elements such as air and water are especially useful as concretizing resources. Air can be experienced as peace or calm inducing and may be especially helpful in dealing with anxiety, with a smoking habit, or with any conditon that involves taking something into the body. In the form of wind or simply in its stillness, air can be experienced as a vehicle for inspiration (literally "breathing in"). Similarly, drinking or sipping water can give a person a sense of relaxation or fulfillment. With appropriate imagery and association practice, even a feeling of intoxication can be achieved by drinking water.

One of the best ways to find resources that may replace or alleviate a symptom is to have patients search for "unconscious learnings" by going back to a time when they have felt secure, comfortable, and warm inside. They can find images that come to them as they do this. I call the images that trigger the desired effect "positive triggers" or "positive switches"; they are forms of posthypnotic cues. Often these "switches" can be concretized. For example, the sensation of holding a rag doll from childhood may be recalled and then transferred to a ball of wool or some other object that the patient can carry or touch.

CONCRETIZING OF RESOURCES IN CANCER PATIENTS

Immune stimulating forces or healing forces may be visualized or thought of as little animals or fish, such as "blue sharks" (see Achterberg, 1985; Simonton, Simonton, & Creighton, 1978). Technological powers such as those connected with laser beams are often visualized. The cancer itself can be seen as wild animals, which can then be tamed, eaten by the sharks, or diminished in size by laser beams. In the form of a monster, the cancer may be transformed by some technical or magical means into a smaller, weaker form of the same animal or into another harmless or even a helping animal—a nursing mother lion, for example. The patient might imaginally "become" a lion cub who is strengthened by the milk he receives from the nursing mother. Along the same lines the injected chemotherapy fluids can be experienced as that nourishing and strengthening milk.

CASE EXAMPLES

To illustrate how these concretizing techniques can be used, some case examples may be helpful.

A Patient with Abdominal Pain

THERAPIST. Find a color that comes to your mind while you're focusing on that pain. . . . Red? Think of an object or some objects that are colored red. What comes to you now?

PATIENT. A pen.

T. A red pen? Does it write in red ink also?

P. Yes.

T. Pick up the pen and write, in red ink, some words, such as "comfort," "peace," or you may just want to scribble or make some wavy lines until all the red is gone from that pen. As the red leaves the pen it can be interesting to wonder, "Will my pain leave my abdomen also?"

When the pain is very much less in your abdomen, then your right thumb can go up as a signal. (Thumb goes up.)

When you're ready, you can come out of your trance and leave that pen and that pain behind you and you can look forward to dealing with black ink and being in the black. Put some of the situations you've been dealing with into a black hole. And you can know that it's alright for you to succeed. It's alright for you to be happy. It's not written anywhere that you cannot succeed, and if it is written anywhere that can be erased, can't it? And you can replace it with black ink.

(After the patient comes out of trance,)

T. How does your abdomen feel now?

P. It's fine. It doesn't hurt.

T. And that took only about 10 minutes.

P. It felt real bad before.

A Hair-Pulling Compulsion (Trichotillomania)

The patient, a 38-year-old professional woman, sought help in overcoming a hair-pulling compulsion. She also is a compulsive worker and suffers from several psychosomatic ailments, including allergic skin reactions, asthma, and obesity. In previous hypnotic work the patient and I had agreed that her thumbs could move, automatically, to signal "yes" via the right thumb and "no" with the left thumb.

T. You can take that hair-pulling compulsion and put it into some form, if you like. It could be a form which would apply to and which could represent the hair-pulling compulsion. When you have found such a form, you can let your right thumb go up, as a signal. (Pause—20 seconds. Right thumb moves up.) Tell me about it, if you like.

P. Interesting—it's a bird.

T. Does it have a color?

P. Red.

T. Like a cardinal? A scarlet tanager? A red bird.

P. Mmm.

T. Well, we certainly do not want to put a wild bird into a cage. What can we do with that bird. . . to let it keep its energy. . . and freedom, while letting go of its destructive elements.

P. We could feed it and take care of it.

T. That does not mean feeding your body, does it? Substituting overeating for pulling. How could you feed that bird without hurting yourself?

P. Give it gradually increasing increments of food.

T. Small increments of nutrients.

P. Enough space to explore and exercise.

T. Uh-hun. Can you come up with some ritual or movement or an image which could provide the small increments of nutrients and enough space to explore? How would you represent that?

P. Just picturing the bird.

T. When you see that bird, does the impulse to play with your hair become more or less?

P. Less.

T. Would visualizing the bird be enough to take away or stop your impulse?

P. (no answer)

T. Just thinking about it. Would that help?

P. I see it pecking at me. Fluttering around.

T. Pecking at your hair?

P. Yes.

T. So I'd suggest that you picture that bird, pecking at your hair. . . and fluttering around . . . and see to what extent that diminishes your impulse to touch your hair. It may get rid of it entirely. You could redirect your hair pulling energy toward that image. Will you do that?

P. Yes.

T. Can you see yourself and experience yourself doing it right now?

P. (right thumb up)

T. And is the impulse toward your hair . . . is it diminished or gone?

P. Gone.

T. Gone. Good. And every time you do this it's very likely that the same
thing will happen as is happening right now. You can get that same
feeling of pleasure . . . watching that bird pecking . . . . So that you
don't have to peck at yourself . . . . And you can vicariously enjoy the
sense of freedom that the bird has also . . . can't you? And all it needs
is small increments of nutrition. In fact, if you start to identify with
the bird, I wonder if it might not be helpful for you to start to eat like
a bird. And enjoy that. Because you'll then get the extra pleasure of
seeing and feeling your weight diminish . . . . And the sense of lightness and freedom could reflect in your breathing more easily also.
Feeling lighter. More open. It will be very interesting to explore
that, won't it? And all this can revolve around the image which
you've created, which you've just created, just come up with yourself. It *is* your image . . . it is *your* bird. It's your opportunity to utilize
it for your benefit. (Each time I asked "isn't it?" or "won't it?" the
patient's right thumb went up.)

Interestingly, during the next four months the patient not only
stopped her hair pulling, but also lost about 20 pounds. She found that
she was no longer interested in nibbling food, and she ate sparingly, but
enjoyably, at regular meals. Her breathing difficulties were considerably
relieved and she required less medication.

Fear of Height and Allergic Reactions

The patient was an artist suffering from various allergies (skin and upper
respiratory) as well as from a fear of heights which was severe enough to
interfere with her being able to work on a ladder.

T. When you are in at least a moderately deep trance your right thumb
can go up as a signal. That's right . . . deeper . . . and deeper . . . and
deeper . . . good. And are you now in a sufficiently deep trance now,
so that your unconscious mind can, and is able to, relieve your
allergic symptoms to a great degree?
(right thumb goes up)
Good. So I don't have to tell your unconscious how to do that, do I?
It knows how, doesn't it?
You may want to help it a little bit by focusing on some images,

breathing sea air, while standing on a beach, breathing in air that is not permeated with allergens of any kind ... clean fresh air, healthy air. As you do that your nose opens up. Your head begins to clear. It feels good, doesn't it? A cool breeze blowing across your forehead. You can have a warm feeling inside your abdomen. . . . Breathing becomes easier and easier, so that you feel really relaxed, calm and comfortable . . . and as you feel more relaxed and calm, your head becomes even more clear. Breathing becomes still more open. *You can take those allergic symptoms and put them into some form or other.* You can see something or can conceive of some form that represents your allergy symptoms. When you can do that, let your right thumb go up. Color ... form ... beginning to form itself. More and more clearly ... (long pause) ... that's right. And while you're doing that, you can put into that same form your fear of heights, if you like. Add it on or stick it in there. You can evoke that fear by picturing yourself on a very high point ... that's right. . . . What image comes with that?

Can you attach that to the other form? The one that represents the allergies? (Right thumb goes up) Good. You can see it, can't you?

P. I see a big red circle.

T. A big red circle. Is it shaded, or is it evenly red?

P. It looks hot. And there's yellow in the center.

T. Alright. A big red circle. Hot and yellow ... alright now ... can you conceive of a symbol, or another image that represents security ... and freedom ... and openness. The ability to breathe freely?

P. (right thumb up)

T. That's right. What do you see now? Is it your "power piece"? (a piece of jewelry)

P. A canoe.

T. A canoe. (pause) So all you have to do is transform that circle into a canoe. . . . When you've done that, let your right thumb go up. . . . It's not easy, but you can do it. (pause) That's right. . . . (thumb goes up) Yes. Good. And every time you touch that power piece it could remind you of a canoe. It has a similar shape, doesn't it? So, you have at least two ways of evoking your canoe. You can do it just mentally ... or with the help of a touch ... and as you come out of your trance, by counting from 20 to 1, you can bring back that knowledge with you, that readiness ... to feel secure, to breathe easily ... to be reminded of that, by calling upon your canoe. You'll do that, won't you?

P. (right thumb goes up)

T. Good. So I will count from 20 to 1. You can let your eyes open on the count of 1 feeling relaxed, alert, refreshed, and wider and wider awake. 20, 19, 18, 17, 16 (then faster) 15, 14, 13, 12, 11, 10, 9, 8, 7, 6, 5, 4, 3, 2, 1. And, while you are feeling strong and secure and well supported, you might, after a moment, picture yourself on the top of that ladder, working on your painting. Focusing on the painting. Not needing to think about it. Realizing that you *are* secure.

P. I saw a connection between the ladder and the canoe also.

T. Yes?

P. It was sort of funny. It's uh . . . totally irrational. Completely irrational. But you'll understand it. What I was seeing was a canoe . . . that was . . . I couldn't get it to be a red canoe, and I have *seen* red canoes. The old ones, the heavier ones were painted. They were wood, but they were painted. Red or green usually.

T. Green, yeah.

P. But, by the time I was in camp, we also had aluminum canoes. Which was why it was so funny, because they were lighter to pick up and were easier to deal with.

T. Right.

P. In my mind, all the time I thought, "How can I get that circle to turn into a canoe?" which I eventually was able to make a red canoe out of it. But I kept seeing the ladder. And I have a wonderful wooden ladder. That's the very big one. It's the wooden one. The one that I usually use, that doesn't frighten me, but I don't go up that high, is aluminum, but it's not as big as the one I'm using now.

T. mmhmm.

P. I thought for a minute, "How funny, because the ladder looks more like a canoe."

T. Because it's made of wood.

P. Yeah, but that's the thing that's so irrational. This looks like, it looks like wood. Yeah. It's a church ladder. A library ladder. It's a great big oak—huge. It's a big thing that stands. And it has a flat top. Very, very big.

T. Maybe it looks like a canoe if you put it on its side?

P. Well, it could look more like a canoe, because it looks really like . . . Oh, God! . . . (whispered) I totally forgot! It's like in your picture! (a painting on my wall which she had done.) Oh, I can't believe it! It's so funny!

T. It's alright. You can take the picture with you, in your mind . . . and let me know how comfortable you really feel the next time you get up there on that ladder.

As can be seen in the transcript, the patient and I found several concrete representations of security, in her mental imagery and also in my office, which itself represented and evoked a feeling of security. The fact that we were finally able to bring together an actual creation of her own—the canoe in her/my painting—undoubtedly added to the power of this concretized representation of security. In any case, she reported at the next session that she had lost her fear of working on the tall ladder and her allergic condition had gone into a stage of remission.

A Cancer Patient with Nausea as the Result of Chemotherapy

(The nausea was intensified after her boss's wife had attacked her verbally, questioning her intelligence, competence, and sincerity.)

T. ... And now you might focus on that nausea. You can feel it in your throat, in the pit of your stomach, your chest, perhaps. ... And, as you focus on it, you notice that it tends to increase, doesn't it? But, as you are focusing on it, you can see an object or symbol or color ... some kind of object, perhaps, that represents the nausea. When you see that, tell me what it is ... put the nausea into some form or other.

P. I just see a pyramid.

T. What color is the pyramid?

P. Gold.

T. Alright. Pyramid shaped and gold in color. Is the surface rough or smooth?

P. Rough.

T. Does the pyramid seem to be made out of real gold, or is it just gold in color?

P. Color.

T. It's a little bit like a yellow color, isn't it? Like the color of vomit? (patient nods) Now, what I think I'd like to ask your unconscious mind to do is to change the color of that pyramid ... perhaps to a color like blue ... or any other color than gold. When you can see that new color let your right thumb go up. ... (thumb up) Good. What color do you see?

P. Red.

T. Red. ... And then ... let the red become diluted ... until it becomes a pink, perhaps a skin color eventually. ... Or it may even disappear altogether ... fade away and be replaced by air, or sky blue. Just notice the changes as they occur. (pause) What color do you see now?

P. No color.

T. Good. So that now you can see. ...

P. (clears throat)

T. It's alright to clear your throat. Breathe in that clear air, that clear atmosphere. It could have a calming effect, as it goes into your throat,
down into your stomach; it may warm your stomach on the inside ... soothe your stomach. You can become more and more comfortable, with every breath that you take in ... clean, healing air-
... and when that nausea is gone completely. ...

P. (swallows and looks restless)

T. Not yet. Is it getting worse again?

P. (left thumb goes up to indicate "No")

T. What's happening now? (tears are seen in patient's eyes) The nausea
is being replaced by some emotion?

P. I just feel teary.

T. And the tears can keep on flowing, like the waters of the Nile. You
started with pyramids. But, as you picture that river, flowing, constantly flowing, you know that it will go on .. and on and on, until
eventually it leads to an ocean. You might even want to go for a
swim in that ocean, as I did when I was in Elat, in Israel, years ago.
You can imagine yourself, in any case, being cooled and rested as
you swim, or float, or just bathe in the fresh, clear, healing water.

P. It seems that someone is always shooting at you.

T. When you're between the Israelis and the Arabs, that's what happens. ... There are people who are going to be shooting at you,
that's true. When you are surrounded by vicious, nasty people. Self-
centered people.
But you don't have to just stay out there as a target. You may decide
to just duck under the water for a while. You could enter into a sub-
marine and go under cover for a while. And wait until the attack
blows over. That's the way her husband deals with it, isn't it. He lets
her spout off and ignores it. Then, an hour later, she may just be
angry at something else, or somebody else, maybe. She will have
forgotten about it. I don't think it's necessary to make every attack
into a battle, or a war.
(The patient confirmed that this is what had happened that
day.)

T. Next time you are exposed to this kind of shooting it would be good to
have some kind of shield.

P. A real one.

T. A real one, or at least a mental one. You could imagine yourself inside a
transparent, protective, bullet-proof sphere. Just imagine yourself
on the inside. She's on the outside—throwing things. Shooting. Yell-
ing. You can't even hear her. It's soundproof also. Or, you hear her
voice coming and you change it into the sound of animals. Don't listen to the words ... (two-minute pause) How does your stomach

feel now? Still feel a little nauseous? That will diminish more and more. You might go back and repeat that pyramid exercise, several times a day. Visualize the pyramid. Change the color. Relax.

The patient was subsequently able to negotiate a better, less stressful job, where she did not have much contact with the boss's wife. She utilized the pyramid image before and sometimes afteremotherapy sessions and was able to complete the series of treatments with minimal side effects.

CONCLUSIONS

The process of concretizing symptoms is an effective technique, but, of course, rarely will it constitute an entire therapy. As therapists we must be familiar with many different approaches and must be judicious in deciding which ones to apply in a given case. I have given only a few examples in which concretizing of symptoms and resources has apparently expedited therapy. Obviously, even in these examples there were many other factors that contributed to the success of the therapy and even to the cooperation between patient and therapist in devising the concretizing.

It occurs to me that Erickson frequently tended to think and to express his communications to patients in literal and concrete forms. Whether or not he was correct in believing that people in trance usually responded literally, he may have been correct in assuming that the unconscious mind operates in a literal, concrete mode and that by speaking concretely we can speak more directly with the unconscious mind. Or it may be that literal and concrete formulations are effective and potent simply because they are simple and clear, or because they are similar to the way we would talk to a receptive child. I truly believe that we often can be most helpful to our patients when we talk to them as if they were children—or at least when we talk to "the child within." Perhaps this is because, as children, we were most flexible, most open and available for new learnings. The magical world of the child is approached agreeably and often elegantly with this game we play, which we call hypnosis.

REFERENCES

Achterberg, J. (1985). *Imagery in Healing: Shamanism and Modern Medicine.* Boston: New Science Library.
Erickson, M. (1980a). Hypnosis: Its renascence as a treatment modality. In E.

Rossi (Ed.), *The Collected Papers of Milton H. Erickson, Vol.* 4 pp. 70–74 New York: Irvington.

Erickson, M. (1980b). Literalness, an experimental study. In E. Rossi (Ed.), *The Collected Papers of Milton H. Erickson, Vol. 3* (pp. 92–99). New York: Irvington.

Korsybski, A. (1933). *Science and Sanity* (4th Ed.) Lakeville, CT: International Non Aristotelian Library Publishing Co.

McCue, P. A., & McCue, E. C. (1988). Literalness: An unsuggested (spontaneous) item of hypnotic behavior? *International Journal of Clinical and Experimental Hypnosis, 36*(1), 192–197.

Rossi, E. L. (1978). Videotape of a teaching seminar with Milton H. Erickson. Phoenix, AZ.

Simonton, O. C., Simonton, S., & Creighton, J. (1978). *Getting Well Again.* Los Angeles: Tarcher.

Stevens, J., & Stevens, L. S. (1988). *Secrets of Shamanism* (p. 82). New York: Avon.

CHAPTER 21

Pain Control Interventions of Milton H. Erickson

Roxanna Erickson Klein

Pain control has been a specific area of my interest as long as I can remember. It may have been the circumstances of my upbringing that sparked my curiosity. I was three when my seven-year-old brother, Robert, was the victim of a hit-and-run accident. He spent months in casts on the sofa. My father, Milton Erickson, also experienced significant and daily pain as a result of his polio and postpolio syndrome. Both Robert and my father adjusted to major invasions of their personal comfort. The daily ongoing exposure allowed me to observe pain not as an occasional intruder, but as a fact of life. From an early age I understood pain as something that can come unexpectedly and can touch anyone. I also saw that it was NOT something that has to ruin one's life: It may be an inconvenience, a problem, a challenge, but there is always room to improve.

I consider myself to have been fortunate, far more fortunate than I realized at the time, to discuss and advance ideas that I had, and to work together with my father in formulating approaches to solving problems. For clarity, I will refer to my father, Milton H. Erickson, M.D., as Erickson, but I do wish to note that I think of him as Dad.

The objective of this chapter is to propose five broad classifications within which hypnotic interventions for pain can be grouped. I will begin with a review of 11 hypnotic interventions for pain that were described by Erickson (1967). I will then show five broad categories within which the interventions can be flexibly invoked. Each category will be illustrated with previously unpublished examples. It is my intent to illustrate the variety and range of possible interventions with pain problems.

Pain control was only one area of Erickson's work. Among his greatest contributions to the behavioral sciences were his study, application, development, and advancement of hypnosis as an ethical, professional tool of therapy.

Hypnosis is a powerful therapeutic tool, the use of which demands much responsibility on the part of the practitioner. First and foremost in any health care setting are the needs and well-being of the patient. Pain control techniques, as well as all hypnotherapeutic measures, must be adjunct to the medical, physiological, and psychological treatment of the patient and are intended for use in synchrony with holistic health care measures by health care professionals.

Prior to working with a patient who is experiencing physiological pain, a therapist must have an understanding of the physiological and pathological processes affecting the patient. The therapist must clearly comprehend the pain process, the specific medical conditions affecting the patient, medications taken and their effects, and the potential ramifications of suggestions. I encourage all therapists seriously interested in working with pain patients to study pathophysiology and to explore the usefulness of pain.

Without this vital information, misapplication of concepts could compromise the natural protective mechanisms and healing processes of the body. Obviously, the therapist must work closely with the physician and other members of the health care team in order to ensure that efforts are harmoniously and accurately directed toward healing and enhancement of comfort.

A major responsibility of any therapist who wishes to diminish a patient's response to pain is to teach that patient to recognize and heed warning signals that become masked or diminished.

Another therapist responsibility is individualizing treatment. In his therapeutic work, Erickson stressed the need to tailor therapy and treatment to complement the individual's personality and situation. This concept is especially important in pain control interventions.

Some of Erickson's (1967) applications of hypnosis for pain control were presented by him in April 1965, in Paris, at the International Congress for Hypnosis and Psychosomatic Medicine. The paper has been reprinted twice and has been elaborated on in *Hypnosis: An Exploratory Casebook* (Erickson & Rossi, 1979). I will briefly review each of these applications and then follow with five broader categories and illustrations.

ERICKSON'S HYPNOTIC PROCEDURES IN PAIN CONTROL

Direct Suggestions for the Total Abolition of Pain

This procedure is suitable for a limited number of patients, and even when effective it may be limited in duration. For the few patients with a strong internal will and discipline, a suggestion or command, "You don't need to feel that," may provide temporary relief.

Permissive Indirect Hypnotic Abolition of Pain

These suggestions, similar in content to direct suggestions, differ in the way in which the information is offered. The suggestions are presented in a manner that may be more conducive to patient receptivity. The delivery of suggestions may occur in metaphors or in other indirect modes. I often use this type of approach: "Wouldn't it be nice if your leg were resting on something soft like a pile of shaving cream?" I have found that this approach often works well on hospitalized patients. The unconscious knows that beyond directing the patient toward medical care, and self-protection, the pain serves no useful purpose. The patient, motivated by the discomfort of pain, has the unconscious resources to mobilize the imagination. Images of more comfortable sensations may be conjured up in response to simple suggestions, such as this one.

Amnesia

Partial, selective, or complete amnesia for past pain may be employed as an element in the overall treatment. This occurs naturally and quite often when patients elect to absorb themselves in external events. Books, movies, and sporting events are examples of vehicles for this process.

Hypnotic Analgesia

Analgesia, or the reduction of the sensation of pain, may be employed through direct or indirect suggestion. Suggesting the patient experience numbness in the affected part of the body is a direct approach. Hypnotic suggestions involving snowdrifts, cool streams, or protective gloves could be utilized as indirect routes. Indirection also might be employed by offering suggestions regarding a different body part than the affected or injured body part. For example, suggestions of comfort directed to the contralateral limb might be as effective as continuation of focus on the injured limb.

Hypnotic Anesthesia

Erickson described anesthesia, or the abolition of sensation, as best accomplished indirectly by building up psychological and emotional situations contradictory to the emotional experience of pain. One of my nephews, who is well versed in the use of hypnosis, described the following situation in which he used hypnotic anesthesia. Michael tripped on a ladder at a construction site and fell, damaging the muscle and tendon of his ankle and calf. Utilizing self-hypnosis, he reasoned that any limb so damaged that it hung limply surely had some nerve damage. If the nerve was damaged, it could not hurt. He sought prompt medical attention and remained entirely pain free for the next few days.

Hypnotic Replacement or Substitution of Sensations

An example frequently cited is that of replacing pain with an itch. The emotional content of the sensation also is diffused by the alteration of the perceived pain.

Hypnotic Displacement of Pain

Displacement of pain from one body part to another is a technique that Erickson used extensively. Erickson (1967) described an example of a patient suffering from metastatic cancer. Hypnotic suggestions were offered that effectively shifted the focus of sensation from the patient's abdomen to the patient's left hand. By shifting the focus, control is intitiated and the threat associated with the central body part is displaced by distance.

Hypnotic Dissociation

Time and body disorientation can effectively produce a feeling of comfort. The patient can be reoriented in time to an earlier stage of illness when pain was a minor consideration. In body disorientation, patients are hypnotically induced to experience themselves apart from their bodies. One of my aunts described her application of body dissociation on the occasion of having stitches removed following major surgery. The suture removal was something that she perceived as painful, and she had fainted on previous occasions. She stated, "I left my body on the bed and took my head and shoulders to the solarium at the end of the hall."

Hypnotic Reinterpretation of the Pain Experience

Full awareness of the patient's perception of pain is a prerequisite for successful reinterpretation of symptoms. Erickson (1967/1980) proposed a series of suggestions providing a transition from an experience of deep distress to one of milder discomfort. The example provided is that of "throbbing, nagging, grinding pain having been successfully reinterpreted as the unpleasant but not distressing experience of the rolling with a boat during a storm" (p. 243).

Hypnotic Time Distortion

The hypnotic phenomenon of time distortion was developed originally by Lynn Cooper and elaborated later by Cooper and Erickson in *Time Distortion in Hypnosis* (1959). The process involved is the manipulation of experiential time in relation to actual or clock time. Patients are encouraged to experience an extension of the time when they are relatively pain free, and to perceptually condense those intervals when the pain is problematic. Erickson found that once patients were trained in these techniques, the actual or clock time of the episodes of pain diminished, as well as the experiential time. This technique often is used in combination with amnesia for past pain.

Hypnotic Suggestions Effecting a Diminution of Pain

This technique involves systematically diminishing pain. The patient may be given suggestions, for example, that over the next hour his or her pain will diminish, perhaps imperceptibly at first, possibly only 1%. Ongoing suggestions are given over the course of therapy in which a larger and larger portion of the original pain fades away.

TYPES OF HYPNOTIC PAIN CONTROL INTERVENTIONS

Erickson's techniques of pain management have been classified into basic categories, but in application the techniques may be interwoven and combined. A variety of techniques may be utilized in any individual situation. The technique selected and the application process are the product of therapeutic skills and goals, in the service of individual needs and personalities.

I propose the following broad categories for the classification of hypnotic pain control interventions. The eleven hypnotic procedures described by Erickson may be used flexibly within these categories.

1. Acceptance
2. Division into parts
3. Dissociation
4. Transformation
5. Resolution

This classification for interventions provides a framework within which the therapist may utilize Erickson's techniques. Additionally, it may prove useful to evaluate case reports, and to stimulate and encourage the creative migration from one sensory modality to another.

Acceptance

Within this category fall techniques focused on adaptation to the experience of pain as part of life. Rather than change or manipulate the pain, changes are made within the life-style toward adaptation to the situation.

Erickson had exceptional abilities in encouraging patients to accept adverse conditions and to go forward in time. He did not distance himself from the individual in pain, but often encouraged the person to feel the pain, as it really was, for a few minutes. By confronting the pain and putting it into perspective within one's life-style; the patient is released to go forward. The pain is reduced to a thread in the fabric of life. The focus of treatment is directed on the perspective of life.

Compromises with pain begin with the onset of symptomatology. Often the patient may choose a favorite pillow or sleeping position that reduces the discomfort. Muscular realignment takes place throughout the entire body, to guard, protect, or splint a weak or damaged part. Accepting the adjustments and the changes as they occur facilitates a positive outlook for the patient. Turning inward to discover "just what it will take to put the feelings into a state of balance and comfort" is a task that may encourage ongoing adjustments. To have already begun this is praiseworthy.

Looking out into a garden, one may see the flowers or the weeds. Finding the flowers in an overgrown weed patch may be a cumbersome task, but once the first flower is found, the next becomes easier to locate. Each comfort measure can blossom to provide reminders of past successes, of the unexpected resourcefulness that we have within, and of the promise of future comfort.

Pain control measures may focus on acceptance of all or part of the sensation, either intact or in an altered form. Acceptance frees the patient to flow with the events and to make choices. Success may be measured not by the presence or absence of pain, but by the degree to which a patient's productivity increases.

For example, over a period of years Erickson treated a young man with Charcot-Marie-Tooth disease, a debilitating and progressive neuromuscular condition responsible for an ongoing, more or less continuous experience of pain and loss of muscular function. The friendly, congenial young man became friends with several of the Erickson family members. Recently John shared his insight into how Erickson helped him to adapt to his condition. John described that prior to working with Erickson, he had developed a coping mechanism of focusing. The focusing process, an intense concentration on the present task, was consuming. It was so well developed that while focusing, John actually experienced tunnel vision.

The handicap of that adaptation technique is that once consumed by the process, it is possible to become totally unaware of the world around—like a poor reader who gets stuck on a single word, the eyes keep moving and the mouth speaks, but the content is lost. The attention is latched on that single word.

John stated, "Because pain can happen to me at any time of the day or night, Erickson taught me to take advantage of the times when I feel reasonably O.K. to be productive. One learns to pick up on the early signs, to ease up, to divert attention, and when the down time passes to become productive again and not look back."

John continued: "I'm a slow worker, and I now realize that it is because I take a lot of short breaks, turning away for a minute to collect my strength. It takes a lot of patience. One of the greatest values that Erickson taught me was patience: letting the moment develop instead of forcing it into a predetermined shape. I am not a patient person, but I have learned to work within that framework effectively."

John went on to say, "He taught me to distinguish deliberate bursts of focused attention from the habitual overfocus that I used. I think there is a broad reach to what that distinction can mean to life skills. I have adapted to a differnt type of world view."

This technique, as with all others used by Erickson, was tailored specifically to meet the needs, personality, and life-style of this intellectual and literate young man.

Division into Parts

Pain is often a variable sensation, waxing and waning over time, sometimes in an identifiable pattern. It is apart from, yet becomes a part of the identity of, the part with which it is associated.

Pain can be separated temporally from the past injury, event, or onset, and from past memory of similar pain experiences. The past memory of a painful injection, or an unpleasant visit to the dentist, may generate negative anticipation: The past memories of pain blend into the future expectation of pain. Anticipation produces muscle tension, an endocrine response, and a cardiovascular response, all of which actually contribute to the negative impact of the injury.

The burden of past memories and future expectations can overwhelm and overshadow the present, interfering with perceptions and with coping mechanisms. On the other hand, most people have at least one memory of an occasion in which pain was experienced and then the sensations faded. Inquiring about occasions in the past in which the resolution process successfully evolved may reframe current events. At the least, it will serve as a reference to validate the existence of such a phenomenon.

The experience of pain can be teased apart from the grief that may be associated with the cause of the pain. It may be separated from the burden of past memories and from future expectation of more pain. Once relieved from that entanglement, the present experience of pain is a much less formidable threat. Broken down, moment by moment, even the most monumental of trials can be tolerated.

Reorienting to the present moment, experiencing the sensations as they occur, unencumbered by unessential cargo, the subject frees his or her resources to attend to the task of mending, healing, and comforting.

For example, separation of the present from the past and future and time distortion were the two key elements in the preparation that Erickson did with me for my anticipated childbirth needs. From the time I was 12 or 13, Dad would ask me what I would like to work on hypnotically. General pain control and labor/delivery were my favorite topics even at that young age. What I remember consciously from that trance work is not words. I have a visual image of a line, in wave form. I can see the peaks and valleys along the line and understand that the peaks represent the muscle contractions (discomfort). As I watch that line, I can see the valleys (periods of relaxation, comfort) extend out sufficiently to provide rest. The peaks sharpen up, the intensity and the sensation remain intact, but anticipation of discomfort is transformed into the expectation of only a brief moment of pain, followed by a comfortable rest. The emphasis is on enjoying the "good times," perceptually stretching them, while simultaneously diminishing "bad times" by perceptually narrowing them.

Pain also can be divided *spatially*. Identification of the area affected by the sensation delineates those areas where pain is distinctly felt from those areas where there is a less clear feeling and from those areas free of pain. The investigation process itself may narrow the affected area. Once identification of a pain-free area is achieved, a reference is provided. Self-image entails a feeling of connection with one's own body and a feeling associated with what "normal" or "usual" or "healthy" feels like. The experience of pain within the body part that is damaged or injured may be a reasonable adaptation to the current situation. Removing pain may expose the part to additional risk or trauma. However, it is not always necessary to continue with a large area of pain when a smaller area will achieve the same degree of protectiveness. By using one's imagination, e.g., through positive visual hallucinations, one may draw a barrier, separating the "hurting part" from the "part that does not hurt." Once that division is firmly set in one's mind, movement of the barrier slowly can advance in the direction that affords the maximum comfort to the rest of the body.

For example, while working at a county hospital we saw numerous "wringer" injuries. Small children playing with an old-fashioned wringer washer can get their arm drawn into the wringer mechanism. The injury typically produces a crushing type of trauma to the entire arm, including the shoulder, and treatment includes elevation of the affected part. The children often are hospitalized, and the arm suspended from an ambulatory intravenous pole. I worked with one of these children and produced a long glove anesthesia, which was effective. On a subsequent case, after consulting with Erickson, I utilized an approach of drawing an imaginary line across the shoulder to the level that the pain extended. I then worked with the child to advance that line distally. Over a period of several hours, the discomfort was pulled back to below the elbow. I did not advance the progress further because the injured limb did require the protection that pain commands.

Dissociation

There are various modalities within which dissociation can be achieved. Perceptual analgesia, anesthesia, and amnesia are all mechanisms that dissociate the patient from the sensation and shield the patient from the negative impact of the pain. All are creative mechanisms for setting the pain aside and expanding perceptual response options.

SEPARATION. The patient may experience the pain, in its intact form, in a different location from the affected part. The patient is thereby released from identifying with the painful experience. The entity of pain is accepted as a part of the present experience, but the patient mutates the perception of pain, interpreting the sensations as occurring in a less vulnerable part of the body. The process of pain, or the procedures initiating the pain, diminish to an element over which some control may be executed. The invasion of the self by these agents is reduced, and the patient attains control by manipulating or juggling the perceptual process.

For example, when I was a child, I suffered from relatively soft enamel on my teeth. Despite a reasonable diet and regular toothbrushing, it seemed as if I had cavities on every visit to the dentist. I know that I received novocaine at least once, and Erickson was not against my receiving standard medical or dental care as it was offered. I distinctly remember him emphasizing the importance of making a choice: Was it the dentist's decision as to whether I would receive the injection, or was it my choice? Whatever choice I made was O.K., as long as it was mine. He then enlightened me as to other choices, and to how to use them.

On a later visit to the dentist, following his suggestion, I did try focusing all of my pain receptors into my hand. It was not an entirely satisfactory experience. Initially I targeted my right hand, which was continually at risk because the dentist sat on that side of me. I was terrified that the dentist, unaware of the hypersensitivity of my hand, would inadvertently bump into it. With tremendous effort I switched over in "midstream" to my left hand. It was not satisfactory for me to have spent the entire time "worrying about my hand," a feeling that was NOT comforting to me.

When I reported back to Erickson, he suggested that on a future visit I "see myself across the room, watching the dentist from over his own shoulder." This proved a much more satisfactory perspective for me, and I have used it successfully over the years. Having a roving perspective allows me to go inside and feel, when I want, and to escape easily when that is my choice.

Transformation

The sensation of pain can occur suddenly, unexpectedly, or abruptly; or it can occur in a gradual fashion, building up, waxing and waning, or coexisting as a presence of its own. Both contain mechanisms that may be useful. The sudden pain offers a more complete respite, while the ongoing pain may more effectively prepare the patient to cope with the sensation. With an ongoing experience there is more of an opportunity to approach and alter the perceptual sense.

One approach may be to enlarge and diffuse or dilute the pain over a larger area. Another approach would be to transform the pain sensation into a more intense experience. An unexpected intervention, such as suggesting more discomfort, initiates control and supplies the reference for reframing. Encouraging the patient to "go back and feel the pain as it was before the intensification" perceptually reframes the experience into one of relative comfort.

Variations of transformation are limited only by the imagination of the participants and can involve any of the sensory modalities. Recurrent sensations offer a great deal of opportunity for transformation into experiences that are more acceptable to the patient. The process of learning to alter the sensations and reinterpret stimuli may be sufficiently engrossing to envelop the patient and provide an interim distraction engrossing enough to meet current needs.

For example, while I was working at a large county hospital in the pediatric emergency area, there were a few children who came in with disseminated coccidioidomycosis, a serious internal fungal infection. They were treated as outpatients with triweekly intravenous infusions. The treatments lasted several hours and were generally unpleasant. The drug used sometimes produced a local burning sensation at the site, nausea, dizziness, and an overall sick feeling. Particularly distressing was the fact that duration of treatment may be indefinite, and at times little or no positive response is apparent. Since then, more promising drugs have been developed to treat the condition.

One child with whom I had contact over a period of time described the sensation of the intravenous infusion to me in vivid, colorful language. The colorless liquid was described by Jerry as being fiery red, burning the bottle, and creeping down the tubing, biting his forearm and painting his body in a systematic sequence, until he himself became all red, "like the devil."

Slowing the intravenous infusion and soothing the child seemed so insufficient that I consulted Erickson for advice prior to the next treatment. Over the next few treatments, I developed an intense interest in the phenomenon of color, wondering how bright the color really was, and eliciting an exacting description of the repetitive process. I began to question the experience and to "seed" questions, like "Is it always such a bright color of red?" and "I wonder how it would feel if it were another color?"

After a short period of time, we discovered that the drug remained "red" but that Jerry could look at it "as if it were green," and by so doing, could paint himself ahead of the medicine's own "painbrush." At the time I left that position, Jerry was still coming in regularly and seemed to be more comfortable before and during his treatments.

Another example of utilizing transformation is an incident that happened to me when I was about five or six years old. My older brother, Lance, and I had collided in a doorway and the impact of the door removed the nail from my big toe. I was crying and upset, particularly because Lance did not express what I felt was sufficient remorse for something I perceived to be clearly his fault.

At this age, Erickson had not yet begun working with me in a formal capacity, but he called me into his office. Somehow he convinced me that if Lance would lift me up on his shoulders, I would find on the ceiling an off/on switch. I was not to tell Lance what I was looking for. Once Lance lifted me, I could find and retrieve the switch. Having obtained the imaginary switch I was free to install and operate it in whatever manner I chose.

As I came out of the office, Lance cheerfully complied with my request to ride on his shoulders. I recall finding the imaginary switch with no difficulty and puzzled only over whether it would be more effective inside or outside of my clothing.

The result of the intervention was that my toe stopped bothering me, and my bad feelings about Lance were "uplifted" into feelings that he had helped me.

Resolution

The healing process follows a natural, rather predictable course. Investigation of a wound offers a chance to see those parts normally hidden and an opportunity to explore the healing process in action. Familiarity with those steps of the healing process, and with actions that can be taken to reduce risk at each step, can enhance the healing.

For example, when I was a teenager, Erickson utilized me to work with one of his patients, a white-haired, overweight lady with stooping posture. We spent a number of afternoons together and she described to me, in detail, the arduous experience of her mastectomy. She had been left with residual pain and swelling in her shoulder and arm. One part of her therapy involved research about the Grand Canyon. She had been assigned to go to the public library to research the Grand Canyon. Apparently she had not successfully completed her homework, and so my role was to tutor her in the use of the library. I was paid a minimal hourly wage and walked with her to the library, showed her how to use the card catalogue, and sat with her while she read to me about the Grand Canyon. We would then walk back to the office and together report to Erickson. He would then quiz each of us about what we had noticed about the walk, the afternoon, and the library. This took place over several days.

Initially I noticed that I seemed to be more aware of the beauty and pleasure of the walk than she was. Later I noticed that Erickson seemed to shift emphasis from the immediate surroundings to the grandeur of the canyon. He talked about the tall mesas that rise above the canyon floor, straight and elegant. I recall the emphasis on the running water that, when blocked, developed alternate collateral routes. He described in detail the beauty of erosion, as it takes place in harmony with the strength of the pillars—the changes that occur over time, and the elegance in each tiny change.

I was aware that this lady suffered from diminished enthusiasm about life. I pondered how her homework could have addressed the problems she described to me. However, as a child and employee of my father, I took my role seriously. My role included "no questions." Retrospectively, I have a better understanding of the physiological issues that were being addressed in the analogies. I suspect that by drawing attention to the beauty and the grandeur of the canyon, Erickson was facilitating the development of a broader outlook on life. The analogies of the tall mesas may have addressed her stooping posture and perhaps the collateral flow provided suggestions to enhance the lymph flow in her affected shoulder. It is speculative because the case was never written up, and to my knowledge, it was never discussed professionally.

Many years later, my mother encountered the lady in a social setting. Mom observed that the woman was attending a dog show with her granddaughter and seemed to be interested in the outdoor activity. I regret that I cannot offer more concrete information as to the outcome of that therapy.

SUMMARY

These interventions can be combined to produce an almost limitless repertoire of approaches to solve any pain problem. I have reviewed the

11 applications of hypnosis in pain control that were described by Erickson. I have presented five broad categories within which the applications described by Erickson can be flexibly used. It is my hope that the broad categories provide a framework for the creative advancement of hypnotic interventions.

As in any hypnotic work, it is necessary to tailor the suggestions and imagery to meet the personal needs of the patient. A technique suitable for one patient may be entirely unsuitable for the next, even though the problem may appear similar. Most therapeutic work with pain requires a delicately woven tapestry of interventions, a unique combination suitable specifically for that patient, at that time.

The effectiveness of interventions depends largely on the preparedness of the patient and the manner in which the suggestions are woven into the trance experience. The patient's ability to make use of suggestions may depend on his or her current receptivity and on the extent to which the therapist has included future-oriented posthypnotic suggestions.

One of the fundamental qualities of Ericksonian psychotherapy is that, though the final therapeutic mechanism may appear simplistic, the preparation and study by the therapist are, in contrast, complex. Complexity is clearly a consideration in the utilization of pain control techniques. The individual patient, with his or her particular background, personality, and individual perception of pain, must be carefully considered in the development of an effective treatment plan. The pain management must be harmonious with the patient's medical treatment and life-style.

Finally, the therapist must remain acutely attuned to the consideration that pain signals are a valuable source of information—a warning of disease or injury, or a signal for protection. A major responsibility of any therapist who undertakes to diminish the patient's response to pain is training the patient to recognize and heed warning signals that are now masked or diminished.

The more psychologically comprehensive the approach, the greater the likelihood of therapeutic results. Erickson believed that continued investigation into the phenomena of pain and into the process of pain management would eventually reveal tools for the empirical measurement of both. He also believed that as understanding of these progressed, mystique would yield to explanation.

REFERENCES

Cooper, L. & Erickson, M. (1959). *Time Distortion in Hypnosis.* Baltimore: Williams & Wilkens.

Erickson, M. H. (1967). An introduction to the study and application of hypnosis for pain control. In J. Lassner (Ed.), *Proceedings of the International Congress on Hypnosis and Psychosomatic Medicine.* Berlin: Springer-Verlag.

Erickson, M. H. (1967/1980). In Ernest L. Rossi (Ed.), *The Collected Papers of Milton H. Erickson on Hypnosis, Vol. 4.* New York: Irvington.

Erickson, M, & Rossi, E. (1979). *Hypnotherapy: An Exploratory Casebook.* New York: Irvington.

PART VI

Models of Brief Therapy

How Can Psychological Treatment Aim to Be Briefer and Better? The Rational-Emotive Approach to Brief Therapy
Albert Ellis

There are many ways in which psychotherapists can help clients to briefly *feel* better, but most of them help for only a short period of time and do not enable the clients to *get* better (Ellis, 1972a). When clients *feel* better, they improve at least temporarily in their presenting symptoms. Thus, they feel less anxious, depressed, guilty, and enraged; they behave less phobically, addictively, and procrastinatingly; and they feel happier and act more constructively as a result of the lessening or removal of these presenting symptoms.

When clients *get* better, they again improve in their presenting symptoms but they also tend to accomplish four other things: (1) They *maintain* their emotional and behavioral changes. (2) They become significantly less disturbed and self-defeating about many *other* events and problems than the ones that originally sparked their disturbed symptoms. In other words, they become much less disturb*able*. (3) When they occasionally fall back to disturbed feelings and actions, they know how to deal with them quickly and effectively and they work at applying this knowledge. (4) Ideally, as they keep applying the lessons they learned in therapy, they become increasingly less disturbable and more self-actualizing as the years go by. However, being human, and therefore vulnerable and fallible, they never become completely happy and undisturbed.

If we make this distinction between temporarily *feeling* better and more thoroughly and permanently *getting* better through therapy, we can use many brief techniques to effect the former condition but only a few to help bring about the latter. Let me first consider some popular brief methods a therapist can use to help clients *feel* better.

BRIEF TECHNIQUES THAT HELP CLIENTS FEEL BETTER

Warmth and Support

Giving clients, particularly depressed and self-deprecating ones, considerable warmth and support will often help them feel attended to, approved, and more capable of coping with adversity. Quick progress may ensue. Because many of them, however, have a dire *need* (rather than a strong *desire*) for love and approval, their irrational belief that they absolutely *must* be cared for in order to feel worthwhile may easily be enhanced by this kind of treatment. They may also become *dependent* on their therapist's warmth and support, on what Schofield (1964) called "paid friendship"—and that may prolong therapy.

Reassurance and Encouragement

Because so many clients feel inadequate about succeeding and therefore denigrate themselves, assuring them that they are brighter and more attractive than they think they are and that they can succeed in work and love often will help bring about a swift change in their negative feelings. But it may also reinforce their devout belief that they have to be achieving and successful before they can accept themselves. So this technique can easily boomerang! And, even when reassurance and encouragement quickly help clients to act more competently, as soon as they fail again—which, as fallible humans, they will!—they tend to propel themselves back to their negative outlook.

Advice Giving and Problem Solving

By giving clients sound advice and helping them to solve practical problems about which they upset themselves—such as school, work, and relationship difficulties—they will often rapidly feel much better. But often they will still tend to, first, depend on the therapist rather than themselves to solve their problems; and, second, they only will feel good when their practical difficulties are successfully resolved. They will tend to return to anxiety and depression when faced again with hassles. Is this a real therapeutic improvement?

Insight and Explanation About the Past

Therapists often can briefly "explain" to clients that they hate their mates because these mates are acting the way their fathers or mothers acted years ago, or therapists can "explain" that the abusive way their foster parents treated them during their childhood makes them abuse their own children today. Whether such "explanations" are right or wrong, clients often buy them and feel that they understand themselves much better and sometimes change their disordered behavior. But these insights, even when factually based, fail to show clients exactly why they upset themselves about early life events, what they did to carry on their early upset, what they are now doing to keep it alive, and how they can change their present disturbance-creating attitudes. So this kind of insight or explanation, though often temporarily productive, usually has little lasting therapeutic effects.

Catharsis and Abreaction

Helping clients get in touch with their deep and perhaps hidden feelings of anxiety and rage often will release their pent-up emotions and encourage them to feel better. But, unless therapists go beyond this kind of catharsis and abreaction, they may actually reinforce the intensification of disturbed feelings (especially anger) or effect only temporary release (Ellis, 1977, 1988; Tavris, 1983). The anxiety- or rage-creating philosophy of the clients may not be resolved or may actually be exacerbated.

Positive Thinking and Imagery

Ever since the heydey of Emile Coué (1923) in the early part of this century, therapists have quickly helped clients with positive thinking and success-oriented imagery (Zilbergeld & Lazarus, 1987). I have no doubt that this technique often works—and works quickly. The problem is that positive thinking usually covers up and temporarily alleviates negative thinking; and it offers false promises of marvelous performance improvements that probably will not be sustained. It also tends to reinforce clients' notions that they *have to* do well in order to accept themselves and leads them to deprecate themselves when they once again fail.

Reinforcement and Penalization

The principles of reinforcement and penalization, stemming from the work of Watson (Watson & Rayner, 1920), Skinner (1971), and Wolpe (1982), have been used to help people change disruptive emotions and behaviors. These techniques often work quite well, especially in the case of certain addictions, such as overeating and procrastination. Unfortunately, the gains thereby achieved frequently are not lasting. Moreover, using reinforcements and penalties with clients frequently induces them to do the right thing for the wrong reason—that is, for immediate gratification or lack of pain. It thereby may encourage their short-range hedonism and low frustration tolerance, which often are the main source of their addictive behaviors. When the therapist's or other people's approval is used as the reinforcer, this technique tends to make clients more suggestible and less able to think for themselves—and hence more disturbed (Ellis, 1983).

BRIEF TECHNIQUES THAT HELP CLIENTS GET BETTER

As noted above, you can use many techniques to help your clients temporarily *feel* better but most of the popular ones have their Achilles heel and often fail to effect permanent change. This is because they fail to bring about a profound philosophic or attitudinal change, which usually seems to be required if clients are to *get better* (as defined in the second paragraph of this chapter). Here are some suggestions for using techniques that easily can be taught to clients and that, if practiced by them for several weeks or months, can help many of them to start making a profound philosophic and behavioral change. None of these methods is a cureall for every psychological ill; and many of them, even when they begin to work marvelously for a while, had better be steadily continued by clients as self-help procedures. But after using these techniques for many years with several thousand clients, I see that they can help many disturbed people feel better *and* get better. No guarantees, of course. But try them and see for yourself!

Acknowledging Self-Disturbability

Teach clients that environmental and biological factors "cause" or contribute to their emotional and behavioral problems and that it is sometimes valuable for them to understand these influences. But, most important, as Epictetus (1890) said two thousand years ago, it was not the things that happened that really upset people during their childhood, but their *view* of these things. People *chose* to see and interpret obnoxious occurrences in a disturbing (rather than a frustrating) way; and to a large degree they still *choose* to do so today. Since people mainly (though not completely) disturb themselves, they fortunately have the ability to control their emotional destiny and to stubbornly persist at *refusing* to do so—now and in the future. If therapists are able to teach clients this one idea, that they largely *make themselves* disturbed, that they *easily* and *naturally* do so, and that they definitely can choose *not* to do so, they can quickly help many clients begin to *take* the road (though not exactly to *complete* the road) to *getting,* and not merely *feeling,* better (Ellis, 1962, 1973, 1988).

Clearly Perceiving Dogmatic Shoulds and Musts

Following Karen Horney (1950), rational emotive therapy (RET) hypothesizes that people mainly disturb themselves not only by the unrealistic perceptions and inferences that cognitive-behavior therapies often display and dispute (Beck, 1976; Meichenbaum, 1977; Raimy, 1976), but more important, by devoutly holding absolutistic "shoulds," "oughts," and "musts" (Ellis, 1962, 1973, 1985a, b, 1987a, b; Ellis & Harper, 1975). If clinicians strongly use this RET theory of emotional disturbance, they can quickly (yes, in a few sessions) see that whenever clients feel very anxious, depressed, or enraged, most probably they are consciously or unconsciously believing one or more dogmatic, unconditional musts. Once convinced that their self-defeating feelings largely stem from rigid *must*urbation, clients have at their disposal an invaluable key to self-upset that can put them on the road to depth-centered recovery.

Active Scientific Disputing of Musts and Other Irrational Beliefs

Once therapists convince clients that they are mainly upsetting *themselves* and that they are doing so by devoutly believing and holding on to imperative musts and other irrational beliefs (most of which are connected with or stem from underlying "necessitizing"), clinicians often can help them to use active scientific thinking to ameliorate and surrender their self-defeating dogmas. They can use, and teach clients to use, scientific questioning and challenging. For example: "Granted that it would be unfortunate if you did not perform well at work or at love, why *must* you do so?" "Where is the evidence that you *can't bear* studying for the difficult exam that your professor *shouldn't* have given you?" "Prove that because you treated your friends fairly and that because you are inconvenienced by their inconsiderate behavior, they *have to* be nice to you and it is the *end of the world* if they're not." "Where is it written that because you were thoroughly rejected by the person you love, that makes you a completely unlovable, worthless person?" By forthrightly teaching clients to scientifically dispute their self-sabotoging irrationalities, and to work at giving them up now and later, clinicians may well undermine their basic tendency to create nonsensical conclusions about themselves, others, and the universe (Ellis, 1988; Ellis & Dryden, 1987).

Referenting

People seem to disturb themselves for two main reasons: (1) ego problems, where they denigrate themselves for not doing well enough or not winning sufficient approval from others; (2) low frustration tolerance (LFT) problems, where they insist that they must get what they want and that they absolutely cannot be happy if they get less. LFT also consists of demanding immediate gratification rather than future rewards and leads to addictions and compulsions, such as overeating, alcoholism, and severe procrastination. The main reason why people vow to give up addictions and then continue to indulge in them is often because they focus on or referent the advantages of, say, smoking—such as quick relaxation and pleasure—and also focus on the disadvantages of stopping smoking—such as immediate tension and pain (Danysh, 1974).

A quick and effective technique of helping them change this kind of focusing or referenting is the RET method of getting them to write down on three-by-five cards or notebook paper many disadvantages of their addiction and many advantages of stopping it. They then strongly review and 10 or 20 times a day think about these pros and cons of, say, smoking. This kind of rereferenting or rethinking about their problem frequently, and in short order, brings about a powerful change in their basic *view* of their addiction and significantly helps clients—especially when combined with other behavioral methods—to give it up and to maintain their habit-free behavior (Ellis, 1985a; Ellis & Abrahms, 1978; Ellis & Becker, 1982; Ellis & Bernard, 1985).

Reframing

Reframing is an attitudinal and philosophic technique in which clinicians show clients how to look differently at the poor conditions of their lives and to see that they have a less obnoxious or good side as well. Thus, people who are depressed about losing a job can be shown that the job may have been a good one but it also had definite bad points—such as long commuting time, a nasty supervisor, and low pay. Clients also can be helped to see that losing this job is a *challenge* they can use to get a better one, to raise skills, to obtain better education and training, etc. They also can come to view this unfortunate event as a challenge they can use to *not* make themselves miserable or depressed but only frustrated and disappointed about their loss. Thereby they can use several kinds of reframing to effect a basic philosophical change about losses and frustrations (Ellis, 1985a, 1988; Ellis & Dryden, 1987).

Teaching Unconditional Acceptance

Carl Rogers (1962) held that giving clients unconditional positive regard, or what RET calls unconditional acceptance, is the best way of helping them to fully accept and stop denigrating themselves. RET agrees but adds that if you, as a therapist, mainly show your clients that you completely accept them, no matter how badly and disturbedly they behave, most of them will conclude (as Rogers rightly contends), "Because my therapist fully accepts me, in spite of my poor behavior, I can legitimately accept myself." But this is *conditional* self-acceptance —dependent on clinicians acknowledging clients' worth as humans. *Un*-conditional self-regard would mean that clients would choose to accept themselves whether or not anyone, including the therapist, acknowledges them and their humanity.

In RET, we not only *show* clients, by the therapist's manner, tone, and expression, that we accept them fully—yes, with or without their behaving well—but we also *teach* them to unconditionally accept themselves even when they behave badly and are subject to disapproval by others. To do this, we teach them: (1) People are too complex to be given a single, global rating. (2) They had better evaluate or measure *only* their individual traits or behaviors. (3) The purpose of rating their deeds and acts is to live and *enjoy* and not to *prove* themselves. (4) If they insist on giving any rating to their *self,* their essence, or their totality (a trap into which they may easily and unwisely fall), they had better proclaim, "I am a good and worthy person just because I am alive and human and not because of any act that I may or may not do." (Bernard, 1986; Ellis, 1972b, 1973, 1985a, 1988; Ellis & Becker, 1982; Ellis & Dryden, 1987; Ellis & Harper, 1975).

This kind of teaching of unconditional self-acceptance may take root in relatively few sessions of active-directive RET. But since most people easily and naturally fall back into negative self-rating, clients had better be forewarned to keep practicing self-acceptance for the rest of their lives.

Shame-Attacking Exercises

Feelings of shame, humiliation, embarrassment, and self-denigration are at the bottom of much emotional disturbance. RET for many years has used shame-attacking exercises to help people feel shameless and thoroughly self-accepting even when they behave foolishly or incompetently (Ellis, 1969, 1971, 1985a). Clinicians quickly can teach RET's shame-attacking technique to clients by persuading them to do one or more practical or silly things in public that they would normally feel too ashamed to do—with the proviso that they are not to get themselves into any real trouble or harm anyone else by doing these supposedly shameful acts. Thus, clients can wear outlandish clothing, ask people silly questions, refuse to tip for poor services, use an umbrella on a sunny day, openly read a pornographic book in public, ask a stupid question at a lecture, or do anything else they consider shameful. If they will frequently do these normally embarrassing acts and simultaneously work on their thoughts and feelings to make themselves *not* feel ashamed, they may in a short period of time make tremendous inroads against some of their basic tendencies to direly need others' approval (Ellis, 1988; Ellis & Dryden, 1987).

Rational Emotive Imagery

Since 1971 RET has been using and adapting Maultsby's technique of rational emotive imagery (REI) to quickly and profoundly help people change inappropriate and disturbed feelings to appropriate and undisturbed feelings (Maultsby, 1971; Maultsby & Ellis, 1974). To employ the RET version of REI, you can try the following procedure. Take, for example, a client who is depressed about failing a test and possibly, therefore, of failing an important course and say: "Imagine the worst.

Vividly fantasize that you take this exam over and fail it again. Worse yet, you fail the entire course and your teacher and fellow students are very critical of you and think you're an idiot for failing. Vividly imagine this grim event actually happening! How do you honestly feel as you strongly visualize this event?"

Most of the time, your client will reply, "I feel very depressed."

"Fine! Now really get in touch with that feeling. Make yourself feel very depressed. Really *feel* it."

Wait till the client acknowledges this intense, self-defeating feeling. Then say, "Good. Now keep the same image. Don't change it! But *do* change your feeling! Instead of feeling depressed and self-downing, make yourself feel *only* sorry, *only* disappointed, but *not* depressed."

When your client has changed his or her feeling to that of sorriness and disappointment, ask, "How did you change it? What did you do?"

People who know the principles of RET will see that when they say something like "I told myself it was too bad but not the end of the world!" or "I said to myself, 'That's very unfortunate but I can still live with failing and accept myself as a fallible person',," they really have properly changed their feeling from inappropriate depression to appropriate disappointment. For only by modifying their *view* of what has happened are they likely to change their depressed feeling about it.

Getting clients to do rational emotive imagery many times—preferably, at least once a day for 30 days in succession—may well help them to make a profound change in their disturbance-creating ideas (Ellis, 1985a, 1988).

Implosive In Vivo Desensitization

According to the principles of RET, people can effectively change dysfunctional behaviors by changing their irrational, *must*urbatory beliefs. But since thoughts, feelings, and behaviors are interactional, they also can change their disturbed thinking by forcing themselves, in spite of their discomfort, to modify avoidant or compulsive actions. RET theory also says that if clients engage in implosive or flooding in vivo desensitization, often they will quickly make crucial changes in their irrational beliefs.

Thus, therapists who have a male client who is terribly afraid of rejection by women—who thinks that he absolutely can't encounter them socially and that he is a complete failure if he gets rejected—can try to persuade him to follow through on the homework assignment of talking to a minimum of five women every day. If he follows out this assignment for a month or two, most probably he will not only give up the idea that he can't speak to women, but also will surrender the irrational belief that he is a worthless slob if he gets rejected. His forcibly changed behavior will greatly encourage him to modify his long-held ideas about rejection.

Similarly, with a female client who is deathly afraid of using elevators, persuading her to go up and down in an elevator 20 times a day for a number of days in a row will change significantly her extremely phobic ideas about elevators—and perhaps about several other "dangerous" behaviors (Ellis, 1985a, 1988).

CONCLUSION

It is hypothesized that psychotherapy frequently is beneficial by helping people to *feel* better but that it much more rarely helps them to *get* better—that is, to maintain and extend improvement and become less disturb*able*.

Clients can be helped significantly with several relatively brief techniques of therapy, including warmth and support, reassurance and encouragement, advice giving and problem solving, insight and explanation about the past, catharsis and abreaction, positive thinking and imagery, and reinforcement and penalization. However, these popular methods all have serious limitations even when they truly help people to ameliorate presenting symptoms and feel better.

Fortunately, RET includes several brief methods of therapy that not only help many clients to *feel* but to *get* better and set them on the road to less present and future disturbability. These more elegant and more depth-centered techniques of RET include showing clients how to acknowledge their self-disturbability; to clearly perceive their dogmatic "shoulds" and "musts"; to actively and scientifically dispute their "musts" and other irrational beliefs; to use referenting; to employ reframing; to engage in shame-attacking exercises; to use rational emotive imagery; and to carry out implosive in vivo desensitization. None of these methods, individually or collectively, is a panacea for minimizing emotional and behavioral disturbance. But it is hypothesized that they certainly will help!

REFERENCES

Beck, A. T. (1976). *Cognitive Therapy and the Emotional Disorders.* New York: International Universities Press.

Bernard, M. E. (1986). *Staying Alive in an Irrational World: Albert Ellis and Rational-Emotive Therapy.* South Melbourne, Australia: Carlson/ Macmillan.

Coué, E. (1923). *My Method.* New York: Doubleday, Page.

Danysh, J. (1974). *Stop Without Quitting.* San Francisco: International Society for General Semantics.

Ellis, A. (1962). *Reason and Emotion in Psychotherapy.* Secaucus, NJ: Citadel.

Ellis, A. (1969). A weekend of rational encounter. *Rational Living, 4(2),* 1–8.

Ellis, A. (Speaker) (1971). *How to Stubbornly Refuse to Be Ashamed of Anything.* (Cassette recording). New York: Institute for Rational-Emotive Therapy.

Ellis, A. (1972a). Helping people get better: Rather than merely feel better. *Rational Living, 7(2),* 2–9.

Ellis, A. (1972b). *Psychotherapy and the Value of a Human Being.* New York: Institute for Rational-Emotive Therapy.

Ellis, A. (1973). *Humanistic Psychotherapy: The Rational-Emotive Approach.* New York: McGraw-Hill.

Ellis, A. (1977). *Anger—How to Live With and Without It.* Secaucus, NJ: Citadel Press.

Ellis, A. (1983). The philosophic implications and dangers of some popular behavior therapy techniques. In M. Rosenbaum, C. M. Franks, & Y. Jaffe (Eds.), *Perspectives in Behavior Therapy in the Eighties* (pp. 138–151). New York: Springer.

Ellis, A. (1985a). *Overcoming Resistance: Rational-Emotive Therapy with Difficult Clients.* New York: Springer.

Ellis, A. (1985b). Expanding the ABCs of rational-emotive therapy. In M. Mahoney & A. Freeman (Eds.), *Cognition and Psychotherapy* (pp. 313–323). New York: Plenum Press.

Ellis, A. (1987a). The impossibility of achieving consistently good mental health. *American Psychologist, 42,* 364–375.

Ellis, A. (1987b). A sadly neglected cognitive element in depression. *Cognitive Therapy and Research, 11,* 121–146.

Ellis, A. (1988). *How to Stubbornly Refuse to Make Yourself Miserable About Anything—Yes, Anything!* Secaucus, NJ: Lyle Stuart.

Ellis, A., & Abrahms, E. (1978). *Brief Psychotherapy in Medical and Health Practice.* New York: Springer.

Ellis, A., & Becker, I. (1982). *A Guide to Personal Happiness.* North Hollywood, CA: Wilshire.

Ellis, A., & Bernard, M. E. (Eds.) (1985). *Clinical Applications of Rational-Emotive Therapy.* New York: Plenum Press.

Ellis, A., & Dryden, W. (1987). *The Practice of Rational-Emotive Therapy.* New York: Springer.

Ellis, A., & Harper, R. A. (1975). *A New Guide to Rational Living.* North Hollywood, CA: Wilshire Books.

Epictetus (1890). *The Collected Works of Epictetus.* Boston: Little, Brown.

Horney, K. (1950). *Neurosis and Human Growth.* New York: Norton.

Maultsby, M. C., Jr. (1971). *Handbook of Rational Self-Counseling.* Lexington, KY: Rational Self Help Books.

Maultsby, M. C., Jr., & Ellis, A. (1974). *Technique for Using Rational-Emotive Imagery.* New York: Institute for Rational-Emotive Therapy.

Meichenbaum, D. (1977). *Cognitive-Behavior Modification.* New York: Plenum.

Raimy, V. (1975). *Misunderstandings of the Self.* San Francisco: Jossey-Bass.

Rogers, C. R. (1962). *On Becoming a Person.* Boston: Houghton-Mifflin.

Schofield, W. (1964). *Psychotherapy: The Purchase of Friendship.* Englewood Cliffs, NJ: Prentice-Hall.

Skinner, B. F. (1971). *Beyond Freedom and Dignity.* New York: Knopf.

Tavris, C. (1983). *Anger: The Misunderstood Emotion.* New York: Simon & Schuster.

Watson, J. B., & Rayner, R. (1920). Conditioned emotional reactions. *Journal of Experimental Psychology, 3,* 1–14.

Wolpe, J. (1982). *The Practice of Behavior Therapy,* 3rd edition. New York: Pergamon Press.

Zilbergeld, B., & Lazarus, A. A. (1987). *Mind Power.* Boston: Little, Brown.

CHAPTER 23

Getting the Important Work Done Fast: Contract Plus Redecision
Mary McClure Goulding

In brief psychotherapy the essential work is pinpointing the problem, finding the solution, and helping the client develop the self-esteem necessary to maintain the gains he or she has made after therapy is ended. In this chapter I describe the way we use transactional analysis and redecision in brief psychotherapy. The major components are: establishment of a treatment contract, enhancement of self-esteem and altruism, recognition of personal autonomy, and redecision in order to fulfill the specific contract. Case histories are used to illustrate the process.

CONTRACT

The first step in transactional analysis and in redecision therapy, once the client feels safe, is negotiating a therapeutic contract to accomplish a specific goal. This goal needs to be measurable, testable, and possible to attain from the therapy. It usually includes changes in the client's way of thinking, feeling, and behaving, although sometimes the change may be in only one of these. In short-term therapy the contract also must be one that the client can accomplish quickly. If this is not possible, intermittent therapy can be substituted for short-term therapy. In intermittent therapy sessions are spread out, and the client has more responsibility in working alone toward achieving the long-term goal.

Whether intermittent or regularly scheduled short-term therapy is indicated, the final session, after the contract is fulfilled, will be focused on strokes for accomplishment, and on any work necessary for sustaining the client's success.

My husband, Bob Goulding, asks each client, "What do you want to change about yourself today?" This question affirms the belief that: (1) the client is in charge of her or his own changing; (2) change is possible; and (3) change is possible today.

Therapist and client are partners in negotiating the contract in that the client is entitled to my honest opinion at all times. I don't keep secrets. Since I do not believe in fooling the client, I don't have secret agendas or use strategies that put me in a one-up position. I will explain to the client any strategy I use and I won't pretend to work on one issue while secretly working on another. If I had supervisors or consultants, I'd use them to assist me in looking at my countertransference issues and to help me find the best possible ways to implement the client's goals, and I would also explain their strategies to the client. I would not use anyone to help formulate the contract without the client being a full participant in the process.

I emphasize this because some therapists at the Evolution of Psychotherapy Conference in 1985 suggested that the therapist alone sets treatment goals or even that the therapist's supervisor sets the goals. I think such therapy is a discount of the ability of clients to run their own lives.

Successful short-term therapy begins with a good contract, much as a successful dissertation depends on a good proposal. I can usually tell, as soon as doctoral candidates begin talking about their dissertations, which candidates will graduate on schedule and which ones will struggle for years and often end up in the "all but dissertation" (ABD) enclave. The ones who will achieve their goals on time know exactly what they are researching and why. They can describe their research in a way that a third grader would understand. The strugglers and the ABDs, on the other hand, pick dissertation topics that can be described as "all there is to know, explained polysyllabically, about almost everything, including whatever turns up along the way."

I think graduate schools that take a candidate's money while not teaching that candidate how to write a dissertation in at most one year are cheating their students. Similarly, I think that therapists who do not help their clients pick quick, achievable contracts are likewise cheating their clients.

When clients want to "know myself better" or "find out why I ... ," they are not talking about personal change. The therapist needs to ask them, "Know yourself better in what specific areas of your life?" and "Once you know yourself better and have found out why you do what you do, what changes do you plan to make in yourself?" If the client responds with "You know, kind of like I want to sort of live more or something like that," it is the responsibility of the therapist to teach this client how to make small, discrete, definite, testable, short-term goals.

During the contract-setting process, clients learn to think creatively about their present lives. "What precisely is my life like? What do I like and dislike about it?" This includes health, work, love, and social life. "How, precisely, do I want to change in order to enrich the life I have today?"

This exploration of the present can continue between sessions. The therapist may suggest specific assignments. "You've talked about your relationship with your son. You're clear there. You are less clear about what goes on when you and your husband start arguing. Listen to you and to him during the next few days, and take notes if you like. Figure out exactly how your arguments start, what happens next, and how they end." Or, "Between now and next week, ask your physician the questions you've asked me, and write down exactly what she says. Bring your notes to the next session." Or, "Between now and next week write down five good things about yourself and five good things you have done for yourself. Be specific." Or, "Now that you've learned a bit about imagery, practice five minutes every night imagining yourself doing something exciting. Make up specific scenes, and don't trash your fantasies when you have finished. Next week, if you like, we'll discuss what you imagined."

While establishing contracts, clients also learn to think about their futures. "How do I want to be tomorrow, next year, the year after?" One easy format is to ask clients to pretend that they have just terminated therapy and that it was overwhelmingly successful. Everything they could possibly have wanted to change about themselves has been accomplished. Then ask, "Where are you living?" "With whom?" "What are you doing in your new, successful life?" "How are you different in your thoughts, your feelings, and your behavior from when you began therapy?" Next, suggest that it is 5, 10, or 20 years from the time the client terminates therapy. "How did you sustain your accomplishments?" "What else did you accomplish for yourself after therapy?"

Assignments can also be made about the future. "Write yourself an Emancipation Proclamation and make it specific." Or, "You are unclear about jobs. Between now and next week find out exactly what jobs are available and what skills you need to get the jobs you want." Or, "Go to your library, your Chamber of Commerce, and your phone book, and make a list of activities you have never undertaken but might enjoy."

While you and your clients are exploring present and future, you can, of course, bring into the open any transference issues that are important to resolve. "When I ask you about the future, you tell me about the past. When I ask you to speak up, you speak more softly. I'm guessing that one way you've been dealing with people is to do the opposite of what they expect." Or, "You keep asking if you should have one more AIDS test. From what you've told me, there's a 99.99% chance that another AIDS test will be negative and there's also a 99.99% chance that you won't believe that test either. So one big problem we may run up against here is your unwillingness to believe other people." Or, "Have you noticed that you consider my opinions more important than yours? And it's your life! One goal I'd suggest is that you decide to value your own ability to think."

SELF-ESTEEM AND AUTONOMY

Clients must love themselves as they are today, before they start to make the changes they desire. Without self-love, their triumphs in therapy often backfire. If they believe, "I have to be different to be OK," they will expect too much from therapy and end up disappointed, like the person who believes a reconstructed nose will bring popularity, sex, and happiness forever instead of simply a nicer nose. Until clients believe in their own intrinsic worth, each fulfilled contract gives only momentary pleasure, before they find in themselves new blemishes that need correcting.

Self-care includes deciding against suicide and self-destruction, whether or not therapy is successful. To base one's life on maintaining a marriage or changing a life-style or even overcoming a phobia is overwhelmingly dangerous. Getting a good job may be important, but staying alive with or without a good job is more important. Further, when a client stops using suicidal rumination as an alternative "if things don't get better," that client can put all his or her energy into making desired changes instead of being suicidal.

Self-care also means that the client will do whatever is necessary to be healthy, including stopping food, alcohol, nicotine, and drug addictions. Therapy may need to be postponed until the person has been treated for alcoholism or drug abuse.

Personal autonomy includes a clear recognition of the limits of one's own power and the limits of the power of others. Autonomous people know and accept that all human beings are in charge of their own thinking, feeling, and actions. No one can make a client feel, think, or do, although, of course, others may work hard to "grease the skids." By the same token, a client is not in charge of the thoughts, actions, and feelings of others. Father may be furious, suicidal, or stolidly indifferent when his son announces that he is gay. The stimulus comes from the son; the reaction is chosen by the father and is the father's responsibility.

Every one of us would like to change other people. That is one of the primary reasons people become therapists. When clients want their spouses, offspring, neighbors, and bosses to change, their longing is natural. Of course they want their loved ones to be sober, kinder, and more effective, or at least they'd like the kids to get to school on time. A part of therapy may be the exploration of how to make it easier for the other to choose to do as the client wishes. But ultimately the others are in charge of their own thinking, feeling, and doing. The crucial question to the client is "Whether or not the others in your life change, how do you want to change yourself?"

ALTRUISM

What are the client's goals for the good of people beyond the family? I have noticed that people without such goals are the ones who spend their days fussing about the lint in their navels. Short-term therapy does not sustain them simply because they have nothing exciting in their lives except their own pathology or the pathology of those around them. They need altruistic quests in order to be sufficiently fulfilled to overlook and work around the leftover neuroses, characterological quirks, and basic limitations of themselves and the people they love. Therefore, it is important to explore with each client what altruistic pursuits will make life more meaningful. Usually I'll bring this up in the beginning of therapy, although it may be postponed when clients are too distressed to look beyond their present pain. In such cases, once pain is relieved and the contract fulfilled, altruistic goals can be set as the therapist and client assess how the client will function when therapy is concluded.

FULFILLMENT OF CONTRACT

Short-term therapy requires a skillful therapist. To help the client effect personal changes in the shortest possible time, the therapist must work precisely and efficiently, focusing only on material that is relevant to the contract. There is not time to get involved in all the characterological idiosyncracies that might be dealt with in long-term therapy. This is not necessarily a weakness of short-term therapy. I am impressed with the fact that clients continue to make important changes after therapy has ended, if they have learned to believe in their own ability to change their lives.

There are lots of different therapies designed to achieve the goal of rapid personal change. My primary method is redecision therapy, in which I use childhood scenes as settings for change in the present.

Although I know standard diagnostic categories, I don't consciously think in those terms. Instead, I ask myself what specifically could have happened to this client to render her or him incapable of solving a particular problem that has been solved by millions of people in this world. Why is this reasonably intelligent person pursuing a course that any untrained observer could predict would lead to disaster? What happened that a lovely little baby, as all babies are, grew into this bombastic bore? What happened that this person, who may well have a much higher IQ than I have, can't seem to use that IQ to keep a job? What happened that someone with all the outward trappings for happiness looks for ways to be depressed? Why, in a world full of couples, can this person find no one to love? How is this person's nonsuccess of today related to decisions made in childhood? What scenes from the past will illuminate the present?

There are several ways to find early scenes that answer such questions:

The therapist can ask simply, "Does this problem fit anything you remember from your childhood?" If the client believes that it does, ask for a specific scene.

The therapist can use key words spoken by the client. "You said,'He doesn't respect me or like me, so I guess I am no good. I feel very sad.' Now let yourself drift back in time. You are a little kid, and you say to yourself about someone important to you, 'He doesn't respect me' or 'He doesn't like me, so I guess I am no good,' and you feel sad. What's the scene?"

The therapist can begin with what goes on between the two of them and take this to the past. "You leave long pauses between your words. I have an impulse to finish your sentences for you. Did anyone do that when you were a kid?" If the client says, "Yes," ask for a specific scene, remembered from childhood. If the client says, "No," ask if it is all right to explore how it might fit. Then suggest that the client go back to childhood, bring the whole family to the dinner table, and imagine beginning to speak very slowly. What do the others at the dinner table say and do?

Occasionally, a client doesn't remember childhood scenes or doesn't choose to work with the past. In such cases we can use present scenes in the same way that we usually use childhood ones. However, my husband Bob and I find that almost all clients work well in the past, if they are positively stroked by the therapist for whatever scenes they do remember. If the problem is not memory but lack of desire, go back to the contract. Chances are that it was parental, something the client SHOULD want and really doesn't. In that case, therapist and client will have to find a new contract or find a way to make the present contract more palatable.

Some clients learned early to resist just about anything. In that case, the contract will be "I will fulfill my contract even though this will please my mother, my father, my God, and my therapist." You and the client may choose to look for the early scenes when the person learned to fight back, so that the person can redecide to fight only when it is advantageous to the client to do so.

In redecision therapy, the client finds a relevant early scene and returns to it in fantasy, experiencing the original thoughts, feelings, and actions. The redecision occurs when the client then alters the scene, not by changing others but by changing herself or himself. The scene, then, will be complete in a new way.

The following brief examples illustrate this process:

Ann remembers a typical scene in her childhood and returns to it in fantasy. She is attempting to cook and is scolded and derided for her unsuccessful efforts. As a result, she decides that she is "stupid" and says to herself, "I'll never be able to do anything right." First, she reexperiences that humiliating scene, and then she reenters the scene as a spunky little kid who tells everyone, "Look, I can't help that I am the youngest. I'm intelligent and capable. Instead of acting stupid, this time I am reading the cookbook, because I can read already. I'm not dumb. I am looking up how to make a cake and I am doing it right. The rest of you big guys, get out of my way! I can do lots of things right. I won't be your incompetent baby sister any longer!"

Bill takes care of his little sisters and brothers, sadly and resentfully. He says, "It's not fair I can't ever play baseball with the other kids." He goes back into the scene and tells his mother, "These are your children, not mine. When I was their ages, I took care of myself. They can do the same or you can take care of them, Mom. I'm signing up for Little League."

Cora goes into the scene where she accidentally hears her grandmother say to her grandfather, "Why was she ever born? I'm too old to have to raise another kid." She goes back into the scene as herself today and tells little Cora, "It's not your fault you had an irresponsible mother and a tired grandmother. You are a lovely, valuable little girl, and from now on I will care for you."

Don tells his mother, "Sorry you didn't get a girl, but I am not your girl. I am a boy and I am not guilty about that." He struts around the room, telling group members, "I am proud to be male."

Estelle is in the shop where her mother is picking her clothes. She returns to the scene and says, "I do not want a red dress. You can buy it if you must, but it is not my choice. I am no longer pretending to want whatever you tell me I should want. I am a separate person and my wants are different from yours."

Fred is at his mother's funeral. He doesn't mourn, doesn't say good-bye, and tells himself that he's never going to love anyone else ever again. Returning to the scene, he mourns, says goodbye, and gives himself permission to seek love with others.

After redeciding the childhood scene, the client needs to translate the redecision into new action in the present.

Ann enrolls in night school. Her Christmas note to the therapist says that she is doing well.

Bill understands the origin of his compulsive caretaking, but continues to take responsibility for all the "little kids" in his life, including his brother, who goes right on borrowing Bill's money and not repaying him. Bill terminates therapy without fullfilling his contract. Someday, if he chooses, he may change either by giving up the caretaker role or by permitting himself to be a happy caretaker instead of a sad and resentful one.

Cora makes a no-suicide decision and also decides to eliminate sugar and fatty food from her diet in order to lose weight and be more healthy. She opts for long-term therapy in order to get some overdue parenting, while she practices making friends and having fun in life.

Don considers his short-term therapy in a five-day workshop to be brilliantly successful. As he learns to love his own manhood, he also loves others more. He marries well and is having a joyous time with his baby son.

Estelle writes a "wants" list and works out how she will get things she wants. She terminates happily after the next session, although she has many remaining problems.

After saying goodbye to his dead mother, Fred looks for friends and lovers with whom he can be intimate.

CASE EXAMPLE: SUSIE

Susie had been in therapy with two of my trainees, who left the area. She has a long-term marriage, a daughter with whom she quarrels regularly, and a husband she loves. She is markedly overweight.

FIRST SESSION: She talks at length about her life, demonstrates a sparkling humor, and says that her therapists helped her use her humor to save her marriage. "I stopped being so serious about our problems." Her husband is obviously indulgent toward her and likes the role of caretaker. He had some therapy with her, but didn't like it. Her major problem is, she says, "I'm overweight, but there is no use even mentioning it, because nothing works." I explore this with her and learn that she has been contracting to lose weight and failing to do so for a number of years.

I ask what she is willing to accomplish with me. She argues that she knows I can help her with her weight, although she also knows I can't. I tell her that if she decides to lose weight I'll put her in touch with a local physician who specializes in weight reduction. I then say, "Since I'm an ethical person, I am not going to take your money on false pretenses, yours or mine. So let's get on with establishing your contract." (Since she has had therapists with the same orientation as my own, I am more abrupt than I might be with other clients.)

She decides that she wants to be cured of mouse phobia, since she has heard that I specialize in curing phobics. I agree and begin the desensitization work immediately. I ask her to imagine a cage for a mouse. She and I play with her fantasy, making it more and more grandiose until the cage became a palace with a basement exercise room equipped with every device a mouse could possibly want. She imagines that the cage is outside the glass doors in my office, visible to her but safely distant. Next, she imagines that there is a small gray mouse in the cage. She chooses to name it "Missie Mouse." I ask her to imagine the mouse dressed in some fine costume, and she chooses a bright yellow leotard with "Missie" embroidered on the front. The mouse wears four tiny yellow ballet slippers on her feet and a yellow and blue polka dot ribbon over one ear. Standing up, Susie practices moving closer to the glass and then retreating, as she tests out what is a comfortable distance from her fantasied mouse. Eventually she imagines the cage beside her chair, without making herself fearful. She and I both laugh a lot, as she reports her fantasies of Missie doing backflips on a miniature trampoline. Her assignment between sessions is to go to a pet shop and stand as close as is comfortable to a live mouse.

As she starts to leave she says that her real problem is weight. I suggest that she consider a second assignment: find noneating ways to nurture herself and others.

SECOND SESSION: She is delighted to report that she actually held and petted a mouse in the store, though "It wasn't half as cute as our Missie Mouse." She reports no fear and is amazed that she stopped a lifetime phobia in a week.

She then tells of events of the week, including a quarrel with her grown daughter. When I ask if there is anything about herself she wants to change in her relationship to her daughter, she says, "You sound just like my other therapists." Exploring that, she realizes how much she wanted them to say, "You don't have to change because you are right and your daughter is wrong." I try to get her to track that back to her childhood, and she refuses. I laugh, and admit that I was doing exactly what I had said I wouldn't do during the previous session: I was working without a contract. We look at how successfully she worked with the mouse phobia, partly because the contract was clear to both of us.

She reports on her second assignment, finding noneating ways to nurture herself. She doesn't remember the part about nurturing others. Because she has no contract for future work, I suggest that she decide during the week if she really needs or wants more therapy and, if she does, exactly what she wants to change about herself.

THIRD SESSION: She decides, between sessions, that she wants to be happier with herself and her daughter. She discusses current family difficulties and I teach her some game theory and discuss with her the book I am writing on family games. She likes this and says her contract for the next few sessions is to explore ways in which she can step aside and not be involved in trying to run her daughter's life, in order to avoid their games.

FOURTH SESSION: She reports superb ways she has found to use her humor (secretly and silently, to herself) in order to avoid being angry at her quite provocative daughter. She reports that for the first time she recognizes that she escalates her own anger and sadness with her daughter so that her husband will take her side. She says she doesn't need that any more. "He always takes my side anyway, so what's the big deal?" She asks for the name of the physician who specializes in weight reduction.

FIFTH SESSION: She seems to be doing well at home. She doesn't like the physician, who is parental to her. I tell her I am not going to take sides, and she laughs.

SIXTH SESSION: Her home life continues to improve. I ask at length about her life outside the family and learn that she does nothing outside the home except party and has no interest in altruism.

Because she does have difficulty loving herself and her daughter, I suggest she imagine both of them as new babies in adjoining bassinets in the hospital. She is to imagine holding each of them and telling them they are lovely, unique, lovable, and OK. She is tearful during this exercise and says it has real meaning to her.

SEVENTH SESSION: In an early scene she affirms her own worth even though she is a disappointment to her mother, because she is a plump little girl who has to wear glasses. Mother wants her to be a Shirley Temple. Susie feels tremendous relief and joy from this work, which is child redecision work.

EIGHTH SESSION: She reports that she is getting along much better with her daughter, because she has stopped looking for her daughter's blemishes. She recognizes that in some ways she has parented her daughter like her mother parented her. Her daughter is beginning to accept Susie's positive strokes. Susie is tearfully grateful about this. Because she has no further agenda, we terminate. She agrees to telephone in about three months, to report how she is doing.

FINAL SESSION: In three months, she comes for her final session. She, her daughter, and her husband are enjoying each other. She has a funny tale about a mouse that got in her house and ran back and forth frantically in the kitchen while she tried unsuccessfully to sweep it out the back door.

She is still overweight, did not continue with the physician, and is now going to Overeaters Anonymous.

CASE EXAMPLE: JOHN

FIRST SESSION: John begins by telling of his mother's physical cruelties to him when he was a child. I listen sympathetically and say that his mother certainly was sadistic and maybe crazy. I sympathize with him for having to endure such a childhood. He runs from my sympathy by reminding both of us that all of this happened 45 to 55 years ago, and that he wouldn't be thinking about it at all except that he wonders why he was such a dope as to have discounted his mother's cruelties during his mother's lifetime, probably because his stepfather had been worse. Ten years ago, John was in therapy for a year, because he was depressed. During the course of therapy, he dealt with his feelings about his stepfather but insisted that his mother was OK. He has warm feelings about his therapist, but doesn't want to return to him because "he took too long."

I agree to work as quickly as possible and ask about his current life. He has always been single, has had lovers, does not want a lover now, and has many good friends. He is an accountant and plans to retire within the year. He is very involved in local political affairs and in other activities. As he talks, I think that the word "effective" describes him best. When I ask if this is true, he laughs deprecatingly and puts himself down.

I ask my standard question: "Pretend that you get everything you want from this therapy. You deal with your mother just the way you'd want to, and you deal with whatever else may be important. You make all the changes you want to make in yourself. As you walk out of this office for the last time, how are you different from when you walked in?" He says that he wants to walk out knowing he has laid to rest his feelings about his mother. "Great. Let's assume you are successful in laying to rest your feelings about your mother. How are you different as a result of this?" He says, "I'll have self-respect."

I agree that this is a fine goal and wonder if he's willing to be more specific. He's vague because he doesn't have concrete examples. I bring up his running from my sympathy and putting himself down when I call him "effective," both of which seem to point toward difficulties in "self-respect." He responds that he feels uncomfortable with praise and with the idea of loving himself. Tentatively, we agree that he will deal with his feelings about his mother, and also find ways to be comfortable with the praise of others, as well as to practice praising himself.

He then asks about his insurance covering the cost of therapy. I explain that I don't send in insurance forms, but he can send them in himself if he wants to. I tell him that one of the negatives about seeing me is my unwillingness to fuss with insurance and one of the positives is that I do very good short-term therapy. Then I say, "We've got 25 minutes left, so let's get started on your mother." He agrees. I say, "Bring her into the room and tell her, 'You abused me.'"

He explains that he can't do it because he can't ever see people who aren't there. I say, "Oh, dear, I'm moving too fast. I'm sorry about that. How about starting with something more simple than a mother? Let's start with an orange. Shut your eyes, pretend you are holding an orange, and tell me if you can see it." He can't. "Feel it warm, right off the tree, in your right hand." We go on from there, with me praising everything he does, including his honesty in telling me what he can't do. I do this so that he will feel sufficiently comfortable to let himself fantasize, and also I am fulfilling my part of the contract by offering the "praise from others." Within five minutes, he is ready to talk to his mother. He sees her "outline" and that is good enough for us to proceed. I suggest he say, "You abused me."

He blinks rapidly, ducks, and says, "I'd be scared to say that." I ask how old he feels himself to be, and he responds, "Seven." We bring in, as support for the seven-year-old, his grown self and two other adults from his life today. As the seven-year-old, he then feels protected, but says, "I don't even want to talk to her." I say, "Of course, so tell her that." He does, and works for some time in this scene. He lets himself experience his fear and especially his sadness at not having been nurtured well. "I am not loved, that is the worst," he says. He doesn't experience anger.

He switches back to being his competent adult self and reports that he learned in childhood to suppress anger. "If I were angry, she'd have killed me." He tells of her holding knives against his throat, so that he couldn't move without being cut. He tells of terrible beatings. He says, "I was always a good child. There was no reason for any of this. And even as I say this, there is no anger in me." He asks if he has to get angry in order to get well. I assure him that he can let his mother go even if he doesn't get angry at her. (I believe this, just as I believe that people can accomplish their therapeutic goals without shedding a tear, if they can't cry. I work with what people can do, not with what they should do.) I also say that it is freeing to feel all one's emotions.

His assignment between sessions is to get to know that seven-year-old child and to love him. "The child still lives in you and needs from you the assurance that he will never again be abused." I suggest that he experience the richness that comes from loving a little boy.

Between sessions he phones to say that he has arranged for insurance payments if I am licensed. I am, and I say I am glad he can do this. He sounds happy as he reports that he has a lot to tell me at the next session.

SECOND SESSION: He reports what he did during the week. The first evening, when he promised "that kid" that he would love and protect him, he began to cry and spent the whole evening crying for himself. "The next day I woke up absolutely furious with my mother. It was so amazing, you wouldn't believe it! I could have killed her! Treating a kid that way! She was a selfish, inhuman slob." He says that the house was always filthy, the sheets were never washed even when kids urinated in their sleep, and the children were always hungry. He says the children survived because they took care of each other.

"Most of the week I was consumed with anger, and then I was done. Now, I really am done with that miserable woman. I'm not even glad she's dead. I don't care either way."

He says he is ready to say goodbye to her, so I help him reconstruct the funeral scene. He has no trouble visualizing her in an open coffin. Imagining we are among the mourners at the funeral, he and I talk more about his mother, and I ask if he is in touch with any positives. He says, "Well, she birthed me. I don't know where I got my intelligence. My real father was supposed to have been an even worse slob. He was a bum in the U.S. Army. I got intelligence from somewhere. My mother doesn't have any, but I can thank her for my birth." He imagines saying to her body in the coffin, "You are dead, and I thank you for giving birth to me." He has no other appreciations, and doesn't want to repeat his resentments. I ask if there is anything else he needs to do or say or feel before letting her go. He is clear that he is ready to say goodbye, and he does.

Because he is moving much more quickly than most clients, I slow him down by having him visualize the graveyard and the coffin beside the open grave. Again, I ask if there are any last-minute reasons not to say good-bye quite yet. He can't think of any. He doesn't bother with either appreciations or regrets, but simply acknowledges, "You are dead." After saying goodbye, he imagines the coffin being lowered and himself throwing a handful of dirt on it. When he is done, he says, "I am free. I am a real person now." He isn't surprised that he worked so quickly and well. It is as if he expected to complete his work in this session.

We spend the rest of the hour discussing his current life and how to build in nurturance for himself in the future. He has thought about my observations in the previous session that he discounts positive strokes, and he mentions similar examples from work. He decides to practice accepting strokes. I suggest that a clue for him, when he is turning down a stroke, is his self-deprecating laugh. He says that he'll be aware of his laughter and only laugh "when I am pleased with myself."

I ask if he is satisfied with the lack of intimacy in his life, and he says, "Why would I want a lover at my age! I can't imagine sharing my home with anyone, expecially now when I am ready to retire." He decides to expand his friendships to include people who stroke well. He mentions some of the work he is doing for others.

I tell him how much I admire his ability not only to survive, but to live a rich life. He smiles and says, "I'll cherish what you say, instead of discarding it."

He says he accomplished what he came for. I wish him well, and let him know that he can return any time he wants additional therapy.

CONCLUSION OF THERAPY

The conclusion of therapy, as with John, may occur when the therapeutic contract is fulfilled. Sometimes, as with Susie, the client gets some things she wants, such as the cure of a mouse phobia and a happier relationship with her daughter, and doesn't get others, such as the weight loss she wanted most.

Short-term therapy is achievable when a therapist truly believes that the conclusion of a contract is a great time for termination. I am not willing to play out the parental game of "one more thing," in which I would say, "Now that you've made your bed, how about cleaning the closet?" Instead, I congratulate clients on what they have done, and let them leave with pride in their accomplishments.

Clients are appreciative and send other clients who expect to change quickly. Therefore, I get to know interesting "winners." Further, working quickly means being involved every minute of the therapy hour, as I look constantly for newer and better ways to work. This keeps me interested and satisfied with what I do.

BIBLIOGRAPHY

Goulding, M. M., and Goulding, R. L. (1979) *Changing Lives Through Redecision Therapy.* New York: Brunner/Mazel.

Goulding, M. M., and Goulding, R. L. (1989). *Not to Worry.* New York: William Morrow, Silver Arrow Imprint.

Goulding, R. L., and Goulding, M. M. (1978). *The Power Is in the Patient.* San Francisco: TA Press.

Kadis, L. B. (Ed.) (1985). *Redecision Therapy: Expanded Perspectives.* WIGFT Press.

CHAPTER 24

Short-Term Anxiety-Provoking Psychotherapy (STAPP) Termination—Outcome— and Videotaping

Peter Sifneos

A brief overview of a type of brief dynamic psychotherapy called short-term anxiety-provoking psychotherapy (STAPP) is presented in this chapter. It was developed 35 years ago. It has been researched systematically by control studies and has been demonstrated to mental health professionals and to students as an effective treatment modality by the extensive use of videotapes (Sifneos, 1972, 1987).

The criteria for selection of appropriate candidates and the requirements and techniques used are listed below. Also, the outcome findings of this brief dynamic psychotherapy are discussed.

All these aspects have been reported in numerous publications particularly over the last 15 years, so the question may be asked as to what exactly is new in this chapter (Sifneos, 1987). In answer to this question, I will address the issue of termination in this form of psychotherapy in more detail, because it plays a crucial role in making treatment brief and therefore cost-effective. The use of videotapes for educational purposes also will be discussed and an attempt will be made to point out which of the selection criteria utilized in STAPP might be used effectively for choosing and treating more severely disturbed patients, for whom long-term psychotherapeutic interventions have been commonly used.

STAPP was developed at the Psychiatric Clinic of the Massachusetts General Hospital in the mid-1950s, following a successful three-month treatment of a patient who developed an acute onset of phobias about all forms of transportation, at a time when neither psychopharmacological agents nor behavior modification techniques were available for the treatment of phobic disorders. The only treatment available then was long-term psychodynamic psychotherapy (Sifneos, 1972).

As a result of this successful intervention we completed three systematic investigations dealing with patients who had the same type of character structure as this first patient, as well as similar symptoms or difficulties in their interpersonal relations (Sifneos, 1987).

CRITERIA FOR SELECTION

The criteria used for the selection of appropriate patients included the following: The presentation of a circumscribed chief complaint and the ability of the patient to assign top priority for its resolution. The identifications by history of at least one meaningful (give and take, altruistic) relationship during the patient's early childhood and the demonstration of the patient's capacity to interact in a flexible manner with an evaluating mental health worker constituted additional criteria for selection. Finally, psychological awareness and particularly a motivation for *change* and not for symptom relief, or any other kind of relief, were considered to be essential ingredients for the proper evaluation of appropriate candidates to be offered a rapidly progressing dynamic therapy of brief duration.

After establishing the fact that a patient fulfilled the above-mentioned selection criteria on the basis of information received during a systematic developmental history, the therapist also had to specify a therapeutic focus around which the treatments would concentrate and revolve. Such a focus signified that the therapist had arrived at a psychodynamic formulation of the emotional conflicts underlying the patient's psychological difficulties and was convinced that if these conflicts were resolved, the treatment would be successful. The most common foci found to be used effectively by short-term dynamic psychotherapeutic interventions involved such problems as unresolved Oedipal conflicts, loss and separation issues, and grief reactions.

Another task of the evaluator had to do with the ability to communicate to the patient his or her dynamic formulation and get an agreement of cooperation to work on its resolution so as to establish a working alliance to help examine and eventually eliminate the conflicts underlying the therapeutic focus.

In recent years at Boston's Beth Israel Hospital and the Psychiatry Department of Harvard Medical School, in an effort to investigate the results of STAPP on a homogeneous population of patients, we selected for treatment individuals with unresolved Oedipal interactions, i.e., triangular types of interpersonal difficulties in their adult life emanating from similar difficulties that the patient had encountered during their early childhood with parents.

THERAPEUTIC REQUIREMENTS AND TECHNICAL ISSUES

The specific treatment requirements involved weekly 45-minute face-to-face interviews continuing over a few months. Usually neither a time limit nor a total number of interviews was specified, and no termination date was set. The patient was told that the therapist did not know how long it would take for resolution of the focal conflicts agreed upon, but because the patient was found to be a good candidate to receive STAPP, it was the therapist's impression that the problems could be solved over a brief period of time, from two to six months. In the five research studies of STAPP conducted during a 25-year period, only one patient needed 20 sessions of therapy.

The techniques used involved the development of a therapeutic alliance, which was actually an extension of the working alliance that had been established during the evaluation interview, as well as anxiety-provoking confrontations. In addition, the therapist actively helped the patient to concentrate on the agreed-upon therapeutic focus by use of early transference clarifications. Patients were encouraged to observe the similarity in the patterns of their behavior to people during their daily life, with key people in their childhood, such as parents or parent-surrogates. These observations, mingled with the already mentioned transference clarifications, helped in establishing the development of "past-present links," which have been found by several investigators to be invaluable therapeutic tools and which usually lead to a successful therapeutic outcome (Malan, 1976).

Another basic technique of STAPP had to do with the activity of the therapist, who was viewed not as the caricatured passive "sounding board," but rather as a relentless pursuer, urging the patient to stay on focus, despite the anxiety generated by such a technical intervention. Based on the evaluation of the patient's character, strength, and strong motivation to change, the therapist felt confident in being able to keep the patient working hard on the resolution of his or her conflicts which underlined the focus and which were thought to be responsible for the patient's circumscribed psychological difficulties. Of course, patients, because of their anxiety, sometimes attempted to escape from it by utilizing pseudoregressive or other evading maneuvers. Therefore, the therapist had to be active, anxiety-provoking, and stimulating in his therapeutic efforts.

Problem-solving was used extensively. Because of the therapist's anxiety-provoking interpretations, when the patient's resistance became strong, it was helpful to point to problem-solving techniques that have given rise to conflict resolution during the course of psychotherapy in the past as well as recapitulations of what already had been learned. At such times the therapist repeated verbatim statements made by the patient about memories, past episodes, fantasies, relationships, and so on, so as to be able to convince him or her that the interpretations were correct. Such recapitulations, as well as the use of problem solving, helped circumvent resistances and produced satisfactory progress in the form of tangible evidence of behavioral change.

To be able to use correct interpretations, the therapist had to repeat the exact words used by the patient. Note taking was therefore imperative: It enabled the therapists to study their notes before every session to review the patterns of associations as well as the process of the previous therapeutic interview, so as to be able to discuss them explicitly with the patients.

Finally, if there was adequate evidence of behavioral changes acknowledged by both therapist and patient, the time arrived for the treatment to end.

TERMINATION OF STAPP

In reference to the subject of termination, one should compare and contrast it with the termination process involved in other psychotherapies, including psychoanalysis. In this paper "Analysis Terminable and Interminable," Freud (1950a) discussed some of the problems of ending psychoanalysis. He emphasized that *three* factors were likely to determine the ending of the analysis. These were (1) strong instinctual impulses and traumatic environmental factors which were thought to influence the patient's resistances and give rise to problems with a successful termination of the psychoanalytic process. (2) He also observed that there was a necessity for modification of the patient's ego, in the face of strong defensive maneuvers which resisted recovery. (3) This task was furthermore complicated at times by the analysts' own defense mechanisms, which could interfere with their ability to analyze successfully a strongly resisting patient. He concluded, therefore, that "the business of analysis was to secure the best possible psychological conditions for the functioning of the patient's ego" (Freud, 1950a, p. 254) and that when this had been achieved, analysis was complete.

It may be valuable, therefore, to see how these principles in terminating psychoanalysis have a bearing on the termination of STAPP. First, in contrast to the usually haphazard way by which analysts evaluate patients, in STAPP elaborate efforts have been made to use strict criteria for selection, as well as a choice of a specific focus and an agreement with the patient to work on it, this eliminates, for all intents and purposes, the possibility that STAPP candidates will have strong instinctual impulses to deal with, or that they would have encountered, such strong and traumatic environmental factors in their lives. Thus, it is unlikely that their ego structure would have developed strong defense mechanisms that would create difficulties in the successful termination of the treatment. STAPP candidates, as has already been seen, are flexible, highly motivated individuals capable of experiencing anxiety and eager to cooperate with their therapists for resolution of their conflicts.

If STAPP candidates are not likely to create problems with the termination of their therapy, then if such difficulties take place, they must be more likely to emanate from their therapists' need to prolong the treatment. Looking at the possible factors that may play such a role, one should consider the therapists' narcissism, that is, their viewing themselves as indispensable to the patients and thinking that the patients cannot function separately, independently, and effectively without them. In addition, there might also be an element of therapeutic perfectionism, which is a notion that the patient must be "99% cured" and anything less would not be considered satisfactory. Finally, countertransference feelings also may have to do with separation problems from an individual who is likable, who develops insight rapidly and who demonstrates all the principles of psychodynamics that the therapist has been taught to observe. It is therefore the potential loss of such a "good patient" which makes terminating difficult to contemplate. Such problems, which Freud (1950a) considered to be the personal characteristics of the analyst, also may play an important role in the therapist's attitude for the termination of any kind of psychotherapy.

Freud (1950a) concluded that analysts in their own personalities do not completely achieve the highest standards of psychical normality that they set for their patients. If this is the case, then the same can also be said about psychotherapists in general, and STAPP therapists in particular.

OUTCOME OF STAPP

Regarding the outcome of STAPP, the question, of course, is whether in this type of psychotherapy we secure "the best possible psychological conditions for the functioning of the patient's ego." The answer to this question is an unequivocable "yes."

The most important finding of the results of STAPP has to do with the patients having developed an ability to utilize what they have experienced and learned during their therapy, in order to solve new emotional problems they are likely to encounter during their lives.

This type of problem solving, which has been described as a special aspect of the technique of this brief dynamic psychotherapy, also can be found to be an important outcome finding of this therapy: Once problem solving during the course of STAPP has been learned and found to be helpful, it can be used effectively over and over after the treatment has come to an end.

The value of short-term psychotherapies in general (and STAPP in particular) is not that they conform to the current social demands and pressures we hear about daily, such as saving time and money for third-party payers. The value of these brief treatment modalities has to do with their challenge to the myth that psychotherapy must be of long duration in order to produce behavioral change. The notion that human beings are so rigid, so inflexible, and so unyielding that they require a great deal of time to learn and change is an insult to the human mind. The obvious fact is that all human beings are not the same. The fact is that there are millions of people who are flexible, creative, bright, hard working, and changeable. These individuals contribute greatly to their communities but also may have developed certain circumscribed emotional problems, which although they might interfere with their psychological functioning, are not so serious so as to require a long time to change. For these kinds of patients, STAPP is one of the best forms of assistance one can provide to them.

To those who read this chapter and who are not familiar with short-term dynamic psychotherapies, all this may appear to be a familiar boast of psychiatrists about the value of one of their therapies. This is not the case, however. The value of STAPP lies in its ability to present the evaluation of the patient, to show the whole process of the therapy, and most important to demonstrate its outcome, by use of videotapes, so that everyone can see and draw conclusions objectively. Thus, before ending I would like to describe briefly how videotapes have been used for learning, for teaching, and for research.

VIDEOTAPING OF STAPP

Until the late 1960s most of what we knew about what transpired during psychotherapy was based on anecdotal information. There were almost no systematic research studies of the results obtained. In order to assess the success or lack of it in any psychotherapeutic intervention, one had to rely on the reports of therapists, hoping that such communications were objective.

The introduction of videotape, however, has revolutionized psychiatry in general and psychotherapy in particular. It was particularly in short-term dynamic psychotherapy that videotapes were first used, and it must be clear why this has been the case. The short-term duration made it possible to show not only an evaluation interview, but actually session after session, the whole length of the treatment, and finally follow-up findings. Thus, the objectivity of outside observers could be tapped in order to ascertain not only what exactly had taken place during the course of the psychotherapy, but also to find out how successful such treatment had been.

It is therefore surprising that instead of welcoming videotaping with open arms, psychotherapists initially shied away from using videotapes and often tried hard to suppress their use, claiming the usual and time-worn excuses and clichés that taping interfered with the doctor-patient relationship and violated the confidentiality of the interaction.

An informed consent form is always used to obtain the patient's permission for videotaping the sessions, and it is my experience that only rarely did patients refuse to sign such forms. What is even more striking, however, is that during the course of the psychotherapy, rarely if ever did patients complain or even mention the fact that they were being videotaped.

It seemed clear, therefore, that it was not the patients who objected to the use of videotapes, but the therapists who were frightened to expose their techniques and demonstrate what they were doing in the course of treating their patients.

During the last 20 years, however, videotaping of psychotherapy has become progressively more popular and is used more extensively. The advantages, of course, as mentioned already for teaching and research purposes cannot be overemphasized.

For example, in teaching trainees who have videotaped their interviews, a supervisor has the opportunity to observe how the student has handled the interview. Such technical issues as the handling of transference feelings, making adequate past-present link clarifications, being able to deal with resistances, making appropriate interpretations, and dealing with termination, which are usually difficult for trainees to learn, can be seen on the TV monitor and can be discussed during the supervisory session.

It not surprising that at times, although a trainee may have described dealing with a technical issue in one way, when one observes the videotape it is common to see that the issue had been handled in an entirely different manner. Such discrepancies can be used effectively to educate psychotherapy trainees by helping them to see during their supervisory interview how they may have mistakenly or successfully dealt with a technical aspect, so they can learn how to correct their mistakes or reinforce their own successes.

The second area where videotapes play a major role is in psychotherapy research. It is obvious that the assessment by objective means of the outcome of psychotherapy is a crucial component of demonstrating whether or not such a treatment has any value.

Today psychotherapy is besieged by those who discuss it as a useless process that can be performed by just about anybody. Alternately it is criticized by those who consider helpful only biological interventions such as pharmacotherapy. In 1904 Freud wrote: "To many physicians even today psychotherapy seems to be the offspring of modern mysticism, and compared with our physico-chemical specifics which are applied on the basis of physiological knowledge appears quite unscientific and unworthy of attention of a senior investigator. Allow me . . . to point what is unjust or mistaken in this condemnation of it." (1950b, p. 250). It is ironical to see that in 1989 this statement and the saying that "the more things change, the more they stay the same" are both true. Exaggerated and naïve as these critical viewpoints about psychotherapy may be, they have considerable impact in helping devalue the use of psychotherapy because it is feared and because money can be saved by not more extensively supporting its use. It is unfortunate, however, that it is the patients who suffer from such misguided opinions. Thus, the use of videotapes in short-term dynamic psychotherapies helped to decrease, and it is hoped to eliminate, once and for all, such prejudices.

Finally, it should be mentioned that the question whether or not the focalized technical interventions described in this chapter and found to be of help for fairly healthy individuals with circumscribed psychological problems also can be used to treat some more seriously disturbed patients.

Here the generally held idea that only long-term psychotherapy can help seriously disturbed patients, with or without the use of medication, is essentially correct. Because no systematic efforts have been made to modify the techniques being used, it is possible that some, but certainly not all, could be helped by some modifications in the techniques being used to treat such patients.

From our preliminary investigations we have discovered that there are certain borderline individuals who benefit from a more focalized kind of psychotherapeutic approach. Such individuals, who despite chaotic functioning have an ability to be successful in at least one area of their lives (e.g., work or academic performance), may be able to be enticed during their therapy to work hard to improve or change their defective behavior patterns and succeed in other areas of their lives in the same ways in which they already have been successful.

Another criterion we found to be helpful in choosing borderline patients who could benefit from a brief psychotherapeutic intervention has to do with their motivation for change. The same criterion we discovered to be of such a great value in selecting STAPP candidates may be helpful in choosing some of these sicker patients. If they show evidence of a motivation to change, this may signify that they are tired of their erratic functioning and chaotic behavior and are willing to make an effort to cooperate with their therapists so as to overcome their psychological difficulties.

In this chapter I have tried to present an overview of short-term anxiety-provoking psychotherapy. It is hoped that it will arouse some interest and that therapists will experiment with it and put it to use in their everyday practice.

REFERENCES

Freud, S. (1950a) Analysis terminable and interminable. In J. Strachey (Ed. and Trans.), *Collected Papers* (Vol. V, pp. 316–358). London: Hogarth Press.

Freud, S. (1950b). On psychotherapy. In J. Strachey (Ed. and Trans.). *Collected Papers* (Vol. I, pp. 248–284). London: Hogarth Press.

Malan, D. H. (1976). *The Frontier of Brief Psychotherapy.* New York: Plenum Press.

Sifneos, P. E. (1972). *Short-Term Psychotherapy and Emotional Crisis.* Cambridge, MA: Harvard University Press.

Sifneos, P. E. (1987). *Short-Term Dynamic Psychotherapy Evaluation and Techniques* (2nd ed.). New York: Plenum Press.

CHAPTER 25

Time-Limited Dynamic Psychotherapy: Development and Implementation of a Training Program*
Hans H. Strupp

This chapter describes a training program in time-limited dynamic psychotherapy (TLDP) and explores some of its broader implications. This program is the centerpiece of our current research project (Vanderbilt II) at the Vanderbilt University Center for Psychotherapy Research, whose major aim is to study the effects of specialized training on the therapist's behavior and, in turn, on the process and outcome of psychotherapy. Before describing our current research in greater detail, we will sketch the background of our investigation.

BACKGROUND

In a project extending over a number of years, the Vanderbilt research team studied in considerable detail and depth the performance of a

*Presented as the sixth B. Ruth Esser Memorial Lecture, Department of Psychiatry, Mount Sinai Hospital, Toronto, November 6, 1987.

Important contributors to the work reported in this chapter include Stephen F. Butler, Jeffrey L. Binder, Thomas E. Schacht, and Cären L. Rosser.

small group of highly experienced psychotherapists ($N = 5$), comparing them with a group of college professors who were known for their warmth and understanding but who had no training in psychotherapy. There also were untreated controls. The results have been presented in numerous publications (e.g., Strupp & Hadley, 1979; Sachs, 1983; Gomes-Schwartz, 1978) and will not be repeated here. Particularly revealing were comparisons of good and poor outcome cases treated by the same therapist.

We found that poor outcomes were achieved with patients who emerged as hostile, resistant, and negativistic early in therapy. Such behaviors point to deep-seated characterological disturbances, which made it difficult for these patients to form a good therapeutic alliance with the therapist. Since the therapy was time-limited (up to 25 weekly sessions), it was critical for patient and therapist to develop a viable therapeutic relationship early in therapy. We found that unless a good therapeutic alliance had been established by the third session, the outcome tended to be poor or unremarkable. Furthermore, therapists were generally unable to deal effectively with early negative transference. Conversely, professional therapists were particularly effective with patients who were able to form a good therapeutic relationship by the end of the third hour.

Of perhaps even greater importance was the finding that therapists tended to respond with negative countertransference to the patient's negative transference. We concluded that the handling of negative transference is of overriding importance in time-limited psychotherapy and perhaps in other forms as well. Finally, we noted that professional therapists proceeded in time-limited therapy as presumably they would have in time-unlimited therapy; that is, they practiced an open-ended form of psychodynamic therapy. This should have occasioned no surprise since none of the therapists had any experience in time-limited psychotherapy nor did they claim such expertise.

THE VANDERBILT II STUDY

Our next study, called Vanderbilt II, was started after several years of developmental work and is now nearing completion. It is a five-year project involving 16 therapists and 80 patients, its primary focus being the study of process and outcome in time-limited psychodynamic psychotherapy.

Central to this project was the development of a treatment manual in which we endeavored to specify as stringently as possible a set of therapeutic principles and techniques that might serve as a model for therapists. The manual has been published in book form and is entitled *Psychotherapy in a New Key,* by H. H. Strupp and J. L. Binder (1984).

Drawing on elements from psychodynamic, psychoanalytic, interpersonal, object relations, and general systems approaches, our present approach views patients' problems as a function of disturbed interpersonal relationships, which, harking back to childhood, are unwittingly reenacted by the patient in relationships with significant others in the present, including prominently the therapist. These enactments, called cyclical maladaptive patterns (CMP), are the principal area of interest to the TLDP therapist. As these patterns are reenacted in therapy and better understood by patient and therapist, and as the therapist is able to mediate a constructive experience (i.e., a corrective emotional experience), the patient is therapeutically benefited.

The focus in our form of time-limited dynamic psychotherapy (TLDP) is on the transactions between patient and therapist in the here-and-now. Crucially important, too, are the therapist's emotional reactions to the patient's transference maneuvers and the therapist's ability to resonate to and communicate with the patient about these transactions. In addition, special attention is given to such topics as the therapist's stance vis-à-vis the patient, the identification and management of CMPs, how to turn countertransference reactions to therapeutic advantage, and such topics as setting time-limits and termination. By helping therapists to manage more effectively transference and countertransference phenomena, we also hoped to bring under better control, if not eliminate, the problems we had observed in the Vanderbilt I study.

Basic Design

Based on these views, we designed the investigation diagrammed in Figure 1. We enlisted 16 reasonably experienced psychodynamically oriented therapists, all of whom were in private practice. There were 8 psychiatrists and 8 clinical psychologists—10 men and 6 women—ranging in experience from 2 to 14 years postresidency or postinternship. Patients were carefully selected adults who met stringent selection criteria. In terms of disturbance, motivation for therapy, demographic factors and other variables, they were comparable to reasonably promising patients who apply to mental health centers or therapists in private practice. About 80% were women, and the typical presenting complaints included anxiety, depression, and interpersonal difficulties.

All were moderately disturbed and a number had additional diag-

PHASE I	PHASE II	PHASE III
"Therapy as Usual"	Training	TLDP Therapy
Therapist 1— "Good" Patient "Difficult" Patient	Therapist 1— Training Patient	Therapist 1— "Good" Patient "Difficult" Patient
Therapist 2— "Good" Patient "Difficult" Patient	Therapist 2— Training Patient	Therapist 2— "Good" Patient "Difficult" Patient
•	•	•
•	•	•
•	•	•
Therapist 16— "Good" Patient "Difficult" Patient	Therapist 16— Training Patient	Therapist 16— "Good" Patient "Difficult" Patient

Figure 1. Design of the Vanderbilt II Psychotherapy
Research Project

noses on Axis II of the DSM-III. Patients were categorized as relatively
"good" or relatively "difficult," based on ratings made by the screening
clinician (Butler, Thackrey, & Strupp, 1987). Extensive assessments
were made prior to therapy, during therapy, at termination, and at one-
year and two-year follow-ups. All interviews were audiotaped, and all
assessment and selected therapy interviews were videotaped.

The basic design of the study consisted of three phases. In Phase I,
each therapist was assigned two patients and asked to treat them in up to
25 weekly sessions, as they ordinarily would treat such patients. Each
therapist was assigned a relatively "good" patient and a relatively "difficult" one. During Phase II, therapists went through a specialized training program. Phase III was an exact replication of Phase I (with different
patients), except that the therapists were expected to have learned and
to be practicing TLDP. We were interested in studying effects of training as these would manifest themselves in process and outcome.

The training program, Phase II of the study, was designed to last about
12 months. For logistical reasons, we carried out the training in four
groups of four therapists and two trainers each. J. L. Binder and a psychiatrist co-led two groups, and the other two were led by S. Butler and
H. Strupp. Each group met weekly for two hours.

The training program was divided into two parts—a didactic portion (lasting three months), followed by case supervision. We reasoned that a didactic approach would be the most expedient way to impart the necessary TLDP perspective to the therapists. This portion included discussions of the principles and strategies prescribed by TLDP and examination of each therapist's videotapes from Phase I, as well as videotapes of so-called "model" cases conducted by one of the supervisors. The didactic portion of the training essentially covered the following topics:

1. Patient's problems as a function of disturbed interpersonal relations
2. The therapist's stance
3. Assessment
4. Dynamic Focus
5. Technique
6. Termination

Following the didactic part of the program, each therapist was assigned a "training case" and encouraged to put into practice what he or she had learned about TLDP. Because each group met once a week for two hours, it was possible to discuss each case for one hour every two weeks. During these discussions, the therapist would summarize the therapy progress and play a portion of an audio- or videotape of the session, and the group would discuss the therapist's attempts to implement the TLDP strategies. Although weekly individual supervision clearly would have had certain advantages, it was our hope that the group format would benefit from peer support (the group members did develop something of a group identity) and the exposure to the technical problems that arise with different patients.

All phases of the study have now been completed and major process and outcome analysis are underway. In addition, two doctoral dissertations and two masters' theses have been completed. All four groups had aproximately one year of weekly training sessions (mean = 51 training sessions per group; range = 45-57 meetings) and each therapist completed a training case.

Data Sources

In order to begin to understand the supervision process, we looked at the following three sources of data:

1. Supervisors' ratings of each therapist after training. This included ratings of retrospective assessments of the therapist's competence *before* training and *motivation* for the training experience, ratings of therapists' personal qualities (degree of *empathy, warmth, and flexibility*), ratings of *mastery and skill* in TLDP, as well as *overall competence* after training.

2. *Ratings by the therapists of their training experience.* This included the degree to which they *liked* the training program, the extent to which they felt *comfortable* using the methods prescribed by TLDP, the degree to which they felt the training *influenced* their practice of psychotherapy and the degree to which they *benefited* from the training experience.

3. *Independent ratings of the therapeutic process by trained judges on the Vanderbilt Negative Indicators Scale* (VNIS; Strupp et al. 1981).[*] These ratings were based on the therapeutic process during the third session of Phase I of the study (i.e., before training). Also included was a measure of therapists' comments about their own performance in the session they had just completed. The latter data were obtained by asking therapists to comment on the session and their performance immediately after the patient had left.

Results

Examination of these data revealed the following findings:

1. There were no significant differences between the two senior group leaders on any of the measures or ratings. Thus, none of the responses to the training experience could be accounted for by the particular supervisor.

2. *Supervisors' ratings:* The subjective experience of the supervisors suggested that therapists rated as competent before training were those therapists with more years of postgraduate experience ($r = 0.49$).[**] Also, competence before training was inversely related to negative attitude on the VNIS ($r = 0.47$). Therapists rated as competent before training were more likely to indicate greater comfort using TLDP ($r = 0.51$) and were more likely to express regrets ($r = 0.49$).

Overall competence in TLDP posttraining was highly associated with competence before training ($r = 0.84$), although these ratings were made at the same time and thus are not independent. Nevertheless, this

---

[*]These data were collected by Lydia Flasher as part of her doctoral dissertation (Flasher, 1987).

[**]Unless otherwise specified, all correlations are significant at $p < 0.05$ or better using a one-tailed test of significance.

association suggests that, like patients' responses to therapy, the familiar wisdom that "the rich get richer" may be true for therapists' responses to training and supervision. Interestingly, those rated more competent after training were also more likely to have expressed regrets (r = 0.45).

3. In this regard, *regrets* turn out to be an interesting measure. It appears to represent a therapist's willingness to be critical of his or her own performance. It was quite consistently and positively related to supervisors' ratings of *motivation* (r = 0.46), *empathy* (r = 0.59), *warmth* (r = 0.52), *skill after training* (r = 0.47), and *competence after training* (r = 0.45). Thus, at a minimum, a willingness to express regrets seems related to supervisors' reactions toward trainees. It was also positively related to therapists being in outside supervision before the training began (r = 0.43) and negatively related to the total of therapist subscales on the VNIS (r = 0.43). These interesting data suggest the possible importance of a self-observing and, within limits, a self-critical stance on the part of the therapist.

4. *VNIS* ratings made of sessions conducted *before* the TLDP training did not correlate significantly with supervisors' ratings of response to training.

5. Therapists' ratings of the training program as reported to a graduate student on our research team (Rosser, 1987) in individual interviews tended to be uniformly positive. On a scale of 1 (not at all) to 5 (very much), 15 of 16 therapists rated a 4 or 5 on the items *liked the training* and *benefited from the training*. These possibly "idealized" ratings yielded little in the way of correlations with the other measures, perhaps because they were so uniformly high. However, these ratings may reflect a generally positive attitude on the part of therapists toward the training experience, rather than being simply an artifact of the method used to obtain the ratings (i.e., reporting them to a research team member).

For example, in three years of participation with the project, none of the participating therapists dropped out of the project. There was consistently good attendance at the supervision meetings, with some therapists expressing unsolicited praise of the training experience and disappointment on termination of the training program. The therapists rated by supervisors as more competent *before* TLDP training rated themselves as *more comfortable using TLDP* (r = 0.51). (Also, a significant correlation of -0.50 was obtained between therapists reporting *benefit from the training program* and low ratings on the *negative therapist attitude* subscale of the VNIS, but the constricted range on the "benefited" item makes this difficult to interpret.) The main observation of the therapists' ratings of their own response to the training was a general tendency to *tell us* that the training experience had been good.

6. A final observation is that the *didactic portion* of the training program was relatively *unpopular* with our therapists. The ideas underlying TLDP are not radically different from other dynamic approaches to therapy, and some therapists indicated they were already familiar with these ideas, understood them, and incorporated them into their work. By contrast, in the supervisors' view, the therapists' *understanding of the concepts was fairly superficial,* and they rarely, if ever, dealt systematically with the therapeutic relationship. For our project therapists, supervision of an *ongoing case* was more worthwhile because we were able to focus the discussion on specific, concrete suggestions of how the therapist might *act* differently. We concluded that lectures and abstract discussions of clinical issues are generally of limited value.

Our ability to instill TLDP principles and techniques in a group of relatively experienced therapists also was limited by the fact that *we* had solicited their participation in our research/training program instead of *their* applying to us for specialized training in time-limited therapy techniques. We believe that far greater training effects might be demonstrated with beginning graduate students or junior residents.

IMPLICATIONS FOR TRAINING

While the analyses of our data are far from being complete, the study has already deepened our thinking about the training of psychotherapists. For example, what does a psychotherapist need to know? How is training best imparted? How can we assess the effects of training? What personal and professional characteristics should we look for in applicants?

In a recent review of the literature, Strupp, Butler, and Rosser (1988) found that solid research on the training of psychotherapists in psychodynamic psychotherapy is conspicuous by its absence and that most training programs remain wedded to the master-apprentice model. In other words, there is as yet little hard evidence of what novices need to learn, how they can best learn it, and what a reasonable criterion of competence might be. To be sure, there is as much clinical wisdom in this area as there is about the conduct of psychotherapy itself, but one would be hard put to find research-based specifications of teaching and learning. In a nutshell, we are dealing with a largely *uncharted* area. Considering the rapid rise and expansion of psychotherapy training programs, the growing demands for accountability and cost-effectiveness, and the continuing criticism of psychotherapy in many quarters, it is high time that the field bestir itself in correcting these deficiencies.

The remainder of the chapter will thus be devoted to psychotherapy training which, in our judgment, holds considerable promise.

The SASB System

Our approach has been significantly influenced by Lorna Benjamin's Structural Analysis of Social Behavior (SASB, 1974), which is a sophisticated system for analyzing the process and content of interpersonal transactions. This system has had significance in the analysis of our data in the Vanderbilt II study. The system (and our approach) assumes that, stripped of technical jargon, psychotherapy may be seen simply as a structured relationship between two people. Most major therapeutic camps have come to recognize the crucial importance of the quality of this therapeutic relationship in facilitating change.

It is clearly difficult to operationalize such an ineffable concept as "the relationship" and numerous attempts to do so have failed (e.g., in trying to use measures such as the number of accepting statements, percent of emotional words, latency time per response, etc.). Yet psychotherapy researchers (e.g., Beutler, Crago, & Arizmendi, 1986; Orlinsky & Howard, 1986) have continued to stress the importance of explaining exactly what it is a therapist *does* to create a favorable therapeutic alliance (Hartley & Strupp, 1983).

Two basic questions must be faced: (1) Why is the relationship important; that is, what is the role of the relationship in effecting patient change? (2) What does the therapist do that can be meaningfully operationalized and measured?

Sullivan (1953) defined personality as "interpersonal process" and stated that personality consists of the "relatively enduring patterns of recurrent interpersonal situations which characterize a human life" (p. 110). He further believed that the "self" is made up of the "reflective appraisals" of others encountered in interpersonal transactions. Thus, we come to think about and to treat ourselves as others have treated us, particularly in infancy and early childhood.

The resultant self-system has the ability to selectively perceive and distort one's interpersonal relationships so that similar cyclical transactions tend to occur which confirm a stable self-concept, thus reducing anxiety. In this view, psychiatric "symptoms" may be seen as a "complex subjective experience that consists of interrelated cognitive, affective, and interpersonal elements" (Horowitz & Vitkus, 1986, p. 444). Interpersonal interactions activate components of the symptom, maintaining distress, while at the same time predisposing the patient to particular types of interpersonal transactions. For these reasons, interpersonal transactions become an *important* unit of study. It is this unit that defines the personality (for Sullivan), the unit in which cyclical pathology may be directly observed, and the unit that may serve to operationally define "the relationship" for research purposes.

In this interpersonal view, patients enact with the therapist cyclical maladaptive patterns and in so doing tend to evoke complementary maladaptive reactions from the therapist (Kiesler, 1982). An important quality of the competent therapist is the ability to resist the "pulled for" response by giving what Young and Beier (1982) call an "asocial" response. Thus, by declining to participate in the patient's maladaptive patterns and by his or her benign attitude, the therapist over time facilitates changes in the patient's self-system (introject). The introject is analogous to self objects postulated by Kohut (Baker & Baker, 1987).

Historically, circumplex models (e.g., SASB; Benjamin, 1974) have provided a theoretically coherent and psychometrically sound approach to measuring interpersonal behavior. In this approach, behaviors are arrayed in circular fashion around two axes representing the basic interpersonal dimensions of dominance (control) and affiliation (love-hate) (see Figure 2.) Thus any point in this two-dimensional Euclidian space represents the joint action of these two so-called primitive basics. Similar behaviors (or behavioral types) are adjacent to one another, while negatively correlated behaviors lie opposite one another.

Interpersonal theory posits that any given action tends to evoke or pull for a reaction that is similar on the affiliation dimension and reciprocal (opposite) on the control dimension. For example, hostile dominance pulls for hostile submission. This is the principle of complementarity.

SASB takes the circumplex idea and expands it to three separate but interrelated and structurally homologous surfaces: self, other, and introject. The introject surface represents the surface 1 (actions of others) turned inward and directed at the self. For example, the hostile control (or blame) of others becomes self-blame from the perspective of the introject.

The *process* as well as the *content* of therapeutic interviews can be coded by SASB. Benjamin also has developed coordinated questionnaires (called INTREX) by means of which patient and therapist can describe their relationship with each other as well as with significant others in their present and past life.

TLDP Training

We found that TLDP training, conducted in a mode similar to graduate training (seminar, discussions, readings, tape watching, supervision) in-

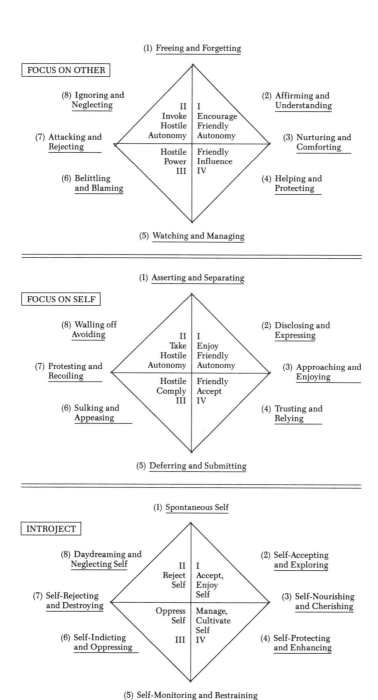

Figure 2. Surface 1 (focus on other), Surface 2 (focus on self), and Surface 3 (introject) of the structural analysis of social behavior (SASB).

fluences therapists' "technical skill" (as measured by our adherence scale, a measure specifically developed for this purpose). However, even though the training involved discussion and attention to interpersonal dynamics, it did not significantly change the manner in which therapists actually related to their patients. For example, a therapist who was subtly controlling and critical before training remained so after training—the training simply changed the technical agenda around which the controlling and criticism occurred. Furthermore, some evidence (Christenson, 1987) suggests that therapist's *interpersonal styles* with patients are a function of the therapists' *own interpersonal experiences* in his or her family of origin, which presumably have skewed the therapist's perception of interpersonal events (Henry, 1986).

Similar problems have been long recognized and discussed as part of the question of whether therapists need *personal therapy* as part of their training. The implication is that personal therapy is the only way to address the question of interpersonal perception (conceptualized as "transference"). Unfortunately, research on this topic has been equivocal because of severe methodological shortcomings (Strupp, Butler, & Rosser, 1988).

The issue is centrally important because the field of psychotherapy research is moving rapidly in the direction of *manualized* psychotherapy. If, as our data suggests, there are fundamental interpersonal skills that stand in a metarelationship to manualized skills, then the field may reach erroneous conclusions about the effects of *manualized therapies*, attributing outcomes to the therapies rather than to underlying interpersonal events that the manuals do not address. *No one* has as yet manualized *basic interpersonal skills*. Our data indicate that we cannot assume that trained therapists automatically possess high levels of therapeutically important interpersonal skills.

CONCLUDING COMMENTS

To reiterate, our *attention* was forcefully drawn (in the Vanderbilt I study) to surprisingly high levels of *destructive interpersonal processes,* such as hostile *blaming* or mixed messages by the therapist, even among well-trained and otherwise skilled clinicians. These undesirable interpersonal processes were inevitably linked to poor or inconclusive outcomes (Strupp, 1980a–d). In the Vanderbilt II study, we endeavored through training in a manualized form of therapy to assist therapists in working with the kind of interpersonally difficult patients who had proved so problematic in the Vanderbilt I study. Although therapists succeeded in mastering TLDP principles, they often were unable to cope effectively with the foregoing difficulties posed by their patients (via negative transference).

We are currently exploring further steps to identify these recurrent *interpersonal dilemmas* (typically found in patients diagnosed as having one of the personality disorders) and to teach therapists how best to cope with them. We plan to accomplish this objective through a specialized training program in interpersonal skills that is grounded in the SASB system. Pilot efforts in training undergraduate students to become SASB coders and in teaching graduate students as well as residents in basic therapeutic skills have been enormously gratifying. The SASB model provides an excellent theoretical base for sharpening the trainee's understanding of desirable, as well as undesirable, kinds of therapeutic process. The SASB model may indeed be the first systematic attempt to provide a theoretically coherent rationale for helping therapists deal more effectively with the all-important transference challenges posed by the difficult patients who make up the majority of individuals whom the contemporary therapist is called upon to treat.

REFERENCES

Baker, H. S., & Baker, M. N. (1987). Heinz Kohut's self psychology: An overview. *The American Journal of Psychiatry, 144*(1), 1-9.

Benjamin, L. S. (1974). Structural analysis of social behavior. *Psychological Review, 81*, 392-425.

Beutler, L. E., Crago, M., & Arizmendi, T. G. (1986). Therapist variables in psychotherapy process and outcome. In S. L. Garfield & A. E. Bergin (Eds.), *Handbook of Psychotherapy and Behavior Change* (3rd ed.). New York: Wiley.

Butler, S. F., Thackrey, M., & Strupp, H. H. (1987, June). Capacity for Dynamic Process Scale (CDPS): Relation to patient variables, process and outcome. Paper presented at the Society for Psychotherapy Research International Conference, Ulm, West Germany.

Christenson, J. (1987). Pre-therapy interpersonal relations and introject, as reflected in the therapeutic process. Unpublished Masters Thesis, Vanderbilt University, Nashville, TN.

Flasher, L. (1987) Negative factors in short-term psychotherapy: Focus on therapist interventions. Unpublished doctoral dissertation, Vanderbilt University, Nashville, TN.

Gomes-Schwartz, B. (1978). Effective ingredients in psychotherapy: Prediction of outcome from process variables. *Journal of Consulting and Clinical Psychology, 46*, 1023-1035.

Hartley, D. E., & Strupp, H. H. (1983). The therapeutic alliance: Its relationship to outcome in brief psychotherapy. In J. Masling (Ed.), *Empirical Studies of*

Psychoanalytical Theories, Volume 1 (pp. 1-38). Hillsdale, NJ: The Analytic Press.

Henry, W. P. (1986). Interpersonal process in psychotherapy. Unpublished doctoral dissertation, Vanderbilt University, Nashville, TN.

Horowitz, L. M., & Vitkus, J. (1986). The interspersonal bases of psychiatric symptoms. *Clinical Psychology Review, 6,* 443-469.

Kiesler, D. J. (1982). Interpersonal theory for personality and psychotherapy. In J.C. Anchin & D. J. Kiesler (Eds.), *Handbook of Interpersonal Psychotherapy.* New York: Pergamon Press.

Orlinsky, D. E., & Howard, K. I. (1986). Process and outcome in psychotherapy research. In S. L. Garfield & A. E. Bergin (Eds.), *Handbook of Psychotherapy and Behavior Change* (3rd ed.). New York: Wiley.

Rogers, C. R. (1957). The necessary and sufficient conditions of therapeutic personality change. *Journal of Consulting Psychology, 21,* 95-103.

Rosser, C. L. (1987). Therapists' personal attributes and attitudes in relation to psychotherapy process, training, and supervision. Unpublished Masters Thesis, Vanderbilt University, Nashville, TN.

Sachs, J. S. (1983). Negative factors in brief psychotherapy: An empirical assessment. *Journal of Consulting and Clinical Psychology, 51,* 557-564.

Strupp, H. H. (1980a). Success and failure in time-limited psychotherapy: A systematic comparison of two cases: Comparison 1. *Archives of General Psychiatry, 37,* 595-603.

Strupp, H. H. (1980b). Success and failure in time-limited psychotherapy: A systematic comparison of two cases: Comparison 2. *Archives of General Psychiatry, 37,* 708-716.

Strupp, H. H. (1980c). Success and failure in time-limited psychotherapy: With special reference to the performance of a lay counselor. *Archives of General Psychiatry, 37,* 831-841.

Strupp, H. H. (1980d). Success and failure in time-limited psychotherapy: Further evidence (comparison 4). *Archives of General Psychiatry, 37,* 947-954.

Strupp, H. H., & Binder, J. L. (1984). *Psychotherapy in a New Key: A Guide to Time-Limited Dynamic Psychotherapy.* New York: Basic Books.

Strupp, H. H., Butler, S. F., & Rosser, C. L. (1988). Training in psychodynamic psychotherapy. *Journal of Consulting and Clinical Psychology, 56,* 689-695.

Strupp, H. H., & Hadley, S. W. (1979) Specific vs. nonspecific factors in psychotherapy: A controlled study of outcome. *Archives of General Psychiatry, 36,* 1125-1136.

Strupp, H. H., Moras, K., Sandell, J., Waterhouse, G., O'Malley, S. S., Keithly, L., & Gomes-Schwartz, B. (1981). Vanderbilt Negative Indicators Scale (VNIS): An instrument for the identification of deterrents to progress in time-limited dynamic psychotherapy. Unpublished manuscript, Vanderbilt University, Nashville, TN.

Sullivan, H. S. (1953). *The Interpersonal Theory of Psychiatry.* New York: Norton.

Young, D. M. & Beier, E. G. (1982). Being asocial in social places: Giving the client a new experience. In J. C. Anchin & D. J. Kiesler (Eds.), *Handbook of Interpersonal Psychotherapy* (pp. 262-273). New York: Pergamon Press.

CHAPTER 26

Ecological Therapy
Carol H. Lankton

Ecological Therapy is a label I have chosen to describe any kind of comprehensive therapy that focuses on how clients need to deal creatively with current demands and pressures in their life. An equally important focus is on how therapists can communicate so as to stimulate thinking, emphasize abilities, and help clients organize new relational patterns in response to current and predictable future demands. Ideally, this can be accomplished briefly. Ecology, generally defined, is concerned with the interrelationship of organisms and their environments, especially as manifested by natural cycles and rhythms, community development and structure, interaction between different kinds of organisms, geographical distributions, population alterations, and other factors. Discovering the pattern of relations between living things and their environments is an ongoing process.

Sometimes therapists use techniques without keeping sight of ecological issues such as developmental tasks, interpersonal pressures, personal resources, and global variables (e.g., neighborhood, recent history, and even worldwide affairs). This often results in ineffective therapy. Thus, ecological therapy involves retrieving experiences (resources) that are developmentally relevant and connecting them to the contexts in which clients need them.

People usually come to therapy in response to a symptom or problem that has resulted from their being unable to generate or organize needed experiences. Perhaps their context has changed or new challenges are being encountered at a transition in development. Symptoms and other problems indicate that individuals are "out of sync" with their

342

environment, but it is not always clear what needs to change or what resources need to be retrieved. It's just clear that there seems to be a block or obstacle to a desired goal.

To illustrate with an example outside of the therapy context, my child returned home from his three-year-old preschool class and announced that he had just learned from his teacher that there was no such word as "can't." While the teacher's goal was apparently to engender a sense of potential or encouragement, the outcome seemed to be the loss of an option for communicating a need. Besides, what she told the child was wrong: "can't" is a word! In fact, it may be a three-year-old child's means of saying in a simple way: "I really don't know how to respond to this situation. I do not have the necessary experiences sufficiently available or developed in order to solve this problem. I'm not even really sure what is required here. Please help me." This process can be seen as similar to the symptom development process by which people indicate a lack of option in solving problems by metaphorically saying "I can't" with some symptom or problem presented for therapy.

But back to preschool. The next day, I praised the teacher for suggesting that kids can do what they set out to do. I then suggested that as she continued to suggest this, she also might identify and access what a child would need to succeed in a given area. Specifically, I encouraged her to respond to the child saying, "I can't" with the question: "What do you need in order to?" Such a question, whether addressed directly to the child or pondered internally by the teacher, would initiate the development of skills and resources needed to translate "I can't" into "I can."

This simple intervention underlies a philosophy that is important enough to serve as the foundation of a therapeutic approach for people of all ages. It is a philosophy that appreciates a person's perceived limitations while assuming that people have the necessary resources to generate creative solutions to their difficulties. In this approach, a symptom or problem is seen as a relational pattern, learned at some point for an adaptive purpose. It is not a learning deficit, but a learning that can be unlearned. Within this view, therapy focuses on what is needed to motivate new learnings and stimulate new relational patterns.

THERAPEUTIC GOALS

In each session with a client, I pose the question, "What do you *really* need to change or to solve that problem?" Sometimes it is asked aloud, sometimes only to myself as I observe the person. Often the client and I have similar responses, though sometimes our ideas are quite different. I frequently find that clients underrate their resources and tend to take a "minimalist" route on their journeys through life; that is, they pack only the barest essentials of choices.

Similarly, many therapists needlessly limit their focus to one type of goal when a more comprehensive array might better facilitate the client's growth. For example, I routinely set specific goals in areas of affect retrieval, attitude restructuring, behavior development, family structure change, self-image change, and changes related to discipline and enjoyment (Lankton & Lankton, 1986). By contrast, proponents of some therapies often focus on just one of these areas. These therapists usually maintain that successful change in that one area will automatically lead to a reverberating change throughout the other, ostensibly secondary, areas (Bandura, 1969; Ellis, 1971; Perls, 1973; Wolpe, 1982). This is analogous to assuming that if one gets a new job, all housing, interpersonal, and money management matters will automatically be improved.

Setting relevant, specific therapeutic goals in areas of behavior, attitude, affect, family structure, self-image, discipline, and enjoyment is an ongoing process that is accomplished as a result of asking clients the question "What do you need in order to really solve your problem and change in desired ways?" I can briefly clarify what I mean by specific goals. A specific behavior goal might be for a woman to cry in front of her husband, or for the husband to say, "I need help with this." Specific affect goals might involve experiencing anger, grief, or tenderness. An attitude change goal might involve changing the belief of "If you show your feelings, people won't respect you" to "Only to the extent that you show your feelings will other people be able to truly know and relate with you." In setting such goals, it is important to be specific, usually much more specific than the client's initially stated goals (Lankton & Lankton, 1986).

Therefore, ecological therapy is a strategic therapy that involves setting specific goals and revising them based on continuing feedback from the client system. The goal-setting phase of therapy is the most difficult. Each case deserves and requires all of the observation and diagnostic skills that the therapist can muster. Goal setting is that all-important phase of therapy that Kristina Erickson (1985) has termed "thinking very hard" (p. 379) about what is needed. While there are times when it seems "crystal clear" what is needed, it is important to remember that each seemingly "transparent" person may conceal many complexities and systemic entanglements. Once a (tentative) set of specific treatment goals is developed, the "hard" part of therapy seems over even though the main "work" has barely begun. But specific goals make it a lot easier to generate a relevant plan of interventions (Haley, 1976).

Depending on the therapist's skills and the client's availability of resources, the ensuing therapy can be comprehensive *and* brief. (On the average, I spend six sessions with clients in my practice.) I always hope the first session will be effective enough to be the last session, though I'm prepared to work with a client as long as needed to achieve the designated goals. Sometimes the feedback indicates the need for designating new or different goals as well.

Frequently therapists, especially when new to an approach, are so overwhelmed or fascinated by the array of possible interventions that they "leap without looking." That is, they apply an intervention without first "thinking real hard" about a case. Or else they grow overly concerned about "how hard this whole line of therapy is" and how they "will never be any good at it." In either case, they tend to bypass the goal-setting stage and then find themselves floundering about like a ship with no direction, unable to "set the sails" so as to channel the available energy. Though the ship may seem to drift along without obvious difficulty, therapy becomes aimless. When the goals are vague, nonexistent, or so large that small changes are barely noticed, therapists and clients experience uncertainty about when therapy has been accomplished.

One typical goal in therapy is cessation of the symptom or presenting problem. This goal might better be considered the treatment contract, and the question of "What is needed in order to accomplish this reduction of the symptom?" may then be asked to generate the setting of specific subgoals. Because symptoms represent complex relational patterns, it is difficult to make "stopping them" the focus of therapy. A more helpful approach might ask, "What goes into the making of a symptom?" and, "Which resource experiences need to be retrieved and associated to particular contexts in which they are not now available?" (Quite often, the client does not seem to notice or recognize the importance of the larger context.)

When treating a family, I think in terms of ongoing developmental stages through which they are moving—like logs down a winding river, moving with the force of the current, negotiating the bends, dealing with the dams and other challenges. When the river requires a "flexibility" the log doesn't have, a jam occurs. What does it need in order to get moving again? The log would only need a little shove to dislodge it and send it back into the mainstream. But a family is more challenging, and in order to "unjam," members must develop or retrieve needed experiences and transactions necessary to deal with the current demands. We often can do briefer and more ecological therapy by including in our focus events and variables seemingly outside the symptom context, rather than moving in and shoving the symptom out directly. It's what I call the 80% to 20% ratio. That is, I spend approximately 80% of my interventions on helping clients retrieve and organize experiences that, when combined and associated to relevant contexts, will hopefully render the symptom no longer necessary. I typically spend only 20% of interventions directly working to disrupt, relieve, or remove the symptom.

It is in this way that ecologically comprehensive therapy differs from symptom-focused treatments in which direct suggestions for symptom removal are given. Though direct suggestion may sometimes appear to be effective, at least temporarily, additional assistance is often needed to develop better ways of satisfying whatever needs were represented by the symptom. In other words, the short-term "solution" does not always make for the briefest therapy. This is particularly evident in habit control cases, such as overeating, where the treatment contract specifies the reduction of a particular behavior or "symptom." Clients seeking hypnotherapy for such conditions typically do so with the expectation that therapy will be brief, symptom focused, and involve "taking away" the undesired pattern. However, I prefer not to take away a developed choice, but to ask what it is accomplishing and what the person will need to do to accomplish the same outcome without having the symptom. Therefore, it may come as a surprise to many clients that a far more comprehensive assessment is done than they may have expected in areas they did not think about as being part of or influencing the problem in any way.

CASE EXAMPLE

A chronically overweight woman in her early forties recently consulted me regarding her midlife desire to finally resolve the weight problem she had experienced most of her life. Each time she had lost weight in the past, she had grown intensely anxious and then regained the weight. She had never married. She managed a small staff of therapists in a hospital setting. Though quite skilled at taking care of others, her ability to express her own fear, tenderness, or desires was notably underdeveloped. Though she had a network of friends, she did not experience herself as being close with anyone. Food was a dependable means of gratification and self-nurturing. Coming to therapy was an awkward process for her, possibly because of her anxiety about expressing her fears, sadness, and needs to another. At some level, she hoped that therapy would be a brief, effortless event in which the "magic" of hypnosis would somehow change her life in desirable ways. It was clear that she did not need technical information on dieting; she had a lifetime experience of doing that. What she really seemed to need was to learn how to be comfortably vulnerable and appropriately dependent, take emotional risks, express needs, and use some of her caretaking abilities with herself. These needs inherent in human relating might clearly provide more gratification than food.

Addressing goals related to the development of joy and intimacy represented at least 80% of the ensuing therapy. In fact, the only intervention directly related to her weight complaint involved an assignment to eat, at the minimum, three nutritious meals each day, or whatever the "nutritionist part" of her decided that a normal person should eat to remain healthy. Additionally, she was to eat these three meals in the thoughtful manner to which she deserved to become accustomed: for example, sitting down; using placemats, napkins, and china; with friends or comfortably alone; in pleasant surroundings; and so forth. Then, and only then, she was free to consume anything else that she might feel the urge to eat, no matter how "fattening" it might be. In fact, she was not to refrain from eating anything she really wanted but she was to eat the three nutritious meals even if she thought she did not want to. Above all, she was not to stop eating (as she had done repeatedly during previous weight loss binges). Even this one intervention designed to specifically alter and disrupt her routine with food (the 20% aimed at the symptom) was simultaneously part of the 80% aimed at developmental needs, since it clearly involved the development of a long-awaited and needed self-nurturing. This, of course, is opposed to the deprivation and binge model this client had lived with for so long.

It may not have been clear to a casual observer of these sessions just what the presenting problem was, for it was rarely addressed in therapeutic conversations. Instead, it was pointed out to this client in a metaphor that she had been able to successfully "lose" plenty of times in the past, but that now she could use her ability to love (others) to "win" her weight goals by finally loving herself. This somewhat general goal of "loving herself" was specified by many tangible feelings, behaviors, attitudes, and self-image adjustments and therefore took many specific tangents during the course of this brief therapy (three sessions).

A BRIEF ASIDE ... TIME CONSIDERATIONS

The brevity or length of the therapy is, to me, always a secondary consideration to how the limited commodity of time is invested. For example, some people may become millionaires with a few well-placed investments while others may compulsively invest for a lifetime and still come up short. It all depends on how, when, and where you place your bets. It is therefore surprising that many physicians and other health professionals maintain that they cannot deal with a patient's psychological needs because of limited time. They thus ignore those psychological aspects of their patients altogether. However, as every busy parent knows, the quantity of time is not necessarily as important as the quality of time spent.

In every encounter, no matter how brief, communication occurs. The opportunity to communicate can simply be squandered or even used negatively. A preferred way to use the opportunity to communicate is to determine specific goals and let each intervention, however brief, proceed accordingly. No therapist, even in long-term therapy, is able to be truly comprehensive in the sense that he or she stimulates all of the resources a client will need in all situations. We are influenced by a plethora of figures in that regard, from parents to health care technicians who only interact with us about specific forms of treatment.

Both positive and negative communications can snowball or set off a "domino" reaction that influences a chain of responses and adjustments. It is often possible for therapy to be ecologically relevant and truly brief (one to five sessions), even when the person has a sizable "disorder" that is "supposed to" be treated for much longer. A real disservice can be committed when therapists unquestioningly accept that clients have preassessed "conditions" that are "known" to be caused by specific circumstances and curable only by a certain treatment of a typical, predetermined duration. People are unique and develop patterns in an idiosyncratic way and may or may not require therapy in order to change.

Though categorization and diagnostic labeling can sometimes be helpful with regard to understanding possible tendencies and similarities, it is important for therapists to assess each individual with regard to unique history, resourcefulness, motivation, and so forth before deciding on the length and course of therapy that might be prescribed by an arbitrary diagnostic category. For example, consider the relatively new diagnostic category of "adult children of alcoholics" (ACOAs). I suspect that, as with other diagnostic categories, there are some people who didn't particularly experience themselves as having a problem until they encountered the now abundant literature describing and defining an ACOA and the kind of treatment required for this condition. Then, because they were able to identify with some of the commonalities, they concluded that "this is what people like me have and therefore I need therapy of the specified duration." This reaction could conceivably happen to an extent that people would discount or deny obvious abilities or positive traits they have to the contrary.

If we must have such categories, I would suggest a broader category of "adult children of parents" and leave it at that general level of understanding about which we all can agree: There were/are no perfect parents and each failed child must come to terms with how he or she will take what the parents offered, reject what is not of value, learn from the parents' mistakes, "adopt" other parental models in various ways, and put together a composite new being who will move yet again through the developmental stages defined by natural rhythms and impending pressures from the changing world around us. Some will make this adjustment in therapy quickly. Others will do this without therapy. Some never will, whether in brief or long-term therapy or in no therapy at all. Some may do it with brief intermittent therapy throughout the life cycle. And if these adjustments are completed, then there are the imperfections of the global and political society with which each individual must cope. This being a paper on ecological therapy, it is appropriate to mention, at least briefly, some of the ecological challenges at the global level.

THE BIG PICTURE

When we consider the broadest definition of ecological therapy, perhaps we need to propose another category that describes the common difficulties experienced by adults and children living in a world that is increasingly polluted, overpopulated, and apparently on the brink of destruction. Hostile, competitive, self-indulgent, biased, wasteful, irresponsible attitudes and actions are threatening our very existence. What do we need in order to remove the symptoms of societal, political, environmental imbalance and disease? What do we need to get along, conserve resources, recycle sensibly, and curb extravagant appetites for various commodities that are irreversibly poisoning our world? I am sad that my children must grow up in our current world and sooner or later discover and be influenced by its disease. I don't like to read the ever-increasing number of species added to the "now extinct" chart. I don't like watching tender seedlings choked out by weeds, poisons, and generally infertile or hostile conditions before they have a chance to grow and unfold their genetic inheritance.

One of my favorite plants is the sea oat. It manages to thrive on beaches around the world in shifting sand that is void of apparent nutrients, with harsh winds, baking sun, and occasional flooding. And yet time and time again, it finds or seemingly creates what it needs in order to grow, flourish, and contribute to the ecological balance of the beach system. The sea oat is a symbol of hope to me, as are those people who similarly manage to thrive and flourish in unlikely environments.

Family therapists often emphasize that intrapsychic individual therapy is an inadequate way to treat problems that are generated, reinforced, and continued in a family system. Thus, apparent "progress" accomplished in such a therapy is destined to be undermined, sabotaged, or ultimately weakened when the individual returns to that family ecosystem and to the established hierarchy of power, rules of conduct, and generally negative consequences for new behaviors. If this is true, then by the same logic, when families return to the untreated cultural environment in which the problem was born, why are they not as unlikely to succeed as when an individual returns to his or her untreated family environment in which the problem was born?

Can we change cultural and personal habits significantly and rapidly enough to reverse the poisoning of our environment and the destruction of our planet? What is needed in order to do that? These are not questions we usually ask on a daily basis as therapists working with clients who present various symptoms of discomfort and imbalance. It is all too easy to become preoccupied with a focus on the diseases of the individual trees without considering the larger trends that feed, influence, and determine the healthy balance of the entire forest and its relationship to the other organisms sharing the planet. And, sometimes the short-term treatment for a symptom of imbalance may, in fact, contribute to a greater overall imbalance (Bateson, 1972).

Recently, much attention has been addressed to various natural disasters, such as the droughts of 1988 and the later flooding that some scientists call the first symptoms of the "greenhouse effect." They predict that these and other ostensibly "isolated" disasters will become more widespread as planetary conditions worsen. Whether or not any kind of "therapy," ecological or otherwise, successfully can facilitate a system-wide return to healthful balance, once the real needs are discovered, is uncertain. At a recent international conference concerned with reversing or at least slowing the greenhouse effect, activists stressed the need for a "truly global response," a "fundamental change in attitude and life-style." "For example," the very next speaker proposed, "we could put a 2% sales tax on gasoline." This intervention hardly seems to represent a fundamental change in life-style or even the beginning of one. What we really need is for people to universally comply with simple measures that may sound like a return to basics—practices such as responsible garbage sorting at the very least, recycling, composting, increased vegetarian habits, giving up a few lethal conveniences like plastic and aerosol. But I wonder if we can ever hope to successfully develop adequate emission control and clean air policies on a global level when so many individuals continue to voluntarily pollute their personal air (and the air necessarily shared by anyone in their vicinity) with cigarette smoke. By the same token, I wonder if we will ever achieve peaceful relations between humans until we discover that we should respect the rights of all living things.

Obviously this is not the conference to answer the questions of what is really needed at the global ecological level to restore physical balance on the planet. However, the process of symptom development and resolution briefly discussed at this global level is analogous to therapeutic change in individuals and families. It is equally ineffective, at either level, to focus our efforts on eliminating or patching symptoms of imbalance. We must facilitate a fundamental change in relational patterns.

BACK TO THE CONSULTING ROOM

I mentioned earlier that the "hard" part of doing psychotherapy, for me, is assessing and understanding just what clients need to learn, retrieve, or develop in order to respond to life's challenges creatively and without symptoms. The phase of therapy involving the retrieving of those experiences is "easy" because people are flexible and resilient beings with an abundant array of emotional, intellectual, and behavioral abilities. Operating from this belief and with a wide variety of effective interventions, it is possible to rapidly stimulate a client's thinking so as to restructure, retrieve, or develop needed experiences and transactions. Then, if the assessment has sufficiently considered the various factors involved, the person can apply these needed experiences in ways that do not require the continuation of the presenting problem. If this ideal result does not develop, it suggests one or more of the following: insufficient assessment of needed experiences, insufficient retrieval or development of resource experiences, or insufficient association to the desired context. It is *not* an indication to me, as I heard one therapist explaining about her clients, "that their resistance lies in their failure to use the insights that have been gained to stop the problem behaviors." It simply means that (1) additional experiences need to be retrieved, (2) the originally assessed experiences need to be more congruently developed, or (3) those experiences need to be more strongly associated to the desired context.

This may sound like a fairly utopian expectation, especially in contrast to the somewhat grim picture of the larger environment just painted. Sometimes an ideal adjustment is possible and sometimes, of course, it is not. There are limitations within which we must operate, though they are usually far less rigid than we have been led to believe. The "how long have I got (to live)?" question and the conservative answers that have been given to many patients illustrate this phenomenon. Milton Erickson is one well-known example of a patient "proving the doctors wrong" with regard to expected time of demise. He lived on "borrowed time" for 50 years if we count the first doctor's prediction that he would not live to see another sunrise (during his first bout with polio at age 17). And though I delight in helping my clients discover ways to unlimit themselves and disidentify with prejudices and biases about how they cannot change, I also acknowledge with them those "unmovable objects" against which even an unrelenting force effects little change.

A most cogent example of this occurred last summer with a resourceful woman who sought therapy in the latter stages of cancer. She congruently believed that it was possible to align her psychological abilities such that she might reverse the cancer and reclaim her energy. Though it is not possible to know with any certainty what physiological and psychological variables had combined to cause or contribute to her development of cancer, I still looked upon it as a possible symptom as I searched for some clue regarding her psychological adjustment and needs. What might she be expressing with her cancer or how might it be a "best choice" for needs that she was unable to express otherwise? What psychological imbalance might it be a symptom of and what might she need in order to create a balance without having cancer? What psychological resources might be beneficially applied to increase her congruence about living? These questions were in my mind as I observed her in her home environment interacting with her husband and still working to a restricted degree on various research projects in her profession. The most striking thing about this woman was her apparent lack of any emotion (neither sadness, anger, fear, resignation) about her illness, possible death, relationship with her husband, family of origin, professional goals, or the fact that she had never had children.

Though obviously a strong woman who wanted to live, she calmly described an almost complete lack of intimacy in her marriage but did not consider this to be a problem since she had decided in childhood to be "existentially alone" and not need anyone. While this may be a viable choice for some, it appeared to be inconsistent with her desire to optimally align psychological resources so as to alter the course of her cancer. Influencing the course of her cancer was, of course, an abstract and perhaps unrealistic goal since the origin and cause of cancer is far from clearly understood. However, her chronic failure to express needs or even to acknowledge their existence, coupled with the tendency to avoid or deny her emotions, though perhaps a best choice at the time it was adapted, was now representing an imbalance that was significantly affecting her life-style undesirably.

This woman had previously worked in therapy on a chronic cough seven years earlier. The cough had abated. However, when she reinitiated therapy related to the cancer, she indicated that the cough had been gone but came back *because* her husband had not given her the "support" she needed. But operating under her "existentially alone" policy, she had not told him of her need and he had failed to respond in a manner she considered to be "support." Clearly, his participation in the later therapy was required for it to be ecological.

And, though she denied any feelings of anger toward her husband, or fear or bitterness about the cancer, or a need to develop a closer relationship with her husband or others, she sent me a book entitled *Love, Medicine, and Healing* by Bernie Siegel, M.D. This was, she explained, to give me an idea about the kind of therapy she intuitively thought might prove helpful for her. The book was replete with stories of cancer patients who learned to express their needs and feelings and to take care of themselves better, and who sometimes had a remission of cancer. Sending me the book, combined with her statement about needing her husband's support, seemed a far clearer expression of her needs than her conscious mind could give.

And so, the work of therapy began, including suggestions to detail and intensify her use of cancer-related guided imagery, but primarily focused on the retrieval and development of attitudinal, emotional, and behavioral resources and on congruently applying herself to living as fully as possible. She responded in guarded but promising ways to stories and assignments to facilitate thinking, attitude restructuring, behavior change, and so forth. Her husband was involved. Their communications were analyzed and restructured. Intimacy was facilitated. Emotions and desires were expressed. The therapy was brief, but intensive and ecological. Happily, she reported a complete remission according to all lab work done for the next several months, regained desired energy, and yet died of cancer five months later. Her husband reported that she had died peacefully and at home. He described the quality of their remaining time together as vastly improved and her attitude as consistently positive. Was this therapy successful? What else was needed? Could any therapy have made a greater difference? I don't know the answers to these questions. Obviously, there are physical limits. None of us know how much time we have to live, and we should neither take for granted a long life nor readily believe what medical "experts" may pronounce in the case of what is supposed to be a terminal illness. Hopefully, medical experts are beginning to realize how much these predictions become powerful hypnotic suggestions that shape expectations and behaviors, rather than simply a comment on some predetermined reality (Rossi, 1986). We have a responsibility for our communication and must accept that we participate in creating the current reality.

POWER AND MANIPULATION

As therapists, we face a difficult paradox with regard to power. Many times the therapist's greatest frustration is feeling inadequate or helpless in the face of devastating problems brought by clients. And yet, there is often a feeling of apprehension and concern when therapists learn techniques and interventions that they fear will be "too powerful." The concern is that the degree of power will lead to undue manipulation of clients and too much control on the part of the therapist. This value conflict is, to some degree, shared by some clients who both hope that the therapist will be powerful enough to effect solutions yet fear that the therapist will be too powerful and will control or otherwise affect them negatively.

So how do we come to terms with power? I believe that the ultimate power is always with the client. That is, no matter how clever, enchanting, or well designed my interventions might be, clients are free to disregard my suggestions and respond in ways that are relevant for them. I have power but it is not absolute. I cannot make anyone do anything. This belief is somewhat freeing for me as the therapist in the sense that it relieves me of the burden of being perfectly accurate in my assessment and subsequent interventions. My "mistakes," or deviations from perfection, become stimuli to which clients respond with diagnostically relevant feedback. Still, I have the responsibility to carefully communicate in a way that does not inadvertently divert clients from the full range of personal potential that is rightfully theirs. This belief translates to setting positive, ecologically relevant goals and then fully applying my power in a cocreative or coconstructive process that involves working together to facilitate the retrieval and association of desired experiences.

So where does the therapist develop "power"? Some therapists identify themselves with particular interventions to be employed with each client, regardless of the situation. This offers the illusion of power since the therapist knows exactly what he or she is going to do. Of course, all clients won't respond the same way to a given approach, and thus the illusion of power is threatened and a familiar frustration is encountered instead. By contrast, would-be "Ericksonians" are plagued by the concept that, according to Erickson (Erickson & Rossi, 1979) himself, there should be no theory, that you should make up a new theory and a new approach for each client. This can seem like an overwhelming task. And it may mean that you won't know how you're going to proceed with some clients ahead of time. Sometimes, you'll have to "think on your feet," so to speak, or design interventions "under fire." Not knowing how you're going to stimulate in advance can create some anxiety that does not seem consistent with a feeling of power. (Nobody ever said you get to feel secure just because you have power.) Also, not knowing what will be said or done in advance does not seem wholly consistent with the idea of strategically setting goals and working systematically toward them, as I have suggested. But the open-ended approach (with regard to interventions selected) for each client is not the same thing as "flying by the seat of one's pants." There are goals which may or may not change as continuing diagnostic information is observed, but therapists must be free to respond intuitively, unpredictably, and creatively as they choose from an unlimited number of techniques and interventions. Sometimes, the interventions result from a great deal of personalized preplanning for each client, and other times the interventions are selected intuitively and congruently in immediate response to the client. Neither way is better; power takes different shapes and forms. There is just as much power involved in listening, observing, and thinking very hard about what is needed as there is in strategically intervening toward that end.

This chapter is not written to endorse or suggest superiority of particular interventions. I have instead indicated that there is a wide variety of possible interventions that therapists can use to enhance their sense of option and power in dealing with the ecological, developmental, and relational concerns represented by clients' problems and symptoms. Interventions can range from empathy to confrontation, from indirect methods such as metaphor and ambiguous function assignments to rational emotive analysis. Treatment may include hypnosis, family therapy, age regression, redecision, reparenting, assertiveness training, behavior management, modeling, paradoxical assignments, ego state analysis, play therapy, jokes, caring, and "just talking." The possibilities are endless.

Ecological therapy can be practiced across disciplines. It need not become a discipline in itself. All therapy is presumably oriented toward helping clients solve problems and experience relief, positive change, balance, and creative adjustments. Dividing boundaries can become arbitrary when we examine our commonly held beliefs and values. We must believe that people are inherently interested in living the best life they can create and that each symptom or difficulty presented for therapy represents their best choice under current circumstances for adapting to the demands and pressures of the ecosystem.

When we become curious about what is needed to help people

organize better choices, we tap into a great storehouse of unconscious resources, both therapist-and client-based. With this kind of power, perhaps we can find the courage to cocreate that fundamental change in attitude and life-style that will result in people using their resources and relating to each other in such a way as to not only be free of symptoms, but to create a healthy balance in a healthy environment.

REFERENCES

Bandura, A. (1969). *Principles of Behavior Modification*. New York: Holt, Rinehart & Winston.

Bateson, G. (1972). *Steps to an Ecology of Mind*. Part Five: "Conscious purpose versus nature." New York: Chandler.

Ellis, A. (1971). *Growth Through Reason*. North Hollywood, CA: Wilshire.

Erickson, K. (1985). One method for designing short-term intervention-oriented Ericksonian therapy. In J. Zeig & S. Lankton (Eds.), *Developing Ericksonian Therapy* (pp. 379–396). New York: Brunner/Mazel.

Erickson, M., & Rossi, E. (1979). *Hypnotherapy*. New York: Irvington.

Haley, J. (1976). *Problem-Solving Therapy*. San Francisco: Jossey-Bass.

Lankton, S., & Lankton, C. (1986). *Enchantment and Intervention in Family Therapy: Training in Ericksonian Approaches*. New York: Brunner/Mazel.

Perls, F. (1973). *The Gestalt Approach and Eye Witness to Therapy*. Palo Alto, CA: Science and Behavior Books.

Rossi, E. (1986). *The Psychobiology of Mind-Body Healing*. New York: Norton.

Wolpe, J. (1982). *The Practice of Behavior Therapy* (3rd ed.). New York: Pergamon Press.

PART VII

Distinguishing Features of Brief Therapy

CHAPTER 27

Coevolution of Primary
Process in Brief Therapy
Stephen G. Gilligan

An aged man is but a paltry thing
A tattered coat upon a stick, unless
Soul clap its hands and sing.
— W. B. Yeats

When I met Milton Erickson in the mid-1970s, he was an aged man, beset by physical illnesses. But far from tattered, Erickson exuded a strength and wisdom that touched and inspired many around him. Part of his influence was due to remarkable technical skills: He learned how to master therapeutic communication. But something else about Erickson, call it "soul" if you will, was even more powerful than his technique. One could not help being impressed by the way he thought, the way he looked at people, the way he spoke. Simply stated, his approach to psychotherapy was highly effective and intensely personal.

While some of Erickson's style was idiosyncratic to him and therefore of little direct value to the average practitioner, his approach also contained highly original ideas about psychotherapy. His personal style and creative ideas constitute a context for psychotherapy that is quite different from traditional approaches. This difference in context can significantly affect how technique is used and received: Techniques of Ericksonian psychotherapy may have a positive effect within one context, but may be misused and even have negative effects when applied

359

within a more traditional context. This idea was suggested by Gregory Bateson during a 1976 interview with Brad Keeney:

> *Keeney*: You're saying that people who go see Erickson come away with a craving for power?
> *Bateson*: Yes! They all want power.
> *Keeney*: Is there something about seeing [Erickson] that induces this power hungriness?
> *Bateson*: Well, it's the skill which he has of manipulating the other person which really in the long run does not separate him as an ego dominant to the other person. *He works in the weave of the total complex and they come away with a trick, which is separate from the total complex, therefore, goeth counter to it and becomes a sort of power.* I think it's something like that. (Italics added) (Keeney, 1976, p. 49)

I find Bateson's comments especially relevant to the current state of Ericksonian psychotherapy. At this point we have many sophisticated techniques: We know how to induce hypnotic trance in many ways, how to give indirect suggestions, and how to weave marvelous metaphors. We know 101 ways to assign homework, how to paradox and counterparadox, and so forth. At the same time, we have considerably less sophistication regarding the personal context of the therapist applying such techniques. More attention has been paid to the "suggestions" therapists give clients than to the suggestions therapists might give themselves to best work with clients. There has been greater emphasis on joining and utilizing the client's unconscious processes than on tapping into the *therapist's* unconscious creativity. And, there has been more focus on how therapists may influence clients than on the reciprocal effect of clients on therapists.

Such an imbalance is unnecessary and perhaps dangerous, because it fosters the illusion that experience resides exclusively within the client, thereby denying or ignoring how the therapist participates at every level in the relationship. Such a dissociation gives rise to further illusions of power and attempts to control others. This "goeth counter" to the spirit and example of Erickson's work and may result in ineffective therapy. To avoid such peril, I believe it is important to explore how the therapist may participate, in Bateson's words, within the "weave of the total complex" of the therapy relationship.

This chapter is devoted to such an exploration. The first part identifies some suggestions that therapists may give themselves to shift into a personal context conducive to conducting effective Ericksonian therapy.

The second part describes a case history that illustrates the type of therapy that arises from giving oneself such suggestions.

ACCESSING THE THERAPEUTIC SELF OF THE THERAPIST

To begin, let us imagine a therapist sitting in his office, waiting for a client to arrive. This therapist, like most, is conscientious, hard-working, and concerned. He wants to do a good job. He has read 143 of Erickson's success stories, has attended 31 workshops within the past five years, and has listened to 92 different hypnotic inductions (including a few political speeches) in the past year. Yet sitting in his chair, waiting and wondering, a nagging idea begins to creep into his consciousness: All this is not enough! The factual knowledge he has accumulated is not enough to make him effective. He must have a way to use this knowledge, to access this information while immersed in the therapeutic relationship. He must be able to tap into not only his own resources, but those of the client, because both will be needed for successful therapy. The question is, how can he do this?

One way involves a self-referential series of hypnotic-like suggestions. These suggestions are meant to be self-dissipating; that is, fairly rapidly they should disappear from conscious thinking and move into unconscious thinking, to reappear only when the therapist is stuck. The purpose of using such suggestions is to develop a way of being that allows techniques and solutions to arise from the integrity of the relationship, rather than from the therapist as an individual.

Cooperation

The first suggestion is: *cooperate.* By this I mean something different from what my father (and perhaps yours) meant when he said, "You'd better cooperate!" The underlying idea here is that therapists and clients cocreate realities; each unavoidably influences the other (Gilligan, 1987). By appreciating this mutual influence, therapists can take advantage of it. They can set aside the limiting and erroneous assumption that the therapist is responsible for developing all techniques, resources, and solutions and instead find ways to join with the client so that both contribute equally.

A helpful image here might be the potato sack race that most of us have participated in at a picnic or county fair. In such a race, you and your partner each have one leg inside the sack and one leg outside.

When you are synchronized with your partner in this three-legged race, progress is made; when you're out of rhythm, both of you fall down.

The situation is similar in therapy, where both therapist and client have one foot inside the system and one foot outside. In this view, progress is made by *cooperating with* rather than *operating on* another person. The client has ways of being, as does the therapist; the task is to find ways to blend those patterns so that two "I's," rather than one, focus together to provide a deeper vision of possible futures (cf. de Shazer, 1982). Neither "I," neither point of view, is superior to the other; but working together, "apart from and yet a part of" each other, they constitute an effective team.

This notion of cocreating realities has applications in every phase of therapy. One phase is diagnosis, which in general terms means accurately describing where clients are and where they want to go. As O'Hanlon (O'Hanlon & Wilk, 1987; O'Hanlon & Weiner-Davis, 1988) has cogently pointed out, representations of problems and possible solutions are negotiated between therapists and clients; they do not have an independent existence. Thus, a man complaining of work difficulties may be "found," depending on the therapist who interviews him, to suffer from an anxiety disorder, unfinished business with his father, poor self-image, negative self-talk, or even marital discord. None of these diagnoses is "true" or inherently better than the rest: their values lie in how well they accurately portray the difficulty while also allowing change. Since both therapists and clients will have individual preferences in this regard, it is important to work together to find a mutually helpful representation.

This same cooperational approach applies to technique. Therapists can blend with the "techniques" clients are already using to create their experience, complementing or modifying them in ways that allow solutions to emerge. For example, say the client complaining of job anxiety specifies that this process includes the following: (1) making pictures of what might (or might not) happen at work in the next months, (2) shaky hands, and (3) stomach nausea. The Ericksonian therapist might regard these as hypnotic techniques: the "making pictures of the future" technique is a version of hypnotic future orientation (Erickson, 1954), the "shaky hands" technique is an instance of ideomotor signaling (Rossi & Cheek, 1988), and the "intense feeling in the guts" technique is an example of ideosensory signaling (Gilligan, 1988a). Based on the cornerstone assumption that the same techniques can lead to problems or solutions (Erickson, 1965; Gilligan, 1987, 1988a,b; Zeig, 1988), therapeutic interaction can use these very techniques to develop a solution. For example, the client might hypnotically learn a variety of other forms of future orientation. At the same time, he could learn to let automatic movements of the fingers signal and access resources of security, while discovering how feelings in the stomach could become a comfortable warmth spreading throughout his body. This is one of many ways that therapeutic techniques are cocreated: The therapist accepts and utilizes what the client is already doing to develop solutions where problems were.

In this cooperational view, the traditional idea of resistance has no place (de Shazer, 1984). It is a concept that emerged from a different sense of the term "cooperation," namely, the one my father used. In this old view, the client was resistant if he didn't follow the therapist's directives. In the present view, "resistance" merely signals that therapist and client are not cooperating, i.e., not working together very well, a problem that adjustments by either therapist or client can remedy.

Experiential Participation

A second suggestion therapists can give to themselves is: *experientially participate*. That is, do not confine yourself to an analytical mode; find ways to get out of your head and into the interpersonal connectedness of the relationship. Rather than being merely an outside observer or an inside participant, become an observer/participant immersed in what Mary Catherine Bateson (1988) calls "disciplined subjectivity." This, of course, is one of the major suggestions Ericksonian therapists give clients. It is based on the idea that the analytical mind is basically conservative. It tends to see things from one perspective and acts to preserve that perspective. This is fine in many instances, but not when recurrent problems are indicating a need for a change. In such instances, a "deframing" into direct experience is called for. While we generally agree that it is important for clients to do this, we sometimes forget that it is equally important for therapists. As Erickson commented:

> Too many psychotherapists try to plan what thinking they will do instead of waiting to see what the stimulus they receive is, and then letting their unconscious mind respond to that stimulus. (In Gordon & Meyers-Anderson, 1981, p. 17)

By shifting into a receptive, experiential mode, therapists are modeling the creative state that they are asking clients to experiment with. The general attitude is: "The water's fine. Come on in and try it at your rate and in your own style." An experiential mode also lets therapists sense the client's reality from multiple perspectives, something crucial to being helpful.

In the tradition of Ericksonian psychotherapy, hypnotic processes are a major means for shifting from analytical rigidity to experiential fluidity. Both clients and therapists can use and benefit from them, albeit in different ways. As Erickson noted:

> If I have any doubts about my capacity to see the important things I go into a trance. When there is a crucial issue with a patient and I don't want to miss any of the clues I go into a trance. . . . I startkeeping close track of every movement, sign, or behavioral manifestation that could be important. (Erickson & Rossi, 1977, p. 42)

I devoted an entire chapter in my book, *Therapeutic Trances* (Gilligan, 1987) to talking about how therapists can use hypnotic processes responsibly. What I'd like to emphasize here is that learning these skills is an art that requires commitment and rigor. Contrary to the mistaken perceptions of some critics (e.g., Hammond, 1988), "trusting the unconscious" is not a substitute for careful planning or strategizing. It is an additional skill that, when used responsibly, can significantly improve both the sensitivity and influence, the receiving and the giving, of your communication.

Future Orientation

In experientially cooperating with clients, therapists need to have some clear sense of intention. In this regard, a third helpful "mantra" is: *orient to the future.* This is a basic value that distinguishes Ericksonian psychotherapy from the primary orientation to the past emphasized by traditional approaches (Gilligan, 1987; O'Hanlon & Wilk, 1987). It also differs from the major focus of most clients, who enter therapy fixed on a troubling past. Thus, I emphasize this basic value of future orientation in initial interviews with clients and then devote a good deal of time and effort to making it experientially come alive during the therapy. One way I've been doing this lately involves literally hypnotically hallucinating the client's "future self" in the room. It's a sort of three-ring circus: One ring is the therapist, a second is the client system, and the third ring is the future self. Conversation between the first two rings is used to generate the third, guided by the general underlying question "What does your desired future self look, sound, and feel like?" Once the future self is hallucinated, I treat it as an actual "living presence" and try to develop a balanced experiential connection between it, the client, and me.

This orientation to a "future self" enhances my trust in my unconscious processes by serving as a positive constraint; that is, it provides an image of achievement around which the unconscious can weave patterns. In doing so, it moves experiential communication from a wide-open free association to controlled spontaneity. By expanding the therapist's attention beyond the client, it also reduces the likelihood of getting dragged into the undertow of some relationships. For example, many therapists have experienced getting lost in a relationship with a borderline or depressive personality. Part of this owes, I think, to the instability of a dyadic relationship. By sensing a "future self" as fully as you sense the client's presenting self, you can be "a part of, yet apart from" the client's present reality. This will allow you to support and utilize where clients are, while at the same time orienting to where they can also be.

Solutions

A fourth suggestion therapists might give themselves is: *think in terms of solutions rather than problems*. Clients present problems, emphasizing what they can't do; Ericksonian therapists organize in terms of solutions, thinking in terms of what the client can do. The basic difference here has been nicely described by Joseph Chilton Pearce (1981). Pearce pointed out that each of us is born with a set of "neural injunctions," or what we call in hypnosis "irresistible suggestions." Regardless of name, nationality, religion, politics, race, or whatever, you *will* respond to these suggestions. They include "walk," "talk," "construct a world image," and "generate a self-image." Each task involves primary and secondary processes. For example, the primary path in walking is, simply, to walk; secondary paths include balancing, shifting weight, and falling. As long as attention remains tuned to the primary process of walking, falling is a solution, not a problem; it is essential to learning to walk. But if primary attention becomes somehow misdirected from walking to falling, problems become dominant. Pearce (1981) describes this as the movement from the "fall" to "The (Biblical) Fall" from grace. To move back into one's "good graces," then, involves reorienting to solutions, i.e., to the developmental skills and challenges a person is facing.

Resources

A related suggestion is: *think in terms of resources rather than deficits*. The general question is, How can I use my processes and patterns and the client's processes and patterns, whatever they may be, as the basis for therapeutic interaction? A good rule of thumb is to claim as a resource any experience or skill involving emotion, either positive or negative, since emotion indicates the self is involved in the process (cf. Gilligan, 1982). In the client's experience this might involve clearly positive resources, such as the memory of a success, an empowering symbol, or a positive figure in the person's life. Symptoms, however, qualify as equally powerful resources. For example, a depressed client complained of an nagging inner voice that recurrently incanted, "You can't do it . . . you can't do it . . . you can't do it." Approaching this "tape loop" as a potential resource, trance was initiated in the following way:

> *Therapist*: John, there are many things that should and could be done, but we both know that *you can't do it*! What do I mean by that? Well, I'd like you to sit there in that chair and look at me without blinking your eyes. But I bet *you can't do it*! I'd like you to not listen to my voice, but you probably *can't do it*! I'd like you to try not to think of not listening at an unconscious level, but *you can't do it*! I'd like you to not signal by lifting a finger when you're ready to go deeper into trance, but you can't do it, can you not know?

These suggestions, offered in an intense fashion, absorbed John's attention and were further used as an element of the solution. For example, John had several minor relapses during the course of the therapy. On these occasions, I told him with great intensity, "I thought that maybe you might be the first person to learn how to walk without falling. But you can't do it, can you!? You can't be the first perfect person on the face of the earth, can you?" Detecting both my seriousness and humor, John responded with both a tear and a smile. "I guess not," he replied. "That's right," I softly emphasized. "It's nice to know that you *can* sense and appreciate how important your falling and failings are in learning how to walk your own path." In this way, John's pattern of using "I can't do it" in a self-defeating manner was recontextualized as a part of learning new ways of being.

Just as the client's ongoing processes can be regarded as resources, so can the therapist's. For example, I was working with an elderly Irish gentleman whose legs were, in his words, "howling at him." It was a strange and intense pain that baffled the neurologists, occurring precisely from the knees down and being unresponsive to medicine and psychological interventions by other specialists. While I felt confident that hypnotic pain control could be achieved, every method I introduced—age regression, age progression, dissociation, shifting the locus of sensation—failed miserably.

During these efforts, a 15-year-old memory of the last time I saw my Irish grandfather, right before his death, would periodically filter through my awareness. I wondered what Grandpa Jack was doing "visiting" me, then quickly concluded that I was distracted and thus dismissed him to try to concentrate more on the issue of pain. However, further therapeutic efforts failed and Grandpa Jack continued to return. Finally, I responded to the "minimal cues" indicating that somehow I was "off," gave up my fixed frame of assuming that pain was the issue, and surrendered contemplatively to the recurrent image of Grandpa Jack. Suddenly, it dawned on me: perhaps dying was the issue here, not pain. So I began to softly share stories about my grandfather, including his last trip back to Ireland and his death. As I did, the man's body softened for the first time and tears welled up in his eyes. Thus, Grandpa Jack was a key opening the passage to therapeutic progress.

What I'd like to suggest is that everybody has a Grandpa Jack. By thinking in terms of resources, therapists can discover how their ongoing processes provide many resources helpful in working with clients. This, of course, makes for better therapy.

Context

A sixth suggestion is: *appreciate context as the key to therapeutic change.* This idea here is that meaning is derived from context, so that when you change the context you change the value of an expression. For example, suppose someone complains of withdrawing. The question can be asked, Is withdrawal good or bad? If you think this is a trick question, you're right: Sometimes withdrawal is useful, sometimes not. It depends on the context. Thus, the challenge is to take that process of withdrawing that's self-defeating in one context and cocreate a variety of other contexts, some of which feature withdrawal in more satisfying ways. Maybe she will withdraw into self-appreciation; perhaps she will withdraw for only 10 minutes a day; perhaps she will withdraw into a relationship with a pet or another person. You don't know and they don't know at the outset how they will use withdrawal comfortably and self-supportively; what you *can* realize is that by supporting clients in doing their symptom

BRIEF THERAPY

"more and better," they can find contexts in which it is a solution, not a symptom.

Another application of contextual thinking comes from the observation that people lose a connection to larger contexts when they experience a symptom, and that this may be what's blocking the natural development of solutions (Gilligan, 1988b). For example, suppose someone complains of a migraine headache. In such cases, a question I often ask is, "When you have a migraine headache, how do your hands feel?" The client may look at me as if I'm crazy and ask, "What in God's name do my hands have to do with the pain in my head?" My response is, "Exactly my question!" The idea here is that when people develop chronic pain in one part of their body, they dissociate the rest of their body. Or, when they develop anxiety, they lost their social connection to others. Or, when they access a trauma, they can't access any other memories. In each case, experience is functionally separated from its deeper organismic, social, and psychological contexts. The figure gets dissociated from the ground, the piece from the whole, the conscious from the unconscious, the problem from the solution. A cornerstone idea in Ericksonian psychotherapy is that reconnecting individuals to larger contexts allows change to naturally occur.

Multiple Truth Values

Experimenting with context emphasizes that the primary interest of therapy is constructed meanings, rather than objective reality per se. In this regard, another suggestion is: *appreciate and accept multiple truth values.* Appreciate that your reality, your way of being, your perspective is not superior to the client's. Both therapist and client are operating in "as if" worlds, acting "as if" the world were this way or that way. Assuming that your "as if" world is better or more accurate moves therapy into a competitive power play; on the other hand, letting two different "as if" realities interact allows new "baby" realities to be born, some of which may be more useful to the person's present needs and challenges.

Another application of truth values has to do with the logic you use to organize your experience as therapist. While most of us have been trained to reflexively use traditional either/or logic, this may not be the best way to promote change. The words of Neils Bohr, the physicist who founded quantum mechanics, are useful in this regard. Dr. Bohr suggested that there are two kinds of truth: In the shallow kind, the opposite of a true statement is false; in the deep kind, the opposite is equally true (Wechsler, 1979). This logic, where something and its opposite are equally true, has been pointed out by Freud, Jung, and others to be the logic of the unconscious. It is a logic underlying paradoxical assignments, the logic that allows us to see a symptom as a solution. It is a logic that allows us to encourage clients to both hold on and let go, to change and not change, to appreciate both sides of a conflict. In short, it is a logic of cooperation, a logic of healing, a logic of love.

To summarize, therapists may give themselves a variety of suggestions for establishing a personal context for conducting Ericksonian therapy. These suggestions include: (1) cooperate, (2) experientially participate, (3) orient to the future, (4) orient to solutions, (5) orient to resources, (6) appreciate context as the key to change, and (7) appreciate multiple truth values. To provide some sense of the sort of therapy that arises from using such suggestions, I'd like to shift at this point to a case history.

CASE EXAMPLE

Maureen entered therapy seeking, in her words, more confidence at work. She was 36, the oldest of five children in a strict Irish-Catholic family, married with no children, and a highly successful business-woman. She complained of experiencing debilitating fear and stress when making presentations at work and hoped that hypnosis could help her feel more comfortable in such situations.

Three 90-minute sessions were needed to handle this initial complaint. In the first session, hypnosis was described as a mastery process wherein experiential resources could be accessed and used for therapeutic purposes, and several light trances were successfully developed. A self-hypnosis process was then demonstrated and assigned as a daily homework task.

In the second session, a deeper trance was induced and suggestions to develop a comfortable state were elaborated. As Maureen accomplished this, I suggested that her unconscious mind access an experiential symbol that would help her revivify and maintain this state when making presentations. It was noted that symbols come in many forms—for example, memories, objects, or persons—and that what she came up with might not make sense to her conscious mind. She was surprised and intrigued upon developing a vivid image of a big, friendly bear. I congratulated her and suggested that she hypnotically explore where in the context of making presentations the bear would be most helpful as an ally. After a minute or so of silent exploration, she smiled while describing a big, happy bear sitting in the back of the meeting room while she was making a presentation. I encouraged her to continue this hypnotic rehearsal for another 10 minutes or so and then reoriented her from trance.

The process of envisioning a bear in the meeting room was then repeated. This, time, however, Maureen entered trance with her self-hypnosis technique and kept her eyes open throughout the explorations. Both modifications were designed to help her use the process in the target situation. Upon reorienting from trance, she expressed delight and satisfaction in her newly found hypnotic skills. She was congratulated and encouraged to practice each night in preparation for her presentation later that week.

Maureen returned two weeks later in a happy mood. She had made two presentations since the last meeting, and did surprisingly well in each. Initial doubts and fears seemed to disappear after she hypnotically "discovered" a big, happy bear sitting attentively and supportively in the back of the room. Whenever she needed to bolster her comfort and confidence during the presentations, a brief and unnoticeable orientation to the bear would suffice. She expressed confidence in continued success, and we therefore agreed that the therapy contract had been satisfied. After reviewing the therapy and talking about how to maintain the changes made, farewells were exchanged and the session ended.

About six weeks later, Maureen called to urgently request another appointment. Something terrible was happening, and she didn't know what it was. It had started several days earlier, with the sudden and inexplicable onset of severe stomach pains. So intense were they that she felt compelled to seek help at the emergency room of the local hospital, where a series of tests and examinations all proved negative. When the attending physician discussed with her the possibility of psychological factors being involved, her concern increased and she decided to call me.

I arranged to see her the next day. Since she expressed great interest in knowing what was happening, I began by asking many questions. I obtained a detailed description of the pain, learned that it was sometimes accompanied by self-mutilating images and severely critical internal dialogue, and that it had occurred (to a lesser extent) on at least several other occasions in the past years. Maureen couldn't connect the symptoms to any present difficulties, as she thought her work and family life were going well. She also couldn't attribute them to anything in her family of origin, though she did describe both parents as being alcoholic and physically violent.

Given that the symptoms had a dissociative quality to them, I used the dissociative method of ideomotor finger questioning. After inducing a light trance and using suggestions to establish a "yes" finger, a "no" finger, and an "I don't know" finger, I asked if her unconscious mind knew what the pain was about. Her "yes" finger lifted. I asked if it was alright to let her conscious mind know. The "no" finger lifted. I asked if her unconscious mind was willing to work with me on the matter and let her conscious mind know at the proper time. The "yes" finger lifted.

I therefore elaborated suggestions for her to go very deeply into a trance, deep enough to appreciate that her "unconscious mind was very intelligent, intelligent enough to be able to summon the resources and develop the means to deal suitably with the challenge at hand." I further noted that she had a "body" of experiential knowledge, and that her unconscious could express itself through this body in a variety of ways. I pointed out that while her unconscious could express experience through bodily pains, it could just as thoroughly express ideas through bodily *movements*, as her ideomotor finger signaling showed. I therefore suggested that each night during the week, and also whenever she felt any pains developing, she find a safe and private place to sit down, go into trance, orient to the question "What healthy needs can my unconscious body of experience express?" and then let herself draw or paint for a half-hour or so. When I asked her unconscious mind if this seemed like a good plan, it signaled yes; when I inquired whether anything else needed to be added, it signaled no. So after a few more minutes, she was reoriented from trance, given the same instructions in a waking state, and bid goodbye.

She arrived for the next session with about a half-dozen paintings, each one intense and extraordinary. We sat shoulder to shoulder, examining the paintings with a shared hypnotic absorption. I found myself orienting to the stomach regions of different painted characters, for they were filled with black or red circles. When I gently drew attention to them, she seemed to plummet into a silent, emotion-filled space, her eyes fighting back tears. I asked her what she was aware of, and she said she didn't know. Tuning to my own inner processes, I became vividly aware of a memory of puppies dying. That's when I consciously realized that the holes suggested a dead baby.

Making sure to remain experientially connected, I paused silently for awhile before softly beginning to describe the memory of the puppies. Her tears began to flow and her body was racked by sobs. For the next 15 minutes or so, she cried and I gently consoled her. Slowly her story came out. Fleeing an abusive home situation at 17, she moved into a commune and promptly got pregnant. Despite her guilt and confusion, she and the baby's father immediately went for a medical abortion, after which he insisted angrily that the situation be completely forgotten, for the baby "no longer existed." She never spoke a word about it, though apparently she didn't forget. As we discovered later, on each anniversary of the abortion she had severe depression and physical pains.

Sitting with Maureen, I couldn't help but sense the baby's presence in the room, so I softly suggested, "She's still alive!" These words seemed to touch something inside her, so I continued by gently pointing out that while the baby was indeed no longer physically living, her spirit seemed to continue to exist. She nodded silently and tears reappeared, this time more gently. We talked about burial rituals across different cultures, and I suggested that her baby's spirit was still awaiting one. This idea resonated deeply within her, so I suggested that she engage in four preparation tasks. The first was to use meditation and self-hypnosis to find a name for the baby. The second was to spend some time (I suggested 45 minutes) each day writing letters to the baby, communicating whatever she needed to about her feelings then and now. The third was to make some physical burial symbols to accompany the baby's spirit on its passage to safety. The fourth was to select some living symbols of her commitment to new life.°

She returned five days later with the tasks completed. She reported that deciding on a name and writing the letters were both important and emotional processes for her. She also showed the baby's outfit she knitted and the paintings she painted for burial gifts and noted she had purchased two plants as symbols of new life. We discussed details of the ceremony, and she decided on a nearby wilderness preserve as a burial site. She emphasized that somehow it was important for her to do this alone, but with my presence as a support and witness.

We met several days later at the wilderness preserve. After a brief meditational ceremony, we walked in silence so she could find a proper burial site. She selected a private clearing near a stream, and I knelt down and waited as she dug a hole, laid out an alter cloth, and arranged the ritual items. Beginning the ceremony with about 10 minutes of intense, focused silence, she suddenly let out a piercing cry, followed by words addressed to the baby about what happened, why, how she felt now, what she wanted for the baby's spirit, and so forth. During this process, the baby was named, the burial gifts and new life symbols were placed in the grave, and a goodbye message was offered. The ceremony ended with about five minutes of meditational silence.

As we walked back to the cars, I let her know how deeply touched and moved I was by the whole event. I also suggested that she continue the letter writing during the next week to express any lingering feelings to

---

°The process of enacting rituals to absorb grief and acknowledge death is, of course, an ancient one. Its use in psychotherapy was noted by Erickson (in Zeig, 1980, pp. 287-288), who described how he directed a woman distraught over the death of her six-month-old baby in the grief-absorbing task of planting a tree.

the baby or other individuals (e.g., family members), and that she plant a new seed in her garden each day to honor new life emerging. She returned the following week with reports of experiencing a deep calm and peace since the ceremony, occasionally joined by waves of sadness. The tasks had been helpful, and she had suffered no physical pains or self-denigrating internal processes. After follow-up sessions during the next month showed no return of the symptoms, therapy was terminated.

Four months later, Maureen scheduled another appointment. She had been trying to get pregnant, but with no luck. When medical examinations revealed scar tissue from a previous surgery causing tubal blockage, she and her husband decided to pursue a surgical remedy. A major obstacle, however, was Maureen's terror of doctors and operations. In fact, she had become paralyzed and mute during the most recent medical examination, a condition exacerbated when the physician and nurse impatiently reiterated demands for her to speak. She requested my assistance in changing her responses of terror and paralysis, so that the surgery could be undertaken.

I began by interviewing both Maureen and her husband. I seriously questioned whether the operation was the best choice for them, given that it might not work, that she might miss a month of work, and that it was placing the onus of change primarily on her. I asked them to go home and list the pros and cons of each alternative, then use discussion and self-hypnosis to decide what was best for them. When their choice remained the same, I agreed to work with Maureen on preparing for surgery.

As in most cases, the work was organized around cocreating a vision of the desired future and identifying and accessing sufficient resources to get there. The first order of business concerned the "spontaneous trance" of paralysis into which Maureen would slip. As she reported that her primary experience within this troubling state was a "silent scream," I allowed myself to slip into a "working trance" (Gilligan, 1987) to ponder how this might be used as a powerful resource. Multisensory images of martial arts began to arise in my mind, replete with focused karate "screams." I confessed to Maureen that I had no confidence that her unconscious would stop screaming, since that was an important way to express and protect one's self, and wondered instead how she might be able to "do it more and do it better" (Gilligan, 1987, 1988a). She became attentively absorbed by this statement, so I elaborated stories of martial artists learning to use focused and centered screams in powerful ways. Her scream was in her throat, I noted, but it might be interesting to hypnotically experiment with moving it around in the body, to find the place where it would best protect and support. We engaged in this hypnotic process of shifting the symptom locus for about 30 minutes and discovered that a scream right below her navel provided a calm and centered feeling. I suggested that she practice this process in self-hypnosis during the week, and we ended the session.

The next week, while browsing in a drug store, she described finding and buying a self-hypnosis tape for surgical preparation. But, when she listened to its soothing messages of relaxation at home, she grew increasingly nervous and paralyzed. This was followed by hearing in her head the intense "screaming" of heavy-metal rock music. Though she generally disliked such music, it somehow had a deeply calming effect on her. Intrigued, she practiced her self-hypnotic surgery preparation that week while listening on headphones to heavy-metal music. It worked well: Her unconscious had discovered an even better way to shift the symptomatic scream into a solution.

With this resource in hand, we developed several others. The first concerned her terrifying fear of being invaded by the hands or instruments of the surgeon. Trance was developed and it was noted that while her scream was there to provide a radiating "inner to outer" protection, her unconscious could balance this process by developing a way to receive a life-enhancing gift from outside to inside her body. She developed the image of a healing seed being planted inside her. She felt this would be an excellent way to experientially sense the surgical intervention, as long as the scream was there as a complementary balancing process.

The third symbol had to do with orientation to the future. We discussed how seeing beyond the surgery to its intended outcome, namely having a baby, might be helpful. Through further hypnotic experimentation she discovered the vivid image of a little girl waiting for her in the future. Hypnotically hallucinating this experiential symbol in front of her was empowering: It motivated her while also expanding awareness beyond her body.

She practiced this and the other skills for another week before entering the hospital for what proved to be a most satisfying experience. She felt fairly calm and centered before the scheduled surgery, especially when listening to her headphones and holding her husband's hand. Then, preliminary investigations involving shooting dye through her tubes to ensure that they were blocked revealed that somehow there was no longer any blockage! Thus, the major surgery was canceled and she was discharged later that day.

While I am told that this "tubal unblocking" is not entirely uncommon, it certainly was a cause of great celebration for Maureen and her husband. She thought that her hypnotic imaging had something to do with it; as I told her, all I knew was that she had trusted her unconscious and worked hard to move through a great challenge in her life. I congratulated the couple and suggested they get involved in conceiving.

I wish that this story ended like some of Erickson's case histories, namely that the client was seen at a casual social gathering with three children, expressing a little bit of the symptom for old time's sake. But the pregnancy hasn't happened yet.* They are practicing, though, and that's important. More important, Maureen feels hope for the future and a deepened confidence in her ability to handle life's challenges.

This, I think, is what therapy is all about. My intention in describing this case has been to illuminate how an Ericksonian approach may be especially effective in this regard. The case illustrates some key ideas in this approach: (1) how therapy is a cooperative process between therapist and client; (2) how therapy involves the unconscious processes of *both* therapist and client; (3) how creative unconscious processes may be expressed in inner realities (hypnotic trances) *and* outer realities (rituals); (4) how techniques and solutions are cocreated; (5) how future orientation and resources are primary tools in therapy; and (6) how context determines meaning and how context can be shifted, such that a scream can be a symptom or a solution.

Most important, I hope the case and the suggestions preceding it give some idea of how a therapist becomes therapeutic by operating in two opposite worlds simultaneously: the worlds of inner and outer, self and other, heart and mind, knowledge and uncertainty, giving and receiving, holding on and letting go. Operating in both worlds, an individual can work within what Bateson described as "the weave of the total complex." He or she can find the still point of the self from which new realities are created. This, I believe, was Erickson's shining example; and this, I believe, is each of our challenges. As Eliot (1963, pp. 191-192) suggested:

> At the still point of the turning world, Neither flesh nor fleshless;
> Neither from nor towards; at the still point, there the dance is,
> But neither arrest nor movement. And do not call it fixity,
> Where past and time are gathered. Neither movement from nor towards,

---

*It is a pleasure to report that at the present time (January, 1990) Maureen is seven months pregnant.

Neither ascent nor decline. Except for the point, the still point,
There would be no dance, and there is only the dance.
I can only say, *there* we have been: but I cannot say where.
And I cannot say, how long, for that is to place it in time.
The inner freedom from the practical desire,
The release from action and suffering, release from the inner
And the outer compulsion, yet surrounded
By a grace of sense, a white light still and moving
Erhebung without motion, concentration
Without elimination, both a new world
And the old made explicit, understood
In the completion of its partial ecstacy
The resolution of its partial horror.

REFERENCES

Bateson, M. C. (1988). Interview with Kevin Kelly. *Whole Earth Review, 61,* 136–137.

de Shazer, S. (1982). *Patterns of Brief Family Therapy: An Ecosystemic Approach.* New York: Guilford Press.

de Shazer, S. (1984). The death of resistance. *Family Process, 23,* 79–93.

Eliot, T. S. (1963). Four quartets. In T. S. Eliot, *Collected Poems.* London: Faber & Faber.

Erickson, M. H. (1954). Psuedo orientation in time as a hypnotherapeutic procedure. *Journal of Clinical and Experimental Hypnosis, 2,* 261–283.

Erickson, M. H. (1965). The use of symptoms as an integral part of therapy. *American Journal of Clinical Hypnosis, 8,* 57–65.

Erickson, M. H., & Rossi, E. L. (1977). Autohypnotic experiences of Milton H. Erickson, M.D. *American Journal of Clinical Hypnosis, 20,* 36–54. Reprinted in E. L. Rossi, (Ed.) (1980), *The Collected Papers of M. H. Erickson. Volume I: The Nature of Hypnosis and Suggestions.* New York: Irvington Press.

Gilligan, S. G. (1982). Effects of emotional intensity on learning. Unpublished doctoral dissertation, Stanford University.

Gilligan, S. G. (1987). *Therapeutic Trances: The Cooperation Principle in Ericksonian Hypnotherapy.* New York: Brunner/Mazel.

Gilligan, S. G. (1988a). Symptom phenomena as trance phenomena. In J. K. Zeig & S. R. Lankton (Eds.), *Developing Ericksonian Therapy: State of the Art.* New York: Brunner/Mazel.

Gilligan, S. G. (1988b). Psychosomatic healing in Ericksonian hypnotherapy. *Hypnose und Kognition, 5,* 25–33.

Gordon, D., & Meyers-Anderson, M. (1981). *Phoenix: Therapeutic Patterns of Milton H. Erickson.* Cupertino, CA: Meta Publications.

Hammond, D. C. (1988). Will the real Milton Erickson please stand up? *International Journal of Clinical and Experimental Hypnosis, 36,* 173–181.

Keeney, B. (1976). On paradigmatic change: Conversations with Gregory Bateson. Unpublished manuscript.

O'Hanlon, W. H., & Weiner-Davis, M. (1988). *In Search of Solutions: A New Direction in Psychotherapy.* New York: Norton.

O'Hanlon, B., & Wilk, J. (1987). *Shifting Contexts: The Generation of Effective Psychotherapy.* New York: Guilford Press.

Pearce, J. C. (1981). *The Bond of Power.* New York: Dutton.

Rossi, E. L., & Cheek, D. B. (1988). *Mind-Body Therapy: Methods of Ideo-dynamic Healing in Hypnosis.* New York: Norton.

Wechsler, J. (1979). *On Aesthetics in Science.* Cambridge, MA: MIT Press.

Zeig, J. K. (Ed.) (1980). *A Teaching Seminar with Milton Erickson.* New York: Brunner/Mazel.

Zeig, J. K. (1988). An Ericksonian phenomenological approach to therapeutic hypnotic induction and symptom utilization. In J. K. Zeig and S. R. Lankton (Eds.), *Developing Ericksonian Therapy: State of the Art.* New York: Brunner/Mazel.

CHAPTER 28

Tight Therapeutic Sequences
Erving Polster

In 1953, when I was first attracted to Gestalt therapy, one of its major claims was that it shortened therapy. It contrasted sharply with the more leisurely paced therapy common in those days by accenting immediacy and action, and it provided specific procedures and perspectives that got down to business pointedly. The consequent sharp focus, considered radical when it was introduced, is now recognizable in many contemporary methodologies, especially in brief therapy.

To illustrate sharp focus, when a patient rambles unhappily, only touching on his sadness, the therapist must attend keenly to that sadness, amplifying it in any number of ways. He might guide the patient to describe the sadness more poignantly. Or he might ask the patient to tell his dead mother what he missed in their relationship. Or he might direct him to localize the feeling of sadness in his body. The procedural inventory from which to select is large and serves two purposes: (1) to *accentuate* what might otherwise remain a veiled reference to sadness and (2) to *connect* the sadness to a range of possible consequences—crying, anger, resolve, remembering, rather than settling for chronic and unsatisfying allusion.

Therapeutic pointedness is a corrective for psychological *slippage*, a mechanical term I am adapting. In mechanics, slippage refers to the loss of motion or power through inadequate connection between gears. When gears mesh properly, the rotation of one gear impels the other; the resulting movement is fluid and powerful. When the gears are poorly engaged, power is lost and movement is sluggish and uncoordinated.

In human metaphor, people also must integrate connections among their experiences. When they are able to mesh each experience with succeeding experiences, this produces a confident directionalism. Therefore, the tightening of the experiential connections between one moment and the next is a primary task in psychotherapy. Loose connections often result in feelings of aimlessness or being stuck, omnipresent in neurosis. Session after session, the patient may wander, alluding almost absentmindedly to his life's complaints, struggles, confusions, and so on. The therapist, when not oriented to the tightening of the relevant experiential connections, may collude by offering explanations without observable consequences, often feeding new material to the wanderer.

TIGHT SEQUENCES

In a recent book (Polster, 1987), I introduced the concept of tight sequencing. Tight sequences are those sets of experience where the perceived consequences of any event happen right away—or very soon. The most simple satisfaction of this requirement for consequentiality is achieved by focusing on the transition point between "now" and "next." Each moment serves as a springboard into its future and will announce that future in sometimes clear, sometimes cryptic signals. The therapist reads each of these signals, edging forward, like a detective, to discern the hints for what is going to be next.

But unlike the detective, who is concerned with recognizing what already has happened, the therapist also must help to create new experience by leading the patient into the naturally next expression or feeling. This requires intricate discernment because each moment calls out for a number of possible moves, *arrows*, in a sense, each pointing to a different nextness. Furthermore, the patient may not want to go forward and will use diverse means, familiar to all therapists, to avoid the trip. He may care more about other matters, as does the paranoid person preoccupied with fixed expectations or the anxious person careful to keep his muscles tight against new experience. We well know that any patient proceeding forward might discover dangerous characteristics such as his viciousness if he were to say more about his mother, or his homosexuality if he were to express tender feelings, or his selfishness if he were to satisfy his own needs.

In the face of such fears, pointed and sensitive evocation is required to move the patient's statements gradually in the direction for which he only gives hints. Here is an example of a session where the sequentiality between one statement and another was dogged by slippage. The process of tightening the sequences may often bank on verbally strong interruptions of the evasive process or on experimental arrangements like the empty chair technique, visualizations, or accentuating sensations. But in this case, each step in the tightening process came through a gentle increase in the spiciness or directness of the language. Each remark, small though its force may have been, tightened the connections between one statement and the next until, at last, the ingredients came together to form a moving story.

The patient, Kevin, started the session by talking in his meandering style:

> "Well, um, let's see. Um, today I found myself, a lot, ah, a lot more enthusiastic about coming in today. Um. Yet, as soon as I sit down here and try to tell you that, um, it's it kinda goes. (Laugh) I don't know why but (laugh), damn, I mean it's always, I always get intimidated. I told you that. (Quiet voice) Anyway, um, one of the things I was thinking about was the way I'm here, um, in a way, (nervous, forced words) another way in um that I'm in here that's like being with my Dad, the way I'm like with my Dad. Um, it is ah kind of saying or presenting myself in a way that's um a more innocent or more adolescent or something along those line to you then. I mean it's like I'm purposely trying to be . . . ."

I knew from previous sessions that this could go on and on, so I interrupted to get at the substantive kernel, obscured within. "How do you play innocent?" I asked. His answer tightened the connection somewhat, but his words were anemic. They only thinly disguised the fact that he pretended to need my advice or leadership more than he really does. I said, "(you're) sort of building me up," to emphasize both his generosity in protecting me and the possibility I might not need it. He replied, "Yeah, yeah, yeah," excited this time about the simple truth. The excitement made him somewhat bolder—enough to say he was thinking last night about something, now forgotten, which he had decided not to tell me because it was *too assertive*. That's some riddle, I thought. When I teased him about dismissing me by saying, "How quickly they forget," he guffawed. By now, his assertiveness had overcome his fear and I could confidently tell him his memories would come. He went on, still hazily, and apparently changing the subject, saying, self-congratulatorily, that on the way over he had thought that he was being a good friend to himself these days, though not yet to others. But he still didn't remember.

I guessed aloud that he didn't want to hurt me with his assertiveness. He demurred, unsatisfied with my guess. Based on his earlier confusion between me and his father and my interest in keeping the connections tight, I asked whether his father could handle his assertiveness. The gears meshed perfectly. He remembered a clear example and he spoke, at last, with a marked reduction in slippage. With greatly increased clarity and drama, he told me:

> "Yeah. Sometimes when I do get assertive, oh yeah, times where I have been assertive, it's felt like I've defeated him. I can remember one time when we were, myself, my Mom, and he were sailing. We went for a week on a sailboat up into the coastal islands. And there was one very windy day where we had the big jib up, do you know about sailboats very much?"
>
> (I said, "not much," and his voice became instantly more animated and he continued to describe the events with great excitement. His authority was not only greatly increased as he lucidly instructed me, but he did it with animation and color.)
>
> "The jib is the forward sail. And you can have different sizes of jibs. And the bigger the jib, the more wind it catches and the faster it makes the boat go. But the bigger the jib you have the more unstable the boat can be. Particularly because it pulls right from the very front of the boat. So we had a huge jib on that day. We got up in the morning when the winds came up and it was really rough. But we were screaming along with this huge jib and I loved it. And the boat was kinda shaky. And my dad wanted to take the jib down. And I really wanted it up, I wanted to cruise. So, we got into a fight about it. And he finally just said, (imitates his Dad's angry voice and smiles, also, having found his own angry voice) 'Okay, take the jib down, do what you wanna do, I don't care, leave the jib up.' So we did for a while. At one point, it got caught in something and I had to crawl up front to undo it, and I cut my finger kinda badly when I did it. And that just made him feel worse. He just said, 'Oh God, now you cut your finger, this is awful.' And I just felt tremendously guilty after that point. Like I really usurped his authority."

Once the momentum got going, the of-course quality of his story caught on, just rolling from one incident to the other. This lubricated him to continue elaborating about his father's fragility and the assumptions he now makes about the fragility of others, including me. He was then able to say what seemed unspeakable: that there were some things he didn't like about me. But I turned out to be neither as fragile as he thought nor as wrathful, which was good for both of us.

The creation of consequentiality—words that matter—is a major force for quickening and heightening therapeutic pace. That which in ordinary conversation may proceed airily, with little notice, in therapy takes on great amplitude and is thus transformed into a vibrant, life-determining, fulcrum-creating moment, with the energy to move wherever the individual's direction requires.

The better the therapist swings into the momentum, the more likely will his remarks bring on the naturally next behavior. Therapy in its greatest moments provides masterful examples of what can be called the "*sequential imperative*"—the sense of the irresistible sweep into nextness. Experience appears to be seamlessly and inevitably interconnected. Perhaps the word inevitable is excessive since we all know that experiences have a variety of possible consequences. It is more accurate to say we are seeking, with variable success, the sense of exquisite rightness, so right we would want nothing better. Yet, inevitable or not, the *sense of inevitability* offers relief from the plaguing questions that immo-bilize the mind. Am I going to alienate people, am I going to get promoted, am I going to get sick, fat, or put in jail? Of course, the sense of inevitability also has some harmful connotations and must be distinguished from driven, monomaniacal, and compulsive behavior, where rigidity governs the person's movement. Rather, it represents the simple, unmediated grace that comes with an organic progression, within which all the parts fit beautifully together.

Inducing confidence in this progression is a therapeutic mandate and it impels the patient from the static moment of the present into the engaging experience of nextness. Just as the Olympic diver's taut body is unerringly directed and knifes gracefully into the water with hardly a splash, the therapist's intention is to guide the patient to follow the natural directions of his words and actions, one after the other, with a minimum of circumlocution, qualification, allusion, illogicality, self-suppression—what I have called *slippage*.

This primitive predisposition to be swept into the stream of continuing nextness is the basis for a number of mind-influencing procedures that have in common the invocation of high fascination, a feeling of heightened emergency, and a sense of the inevitable succession of events. These procedures include the induction of hypnosis, as well as meditation, drugs, and brain washing (see Polster, 1987), each of which reduces the interval between stimulation and reaction, between what has happened and what happens next.

Among these high-focus methods, hypnosis is the system most clearly relevant to brief therapy (Erickson & Rossi, 1979). The sense of inevitability is set up through a series of highly narrowed cause-and-effect sequences—counting, giving easily resonant suggestions, and so forth. These are each small in impact or risk but in series they add up to the feeling "of course;" the individual may ride this "of course-ness" into the most surprising consequences (Erickson & Rossi, 1979). Meditation is comparable because the repetition of the mantra creates a sense of ultimately welcome choicelessness, a release from the individual's thought processes or other background influences that distract from narrowed attention. Once this narrowing occurs, the sequence of awarenesses seems altogether natural and conflicts recede into the background.

The phenomenon of no-choice—to be distinguished from resignation—when accompanied by fascination, reduces the awareness of, or anxiety about, danger. While this feeling of safety is advantageous for movement in therapy, one should be mindful not to induce a greater sense of safety than circumstances merit. Dangers do exist, after all: bosses fire assertive employees, sexual fantasies can create debilitating panic, and recognizing rejection can be severely depressing. It is risky to sweep patients into that for which they are poorly equipped.

Before going on to describe some particulars of tight sequences, I'd like to say a few words about loose sequences. Loose sequences are those moments in therapy which do not have observably compelling consequences, even though they may be very interesting and important. Though not always immediately located on the path of problem-solving sequences, these experiences are valuable because they offer unrestrained opportunity for the patient to find his own way while verbalizing and to explore diverse, sometimes chaotic, wisps of experience. Free association is one technique that offers very loose constraints on purpose or communicative style. Loose sequences also exist when the therapist "listens" but inserts little of his own thought into the stream of therapeutic interchange. In loose sequences, inevitability and concern with direction take a vacation and there is freedom for trial explorations and the tentative meandering that allows new thoughts to catch on. Even surrealistic connections may occur and exercise the mind's potentialities. Many specific therapeutic advantages accrue to these and other loosely sequential procedures, but right now I choose to disregard the roaming power of the mind in order to examine the power of narrow focus and tight sequences.

CONTACT-TRANSFERENCE

As I have proposed, the generic source of slippage is discontinuity between one moment and the next. The content that determines the tightness of sequentiality is influenced along three major psychological dimensions. One is the dimension of contact as contrasted with transference. The second dimension is action as contrasted with awareness. The third dimension is abstraction as contrasted with detail.

First, the dimension of *contact and transference*. At one pole—contact—the patient is talking to the therapist as the individualistic person the therapist actually is. At the other end of the pole—transference—the patient is talking to the therapist as though he were someone from his past—a father or mother in many cases. These polar markers were transparently evident in the case of Kevin, who blurred the differences between me and his father, thereby diminishing the tightness of sequential development.

To the extent that the patient operates at the transferential level, there is slippage in his expressive system. He is not accurately guided by his past, so his words are off the mark. The result is flabby existence, where momentum and directionality are reduced. With greater tightness—an improved connection between past and present—each experience contributes support and energy for the series of coming experiences.

The psychoanalyst and the Gestalt therapist have historically approached this problem from opposite ends of the pole. The analyst has tended to expect transference and has often found it, using it to understand the effect of the past on the present. His purpose was to move people from transferential errors into an improvement in current contacts, thereby freeing themselves from the long arms of their parents.

The Gestalt therapist, on the other hand, often expected that in immediate contact with the therapist the patient would learn directly how to live life as it really is. However, that expectation was thwarted by the inevitable unfinished business still influencing the patient. To take account of this unfinished business and to try to finish it through current action is a Gestalt fundamental. When accomplished, this not only enables the patient to rise beyond the past, but it also tightens the patient's connections by synchronizing the present with the past, increasing the coherence and unity of life. Though their procedures are significantly different, both psychoanalysis and Gestalt therapy hold one goal in common, namely that the individual's feelings and actions be up-to-date so they may be wholeheartedly included in the moment-to-moment stream of experience.

Davanloo (1980), a short-term, analytically minded therapist, has shrunk the distance between transference and contact. Though the transference understanding is an important facet of his work, he also holds his patient to the immediate consequences of treating him mistakenly. For example, in the case of a woman handicapped by her passivity with men, he repeatedly points out her evasion of contact. He asks, "Do you notice that you leave things hanging in the middle of nowhere?" When she says "yes," Davanloo says, " ... if you say there is, and at the same time say there isn't, and continue to be vague and evasive, then we won't be able to understand the problem ... " (p. 107). Furthermore, Davanloo stands tough in this patient's denials of his interpretations by specific arguments that are both simple and convincing. When his patient tells about having been booted into the back seat of a car, he guides her to the angry consequences implied.

Through Davanloo's continued focus on the quality of her communications, the conversational momentum grows and blossoms into crucial stories about her past, as though it were the most natural thing in the world. He says, "Though the tone is always gentle, the language is extremely confronting, giving the patient no chance to escape from the impact of what he is saying" (p. 106). *No chance to escape* is an apt way of describing his pointedness and the ensuing sense of sequential inevitability. While giving high emphasis to the transference phenomenon, Davanloo has, by accenting current experience, corrected a common source of slippage in the psychoanalytic system. The slippage between past and present would theoretically be reduced by understanding the past, but the faith was often misplaced because there were too many escape hatches for the person avoiding good-quality contact.

AWARENESS-ACTION

A second major influence on the tightness of sequence is the *integration of awareness and action.* Awareness and action are the results of the generic sensorimotor system, and when they are united, the person reaches an apex of personal absorption. When people act without awareness, their behavior will often be mechanical, empty, purposeless, and unrewarding. On the other hand, to be aware without acting also has troublesome consequences: dreaminess, for example, or implosiveness when the energy becomes strongly compacted. Whether a person favors action or awareness, if the connections are only loosely established, they must be restored for the person to move forward with the power that united function provides.

Here is an example of a poor connection between awareness and action. A woman, admired and well-loved in her community, was disturbed because people did not approach her; she felt isolated because she had to make all the social moves. She was unaware that her face did not offer easy welcome and so people were careful not to approach her uninvited. As she talked about her sense of isolation, she became more and more distressed. Immersed in sadness, she put her hands to her characteristically contracted face without awareness. To heighten her awareness of her face, I asked her to just feel the relationship between her hands and her face.

This awareness itself might have been a therapeutic step, since a strengthened awareness often arouses action. But to facilitate that connection, I asked her to let her face move against her hands just the way it wanted to. Her face stiffened all the more during this movement. Then, swept into memories by the new connection, she began to talk about her drunken father, who would be "all over" her when she was a child. Now she felt both futility and rage, but when the movement of her hands and her face became more vigorous, the rage won out and her face fought what felt to her like a suffocating invasion by his drunken body. Finally, in revulsion, she released a desperate sound and cried. Soon after this, when she was ready again to face the group she was in, it was with an unfamiliar open look and an unreserved connection with the people. Plainly, the amplified *awareness* of her father's oppression and of her own facial sensation became more tightly connected with the *action* represented by her hand/face movements and the accompanying sounds. It was through this heightened connection that she was impelled forward, beyond dispirited complaint into aggression and release.

ABSTRACTION AND DETAIL

A third major impact on the tightness of sequentiality is the *relationship between abstractions and the details they summarize or introduce*. Sometimes the relationship of abstraction to detail is either self-evident or not worth exploring. For example, a man says I love fruit, eat it three times a day, and that's why I am so healthy. One probably would have no concern with the kind of fruit he is talking about or about the manifestations of his healthiness. The danger in therapy, however, is that both therapist and patient may be geared to communicate on an abstract basis about important matters, often settling for the empty and distorted understandings that many generalizations offer. Abstractions are containers of life experiences, and they offer rich signals for what should be happening next.

For example, one patient, Robert, an architect, complained about procrastination, so common a complaint it would have been easy to take its meaning for granted. That would have been fine with Robert, who wanted to talk about procrastination with a shapeless assumption that we both knew just what he was talking about. But the word begs for elaboration. Instead of doing what he is supposed to be doing, he may daydream about alternative things to do, he may converse with his secretary, he may go to the bar for a drink, he may endlessly go over what he has written, he may forget what he wanted to do, and so on.

When I pressed Robert by asking him how he procrastinates, he first felt misunderstood and then humored me by mechanically telling me what he did. He stared into space, he turned business phone calls into social visits, he reexamined design plans blankly, all of which got him no place. But he was just warming up and soon the thought came that, while he was working, *his father was sitting on his shoulder.* In fleshing out this new and more fertile abstraction, he then cited chapter and verse about how his father debunked everything he did, drove him to accept his values, inveigled him to become an architect, and continued to live his life through Robert's work, kicking and screaming all the way about Robert's failure to do it right. Life with father and the anger that Robert had set aside opened new avenues away from procrastination as he transformed this stale abstraction into a fresh one, father-sitting-on-his-shoulder, a new wrapping for rich detail.

Without detail, the "understanding" provided by abstraction is like substituting a title for a story. It is surprising how often therapist and patient settle for titles. Patients are rejected by parents, they have moved nine times during their school years, they have been sexually molested: All these promising abstractions are often colored with only the most spare detail, enough to point to disturbance but not enough to profit from the rekindling effect of story line. The great writer Flannery O'Connor (1974) has some instructive words about the elaborative process:

> It is a good deal easier for most people to state an abstract idea than to describe and then recreate some object they actually see. But the world of the fiction writer is full of matter, and this is what the beginning fiction writers are very loathe to create. They are concerned primarily with unfleshed ideas and emotions. They are apt to be reformers and to want to write

because they are possessed not by a story but by the bare bones of some abstract notion. They are conscious of problems, not of people, of questions and issues, not of the texture of existence, of case histories and of everything that has a sociological smack, instead of the details of life that make actual the mystery of our position on earth. (p. 48)

In the four cases referred to in this chapter, the core realizations came when these patients began to tell the stories their abstractions called out. One was concerned with being innocent and adolescent; one was depressed that people did not invite her places; one suffered passivity with men; and one was bothered by procrastination. As long as they neglected the sequential nature of the events underlying their abstractions, they were missing an important link in the chain of experience, bypassing a source of personal fulfillment. Abstractions are the mind's housing for the stories that furnish it; one may be said to be living in an empty house in the absence of these stories. But the stories are abundantly available. When nextness counts, stories multiply and the suspense of the narrative keeps the mind alert to every new prospect. As the investment in each element of the sequence grows, the patient will almost invariably produce a story of some therapeutically pertinent part of his life. These stories spotlight his life and help him to recognize that he is the central player in its drama. With each realization of this centrality, he becomes more hospitable to the union of disparate events, restoring connections within a previously disjointed existence.

This was implied by the whole of Freud's works long ago. He evoked extraordinarily interesting stories from his patients, and most therapists have subsequently done the same. The value of telling these stories has been variously attributed, among other purposes, to abreaction, to clarifying the reasons for current behavior, and to the restoration of the mind's free associative power. These are all valuable aspects of recounting events and feelings. But the story also helps to confirm the individual's existence, the realization of which has fragile roots in the most ephemeral experiences. People pass through life with flimsy purpose, stereotyped meanings, empty rewards, and unregistered presence. The story serves to give content and organization to that part of a person's life it addresses and restores the energizing effect which events should have on each other.

In conclusion, pointedness, tight sequentiality, and the resulting story line are powerful factors in all therapy. For brief therapy, there is hardly anything more. Though therapists intend to bring the events and feelings of a lifetime together by creating a sense of inevitable consequence, this succession of experiences may be hopelessly derailed within the infinitely intricate lives people live. In the face of these complexities, the artistry of the therapist rests on creating simplicity. While neither unaware nor disrespectful of complexity, he whittles it down in size to the point where the human mind can cope with it. In brief therapy, the therapist is especially directed to this simplification, where he knowingly sets aside some explorations for which the complexities of life might otherwise cry out.

REFERENCES

Davanloo, H (1980). Trial therapy. In H. Davanloo (Ed.), *Short Term Therapy*. Northvale, NJ: Jason Aronson.

Erickson, M. H., and Rossi, E. L. (1979). *Hypnotherapy: An Exploratory Casebook*. New York: Irvington.

O'Connor, F. (1974). The nature and aim of fiction. In J. Hersey (Ed.), *The Writer's Craft*. New York: Alfred A. Knopf.

Polster, E. (1987). *Every Person's Life Is Worth a Novel*. New York: Norton.

CHAPTER 29

Reference Experiences: Guardians of Coherence and Instigators of Change
David Gordon

In tackling the problem of change and personal evolution, the focus of attention is usually on looking for those aspects of personality and cognitive reality that afford a foothold for change, and for those techniques which seem to reliably take advantage of those footholds. Anyone who has worked as an agent of change, either for others or for himself, knows what a frustrating search this can be. The fact is that people are remarkably resilient and tenacious when it comes to maintaining their beliefs and behaviors. For every beneficiary of a one-session miracle cure, there are hundreds of other people who spend hundreds of hours "working" on themselves, trying to change.

Despite the near-continuous influx of information from the world about what to think and how to be, despite the urgings and support of friends and relatives, and often despite our own best judgment and earnest efforts, we stay who we are, as we are, from day to day. When we wake up in the morning we have not forgotten who we are or what we believe and think about the nature of the world and how to get along in it. Why not? What holds us together through time and, generally, in the face of a myriad of contrary input and desires? The purpose of this chapter is to offer a model of experience that answers that question and, in answering it, to provide an avenue for understanding and generating effective change interventions.

MAPS

Clear? Huh! Why a four-year-old child can understand this report. Run out and find me a four-year-old child. I can't make head or tail out of it. (Groucho Marx, in *Duck Soup*)

Many theories and models have been advanced to describe the architecture of the human psyche. Each of these carves out and labels certain aspects of subjective experience and then describes how those aspects interact with one another to create our experiences, personalities, and behaviors. In so doing, these models and theories provide us with ways of understanding, interacting with, and having an impact on ourselves.

Each of these theories or models acts as a map of the terrain of human subjective experience. An atlas offers a variety of maps, each one describing a different aspect of the same terrain. North America is depicted by one map in terms of its annual rainfall; by another in terms of elevation; another shows mean temperature; a fourth population density; a fifth state boundaries and major highways; and so on. No one of these maps is inherently more worthwhile than the others. Each of them is useful or not in relation to what you want to know about North America. If you want to get from Santa Fe to Portland, the rainfall map is fairly useless and the highway map just what you need. On the other hand, if you want to select a dry place to live, the rainfall map is the one you should turn to.

Similarly, the Freudian map of id, ego, and superego makes it possible to find those aspects of experience in ourselves and others. If you use the transactional analysis map you will find parents, children, and adults at work in each of us. As a behaviorist you will notice operant behaviors and the intermittent rewards that reinforce them. And the computer-based models will have you logging input and output of information and seeing flow charts. All of these models and theories are useful in certain contexts and to varying degrees. None of them is immanent in any one of us. They are descriptions that serve to organize our perceptions and thinking along certain lines.

It is a small but significant leap to realize that everything that has just been said about the chimerical nature of models can be applied to our personal psychologies as well. Each of us has our own map of the world that we use to make sense out of that world. The "making of sense" is, literally, our experience, extending from peripheral sensation, through perception, emotional responses, to the sensibility of judgments and abstract thoughts.

What makes our experience *subjective* is the fact that the form and content of our experience is largely determined by the features of our personal maps. That is, an individual's experience is not inherently determined by the fact of being in a particular context, but is a manifestation of what and how he is perceiving in that context.[1] Our individual maps, then, determine to a great extent what our experiences will be. Of what are our maps comprised?

RELIEFS

> Black: He said, "George, we're not going to get to go to school. We're going to have to work for our living." He said, "Let's learn the trade that'll make the most money out of work. That's what we're going to have to do . . . if we stand up, haul ourselves up and make men out of ourselves, if we don't know A from B," he says, "we can make somebody call us 'Mr. Black' someday." So that's what we done. Yeah.

> And now, at ninety-two, Mr. Black cannot take a walk in his hometown without seeing the work of his hands, the bricks he has made, one by one, for more than eighty years.
>
> (Kuralt, 1985, p. 53)

Surely there are aspects of being a human being that are "hard wired." But just what is genetic is still unknown. Though concordance studies often show remarkable similarities between twins raised apart, even those dozen or so similarities do not add up to an entire person, with all of his day-to-day decisions, political views, social views, sensibilities, and so forth.

We can and do look for the texture of human experience in the genetic code, in the spurting of neurotransmitters across synaptic clefts, in the numbers of neural spurs sprouting from dendrites, and in the convolutions of the cortex. But in terms of understanding personality, this counting and poking may amount to little more than modern phrenology. Perhaps now we are counting and measuring the bumps *inside* people's heads as explanations for their characters and personalities.

Clearly, our personalities are not stored at the level of a synapse or lobe in the brain. Although it is likely that genetic factors set certain trajectories for each of us, the particular details and qualities of that trajectory are realized through our interactions with the world, beginning perhaps before birth, proceeding with a voracious rush through childhood's first five or six years, and then continuing on to varying degrees throughout the rest of one's life. What is it, then, that we acquire through these interactions that gives form and direction to our worlds?

It is common parlance to say that we acquire knowledge, experience, understanding, perspective, rules, values, and so on. One man's knowledge, however, is another man's misconception. Knowledge or understanding (indeed, reality), even at the seemingly unequivocal levels of the purer sciences, is nevertheless subject to interpretation. Kuhn (1970, p. 50) cites several examples of this, including that of physicists and chemists disagreeing about what a molecule is.

What we in fact acquire are beliefs about the world and the nature of our experience, ranging from what constitutes a molecule, to how a society should be run, to who we are. These beliefs may not be explicit or in our consciousness, but they are there, defining our worlds. A belief, then, is *any construct that one accepts as being descriptive of the world.* Beliefs take two forms: Criteria and Cause-effect.

Criteria

The world is infinitely rich in terms of the sensory experiences and complexity it has to offer. However, as we look around our world, we do not experience it as a kaleidoscopic cascade of images, sounds, and sensations. It seems quite organized, recognizable, and stable. We know what things are. We are not born knowing most of what we know, however. From birth we learn to see, hear, and feel that which is *marked out* and labeled for us by others. In this way we come to recognize something that looks and feels like the thing you are holding as a "book." Or that to work relentlessly toward a goal is being "determined." Or that people who believe as you do are "allies."

Our distinctions define for each of us what constitutes certain experiences, and these may vary from person to person. For example, the friend who never asks you questions about your feelings and offers little information about his own is considered by you to be "cold." Someone else, however, may consider that same person's behavior to be "respectful."

The difference distinctions make in determining the texture and focus of subjective experience becomes most obvious when looking at other cultures. For instance, the Navaho make a distinction regarding

those individuals who live aesthetically, both in their experience of life
and in how they manifest themselves in the world. Their word for this is
hozh'q (HOE-shk). The Chinese place a high value on *shih* (SHE),
which is the ability to use and present knowledge in an aesthetic way
(Rheingold, 1988). And among the Maori, "parenting" is something that
happens over *generations* (Hall, 1983). Every time some aspect of
experience (sensual, somatic, perceptual, cognitive, spiritual, etc.) is
marked out, a new distinction is added to our maps of the world. In this
way our individual maps change and become enriched, drawing our attention to "new" aspects of experience.[2]

But not all distinctions we make are of equal importance to us.
Although almost everyone knows what it means to be respectful, being
respectful is not important to everyone. Those who do highly value
being respectful notice when they or others are respectful or not and do
things to be respectful and elict respect from others. For these individuals, then, "respectfulness" is a *criterion* they apply to themselves
and others. A criterion is *any distinction that you hold as a standard in a
particular context.*

For example, you may be applying the criterion of "understanding" as
you read this chapter. As long as that is your criterion, you will evaluate
whether or not you understand and will do what you can to understand.
If instead your criterion is "usefulness," then as you read you will be
looking for how you can use the information in the chapter. (Of course,
you could be applying both of those, as well as other, criteria simultaneously.) The significance of criteria is that they establish for us what
is relevant or important in a particular situation. Examples of beliefs
based on criteria include: "It is important to be *friendly*," "People should
be *independent*," and "I *give* all I can give."

Cause–Effect

We observe, or have impressed upon us, that actions lead to consequences. We find relationships between actions (*causes*) and consequences
(*effects*) not only in the physical world (such as the effect of letting go of
a glass when it is not resting on anything), but in our perceptual, emotional, and cognitive worlds as well.

For instance, if you have a sufficiently compelling experience of a
person doing something nice for you because you did something nice
for him, you might extract from those two contiguous events the cause–
effect relationship: "If I treat people well, they'll treat me well." Once
installed as part of your map, this cause–effect will serve as a guide to
your subsequent behavior. That is, you will treat people well *in order to*

be treated well, and you will *expect* to be treated well in return for your being considerate of other people. Furthermore, you will probably hold yourself accountable to respond in kind to those who treat you well. The subjective and behavioral significance of a cause–effect becomes manifest when you consider adopting its opposite. Suppose that, instead of the cause–effect posed above, you believed, "If I treat people well, they'll walk all over me." Presented with the same situation, obviously your response would be very different because of this different cause–effect belief.

Cause–effect relationships can be drawn between any aspects of our internal or external worlds. Examples include: "My feeling bad makes other people notice me," "If you get encouragement you will do better," and "I need to be well regarded in order to feel loved." Each of these cause–effects expresses a belief about how elements of the world relate to one another in terms of consequences. Accordingly, as features of our personal maps of the world, cause–effect beliefs inform and guide our attention, understanding, and responses.

To recap, much of our ongoing experience and behavior is a manifestation of the beliefs through which we are assessing our sensations and perceptions. Our beliefs either establish what is significant by specifying criteria or inform us about consequences by specifying cause–effect relationships. Our criteria attune us to certain aspects of our perceptual world, bringing them to the foreground of our experience, and our cause–effects guide our behaviors along certain lines.[3]

FILTERS

> Man designs for himself a garden with a hundred kinds of trees, a thousand kinds of flowers, a hundred kinds of fruits and vegetables. Suppose, then, that the gardener of this garden knew no other distinction than between edible and inedible, nine-tenths of this garden would be useless to him. He would pull up the most enchanting flowers and hew down the noblest trees and even regard them with a loathing and envious eye.
>
> (Hesse, 1963, p. 75)

Our beliefs about what is significant and what is causal in the world act as filters for our experience. It is no secret that two people faced with the same situation will view it differently and interact with it in different ways. For instance, a couple attends an office party. Both of them start swaying to the rhythms when the music starts, but soon he is jumping up and heading for the dance floor . . . alone. She does not join him, preferring to sit it out, as usual. We can easily lock these two people into their respective boxes by observing that he is a "dancing kind of person" and she is not "that kind of person." Unless we want to believe that there is a gene for "dancing person," this woman's reluctance is not an expression of her intractable genetic heritage, but an orientation she has acquired.

When we ask this woman, "Why do you not dance?" she responds, "You look foolish jumping around out there when you don't know what you're doing." Her response reveals two beliefs she is holding in relation to dancing. One is that it is important to not look foolish (criterion). The second is that if you know what you are doing, then you won't look foolish (cause–effect). *Anyone* who operated out of this criterion and cause–effect (and who did not already know how to dance) would be loath to get out on the dance floor.

When we ask her partner, "Why do you dance?" he responds, "I love to feel my body moving. I always feel kind of cleansed afterward." He is operating out of a set of beliefs that are different than his partner's and that are supportive of dancing. For him, feeling his body move is important (criterion), and dancing makes him feel "cleansed" (cause–effect). *Anyone* using this criterion and cause–effect would feel strongly compelled to get out on the dance floor.

The fact that the man dances while his mate watches is not a function of the music, what they are wearing, or their genetic makeup. Instead, it is the filtering effect of the criteria and cause–effects through which they are perceiving the possibility of dancing that compels them either toward or away from the dance floor. It is as though the opportunity to dance is a white light and he is looking at it through a pair of green-tinted glasses, while the glasses she is wearing are tinted red. The difference in what they see is neither a function of the light (which offers all visible frequencies) nor a function of their visual systems (which are capable of responding to all visible frequencies). The difference in their experience is a function of the filtering properties of the lenses through which they are looking. In the same way, their personal criteria and cause–effects act as filters for their experience of dancing. She "sees" only the possibilities for looking foolish, while he "sees" only the possibilities for feeling cleansed.

COHERENCY

In the natural history of the living human being, ontology and epistemology cannot be separated. His [commonly unconscious] beliefs about what sort of world it is will determine how he sees it and acts within it, and his ways of perceiving and acting will determine his beliefs about its nature. The living man is thus bound within a net of epistemological and ontological premises which—regardless of ultimate truth or falsity—become partially self-validating for him.

(Bateson, 1972, p. 314)

The nature of filters is that they let through only certain information, rejecting anything that is not selected for by the characteristics of the filter. For instance, a red filter allows only wavelengths from the red end of the visible spectrum to pass through. All other wavelengths bounce off or are absorbed into the surface of the filter itself. Similarly, a belief can summarily orient one's attention and thinking according to the dictates of that belief. Anything that is outside the scope of the belief is simply not perceived. For instance, the woman in our office party example may notice only that people are watching the dancers and be oblivious to the fun the dancers are having, or even to the rhythmic movements of her own body.

Unlike an optical filter, however, human beings are not passive pieces of glass. We seek out information and *are* aware of things that are outside of, and even incompatible with, our personal array of beliefs.

Orientations that are incompatible with or challenging to our own can threaten the stability of our personal world. For the most part, our ongoing subjective experience is that the world is as we see, hear, and feel it. It is stable in its structure and functions. That is, we find everywhere confirmation of our criteria and cause–effects. As we have already pointed out, this confirmation is a direct result of holding the filtering spectacles of these criteria and cause–effects up to the world. For the most part, your world seems to you to be *coherent*.

Coherency of our subjective worlds is imperative. If we lived only by the report of our sensory systems, it would not be an issue. Nature imposes its own rules, laying down the law at the sensory level, and a being living at that level does well to respond to those rules, no matter how much they may shift. But human beings live in a far more complex world, one that is forged out of concepts and abstractions and annealed in the nuances of internal representation and emotion. If we adjusted our personal maps to accommodate every new idea or concept that emerged from the kaleidoscopic human environment, we would be living in a maelstrom of shifting criteria and cause–effects. Indeed, we would not even be able to maintain a sense of self.

The coherency of our subjective worlds must, then, be maintained if there is to be any continuity of self, personal experience, and the behavioral manifestations of self and experience. It is the filtering effect of our beliefs, formulated as criteria and cause–effects, that provides that continuity. Where, then, do our beliefs come from?

REFERENCE EXPERIENCES

Although genetics may determine, or at least guide, certain forms and hues of our personal maps of the world, most of the myriads of criteria and cause–effects that give our maps their detail and texture are acquired. We are not born believing in the importance of telling the truth or of hard work or knowing the consequences of touching a hot stove or of treating people respectfully. These are distinctions that we *learn* to hold dear. But what determines whether one learns to hold hard work dear, or to instead believe that it is important to take it easy in life?

It is almost never enough to merely assert a belief to get another person to believe as you do. Over the years, several zeppelins-worth of air has been expended on each of us by our parents, friends, and the media in attempts to impress us with the importance of certain criteria and the validity of certain cause–effects. Once in a while these assertions have some impact on our thinking and experience. But by and large their pleadings and advice do not alter our maps of the world.

What *does* instill a belief is an experience (or series of experiences) that makes the importance of that criterion, or the consequences of that cause–effect, *real* to us. Years ago, while conducting a workshop, I inadvertently called a participant by the wrong name. She immediately became indignant and insisted that she be addressed correctly, adding that she demands that people recognize her for who she is. She was then asked to use the feelings she was having at that moment to take her back to the first time she felt that emotion. A moment later she burst into tears and related the following story: She was one of identical twins. When she was seven years old, her grandmother came to play with her and her sister. Her grandmother confused her with her sister, a circumstance that shocked the little girl. For the first time she realized that her grandmother could not tell the two girls apart. She "realized" that she had no identity distinct from her sister except for her name. These circumstances and events combined to give this woman a very compelling experience, which instilled in her a belief in the importance of being recognized for who she is (criterion).

Any experience that results in a person acquiring or altering a criterion or cause–effect is a *reference experience*. What constitutes a reference experience for one person may be wholly unaffecting for another. You have probably been called by the wrong name at one time or another. But, though you may not have liked being misnamed, it probably was not an experience that compelled you to alter your beliefs about your identity, as it did for the woman described above.

In the above example the experience that the woman had was of sufficient *magnitude* that it installed in her a new belief. Beliefs may also be installed by *repetition*. For instance, a couple repeatedly pointed out to their child what was "new." Everywhere they went, in everything they did, they would draw his attention to what was new by remarking, "Look at that. You haven't seen that before," or, "Now, that's different," and so on. By the time their son was five they found themselves hitting the city's garage sales each weekend looking for toys because their son would play with anything only once or twice before he found it boring and wanted something new and different.

Of course, we all have examples of acquiring new beliefs without the apparent intercession of the external world. All of us have had a concept put to us in a certain way, or have reconceptualized something for ourselves, that has led to a change in our beliefs. Words can be compelling, but only if they generate subjective experiences in the listener. As I have described elsewhere (Gordon, 1988), words can create subjective experiences that have very much the same impact as "actual" experiences. When they do, they too can become the source of reference experiences.

A reference experience, then, is *any experience that is of sufficient magnitude, or has been repeated a sufficient number of times, to compel a change in one's beliefs.*[4]

EVALUATIONS

> It's lovely to live on a raft. We had the sky up there, all speckled with stars, and we used to lay on our backs and look up at them, and discusss about whether they was made or only just happened. Jim he allowed they was made, but I allowed they happened; I judged it would have took too long to *make* so many. Jim said the moon could 'a *laid* them; well, that looked kind of reasonable, so I didn't say nothing against it, because I've seen a frog lay most as many, so of course it could be done. We used to watch the stars that fell, too, and see them streak down. Jim allowed they'd got spoiled and was hove out of the nest.
>
> (Twain, 1959, p. 121)

As we move through our days we have many experienes. Most of them are familiar in form and differ only in slight details. Once in a while, however, we have an exprience that is unfamiliar, one for which our existing criteria and cause–effects are insufficient, or an experience that somehow threatens the stability of our map of the world. If (as described in the previous section) we are able to delete that experience, we are free to move on, our coherency intact.

But sometimes these challenges are not deleted. When we become aware of something that is disconfirming, or possibly even in opposition, to what we believe, we engage in *evaluations* intended to resolve that discrepancy. These evaluations take various forms, such as justification, rationalization, judgment, objective consideration, and so on. The goal in every case, however, is to bring coherency to our personal view of the world. To make these evaluations we draw upon our reference experiences, searching for those that either provide good cause to reject the disconfirming experience as not being true or real or provide ways to distort it so that it is no longer perceived as being disconfirming (in fact, it may even be transformed into a confirmation of one's extant beliefs).[5]

For instance, the woman at the dance can, through her evaluations, conclude that, "He says dancing feels good, but he says that about everything so why should I believe him about this?" She has rejected the reality of the experience and, so, eliminates it as something relevant to the coherency of her subjective reality. She could, instead, conclude that, "I don't really want to dance. I'm just responding to the peer pressure and requests of my partner." In this instance she is distorting the nature of her desire to try out the dance floor. In both cases she draws upon her reference experiences for the "reality" upon which to base her evaluations. The result is that the tug of war between her desire to try dancing and her fear of looking foolish is resolved.

Of course, few of the evaluations that human beings engage in are as uncluttered as the example of the woman just presented. It is probably more useful to think of our individual maps of the world as consisting of *layers* of criteria and cause–effects. The most peripheral layers include beliefs about the minutiae and humdrum aspects of simply moving through the world: "That is a lamp"; "it is important to take out the trash"; "if you turn the key it unlocks the door"; and so on. Behind this layer are other layers encompassing beliefs about social spheres, vocations, avocations, relationships, and so on. Probably at the heart of these layers are the criteria and cause–effects that relate to one's self-concept: "I am intelligent, sensitive, if I treat people well they will like me," and so on. Evaluations occur at each of these levels, and maintaining coherency may require simultaneous evaluations at many different levels of one's map (see Figure 1).

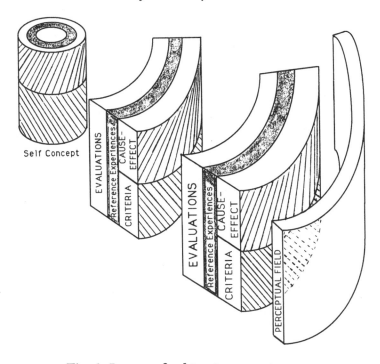

Fig. 1. Layers of subjective experience.

No matter how deep a particular challenge to one's model of the world may penetrate, the prime directive remains the same: Coherency must be maintained. This can be done either by deletion or distortion, or finally, if neither of those proves effective, by change.

CHANGE

What is *always* important is to be sure that the new is not *worse* than the old . . . . Other things being equal (which is not often the case), the old, which has been somewhat tested, is more likely to be viable than the new, which has not been tested at all. (Bateson, 1979, p. 197)

Human beings are generally stable. Stability is an advantage, perhaps an imperative, imposed by nature. Without stability, nothing, including a human being, can maintain its existence. For human beings this goes beyond the question of existence and penetrates to the heart of one's identity. The stability we are talking about here is not that of a rock or a post, which is stable because it is inflexible. Our stability as human beings comes from our ability to respond dynamically to the psychological droughts, gusts, and floods of daily life (see Bateson, 1979).

It is important to keep in mind that the client is asking a great deal of himself when he seeks to change, as are we as agents of that change. That person has had experiences that were so compelling they became reference experiences, thereby altering his map of the world, not just for the moment, but through time. Those experiences, and the criteria and cause–effects they spawned, *are* his world now. Nevertheless, he sits before you, and inside himself, saying, "Alright, help me rend the fabric of my reality and restore it in a better form." This is a lot to ask. How does he know it will be a better reality without having had the experience? Furthermore, as we have described, he is, as a matter of self-preservation (stability), psychologically organized to filter out or distort that which does not fit with his map of the world. Through the utter magic of language and internal representation he nevertheless has ideas about how his experience could be different, but at this point it is still a representation—not sensible, not real. That is, he has no reference experiences for it.[6] This combination of representations outside of one's experiential map and the imperative of maintaining the coherency of that map make change an inherently paradoxical undertaking.

Since it is reference experiences that *naturally* change people, then that is what we need to focus on in terms of therapeutic intervention. Clearly, this was the focus of Milton Erickson's interventions in virtually every case. He often created real-life reference experiences, as when he started a reclusive woman sending African violets to members of the community (Gordon & Meyers-Anderson, 1981, p. 124); intentionally stepped on the toes of a young lady who was embarrassed about the size of her feet and then scolded her furiously for not having feet big enough for a man to see; and had a mother sit on her out-of-control eight-year-old son so he could acquire a reassuring sense of his *being* an eight-year-old (Haley, 1973, pp. 198, 213). Similarly, in his formal hypnotic work, Erickson usually eschewed merely making corrective suggestions in favor of using the trance state as an opportunity to provide his client with hallucinated reference experiences. For instance, he hypnotized a suicidal woman and took her on a walk through an arboretum, the zoo, and to the seashore, all of which were used as opportunities for her to experience the variety, renewal, and mysteriousness of life (Gordon & Meyers-Anderson, 1981, p. 102).[7]

In contrast, too often therapists identify what their clients need to think, believe, or understand and then try *directly* to install that new way of thinking. This ignores a crucial step in the natural process of change, that of embracing a compelling reference experience. The question that needs to be considered is: What *experience* would *naturally* lead this person to think, believe, understand, or behave in the way that s/he needs and wants to?

Compelling Reference Experiences

What elevates some experiences to the level of a compelling reference, while others (most) have no impact in terms of change? Every account of psychological, emotional, and behavioral change with which I am familiar has been either the intentional or unintentional result of the client gaining a reference experience. In comparing these reported and personally witnessed examples with those which failed to foster change, three patterns emerge:

UNDERMINING. Recall that the filtering nature of beliefs and the imperative of coherency create a situation in which disconfirming experiences are either deleted or distorted. It will be far easier for a new idea or experience to "get inside" the system in an undistorted form, then, if the existing, limiting belief is first discredited, or even shown to be "false." This process is called *undermining*. Undermining involves helping the client generate experiences that call into question the reality of what s/he currently believes. For instance, using the woman from our dancing example, if we help her identify experiences in which she did not know what she was doing, and yet did not look foolish, we will be undermining the cause–effect she holds between those two. This creates at least a suspension of the current belief, and often undermines it completely, leaving a void in one's map of the world that can then be filled by the learnings available in the new experience.[8]

RESOLUTION. Our needs, expectations, and goals engage our behavior, keeping us striving. And, it is very satisfying when these needs, expectations, or goals are attained. (Also, it is a great relief when something we dread is avoided.) Naturally, we respond to experiences that lead to such attainments as being especially significant. When an experience makes it possible to resolve a problem (by either attaining or avoiding something), that experience becomes a reference from which we extract lessons about what criteria and cause–effects to operate out of in the future.

FULFILLMENT. We can talk about the "layers" of one's personality, psychology, beliefs, and so on, but of course no such layers actually exist. There is nothing that goes on at a superficial level that is not simultaneously impacting and impacted by the other, deeper levels. We may be organized hierarchically, but all levels interconnect to form a dynamic, coherent whole. Therefore, having some need, expectation, or goal resolved may have personal significance beyond the level at which that resolution occurs. When a person responds to a change s/he has made with comments such as "I feel good about what I'm doing now ... more independent and strong," s/he is expressing that the change has not only resolved the problem, but in some way fulfills aspects of his or her self-concept. Experiences that engage and appeal to the fulfillment of self-concept are inherently significant and, so, compelling.

It is not necessary that all three of these patterns be operating for an experience to become a compelling reference. But at least one will be operating if an experience becomes a reference, and those experiences that involve all three will be extremely affecting.

The concept of reference experiences shifts the attention of the therapist from the dogma of psychological theory, the tyranny of step-by-step techniques, and canned interventions to where it belongs—on the client's subjective experience. The goal should not be to get the client to follow the dictates of a technique, be reasonable, or be agreeable. Whether it is gained through actual interactions in the world, or vicariously through the evocative words of a friend or therapist, it is the *subjective* reality of an experience that makes sense to people and that compels them to change.

SUMMARY

The purpose of this chapter was to provide a conceptual framework for understanding the psychodynamic processes underlying the stability of an individual's personality and behavior. Each of us operates out of a personal "map of the world," the features of which determine our subjective experience. Of paramount importance in defining that map are our beliefs, in the form of criteria and cause–effects. The filtering effects of our beliefs, combined with the imperative to maintain subjective coherency and an evaluative process based on reference experiences, ensures that incompatible experiences are either deleted or distorted to fit the map. If an experience is compelling enough, however, it establishes a new set of beliefs which take their place in the individual's map of the world. It is hoped that this conceptual framework not only will lead to understanding, but will form the basis for practical, effective, and respectful intervention approaches.

NOTES

1. For more on the "map-territory" distinction, see Korzybski (1951).

2. Every distinction is defined by its *criterial equivalence*. A criterial equivalence is that which must be seen, heard, felt, smelled, and/or tasted to recognize a particular distinction. For an in-depth explanation of criterial equivalences, see Cameron-Bandler, Gordon, and Lebeau (1985a,b).

3. For more information on the detection, impact, and use of criteria and cause–effects, see Bandler and Grinder (1975), Cameron-Bandler, Gordon, and Lebeau (1985 a,b), and Gordon (1988). See also Kuralt (1985) for dozens of examples.

4. See Chapter 5 in Cameron-Bandler, Gordon, and Lebeau (1985b) for a typology of reference experiences.

5. Classic examples of people adjusting their evaluations in order to maintain personal coherency can be found in Festinger, Riecken, and Schachter (1956).

6. One of the peculiarities of language is that it can provide us with representations of experience *without actually having had that experience*. The chairbound woman of our example can "know" that it is fun to dance, and the dancing man can "know" that he may look foolish. Being able to convey the representation of experiences through language, rather than through direct experience, creates the possibility of being aware of experiences that are inconsistent with our own subjective worlds.

7. Although examples of using and creating reference experiences will be found in any account of successful psychotherapy, an abundance of excellent examples will be found in Gordon and Meyers-Anderson (1981) and Haley (1973).

8. In reading personal accounts of life-changing experiences, an almost universal feature is that the person "hits rock bottom"; that is, the world as s/he knows it simply does not work, is no longer coherent. See Gordon and Meyers-Anderson (1981), Haley (1973), and Zeig (1980) for examples of Milton Erickson's deft ability to undermine existing beliefs. Also, see Polya (1954) and Hassan (1988) for formal presentations of the dynamics that underly the acceptance of new beliefs, and Clavell (1981) for a chilling example of these dynamics operating in a natural context.

406   BRIEF THERAPY

REFERENCES

Bandler, R., & Grinder, J. (1975). *The Structure of Magic, Vol. I.* Palo Alto, CA: Science and Behavior Books.

Bateson, G. (1972). *Steps to an Ecology of the Mind.* New York: Ballantine Books.

Bateson, G. (1979). *Mind and Nature.* New York: Bantam Books.

Cameron-Bandler, L., Gordon, D., & Lebeau, M. (1985a). *Know How: Guided Programs for Inventing Your Own Best Future.* San Rafael, CA: Future-Pace.

Cameron-Bandler, L., Gordon, D., & Lebeau, M. (1985b). *The Emprint Method: A Guide to Reproducing Competence.* San Rafael, CA: FuturePace.

Clavell, James (1981). *The Children's Story.* New York: Dell.

Festinger, L., Riecken, H.W., & Schachter, S. (1956). *When Prophecy Fails.* New York: Harper & Row.

Gordon, David (1988). The role of language in therapy. In: J. Zeig & S. Lankton (Eds.), *Developing Ericksonian Therapy: State of the Art.* New York: Brunner/Mazel.

Gordon, David, & Meyers-Anderson, Maribeth (1981). *Phoenix: Therapeutic Patterns of Milton H. Erickson.* Cupertino, CA: Meta Publications.

Haley, Jay (1973). *Uncommon Therapy.* New York: Norton.

Hall, Edward T. (1983). *The Dance of Life.* Garden City, NY: Anchor Press/ Doubleday.

Hassan, Steven (1988). *Combatting Cult Mind Control.* Rochester, VT: Park Street Press.

Hesse, Hermann (1963). *Steppenwolf.* New York: Holt, Rinehart & Winston.

Korzybski, Alfred (1951). The role of language in perceptual processes. In: R. Blake & G. Ramsey (Eds.), *Perception: An Approach to Personality.* New York: Ronald Press.

Kuhn, Thomas (1970). *The Structure of Scientific Revolutions.* Chicago: University of Chicago Press.

Kuralt, Charles (1985). *On the Road with Charles Kuralt.* New York: Fawcett.

Poyla, G. (1954). *Patterns of Plausible Inference, Vol. II.* Princeton, NJ: Princeton University Press.

Rheingold, Howard (1988). *They Have a Word for It.* Los Angeles: Jeremy P. Tarcher.

Twain, Mark (1959). *The Adventures of Huckleberry Finn.* New York: Signet Classics.

Zeig, Jeffrey (1980). *A Teaching Seminar with Milton H. Erickson.* New York: Brunner/Mazel.

CHAPTER 30

The Great Simplifying Conventions of Brief Individual Psychotherapy
James Paul Gustafson

MEETING THE CHALLENGE OF THE CASE

I fear the word "great" in the title of this chapter will lead some readers to think I am making claims for myself. Actually, I mean that we all can share in the tradition of psychotherapy which comes before us, which is rich in its breadth and depth of possibilities, like English literature for the common reader, like the history of architectural forms for the builder.

I believe that our field of psychotherapy is most like the field of architecture. Only we are *architects of movement*, rather than of buildings. We are hired to help get the patient out of one place and into another, often when he has but a dim notion of this new place. We have to be expert at finding him where he now lives, at seeing what is confining him there, and designing a lasting way out (Gustafson, 1987a,b). If there is art in finding the patient, and in imagining him somewhere better, there is crafty engineering in improving over the past designs of the patient. We need to know a great deal about what is not likely to work

I thank Nancy Barklage, Lowell Cooper, Ruvi Dar, Pat Jens, Dee Jones, Kathleen Levenick, Helen Vendler, and Mike Wood for their help with this chapter.

408   BRIEF THERAPY

and what is highly probable, between what Sullivan (1954, 1956) called "routinely futile operations" and reliable procedure (Gustafson, 1986; Havens, 1986).

Both psychotherapy and architecture are enormous fields. Both tend to divide into schools, each school with its own conventions of practice (Bordieu, 1977; Foucault, 1982). This following of convention is helpful technically: A discipline can be devised for getting certain clinical results, for training, and for orderly research.

A disadvantage of conventions, however, is that followers of a given school of practice are likely to be badly educated about other conventions for practice that are equally useful. If an individual is skillful at using interaction, he or she may know little about using feeling and thought. The practice may be psychotherapy of the hand, without psychotherapy of the heart and mind (Havens, 1986).

If we compare psychotherapy to another architectural field, namely, the game of chess, we see even further how we have confined ourselves. In chess, there are many kinds of opening moves and many kinds of defenses against these opening moves. But there have developed lines of play for the first 10 or 20 moves which are well known for their opportunities and weaknesses. These are called "conventions," such as the Giuco Piano, the Ruy Lopez, the Sicilian Defense, and the French Defense (Keene & Levy, 1974; Reider, 1959). Indeed, entire books have been written about single conventions in chess, just as entire books (or manuals) have been written about single "lines of play" in psychotherapy.

No serious player of chess would enter a match merely prepared for a single line of play, solely with knowledge of a single convention. He would soon be lost. Yet we do this with patients in our field, as if being well educated about psychotherapy were some kind of liberal education that a skilled tactician could forgo. Such a tactician is not likely to be confused by his patients, because he will structure the game so that it is played to some extent within his convention. However, he will miss playing the complete game.

I propose that *the complete game of brief psychotherapy concerns the entire field of small moves with large effects.* The question is: How does a therapist make small moves with large effects in ways that are reliably helpful for patients, that take them swiftly from bad places to better places? Broadly speaking, I think you don't get rid of bad places on the patient's map. You help him to make *transitions* from such places, more swiftly, decisively, and skillfully. Patients pose problems to us on fields of all sizes from the largest to the smallest scope: from being stuck in huge, even global, problems like war, poverty, racial and sexual prejudice; to being stuck in institutions, in families, in a couple, in negative identity, in an unfortunate behavior pattern, or in states of feeling or mind or in physiological disturbances (Gustafson & Cooper, 1990). *Meeting the challenge of the case*, as Winnicott (1965) would say, *is to get movement on the field in question*. We are called upon as *experts of movement*. I suggest that there are two kinds of conventions for getting movement. I believe they are highly complementary.

THE CONVENTIONS OF THE SINGLE FIELD

The first kind of convention is better known. It consists of finding the best place to give the patient a push. Expertise is knowing where, how, and when to push to get the most successful change.

These marvelous simplicities (Skynner, 1987) are of the greatest importance, like the bicycle to transportation, like penicillin to modern medicine. They are not difficult to put into use; they can circulate rapidly and widely for the benefit of mankind. The critical point of expertise is to look over the relevant fields of the patient's life in search of what Beahrs (1986) calls a "focal point," a place of leverage that will bring about movement that has large, benign effects on other fields of the patient's life, creating what Cronen, Johnson, and Lannamann (1982) call a "charmed loop." In such a loop, the more improvement from the focal point, the more improvement at other focal points, and the more improvement then at the focal point at which the leverage was gotten.

Even though giving someone a well-calculated push is a *linear* activity, subsequent movement travels around the feedback loops to the other fields of the patient's life in fortuitous ways. Linearity of concept can work quite beautifully. Stierlin (1988) calls this "American planning optimism" or "systemic optimism."

These marvelous simplicities of leverage at focal points are mostly used by therapists in combination with one or two other moves which come to define a convention of a school of psychotherapy. This is similar to strategy in chess. About three moves determine a line of play, such as the Ruy Lopez (Keene & Levy, 1974). There are variations or branch points for subsequent moves, but the character of the line of play is clearly established within the first three moves. I hope the reader will appreciate that in a paragraph I cannot possibly do complete justice to the conventions, when entire books have been devoted to each convention.

Let us be entirely specific: Upon the field of global problems, what single, linear activity can transform the lives of our patients? Take the problem of women being regarded and regarding themselves as second-class citizens. A helpful linear activity might be to simply give steady emphasis to the contrary: "You deserve better." "Your brothers seem never to have heard of the women's movement. When are they going to wake up?" Take the problem of blacks being regarded and regarding themselves as second-class citizens: Simply hold and give steady emphasis to the contrary. Archbishop Tutu explains why Christianity is an enormous power against apartheid in his own country: because Christianity says that every man, woman, and child bears God within himself or herself. Whatever is done unto them is done unto Him. Helping someone thus to hold his head up high can be the difference between a broken life and one of great joy.

Upon the field of global problems, such as the demoralization of minorities, what is the usual trio of moves that create a convention? (1) The worthwhileness of the patient must be deeply felt. This arouses hope. (2) The depth of despair must be shared. This places the therapist within the felt experience of the patient. (3) A road out of the wilderness must be shown. This gives the patient something to do. For example, Luther found a way to cleanse both himself and the corrupt Catholic Church. This triad is the very center of Christian practice, for helping those who are lost [James, 1901; Gustafson, unpublished (a)], but it is found to have great reviving power for all peoples who feel themselves to be "lost causes" (Royce, 1936) (e.g., racial minorities, women, Vietnam veterans, the poor, and those who find themselves pushed to the periphery, neglected, and badly used).

Upon the field of organization of work, what single, linear activity can transform the lives of our patients? Helping a patient get a good job, in which a person is doing something that he or she wants to be doing, that is a way of contributing to society (Winnicott, 1971), that is meaningful to that person, that is well paid. So much trouble in America comes from the lack of such possibilities for meaningful work. If you read some of Terkel's (1972) hundreds of interviews of working people, across the entire range of occupations, you will feel a great deal of pain coming from most of the working world. To help a patient overcome this typical unhappiness is to make a huge difference.

Upon the field of work, what convention will be of great help? Here again, there is a perennial triad of moves that can make a difference: (1) Since the struggle for work is likely to be long and often disappointing, the patient must work from her own dream, from her own conception of what she wants to bring into the world. Nothing less will last. This dream must be found. (2) Weaknesses of preparation have to be faced honestly. (3) Finally, a place must be found to show what one can do well, to get the thrill of competence (Gustafson & Cooper, 1990).

Upon the field of the family, what single, linear activity can transform the lives of our patients? All too often, families are caught in vicious circles that seem to be lacking in exits. Usually, it is more accurate to call them "strange loops" (Cronen, Johnson, & Lannamann, 1982), because the very activity intended to free the person from the trouble triggers the very activities of others that make matters worse. A man who belittles his wife to make himself feel better is triggering her endless complaining, which makes him feel worse, which triggers him to belittle her more, and so forth. In the consulting room such a family may frustrate the interview by running on and on in their usual way, discouraging both the therapists and themselves. Their interaction often overwhelms the proposal to be of help. It is imperative to get both the therapist and family out of this strange loop before it runs too long.

Fortunately, there is a marvelously simple way to keep from getting bogged down, most clearly put forward by De Shazer (1987) in his essay "Minimal Elegance." This exit turns on the concept of "The Exception to the Rule." If the rule is to belittle and complain, an *accented transition* (Gustafson, 1986, Chapter 6; Sullivan, 1954) out of this strange loop is achieved by posing questions that *presume* that no rule holds sway all of the time in every place: "Granted that you are usually caught up in this cycle of criticizing her and complaining to him, but when are you not?" "Oh, you always are now! When were you not in the past? After all, you did choose each other!" "Oh, at home you always do this! Where are you different away from home?" Or, turning to her children: "When is father admiring of mother?" "When is mother telling good news to father?" And so forth. The latter questions are so-called "circular questions" (Tomm, 1984, 1987, 1988) in that they invite family members to comment on each other: Everyone witnesses how behavior travels around the circle of the family. Indeed, a break out of the rule of the strange loop into the exception often triggers remarkable relief, as it suddenly travels around the room, like a cool thunderstorm breaking into the dog days of August.

Upon the field of the family, what convention will be of great help? (1) Locating and breaking free of the rule to find the exception to the rule gives a deep breath of hope. (2) Ordinarily some members of the family are in a worse position than others. Our family therapy team calls this the "tilt of the board" (Gustafson, 1987b; Gustafson & Cooper, 1990). An intervention that will bring about momentum within the family thus has to ride the great feeling of the losers to right the wrong of their bitter defeats, for reasons well argued by Selvini-Palazzoli (1985):

... the answer might have come from Montaigne, who already in the sixteenth century said that we move forward more quickly when attracted by desire than when pushed by guilt. In other words, Nina and her father, spurred on by the wish to live, would have moved more briskly than Aldo and his mother, fueled by regrets alone. (p. 31)

(3) The new winners are likely to be terrible in their own way, like certain South American juntas, only driving a new phase of suffering. Therefore, a sequence of sessions is likely to be necessary, allowing the team to recuperate the sequence of losers, who give impetus to the subsequent sessions. Satisfactory life together will become possible only when the family finds a way of winning that is not at the great expense of one or more scapegoats.

Upon the interpersonal field of the individual, what single, linear activity can transform the lives of our patients? Here again, religion has much to teach. To be *called* to do great things often means a lot to a person. The single discovery by a person of something worthwhile that he or she can give back to the world has extraordinary power (Gustafson, 1986, Chapter 7; Winnicott, 1971). You never forget the uncle who took a special interest, or the first-grade teacher, or the coach, or even the university professor. I do not just mean encouragement. I mean someone who sees something individual or important or valuable and helps to bring it out. For me, a remarkable example of this "calling" is a song sung recurrently by Jevetta Steele in the movie *Bagdad* Café, literally "I'm Calling You."

Upon the interpersonal field of the individual, what convention will be of help? Here, many languages compete for the honor of the field (Gustafson & Cooper, 1990, Chapter 1). Not so long ago, the Rogerian triad of positive regard, genuineness, and empathy was taught widely. Now we have self-psychology, with its emphasis on providing the mirroring or idealized self object and careful empathy for breaches in this kind of relationship (Goldberg, 1973; Kohut, 1971; Ornstein, 1974), for "enactments" of the difficulty in using help (Strupp & Binder, 1984). (1) The individual is called forth. (2) Trouble is enacted and shared. (3) The strength of the bond between therapist and patient proves able to contain the grievances.

Upon the field of behavior (smaller than the field of the individual), what single, linear activity can transform the lives of patients? Here the challenge is often to put a complete stop to unfortunate behaviors, such as alcohol or drug abuse, mean punishing of others, phobic clinging to the house, or four hours of hand washing a day. The marvelous simplicity of putting a complete stop to these activities which tend to wreck everything else is to *wait* until such a person can no longer stand it himself, at which time the moment is seized to get him or her to agree to expose him or herself to the triggering difficulties while the behavior itself is strictly disallowed. This combination of *exposure* and response prevention (Marks, 1987) breaks the linkage between the evoking stimuli and the driven behavior, placing what Ashby (Selvini-Palazzoli, 1980) calls a *null-function* between two parts of a tightly driven system, allowing them then to evolve independently.

Upon the field of unfortunate behavior, what convention is highly likely to be of help? (1) There must be faith in the patient, often shown in giving the patient responsibility for being his own doctor, when he is ready. (2) The patient has to agree to put himself within a framework that makes the unfortunate behavior impossible. (3) Once this success of tolerating great anxiety without drinking, compulsive activity, or some other destructive action is achieved, the patient must continue within a framework of abstinence (Bateson, 1971; Beahrs, 1986; Marks, 1987).

Upon the field of intolerable feelings, what single, linear activity can transform the lives of our patients? To *share* them is to lighten their burden for the patient, perhaps to make them bearable, perhaps the difference for the patient between giving up and being able to go on at all. This is the great simplicity of the analytic tradition, especially for its existential doctors, like Semrad (Semrad, Binstock, & White, 1966), Winnicott (1971), Havens (1986), Malan (1979), and Mann (1973).

Upon the field of intolerable feelings, what convention is likely to make a difference? (1) The undermodulated, unbearable feeling must be put into words, gestures, and even sighs, which gives the patient the sense of a burden shared and thus lightened for a while (Semrad, Binstock, & White, 1966; Horowitz and others, 1984). (2) But the patient is likely to take refuge then in overmodulated states (Horowitz et al., 1984) where he is inaccessible, taking up his characteristic constant attitude (Gustafson, 1986, Chapter 4; Reich, 1933) such as passive waiting, or in a security operation (Gustafson, 1986, Chapter 6; Sullivan, 1954, 1956) such as constant complaining. This obliges the therapist to be able to release the patient from such "routinely futile operations" (Gustafson, 1986, Chapter 6; Sullivan, 1954). Some do it by confrontation (Davanloo, 1986; Sifneos, 1979). Others do it by working opposing currents (Gustafson, 1986): If the patient is continuously self-blaming, there was a time when she had confidence; if the patient runs on and on with progress reports, the admiration of everything as being "terrific," even more vociferous than the self-admiration of the patient, will elicit doubts. (3) Finally, there will be hopes aroused that cannot be sustained, undermodulated pleasure that will lead to crashes, unless the patient can be helped to come down from extravagant feeling (Binswanger, 1963; Horowitz et al., 1984). The gap between the highest and the lowest must be traveled with the patient (Mann, 1973): Words and

BRIEF THERAPY

metaphor can carry the patient through these bewildering distances, as from togetherness to utter isolation, from a beautiful world to an ugly world [Gustafson, unpublished (b)].

Finally, upon the field of physiology, what single, linear activity can turn around a life? To give a drug that relieves anxiety or depression. A person may decide he or she is not hopeless, after all. A new start gets underway. This great simplicity is the center of modern psychiatry.

Again, a triad of activities is necessary to the convention which is effective. (1) Careful attention to the patient's experience gives him or her the feeling that this trouble is commonplace and solvable. (2) A modest trial of the drug is proposed, as an experiment. The patient realizes he or she must carry it through, diligently, cautiously. (3) Yet the percentages are proposed as favorable. Hope is aroused.

The great simplicity of modern Ericksonian hypnosis (Rossi, 1986) is comparable to the use of psychotropic drugs. A deep trance alone can give hope for a new beginning, much like the relief from anxiety or depression allowed by a psychotropic drug. The convention of hypnosis will include the same careful attention to the patient's experience (especially the alternation between a background of calm and a foreground of excitation), a modest trial of the procedure, and the arousal of hope.

Now we have before us an entire set of lenses, from the wide-angle lens, which shows the field of global problems, to the narrowest-angle lens, which shows the field of physiological disturbances (Figure 1). No single lens is superior to the others. All disclose useful fields, upon which a marvelous simplicity has been discovered for locating a patient in a problem, loosing him from its bind, and arranging a way forward (Gustafson, 1987a,b).

The virtue of lenses, even one or two, was shown dramatically but simply by Isaac Newton. As Cohen (1987) noted:

> Newton's discovery of the nature of light and color was hailed as being particularly significant because it didn't use complicated, complex, or expensive apparatus, but relied upon a simple device—a prism—and the creative imagination of a single individual. Newton's experimental career illustrates a major facet of the scientific revolution. Knowledge is to be based upon the senses: on what any man or woman can see or hear or touch or smell, on what can be learned by experiment and critical observation. Science progresses by direct interrogation of nature and not on the statements of learned authorities. (p. 22)

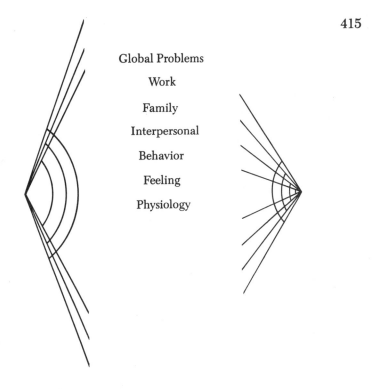

Global Problems

Work

Family

Interpersonal

Behavior

Feeling

Physiology

Fig 1. Available lenses for brief therapy.

THE CONVENTIONS OF THE PATTERN THAT CONNECTS

What if we see that most of our patients do not have isolated disorders, that their problems stem instead from being in a mistreated minority, badly placed at work, or caught in a strange family game; or from having a shaky self, unfortunate behaviors, intolerable feelings, or a physiological panic disorder? What if our average patient is a woman unfairly treated by the world, in a bad job, caught up in a strange loop of mutual blaming with her husband and family, shaken in her confidence, making matters worse by her avoidance behavior, and often feeling intolerably blue or desperate? What if there is no escape from *some* of these findings, from some bleakness or hopelessness concerning physical illness, getting older, bad working conditions, death, taxes? How does one help her morale, while facing up to some of her unfortunate circumstances? Once we have lenses to see troubles at all these different levels or fields, how are we to do reliable work? How are we to secure advantage upon one field without worsening upon another?

416 BRIEF THERAPY

Here we enter the second large class of conventions for brief psychotherapy. Now the emphasis will *not* fall simply on a single problem, on a single field, in a single time, to be directed by an expert doctor. Those are what I have called the restricting conventions of modern brief therapy (Gustafson, 1987a,b). Instead, the emphasis will fall on what Bateson (1979) called "the pattern that connects" all these fields of entirely different scope. This connecting pattern has been given many different *names* depending on the field in which it has been glimpsed: The social theorists, who look most widely, see social class as allowing only certain class variations within a confining set of habits or "habitus," to use Bordieu's (1977) word. The family theoreticians see family games (Selvini-Palazzoli, Cecchin, Prata, & Boscolo, 1978). The interpersonal writers see security operations (Sullivan, 1954, 1956). The individual doctors see the constant attitude (Reich, 1933) or the life story (Malan, 1979). The doctors of behavior see unfortunate behaviors. The doctors of feelings see present and chronically recurring pain (Mann, 1973). Psychiatrists mostly see physiological and personality disorders.

I presume that each of these approaches provides different glimpses of the same *single* pattern that connects what a person can or will do on fields from the largest to the smallest. Presuming such a pattern that connects allows an entirely different set of conventions than those which locate focal points on limited, single fields for leverage. Such conventions take up the "loose thread" of concern upon the field of challenge in which it is presented, but then follow the concern as it moves up and down, into larger and into smaller arenas.

If a patient begins the interview talking about having no self-confidence with young men, this will soon lead in her associations to being unsupported in her family as a child, caught in a war between the parents. She can move into unbearable grief, back up into hopeful starts with peers where her ability to protect herself was weak, directly into the relationship with the doctor whom she tries to put way above her as well, back into rage, and maybe into her feelings about women being vulnerable to physical attack in the university or being given poorer jobs (Gustafson, 1986, Chapter 21).

When you can *follow* such a patient through all the fields of her life, from the largest scope of the problems of women in America, through work, back into her family, to her feeling about herself, to her unfortunate behaviors with men that get her put down, to her great pain and rage, how have you made a difference? What are the advantages of such a convention in brief psychotherapy for following the pattern that connects her life from large to small?

I see three great advantages: (1) She gets a clearer, stronger sense of her own purpose, coherence, mission, or dream, in highly diverse circumstances. She is more deserving of respect than she had seen before. When she has her own boldness, she is also less likely to get lost in other people's purposes. I call this the *updraft*, buoyancy, or resilience of a person. (2) The unbearable feelings become bearable, because transitions are found into them and out of them. In other words, they will pass. I call this the *downdraft*, sometimes of a force like the low-level windshear that slams airliners to the tarmac. A person has got to be able to pick herself up from terrible experiences. A therapy that reaches these (otherwise dissociated) experiences will strengthen that person for the unbearable events of life. (3) Finally, we all get carried away, if we give ourselves over to life with any devotion. We will get up too high. Comedowns must be negotiated. A brief therapy that reaches from bottom to top and back again will prepare the patient for the terrible disappointments that come on the heels of success.

The convention of following the pattern that connects affords, in summary, all the advantages of *transition*, of *freer passage* (Gustafson & Cooper, 1990, Chapter 7), of going forward, of coming back from the depths, of coming down from the heights. Conversely, it shows some of the great difficulties of transition, by providing a large enough set of fields, so that a poorly connected life can be seen.

Such a life may never be seen by those so quick to give a drug or hypnotize or give any kind of push on a field visualized by a single lens. Such a practice was exposed vividly by a man in an audience who asked a well-known clinician how he could justify hypnotizing a patient without knowing anything about him. The doctor argued that he didn't *want* to know the patient, but then admitted that he would never do that in private practice, only in conferences where he was counting on someone else to have looked over the patient's life.

The lives of patients surely must be as important as the lives of children (Dennison, 1969). George Engel (1980) has argued rightly that we owe it to our patients to practice biopsychosocial psychiatry, which means that our preliminary evaluations (Gustafson, 1986) will include at least the fields seen by the physiological, individual, and systemic lenses. The poorly connected life has a chance to be recognized.

Let us briefly bring some of these connecting problems into view. First, there are many patients whose sense of a center in their lives is lost or flattened. By middle age, they look very tired. One patient of mine describes this as being lost in a cloud. In his cloud, one direction seems the same as another. A second patient describes herself as having no momentum. Her life is flattened: That which reaches out to connect is hidden. In classical language, these patients would be described as restricted characters (Reich, 1933).

BRIEF THERAPY

A second class of patients connect, but are always in danger of being overtaken. They are betrayed, overwhelmed, enraged, and often ready to give up on people and on themselves. They feel there is something worthwhile, but the good is so often overrun by the bad that they can hardly stand to try. In classical language, this is the paranoid position (Balint, 1952; Gustafson, 1986, Chapter 8). Perhaps half of my patients can be found here. Their posture is to keep a close watch on the doctor. They eye you all the time. They may be hysterical, obsessive, or morally masochistic (ready to take all blame on themselves before anyone can blame them), but the constant attitude of their character is deeper than the postures taken in hysterical, obsessive, or masochistic modes. Whatever the mode, the eye is looking out for betrayal—whatever the field, large to small.

A third class of patients connect and trust, but are always flying or climbing higher than they can sustain. They never quite reckon the distance between their hopes and what they are likely to find. In classical language, this is the depressive position (Balint, 1952; Gustafson, 1986, Chapter 8).

These are the three great disorders of transition, of free passage, of connectedness: (1) lost connection; (2) betrayed connection; (3) excessively hopeful connection. All come into view within the convention of following the pattern that connects.

Are these disorders of connection helped in brief therapy? Indeed, they have been greatly helped. Freud (1909), Reich (1933) (Gustafson, 1986, Chapters 2, 3, and 4), and later Davanloo (1986) discovered that consistently challenging the patient's constant attitude led them into every aspect of the patient's life, large to small, present to past. Rather than chaotic analyses, they got onto a pattern that connected everything, like a "red thread" that could always be found. Read the relatively brief therapy of Freud's Rat Man (1909) to see such an entire ratlike world, political, economic, family, individual, behavioral, and feeling-wise just like that of a rat. Malan (1979) and Mann (1973) each found a similar thread connecting everything in a patient's recurrent "life story." The patient has tried so hard to realize a certain mission but keeps falling down in the same places.

There seem to be several different lines or threads that have provided the patterns that connect everything: constant attitude or posture, recurrent attempts, and recurrent pain. I call these three aspects of a single pattern that connects: (1) the outside surface, (2) the updraft or dream, (3) the downdraft or collisions with the world (cf. Gass, 1983).

I find it possible to utilize a convention that follows this connecting pattern:

1. You take some time at the outset of every session to find the field on which the patient is *most preoccupied*: Is it some larger political obsession? Is it work? Is it the family or friends? Is it oneself? Is it some behavior that is really getting him in trouble? Is it some feeling that won't go away? Also, the day compartments of the patient's life may not interest him at all, but the night compartment of dreams may freely range over the terrain of the day compartments with great rapidity of movement, turns, and surprises [Jung, 1933; Gustafson, unpublished (b)]. It is simple to take this time to find the patient, but it takes a full range of lenses, large to small, to scan the relevant fields (Gustafson, 1987a,b).

2. If the patient is lost or without momentum, this takes precedence over everything. My patient who was lost in a cloud had to be asked when he last had glimpses of going somewhere. My patient who felt her life at a stop had to be asked when she last had some thrust. Once these patients could be put in touch with direction and momentum, the therapy could go forward. If I didn't do this, nothing else would have happened.

3. Once there is direction and momentum, there are the two risks of transition: going down in unbearable feeling, and going up too high in hopes that cannot be sustained. The first is usually manageable by bearing with the patient, as after a while it can usually be reversed: "You feel so bad about lacking self-confidence. This must mean you once felt a great deal of self-confidence, or you would not feel the lack of it so deeply. You've had it before" (Gustafson, 1986, Chapter 21). This statement, offered to a patient, served to recover childhood feelings of trust. The second risk is usually manageable by riding with the great hope, while giving it a shake to bring the patient back down to earth (Havens, 1986): "You would like to break up with her without giving her any pain whatsoever, as if surgery could be carried out with no suffering at all." This remark was made to a patient quite prepared to bring his wife to couples therapy, as a way of easing his leaving her.

I hope that by now the reader has noticed some redundancy in the triad of moves to bring about movement and direction, whether that triad has been posed upon a single field or whether it has been posed for following the pattern that connects all the single fields. I call this triad of moves "working the opposing currents" (Gustafson, 1986; Havens, 1986). A stuck pattern may be loosened in three ways (Figure 2): (1) By challenging the stabilizing element itself, whether that be considered as the constant attitude, the prevailing security operation, or the strange loop of the family game; (2) by mobilizing the thrust for something else, whether that be intense feeling like hatred or love, ideals like pride and

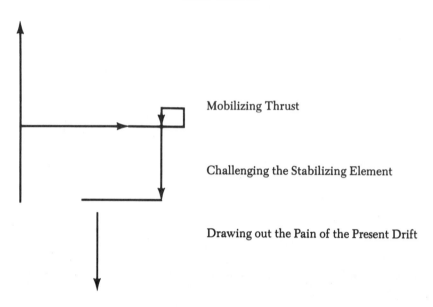

Mobilizing Thrust

Challenging the Stabilizing Element

Drawing out the Pain of the Present Drift

Figure 2. Working the opposing currents.

self-respect, or remembrance of things past that have been better and could be so again; (3) by drawing out the pain of the present drift. Most of us favor one of these three measures, utilizing, as Friedman (1988) has suggested, either the "hard lens" that focuses on how the patient wrecks progress by some stabilizing maneuver or the "soft lens" that looks for the earliest signs of the most hopeful thrust of the patient. Very unusual are Michael White (1984) and Les Havens (1986), who draw upon all three ways of pulling apart the stuck pattern in favor of something better. This is done by working the opposing currents to create a highly fluid situation for testing readiness for change.

SUMMARY

In summary, the convention of following the pattern that connects depends on: (1) finding the patient on the field he is preoccupied, (2) finding direction and momentum, when it has been lost, (3) finding transitions from unbearable pain and from impossible hopes [Gustafson, unpublished (b)].

I see no incompatibility between the Conventions of the Single Field and the Conventions of the Pattern That Connects. If I do not meet the challenge of the case, which is always posed as a focal problem upon a single field, I cannot go on to reach the problems of connecting. The first set of conventions is a necessary element of the second convention. But the first set of conventions can stop us from the most interesting work by unduly restricting attention to feeling, or thought, or behavior, or cleverness.

The other great confinement we need to be wary about is the great call to interpret everything in the language of a particular theory. Some schools of therapy have a way of talking that purports to explain everything. Karl Popper (1963) tells of this with Adler in 1919:

> I reported him a case which to me did not seem particularly Adlerian, but which he found no difficulty in analyzing in terms of his theory of inferiority feelings, although he had not even seen the child. (p. 35)

In this way, the patient may be lost as an individual. As Walker Percy (1975) writes, "falling prey to valid theory . . . What is wrong is a certain loss of sovereignty by the patient" (p. 185).

Therefore, I believe it is extremely important to write and talk about psychotherapy with as full use of the English language as we are capable, and not to confine ourselves or our patients within one interpretation of the world. Susan Sontag (1966) proposes for writing the same deceptive simplicity I propose for psychotherapy:

> Ideally, it is possible to elude the interpreters in another way, but making works of art whose surface is so unified and clean, whose momentum is so rapid, whose address is so direct that the work can be . . . just what it is. Is this possible now? It does happen in films, I believe. This is why cinema is the most alive, the most exciting, the most important of all art forms now. (p. 11)

I believe we can have in psychotherapy what is found both in film and in the remarkable diversity and richness of American lyric poetry in the twentieth century. Helen Vendler (1985) closes her extraordinary introduction to this latter subject in a way that is fitting for our subject, psychotherapy:

> The poem stands before us brilliantly photographic and brilliantly verbal at once . . . "The poetry of a people," said T. S. Eliot, "takes its life from the people's speech and in turn gives

life to it; and represents its highest point of consciousness, its greatest power and its most delicate sensibility." (p. 17)

We may be engineers of transition, but we will not be able to pull off much connection without the poetry of our patients, which will find them in their own words and in their own images. Vendler (1985) puts this most poignantly for me when she writes the following sentence, then cites Robert Lowell's unforgettable lines:

The poet knows that, without the accurate record of art, people subside, as transient statistics, into the anonymous census of history:

"We are poor passing facts,
warned by that to give each figure in the photograph
his living name."

Thus, we can do for our patients what E. M. Forster (1910) urged humanity to do in *Howard's End*: "Only connect." I close with a sentence in Lowell's poem which brings home an individual being:

Yet why not say what happened?
Pray for the grace of accuracy
Vermeer gave to the sun's illumination
stealing like the tide across a map
to his girl solid with yearning.

Or yet another, more down to earth, from William Carlos Williams (1956, p. 206), who overheard a Polish woman say to her daughter: "You bust your coat with your fifty sweaters."

REFERENCES

Balint, M. (1952). New beginning and the paranoid and the depressive syndromes. *International Journal of Psychoanalysis*, 33, 214. Reprinted in Balint, M. (1953), *Primary Love and Psychoanalytic Technique*. New York: Liveright.

Bateson, G. (1971). The cybernetics of "self," a theory of alcoholism. *Psychiatry*, 34, 1–18. Reprinted in Bateson, G. (1972), *Steps Toward an Ecology of Mind*. New York: Ballantine.

Bateson, G. (1979). *Mind and Nature, a Necessary Unity*. New York: Dutton.

Beahrs, J. O. (1986). *Limits of Scientific Psychiatry*. New York: Brunner/Mazel.

Binswanger, L. (1963). Extravagance (Versteigenheit). In Needleman, J. (Ed.), *Being-in-the-World, Selected Papers of Ludwig Binswanger.* New York: Harper & Row.

Bordieu, P. (1977). *Outline of a Theory of Practice.* Cambridge: Cambridge University Press.

Cohen, I. B. (1987). The Newtonian scientific revolution and its intellectual significance: A tercentenary celebration of Isaac Newton's *Principia. Bulletin of the American Academy of Arts and Sciences, 41,* 16–42.

Cronen, V. E., Johnson, K. M., and Lannamann, J. W. (1982). Paradoxes, double binds, and reflective loops: An alternative theoretical perspective. *Family Process, 20,* 91–112.

Davanloo, H. (1986). Intensive short-term psychotherapy with highly resistant patients: I. Handling resistances; II. The course of an interview after breakthrough. *International Journal of Short-Term Psychotherapy, 1,* 107–133, 239–255.

Dennison, G. (1969). *The Lives of Children.* New York: Vintage.

De Shazer, S. (1987, October). Minimal elegance. *Family Therapy Networker,* 57-60.

Engel, G. (1980). The clinical application of the biopsychosocial model. *American Journal of Psychiatry, 137,* 535–544.

Forster, E. M. (1910). *Howard's End.* Harmondsworth, Middlesex, England: Penguin, 1941.

Foucault, M. (1982). The subject and power. In H. L. Dreyfus and P. Rabinow, *Michel Foucault, Beyond Structuralism and Hermeneutics* (pp. 208–226). Chicago: University of Chicago Press.

Freud, S. (1909). Notes upon a case of obsessional neurosis. *Standard Edition, 10,* 152–318. New York: Norton.

Friedman, L. (1988). The clinical popularity of object relations concepts. *Psychoanalytic Quarterly, 57,* 667–691.

Gass, W. (1983). Groping for trouts: On metaphor. *Salmagundi Reader,* 421–433.

Goldberg, A. (1973). Psychotherapy of narcissistic injuries. *Archives of General Psychiatry, 28,* 722–726.

Gustafson, J. P. (1986). *The Complex Secret of Brief Psychotherapy.* New York: Norton.

Gustafson, J. P. (1987a). The rapidly evolving field of brief psychotherapy. *Psychiatric Times,* October.

Gustafson, J. P. (1987b). The neighboring field of brief individual psychotherapy. *Journal of Marital and Family Therapy, 13,* 409–422.

Gustafson, J. P. [unpublished (a)]. Hallucinoia, the release of phantoms in schizophrenonia. Thesis, Harvard Medical School, 1967.

Gustafson, J. P. [unpublished (b)]. Finding and going forward: The two great challenges of long-term psychotherapy.

Gustafson, J. P., & Cooper, L. W. (1990). *The Modern Contest, a Systemic Guide to the pattern that connects individual psychotherapy, family therapy, group work, teaching, organizational life and large scale social problems.* New York: Norton.

Havens, L. L. (1986). *Making Contact, Uses of Language in Psychotherapy.* Cambridge, MA: Harvard University Press.

Horowitz, M., Marmar, C., Krupnick, J., Wilner, W., Kaltreider, W., & Wallerstein, R. (1984). *Personality Styles in Brief Psychotherapy.* New York: Basic Books.

James, W. (1901). *The Varieties of Religious Experience, A Study in Human Nature.* New York: Mentor, 1958.

Jung, C. G. (1933). Dream analysis in its practical application. In C. G. Jung, *Modern Man in Search of a Soul.* New York: Harcourt, Brace, 1974.

Keene, R., & Levy, D. (1974). *How to Play the Opening in Chess.* Albertson, Long Island, NY: RHM Press.

Kohut, H. (1971). *The Analysis of the Self.* New York: International Universities Press.

Malan, D. H. (1979). *Individual Psychotherapy and the Science of Psychodynamics.* London: Butterworths.

Mann, J. (1973). *Time-Limited Psychotherapy.* Cambridge, MA: Harvard University Press.

Marks, I. M. (1987). *Fears, Phobias, and Rituals, the Nature of Anxiety and Panic Disorders.* New York/Oxford: Oxford University Press.

Ornstein, A. (1974). The dread to repeat and the new beginning. A contribution to the psychoanalysis of narcissistic personality disorders. *Annual of Psychoanalysis, 2,* 231–248.

Percy, W. (1975). Metaphor as mistake, and toward a triadic theory of meaning. In *The Message in the Bottle.* New York: Farrar, Straus & Giroux.

Popper, K. (1963). *Conjectures and Refutations: The Growth of Scientific Knowledge.* New York: Harper & Row.

Reich, W. (1933). *Character Analysis.* New York: Farrar, Straus & Giroux, 1949.

Reider, N. (1959). Chess, Oedipus, and the Mater Dolorosa. *International Journal of Psychoanalysis, 40,* 1–14.

Rossi, E. (1986). *Psychobiology of Mind-Body Healing.* New York: Norton.

Royce, J. (1936). *The Philosophy of Loyalty.* New York: Macmillan.

Selvini-Palazzoli, M. (1980). Why a long interval between sessions? The therapeutic control of the family-therapy suprasystem. In M. Andolfi & I. Zwerling (Eds.), *Dimensions of Family Therapy.* New York: Guilford Press.

Selvini-Palazzoli, M. (1985). The problem of the sibling as referring person. *Journal of Marital and Family Therapy, 11,* 21–34.

Selvini-Palazzoli, M., Cecchin, G., Prata, G., & Boscolo, L. (1978). *Paradox and Counterparadox.* New York: Jason Aronson.

Semrad, E., Binstock, W. A., & White, B. (1966). Brief psychotherapy. *American Journal of Psychotherapy, 20,* 576–579.

Sifneos, P. E. (1979). *Short-Term Psychotherapy.* New York: Plenum Press.

Skynner, R. (1987). *Explorations with Families, Group Analysis and Family Therapy.* London: Methuen.

Sontag, S. (1966). *Against Interpretation.* New York: Farrar, Straus & Giroux.
Stierlin, H. (1988). Systemic optimism/systemic pessimism. *Family Process, 27,* 121–127.
Strupp, H. H., & Binder, J. (1984). *Psychotherapy in a New Key. Time Limited Dynamic Psychotherapy.* New York: Basic Books.
Sullivan, H. S. (1954). *The Psychiatric Interview.* New York: Norton.
Sullivan, H. S. (1956). *Clinical Studies in Psychiatry.* New York: Norton.
Terkel, S. (1972). *Working.* New York: Avon.
Tomm, K. (1984). One perspective on the Milan approach. *Journal of Marital and Family Therapy, 10,* 113–125, 253–271.
Tomm, K. (1987, 1988). Interventive interviewing. *Family Process, 26,* 113–125, 167–183; *27,* 1–15.
Vendler, H. (Ed.) (1985). *The Harvard Book of Contemporary American Poetry.* Cambridge, MA: Harvard University Press.
White, M. (1984). Marital therapy—Practical approaches to longstanding problems. *Australian Journal of Family Therapy, 5,* 27–43.
Williams, W. C. (1956). *In the American Grain.* New York: New Directions.
Winnicott, D. W. (1965). The use of the term therapeutic consultation. Course outline, provided by Robin Skynner.
Winnicott, D. W. (1971). *Therapeutic Consultations in Child Psychiatry.* New York: Basic Books.

PART VIII

Special Concerns

CHAPTER 31

"To Thine Own Self Be True . . . " Ethical Issues in Strategic Therapy

Richard Fisch

As the title suggests and this chapter will clarify, strategic therapy calls for a shift in emphasis in ethical thinking from "honesty" as a primary value toward personal responsibility as a primary value. Ethical issues apply to every form of therapy—as well as any other transaction between people—but are more salient in strategic therapies which emphasize the deliberate use of influence by the therapist. Ethical issues regarding therapist influence often are less controversial in traditional insight-oriented approaches since the goal of therapy is principally to aid the client to become aware of, or gain insight into, those factors and events defined as relevant by the particular therapist. In strategic therapies, however, higher regard is given to directives, tasks, and "homework." When therapists are faced with getting clients to *do* things, they are faced with the task of persuasion. With the increasing interest in, and use of, strategic therapies, it is to be expected that more questions of ethical practice will come to the fore.

One example of this concern is Phillip Booth's (1988) presentation at the 1986 Erickson Congress. Another recent, although less extensive treatment of the subject, is a book by O'Hanlon and Wilk (1987). A chapter on ethics has been written by Zeig (1986). Most of my comments address Booth's work because of the extensive and thorough way in which ethical issues are addressed and the way he relates them to theoretical and philosophical considerations. Booth argued:

... for the removal of "trickiness" and manipulativeness from strategic therapy and to rewrite the techniques of strategic therapy according to commonsense and with nontechnical terms. (p. 39)

The intent of this chapter is to argue that (1) manipulation is unavoidable in *any* therapy—and in any human interaction; (2) the measure of its benefit or detriment is in the outcome of therapy; and (3) the choice is not whether or not one is manipulative but whether or not one acknowledges to oneself the use of manipulation. The title of this chapter alludes to this concept. In the course of developing these positions, I will examine the premises on which Booth bases his contentions as well as his own form of persuasion in presenting premises and conclusions to the reader.

BOOTH'S POSITION

Booth appropriately begins his argument with a discussion of philosophical questions regarding reality since they have a direct bearing on ethics. In his criticism of the concept of reality as a subjective matter, he misses the point that this is an alternative *viewpoint* to the traditional *view* of reality as an objective matter. This misunderstanding is apparent in his statement: "if the *existence* of an objective real world is *undermined*, the *objective facts* of that world *become* ephemeral" (p. 43, italics added).

He incorrectly interprets constructivist thought as denying what is factually there. He does not grasp that objective reality and subjective reality are two different *beliefs*. Based on this misunderstanding, Booth proceeds to his ethical position: "*Regard for the facts* is thereby *undermined* and therapists can tell lies with philosophical *impunity*" (p. 43). He warms to this theme with some fervor: "The most serious *attack* on the *obligation* to tell the truth when conducting therapy stems from an *attack* on the notion of 'reality' " (p. 43, italics added).

Constructivism is not a heresy as Booth's language implies. Rather, in offering an opposing view of reality, constructivism opens up an alternative ethical base: *Ethical and responsible therapy involves working with the client's reality (frame of reference, world view, etc.) rather than requiring clients to accept the therapist's reality.* In failing to understand constructivist thought, Booth incorrectly attributes to strategic therapists an adversarial position vis-à-vis their clients.

> ... placing emphasis on truth and honesty. This requires adopting a non-adversarial view of therapy contrary to that which is often promoted by strategic therapists. (p. 40)

Equating "truth and honesty" with being non-adversarial is a questionable position. Webster (1975) defines adversary as: "A person who opposes or fights against another, opponent, enemy." One certainly can oppose, honestly and/or truthfully. More important, attributing an adversarial position to strategic therapists disqualifies the fact that in strategic therapies, as in all therapies, the goal of the therapist and client is mutual; that is, resolution of the client's problem. Booth negates the fact that the therapist uses knowing manipulation to achieve a *mutual* goal. Ironically, the strategic therapist, in deliberately using manipulation, is more likely than the traditional therapist to respect the client's "reality," seeing it as a *different* reality than his or her own rather than an incorrect or "unhealthy" reality. To enhance the client's motivation to accept a suggestion or task, the strategic therapist utilizes the client's "reality" and may say things when explaining the suggestion that do not reflect the therapist's own "reality."

This is anything but "adversarial." Adversarial positions are more likely to arise when the therapist believes the client's reality is "mistaken" or "dysfunctional" and sets about to correct that "reality" in accordance with his own perceptions: "But Joanne, might you be misperceiving your husband's intentions?" "Oh, no. I know him too well. He does that with everyone." "He does that with everyone? You had said that he doesn't do that with your son." "Oh, that's different. Brian knows how to get around him." (I'm sure this kind of dialogue must sound familiar to every therapist. It is an example of the frustrating and counterproductive arguing that often occurs when one tries to get the client to "look at reality." As a handy face-saving device, therapists always can say that they are being realistic and that it is only the client who is being oppositional.)

After disqualifying proposals about alternative views of reality, Booth shifts by implying that philosophy about reality isn't that important anyhow, that the central ethical point is the *intention* of the therapist in what he says to the client.

> Although objective truth is elusive, we *can* know when we are being truthful, that is, saying what we believe or what we know

to be the case and we *can* know when we are lying or fabricating, that is, saying, with the intention to deceive, things that we do not believe or what we know not to be the case. This is a central argument that is quite separate from any philosophical argument about the attainability of objective truth. (p. 45, italics in the original)

I agree that "intention" is the central ethical point, but not in the way that Booth uses the concept: What Booth intends and what strategic therapists intend are quite different. Strategic therapists, for the most part, believe that what the therapist says—regardless of the "honest" intention of that statement—will have some influence on the client. This, after all, is a basic tenet of interactional thought; that is, you cannot not influence. Thus, if the client responds in an unfavorable way, whether or not the statement was "truthful" or "deceptive," the strategic therapist is more likely to reexamine the presented message since, technically and ethically, the therapist accepts responsibility for influencing the client. Booth, it would appear, divests himself of such responsibility since an untoward reaction by the client is secondary in order for therapists to maintain a good feeling about their "honest" intentions or attitudes. He puts this quite succinctly:

My comments on this (i.e., a therapist taking a "one-down" position) as well as on other tactics relate to the therapist's attitude and not simply to some pragmatic criterion of whether that attitude "works" or not. The fact that it *does* is not the justification for it. The attitude cannot be reduced to a tactic or technique. (p. 49)

This obscures to *whom* it is or is not justification and implies that there is some objective standard of ethical practice and that a therapist is either ethical or not. Booth does not leave room for the idea that therapists may have *different* ethics, differences that depend on how the therapist sees his moral obligation to this client. (There are *some* ethical rules that apply to every therapist; e.g., no sex with clients.) Thus, since Booth puts higher priority on "honesty" than on results, for him to say something he does not believe would be unethical. Conversely, for the strategic therapist, results take higher priority than saying what one believes. Thus, to be truthful for the sake of truthfulness, without regard for the outcome on the patient, would be unethical. It is self-deception to believe that if a client responds adversely to a "truthful" utterance, the therapist has not influenced that client in unfortunate ways.

Booth then seems to backtrack from his moral position of truthfulness for the sake of truthfulness by invoking the concept of "unconscious:"

> However, a client's unconscious mind is not fooled by promises made on this basis [referring to a therapist falsely reassuring the client] any more than it is fooled by some affected protestation that the situation is even worse than he or she thought, such as this tactic suggests. (p. 49)

This puts the matter back to the pragmatic necessity of honesty since it would seem to work better than deception—based, of course, on the premise of an "unconscious," which screens for insincere intent. (Wouldn't it be nice if such reliable mechanisms were operating within the voter during political campaigns!)

Since my central point is that manipulation, wittingly or unwittingly used, is an inherent element in human communication, the choice for therapists, ethically speaking, is whether or not to acknowledge to themselves that they are being manipulative. Booth illustrates this self-deception rather clearly:

> For example, to parents who have been extremely worried about their child who has now shown improvement I often say they should give some thought to what they are going to talk about together now. If I want to emphasize the point by hinting that even their sexual relationship may have been neglected because of their preoccupation with their child, I might ask them what they are now going to talk about *when they go to bed at night*. (p. 51)

But why hint? Why not say it forthrightly, as he so strongly defends? I agree with his manipulation in this clinical vignette but he is not saying what he believes, and further, he is saying something he does not believe, namely, that the couple needs to have a conversation when they go to bed. By his own definition, this is "manipulative" and dishonest and therefore unethical. It requires self-deception to deny he is being manipulative.

Similarly, O'Hanlon and Wilk (1987), who are close colleagues of Booth, are caught in a self-deceptive snare. They too take the "dishonest" strategic therapist to task:

> Again, unlike some other therapists, many of whom we respect greatly, we do not try to be tricky in doing therapy. We are not

trying to do something to our clients. Our therapy would not be unsuccessful if our clients found out what we are doing. Our stance is emphatically *not* one of "tricking clients out of their problems." Trickiness is, in our view, disrespectful to the clients and totally unnecessary to carrying out effective psychotherapy. (p. 162)

Yet, earlier they described some of their techniques:

Frequently we "summarize" what a client has been saying ("Let me see if I understand this so far . . . "), but in the summarizing we introduce a significant twist of some kind. Our summary includes all the significant facts of the client's story so far and perhaps some aspects of the story the client has woven around those facts, but introduces a twist in the story—to which we do not draw attention, but which is offered merely as part of the summing up. We get the client to "ratify" our summary and to add "anything we've missed" and then we proceed on the basis of the version of the story so far represented in our summary. (p. 126)

and:

A related operation involves interrupting a client after he has said something significant but before he can go on to specify what he thinks the significance of his statement is or what the implications are for solving the problem. We interrupt to agree with the point made and sometimes stress its importance or insightfulness, and go on to attach a rather different significance to it from which the client might have intended to attach to it. (pp. 126-127)

Again, I agree that these manipulations can be constructive in helping clients resolve their problems. However, my point is that it requires self-deception to state that one is above trickiness and then describe techniques that are clearly "tricky."

In espousing his particular ethical position, Booth recognizes that he is potentially caught in a dilemma because of his high regard for Milton Erickson's work. Not only does much of current strategic therapy stem from Erickson's work, but Erickson himself used manipulation with patients and was quite open about it. In addressing this troublesome disparity between Erickson's manipulativeness and his own commitment to "honesty," Booth most clearly illustrates what I would call self-deceptive reframing. He begins by acknowledging that Erickson used deception in his work: "It is clear, then, that Erickson was not always honest in what he said to his clients" (p. 46). Having had to make that admission, he quickly proceeds to what can only be described as semantic sleight of hand: "But how manipulative was he?" (p. 46), implying that, somehow, it's not quite unethical to be dishonest as long as one isn't manipulative.

However, even this reframing isn't enough since Erickson boldly acknowledged that he was manipulative. This requires another act of self-deception: "It can be argued, however, that there were aspects of Erickson's work that distinguish it from the questionable manipulation of much modern strategic therapy" (pp. 47-48). Booth develops this theme first by acknowledging that strategic therapists, in their use of manipulation, adhere to the moral position that it be used to aid in the resolution of the client's problem and not self-servingly. Yet, after the acknowledgment, he discounts it:

This is fine, but the problem with this view is that, thus defined, manipulation loses its ordinary meaning: The use of underhanded or unethical means to influence people. The illusion is thereby created that manipulation in the bad sense, that of abusing people, does not exist. (p. 47)

The "illusion" appears to be Booth's creation since he had just cited and acknowledged the principal ethical position of strategic therapists that manipulation can and should be used humanely and responsibly, rather than malignantly; to do otherwise is to manipulate without accepting personal responsibility for the manipulation and its outcome.

Booth then arrives at his major argument for distinguishing between Erickson's manipulation and that of strategic therapists. Since, technically, it is difficult for him to differentiate between what Erickson did with or said to patients versus that of strategic therapists, he does an interesting reframe: "There is a profound difference of attitude between Erickson and the strategic approaches referred to at the beginning of this chapter" (p. 48).

He summarizes the "wrong" attitude as one he defines as "adversarial" and, further, identifies a "good" or "bad" attitude by the *explanation* the therapist gives for her interventions, not by the intervention itself or its outcome. Thus, for example, if the therapist explains technical manipulations with the vocabulary of "strategy," "tactics," "games," "maneuverability," and so forth, then one has an "adversarial" attitude and is therefore unethical. Conversely, if the explanation is given in benign terms, "helping the client," "leaving the client to choose," "understanding the client's needs," and so forth, then, one has the "correct," "non-adversarial" attitude and is, therefore, ethical.

(Booth, of course, does not question whether therapists, including Erickson, believe their explanations. For example, since Erickson's explanations most often were responses to his being questioned, was he answering "truthfully" or manipulating the interviewer? Similarly, are many strategic therapists uncomfortable with their "caringness" and compassion for their clients and thus lying when they claim to believe they are really being tough-minded and calculating?)

I deduce from all of Booth's arguments that his central measure of whether a therapist is being ethical or not depends, in the final analysis, not on *what* the therapist says, or its effect on the client, but on whether or not he can convince others that his statements and intentions are "sincere." While he focused on the authors of *The Tactics of Change* (Fisch, Weakland, & Segal, 1982) as the quintessence of manipulative therapy, he did bestow approval of one of their explanations of a tactical ploy:

> One non-adversarial explanation for this tactic is provided by Fisch, et al. (1982, p. 160) themselves when they say it removes a sense of urgency for the patient—a sense of urgency that has probably been fueling his persistent attempts at "solving" his problem. (p. 50)

I suppose the question for Booth is, were the authors of *The Tactics of Change* being sincere?

REFERENCES

Booth, Phillip J. (1988). Strategic therapy revisited. In J. K. Zeig and S. R. Lankton (Eds.), *Developing Ericksonian Therapy: State of the Art*. New York: Brunner/Mazel.

Fisch, R., Weakland, J., & Segal, L. (1982). *The Tactics of Change: Doing Therapy Briefly*. San Francisco: Jossey-Bass.

O'Hanlon, B., & Wilk, J. (1987). *Shifting Contexts: The Generation of Effective Psychotherapy* (pp. 126-127, 160-163). New York: Guilford Press.

Zeig, J. K. (1986). Ethical issues in Ericksonian hypnosis: Informed consent and training standards. In J. K. Zeig (Ed.), *Ericksonian Psychotherapy, Vol. I: Structures*. New York: Brunner/Mazel.

CHAPTER 32

Miracle Cures?
Therapeutic Consequences
of Clinical Demonstrations
Joseph Barber

A miracle cure is one that seems to take place suddenly and for no explicable reason. Single-session therapeutic "cures" sometimes seem "miraculous," both to the therapist and to the patient, because they occur more suddenly than we expect, and because a reason for the "cure" cannot be discerned.

Over the past several years I have had numerous opportunities, in the context of clinical demonstrations in the course of many workshops, to have a single session of psychotherapy with a workshop participant (or, sometimes, a patient of a workshop participant) for the purpose of demonstrating a clinical principle or therapeutic technique. And in the course of such clinical demonstrations, I often have been surprised at the successful clinical outcome. Sometimes it would be evident at the time; other times, the therapeutic outcome would be related to me by a letter from the demonstration "patient" or his or her therapist.

Unfortunately, I have not kept systematic track of all of these demonstration outcomes because I did not expect to observe anything from keeping track, but I now have the distinct impression that the frequency of significant therapeutic change is far higher than I would have expected, based on my own private practice clinical experience. Often, for instance, a demonstration patient will relate a problem to me that leads me to believe he or she will subsequently need further therapeutic help from someone else in order to obtain the hoped-for change. So I am particularly surprised when I later find that he or she felt "cured" or otherwise satisifed with the outcome of our single session. Perhaps I should not be surprised, given the growing evidence of single-session therapeutic success. But, until I began thinking about this issue, in preparation for writing this chapter, I believed that the workshop demonstration is not a particularly benign setting for the creation of such success.

CASE EXAMPLES

One obvious explanation for such successes takes into account the high expectations of both patient and therapist. Though this may sometimes play a role, it is not always so. Consider the following case:

In the course of a four-day workshop in which I was teaching methods for integrating hypnosis and suggestion into psychotherapy, I had the opportunity to work with a patient of one of the workshop participants. She was a woman in her forties who had suffered dramatic injury in a car accident five years previously. Damage to her head and face had required extensive plastic surgery, and she continued to have unremitting pain, even after five years. Of significance is the fact that the car accident was caused by a drunk driver. This woman felt victimized by the recklessness and irresponsibility of the driver. In the course of the workshop demonstration she related, quite dramatically, her bitterness and disappointment over the accident, her multiple surgeries, the fact that her face was "not [her] own" now, her depression, and the fact of her relentless, continuing head and facial pain.

Uncharacteristically for me, a generally caring fellow, I was not very sympathetic to her plight. In fact, I experienced an unusual lack of generosity in my feelings toward her, and although I tried to be "appropriately" kind and gentle and attentive and empathic, I was inwardly surprised by my lack of sympathy to her. I spent less than an hour with her, during which I listened to her tale of woe regarding the accident. ("Tale of woe . . . ," I cannot even talk about this without expressing cynicism about her.) And I used hypnotic suggestion perfunctorily I thought, to help her experience some contemporary perspective, and to put the accident behind her. Since she felt unable to forgive the drunk driver (who had been killed in the accident), I suggested that she find an alternative means of letting go of this experience, so that she could begin to suffer less and less, eventually developing a healthier perspective on the accident.

Afterward, her psychiatrist led her from the room and I talked with the workshop group about my reaction to her, and about my opinion that I had been unhelpful to her and, further, that I thought it unlikely that anyone could help her suffer less pain and depression until she was willing to get over her bitterness about her victimization. Many in the group did not share my feelings; they experienced her rather more sympathetically. When her psychiatrist returned to the room, having spent a few minutes talking with the patient, he expressed his opinion that she would experience significant recovery—that her pain and depression would abate—as a result of the experience with me. Of course, I could not share his optimism. So it was with genuine amazement that, six months later, I received a report from him, relating the details of her recovery soon following our single session. And in another workshop, a year later, she visited the workshop to discuss her "cure." How to account for a significant reduction in pain and depression from a single therapeutic encounter with an unsympathetic, pessimistic therapist? (Her explanation was that she reacted to my lack of sympathy by wanting to demonstrate to me that she would, in fact, improve.)

Another explanatory approach takes into account the optimism and expectation for change of the patient. Though such expectation on the part of the patient undoubtedly is often involved in such circumstances, it is not always so. Consider the following case:

A 48-year-old man, a psychotherapy patient of one of the workshop participants, had told his therapist that he wanted help to quit smoking (a habit he had continued since age 12). He had tried several times previously, but met with frustrated failure each time. He worried that he would be unable to quit. His therapist told him that a "a well-known hypnotherapist" was coming to town, and that he believed this hypnotherapist would be able to help. The patient was initially reluctant, because he did not believe hypnosis was a real phenomenon or a valid treatment (he had considered that a behavioral treatment would be best), and he assured his therapist that he would not be able to be hypnotized, in any case.

We cannot know, of course, whether the patient entertained, at some deeper psychological level, a belief or hope that hypnosis would be able to help him. In any case, he finally acceded to his therapist's advice that he serve as a demonstration patient at my training workshop. When this patient and I met at the workshop, the patient quickly and somewhat apologetically told me that he hoped he did not embarrass me, but that he did not believe in hypnosis.

I expressed complete confidence that this lack of belief was not only permissible, but actually instrumental, if the patient was going to have any significant experience of surprise. I then launched into a brief inter-

440 BRIEF THERAPY

view of the patient, eliciting relevant information from his history, determining his level of motivation, and confirming his somewhat embarrassed pessimism about the whole enterprise. Then, I suggested that, while I was going to employ a reasonably successful hypnotic induction, the patient could feel free to respond or not, as he preferred. The patient did seem to have initial difficulty in responding to the induction, but I began to tell brief, somewhat intermingled stories of interesting, baffling encounters between doubting patients and doubting therapists, interspersing suggestions for comfort and relaxation—and then offering suggestions intended to reduce his interest in smoking, and to reduce the physical and psychological distress of withdrawal. Afterward, the patient was surprised at his experience: He felt a change in his consciousness that was both pleasant and unfamiliar.

Of course, one cannot know "really" what the patient's unconscious expectations may have been. While he was overtly evincing pessimism, perhaps there was a deeply felt, but not consciously known, sense of optimism.

In any case, he did not smoke again, and he reported, on follow-up at one year, that he had been enormously surprised by how easily he had been able to end this noxious habit. I am sure most therapists have experience with such single-session treatment successes. But, given that most psychotherapeutic experience involves an acceptance, even expectance, of multiple-session treatments, how can one explain such sudden "cures"? One can look for explanations among characteristics of the patient, characteristics of the therapist, and characteristics of the treatment circumstances.

DISCUSSION

Among the patient-attribute explanations that have been offered to account for single-session therapeutic success are: The patient is already prepared, psychologically, for change at the time he or she volunteers to be a demonstration subject. The patient invests the clinician with the power to create change. The patient "must" change, since he or she has been treated by a clinician whose clinical effectiveness is manifested by the context of the workshop.

And, regarding therapist attributes: The therapist somehow conveys his or her expectation that this single treatment is all that is necessary to create change.

While many single-session treatment successes have been reported outside the hypnosis literature, I am limiting my discussion primarily to my own experiences of treatments involving hypnosis. What, then, of the attributes of the hypnotic experience that might account for such change?

Does experience of narrowed, focused attention promote change? Does the tendency for the hypnotized person to regress to a more vulnerable ego state lend itself to the desired change? Are there demand characteristics of the workshop demonstration setting that might be accentuated by the hypnotic experience? Does the fact of being faced with the problem in a public way create social pressure to change? As Haley (personal communication, 1988) suggests, might there be a triadic relationship between the patient, the therapist, and the audience?

No doubt the answer is complicated and may involve all of the above possibilities, as well as others yet unspecified. If we can understand what leads to rapid success in these circumstances, maybe we will know something about how to encourage such rapid successes more often, and in other circumstances.

Bloom (1981) took up the question of single-session therapeutic success, and made these suggestions to the therapist whose goal it is to encourage such single-session success. (These may be familiar strategies to anyone who does clinical demonstrations in a workshop setting—but perhaps not necessarily in a "normal" clinical setting.) Ask yourself whether these strategies might be helpful in creating single-session success:

1. Identify a focal problem.
2. Do not underestimate the patient's strengths.
3. Be prudently active.
4. Explore, then present interpretations tentatively.
5. Encourage the expression of affect.
6. Use the interview to start a problem-solving process.
7. Keep track of time.
8. Do not be overambitious.
9. Keep factual questions to a minimum.
10. Do not be overly concerned about the precipitating event.
11. Avoid detours.
12. Do not overestimate a patient's self-awareness (i.e., don't ignore stating the obvious).

Amplifying further on suggestions for increasing the likelihood of single-session success, Moshe Talmon, Michael Hoyt, and Robert Rosenbaum (1988), in their short course presentation at this Congress entitled "When the First Session Is the Last: A Map for Rapid Therapeutic Change," advise us:

1. Expect change.
2. View each encounter as a whole, complete in itself.
3. Don't rush or try to be brilliant.
4. Emphasize abilities and strengths, rather than pathology.
5. Life, not therapy, is the great teacher.

In the context of these suggestions, it appears to me that the clinical demonstration is an excellent opportunity, compared with other clinical circumstances, to carry out these suggestions. And, at the risk of stating the obvious, both therapist and patient *expect* this to be a single session.

I cannot, of course, claim to always be successful at accomplishing the five goals above, although they are familiar enough to me that I know I am usually oriented toward *trying* to achieve them. Perhaps the context of the clinical demonstration is more conducive to significant therapeutic change than I thought. Perhaps the characterisitcs of brevity and orientation to change can account as much as the patient or therapist attributes described earlier for single-session therapeutic success.

To the extent, then, that I have been able to explicate possible reasons for the evident success of so many clinical demonstrations, they are not "miracle cures." But they sometimes seem like it at the time. In the context of what we know about change, though, I now think that the single-session workshop clinical demonstration is probably quite a good vehicle for promoting therapeutic change. Now, I find myself wondering how this public-thinking-out-loud about the process will affect my workshop demonstrations in the future. How will my newly formed expectation of the efficacy of the demonstration affect the process? I'll find out.

REFERENCES

Bloom, B. L. (1981). focused single-session therapy: Initial development and evaluation. In S. H. Budman (Ed.), *Forms of Brief Therapy*. New York: Guilford Press.

Talmon, M., Hoyt, M. F., & Rosenbaum, R. (1988). When the first session is the last: A map for rapid therapeutic change. Short course presented to the Third International Congress of Ericksonian Hypnosis and Psychotherapy, San Francisco, December, 1988. The Milton H. Erickson Foundation, Phoenix, AZ.

PART IX

Mind-Body Healing

CHAPTER 33

From Mind to Molecule: More Than a Metaphor
Ernest Lawrence Rossi

It is well known that major advances in science usually come about by discovering the conceptual links between two or more different disciplines. In physics, one immediately thinks of Clark Maxwell's equations that linked together electricity and magnetism. In the life sciences, one naturally thinks of the integration of biology and chemistry to create biochemistry. Most recently, the integration of molecular and genetic science to elucidate the molecular biology of the gene (Watson, Hopkins, Roberts, Steitz, & Weiner, 1985) is widely regarded as the leading edge of deep discovery in our time. Theoretically profound issues such as the genetic-informational basis of life, as well as the desperately practical problem of finding a cure for AIDS, are now being dealt with on this level of molecular biology.

The implications of this new integration of genetic, molecular, and informational concepts for a practical psychotherapy of the future are not yet well understood, much less accepted. This chapter outlines some of the major conceptual links between our newly emerging Ericksonian psychotherapeutic methods and current discoveries about the pathways of mind-body healing. *The concept of information is regarded as the common denominator that enables us to bridge mind and matter, psyche and soma for a new science of mind/body healing.* This integration enables us to update our entire therapeutic history from classical hypnosis and psychoanalysis to Ericksonian psychotherapy in a manner consistent with recent research on the molecular basis of mood, memory, learning, and behavior.

445

But there is more here than history and arcane theories: 1988 is the year when these ideas made the newspaper headlines. Who will forget how Ben Johnson lost his gold medal at the Olympics in Korea (*Newsweek*, 1988) because of taking steroids (sexual informational molecules)? Who will not acknowledge that Doreen Kimura and Elizabeth Hampson's (1988) finding that women's mental skills are linked to the monthly shifts in their estrogen levels (another sexual informational molecule) is opening a new era in the study of gender and cognition?

AN OVERVIEW OF MIND/BODY INFORMATION FLOW

Figure 1 is an illustration of how we may conceptualize the mind/body as a cybernetic system of information flow. How does the material stuff of the body (flesh, blood, bones) interact with the apparently insubstantial phenomena of mind (psyche, soul, spirit)? This is the Cartesian dilemma that has teased our best intellects since the beginning of recorded philosophy, particularly in the past 200 years since René Descartes proposed mind and body as separate, but parallel processes. Until recently, no satisfactory solution was available because we had no concept to bridge mind and matter. Today we have the concept, though we do not yet know how to use it very well. *Information is the new concept of our age that can bridge mind and matter*; this is the basic insight of cybernetics (Abramovitz, 1974; von Foerseter, 1984) and current molecular biology (Fischer & Lipson, 1988).

Our leading textbooks in biochemistry (e.g., Stryer, 1988), biology (e.g., Darnell, Lodish, & Baltimore, 1986), neural science (e.g., Kandel & Schwartz, 1985), and genetics (e.g., Watson et al., 1985) are now focusing on *information* exchange as the conceptual basis for understanding these disciplines. A generation ago, it was thought that the concept of *energy* was the basis for understanding life processes. *Today, the concept of information is replacing energy as the conceptual common denominator for understanding all life/environmental processes.* The concept of energy is still useful for calculating the results of large statistical interactions of billions and billions of molecular processes. But such calculations become tedious and finally impossible or irrelevant on the more individual level of interaction that takes place between, say, a single hormone molecule and a cell wall receptor. Now, it is conceptually clearer to understand the hormone as a signal molecule (or informational substance: Schmitt, 1984) that transmits information from one place to another to facilitate life processes. Information substances and their receptors, *Is-receptor systems*, are now recognized as the basic communication process for all forms of life on the molecular level.

**All Cells of the Brain
Send and Receive
Information Substances**

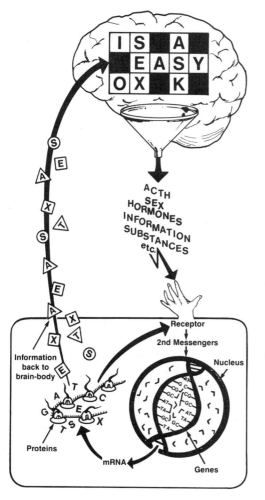

1. MIND-BRAIN CONNECTION
Neural networks of the brain
encode { state-dependent memory
{ feeling-toned complexes
of "mind" (words, images, etc.)
via information substances
(IS's) from all cells of the body.

2. BRAIN-BODY CONNECTION
Neuroendocrinal information
transduction in the brain
converts neural impulses of
the brain into information
substances (IS's) of the body.

3. CELL-GENE CONNECTION
Cells receive information
substances from the brain to
evoke gene information
which communicates back
to the brain for mind-body
health and healing.

**All Cells of the Body
Receive and Send
Information Substances**

**Figure 1. Three levels of the process of information transduction
from mind to molecule.**

The new conceptual challenge is to explore the dynamics of information transduction rather than energy exchange. How is information transformed ("transduced" is the technical term) from one modality to another? This is the basic issue that is illustrated in Figure 1. How does information in the modalities of mental experience (thought, feelings, images, sensations, etc.) transform itself into neural networks of the physical brain and ultimately every cell of the body? How do all the homeostatic modalities of the body (the autonomic, endocrine, immune, and neuropeptide systems that regulate flesh, blood, and bones) communicate their information back to the brain and mind? In Figure 1, I have outlined the process of mind/information transduction on three levels (see Rossi & Cheek, 1988, for a more detailed presentation). Let us explore what we know and do not know about each level.

THE MIND-BRAIN CONNECTION

The first level of mind-brain information transduction in Figure 1 is the basic stumbling block for most theorists, clinicians, and researchers. The nicest people will fight like pit bulls to maintain that we still haven't a ghost of an understanding of the mystery of mind-brain interaction. Rather than fight this attitude, let us simply acknowledge its general truth: The ultimate mystery of mind-body integration is still intact. Science, however, usually proceeds by a series of small, but verifiable steps. In this section, I will summarize a series of such steps that will be useful in conceptualizing a practical psychotherapeutic approach to understanding the mind-brain connection. I have documented in extensive detail the types of clinical and experimental data that enable us to evaluate *the hypothesis that state-dependent memory, learning, and behavior (SDMLB) is the common denominator that bridges the mind-body gap, the so-called Cartesian dichotomy between mind and body* (Rossi, 1986; Rossi & Cheek, 1988; Rossi & Ryan, 1986). Most people respond with a purposefully challenging attitude of drawing a blank when I talk about SDMLB. This nonplussed attitude is evidenced by researchers who are actually doing studies on SDMLB, as well as clinicians who have never even heard of it.

I hope to clarify, therefore, three points about SDMLB:

(1) What state-dependent memory, learning, and behavior (SDMLB) is; (2) how SDMLB can serve as the basis of mind/brain/body information transduction; (3) how SDMLB can account for the basic phenomenology of dissociation in hypnosis as well as reversible memory (repression) and emotional complexes in classical psychoanalysis. Throughout this chapter I note how Ericksonian approaches can utilize this new in-

tegration to facilitate unusually effective and broadly applicable forms of brief psychotherapy.

1. *What is state-dependent memory, learning, and behavior?* Give any experimental animal any drug that is picked up and metabolized in the brain areas associated with memory and learning (alcohol, caffeine, barbiturates, amphetamines, cocaine, etc.), and you will get SDMLB. For the past 40 years, one of the most common studies conducted on a daily basis by most of the pharmaceutical companies throughout the world is to assess the effects of experimental drugs on the behavior of animals before they are used with humans. Of necessity, the test is to determine what effect each drug has on some aspect or other of memory, learning, or behavior. Any drug that passes through the blood-brain barrier usually modifies memory, learning, and behavior in a state-dependent manner. That is, when the drug is present in the brain, the animal responds to training with a certain kind or degree of memory, learning, and behavior. When the drug is metabolized so that it is no longer present in the brain, it is found that what was learned under the influence of the drug is partially lost; we say that the animal has a partial amnesia. Put the drug back into the brain, however, and the memory, learning, and behavior tends to return to its original strength. Researchers explain that the memory, learning, and behavior is now *state-dependent*—that is, its expression is dependent on the *physiological state* of the brain. Memory, learning, and behavior are now *partially reversible* as a function of the presence or absence of a drug in the brain.

2. *SDMLB as the basis of mind/brain/body information transduction.* All this may be interesting, but you could still draw a blank and say, "Well, so what?" What's that really got to do with *normal mind-brain communication* and psychosomatic medicine?

The really important finding that makes SDMLB so significant is that in the past 15 years we have learned that it is not only drugs that can cause a partially reversible amnesia. We now know that dozens of the body's own natural molecules are modulating memory, learning, and behavior in a state-dependent manner. This is the new basis of the molecular biology of memory and learning. In particular, we now know that the stress hormones, the same information substances that are responsible for mediating psychosomatic problems, are at the same time modulating memory and learning (Brush & Levine, 1989; de Wied, 1983, 1987; Izquierdo, 1984, 1989; Izquierdo et al., 1988a,b; Lydic, 1987; McGaugh, Liang, Bennett, & Sternberg, 1984).

The implications of this finding that stress hormones and many other information substances are involved in the memory and learning are profound. I have summarized the research literature that indicates that most forms of learning (Pavlovian, Skinnerian, imprinting, sensitization, etc.) are now known to involve information substances; insofar as these classical forms of learning use information substances, they ipso facto have a state-dependent component (Rossi & Cheek, 1988).

Up to now, we thought that memory, learning, and behavior were mediated by the nervous system—who has not seen the diagram of the reflex arc as a model of stimulus-response behavior? What we now are realizing is that information substances modulate the action of the nervous system. In particular, we now know that many information substances can cross the blood-brain barrier and modulate the neural networks that encode mental experience.

I have outlined a series of researchable hypotheses detailing how information substances modulating the activity of neural networks that encode memory and learning could be the basic process of mind-brain information transduction (Rossi & Cheek, 1988, pp. 50–68). It is important to note that this model of mind-brain communication is a two-way street. It shows how the molecules of the body can modulate mental experience as well as how mental experience can modulate the molecules of the body. In a recent paper entitled "Construction and Reconstruction of Memories," Izquierdo and his colleagues (1988b) summarized the experimental data that document how state-dependent memory, learning, and behavior can be evoked by "cognitive material ('primary') or neurohumoral stimuli" (beta-endorphin, etc.). This is my basis for stating the hypothesis that state-dependent memory, learning, and behavior (SDMLB) is the common denominator that bridges the mind-body gap, the so-called Cartesian dichotomy between mind and body. SDMLB enables us to escape the "Reductionistic Trap" of saying that mind is nothing but the action of molecules. The state dependent concept enables us to create a new "Self-Reflective Molecular Psychology" wherein we can explore how mind modulates molecules as well as vice versa (Pert et al, 1989). An overview of the entire process is greatly simplified in Figure 1.

3. *SDMLB as the psychobiological basis of hypnosis and psychoanalysis.* Table 1 outlines how SDMLB can be conceptualized as a psychobiological common denominator for understanding the classical phenomenology of hypnosis and psychoanalysis. Dissociation, repression, emotional complexes, and partially reversible amnesia are all state-dependent psychological processes. The classical phenomena of hypnosis, multiple personality, neurosis, the post-traumatic stress disorders, psychosomatic symptoms, and mood disorders can all be understood as manifestations of state-dependent behavioral symptoms. Under stress, certain patterns of memory, learning, and behavioral symptomatology are learned and encoded by the release of stress hormones and information substances throughout the entire mind-body. When the stress is

removed, these information substances disappear and the person apparently recovers and seems symptom-free. Reintroduce stress to varying degrees and the mind-body responds by releasing the information substances that reevoke the corresponding degree of SDMLB symptomatology.

These relationships between information substances (Is-receptor systems), memory, learning, stress, and traumatically encoded mind-body problems suggest that we may now be in the first stages of formulating a well-integrated psychobiological theory of therapeutic hypnosis and psychoanalysis: *Dissociation* has been described as the basic mechanism of hypnosis; *repression* has been the central mechanism and model of psychodynamic defense in Freudian analysis; *feeling-toned complexes* have been the units of normal and neurotic emotional life by Jung. What has been the most puzzling about dissociation, repression, and feeling-toned complexes is that they appear to be so variable, insubstantial, and difficult to measure.

I account for this puzzling aspect of the phenomenology of psychoanalytic experience somewhat as follows. As they lay on a couch in a light and usually unrecognized trance, some of Freud's early patients "recalled" sexual trauma from early childhood. Freud used these "data" as the basis for his first theory of the traumatic etiology of neurosis. Later, however, when these patients "awoke" from the light trance of free association (or perhaps when they returned for their next session), they denied the "reality" of their memories. Freud was perplexed by this recall and later denial. He did not realize that his patients were in a therapeutic trance when they were "free-associating." He thought he had given up the use of hypnosis. Actually, he had given up only the use of overt, directive, authoritarian hypnosis and suggestion.

It wasn't until half a century later that Milton Erickson rediscovered the "common everyday trance" that earlier workers such as Charcot and Janet in France had called "hypnoidal states." Janet (1925) proposed that neurotic symptoms were encoded during spontaneous hypnoidal states during everyday life, the so-called *abaissement du niveau mental* (a lowering of mental energy or a narrowing of the field of consciousness). Since Freud did not recognize that his patients were falling into therapeutic trances, which they would later deny when they were "awake," he believed he had to modify his original traumatic theory of neurosis. Freud modified his theory to say that the source of neurosis was in the early *fantasies* of sexual seduction rather than in real, traumatic experiences of sexual molestation.

An unresolved question from the earliest days of psychoanalysis is why people fall into such hypnoidal states (or "therapeutic trances") wherein they can experience spontaneously many of the classical

TABLE 1
State-Dependent Information Transduction from the Sociocultural to the
Cellular-Genetic Level and a Few Quotations from the Research
Literature That Epitomizes the Basic Focus at Each Level

SOCIOCULTURAL	"This state/context dependence theory has other attractive features as well. It creates a bridge between a growing body of laboratory work on neurophysiology and psychopharmacology on one hand, and ethnological field studies on the other hand. It offers a better solution to the problem of rationality. It is not much weakened by the fact that participants' accounts of ritual experience are often at odds with one another, and it easily accommodates evidence that the forms of some rituals change dramatically over time." (Kiefer & Cowan, 1979, p. 55)	Frank, 1963; Kiefer & Cowan, 1979; Reus et al., 1979; Wallace, 1966
MIND-BODY	"Inasmuch as meaningful experience arises from the binding or coupling of (1) a particular state or level of *arousal* with (2) a particular symbolic *interpretation* of that arousal, experience is *state-bound* and can thus be evoked either by inducing—"naturally," hypnotically or with the aid of drugs—the particular level of arousal, *or* by presenting some symbol of its interpretation such as an image, melody or taste. It is interesting to note that hormones that are known to play important roles in homeostatic regulation may also play an important role in regulating memory. This is perhaps not surprising in view of the central role of memory in adaptation." (McGaugh et al., 1984, p. 329)	Fischer, 1971a-c; Gold et al., 1985; Izquierdo, 1984, 1989; Izquierdo et al., 1988a,b; McGaugh, 1983; McGaugh et al., 1984; Rigter & Crabbe, 1979; Zornetzer, 1978
BRAIN-BODY	"Studies of state-dependent physiology are not merely descriptive; they are essential for a complete characterization of the cellular and molecular mechanisms underlying regulatory physiology." (Lydic, 1987, p. 6) "A major conceptual shift in neuroscience has been wrought by the realization that brain function is modulated by numerous chemicals in	Bergland, 1985; Brush & Levine, 1989; Lydic, 1987; Pert et al., 1985; Schmitt, 1984, 1986; Weingartner, 1978, 1986

addition to classical neurotransmitters. Many of these informational substances are neuropeptides, originally studied in other contexts as hormones, 'gut peptides,' or growth factors. Their number presently exceeds 50 and most, if not all, alter behavior and mood states.... Neuropeptides and their receptors thus join the brain, glands, and immune system in a network of communication between brain and body, probably representing the biochemical substrates of emotion." (Pert et al., 1985, p. 820s)

CELLULAR-GENETIC

"Transient expression of genes has been observed in physiological responses to stimuli such as heat shock and hormones....These observations suggest that learning and memory, like other processes of cellular differentiation, may involve a flow of information from membrane receptors to the genome.... By identifying the genes modulated by learning, it should be possible to characterize the cytoplasmic, and perhaps nuclear signaling systems that induce these events." (Goelet & Kandel, 1986, pp. 496–498)

Goelet & Kandel, 1986; Kandel, 1976, 1989; Kandel & Schwartz, 1985

phenomena of hypnosis such as age regression, dissociation and reversable amnesia ("reversable amnesia" is another name for state dependent memory). I have recently discussed (Rossi 1990a) in some detail how patients will commonly fall into the rest phase of their 90-120 minute Basic Rest Activity Cycle (BRAC) in any form of therapy where they are allowed to relax (eg. hypnosis, psychonalysis, the relaxation response, creative visualization, meditation). I have documented how the mental and behavioral characteristics of this ultradian rest are essentially identical with the classical phenomena of hypnosis and the hypnoid state (Rossi, 1982; 1986a and b). Three independent experimental studies have supported these observations by reporting statistically significant evidence that hypnotizability is related to circadian (Aldrich & Bernstein, 1987) and ultradian rhythms (Lippincott, 1990; Rossi, 1990b). These studies support the *Ultradian-Circadian Theory of Therapeutic Hypnosis* which I originally formulated as follows (Rossi, 1982):

> Individuals who override and disrupt their own ultradian cycles (by ignoring their natural periodic needs for rest in any extended performance situation, for example) are thereby setting in motion the basic physiological mechanisms of psychosomatic illness . . . Naturalistic therapeutic hypnosis provides a comfortable state wherein these ultradian cycles can simply normalize themselves and thus undercut the processes of psychosomatic illness at their psychophysiological source.
>
> A more exact understanding of how an individual's ultradian cycles manifest themselves could lead to the development of more deeply involving hypnotic states wherein the ultradian characteristics of therapeutic trance are utilized for psychosomatic healing. (pp. 26-27)

It is well known that state dependent memory, learning and behavior (SDMLB) can be encoded by our normal circadian and ultradian rhythms (Rossi & Ryan, 1986). I now hypothesize that the molecular mechanism for this mind-body process is the Is-receptor system of Figure 1 because so many of the information substances that modulate SDMLB are normally released in pulsate ultradian and circadian rhythms (Iranmanesh et al., 1989). Whether a memory is clear (so that it is recognized as "real") or vague (so that it can be dismissed as "fantasy") depends in part on the degree to which ultradian-circadian encoding of the life experience is similar to the state we are in when we recall it.

This dilemma of real, early events versus fantasies still plagues us today in modern investigation of sexual molestation that are currently shaking the foundations of Freudian analysis (Malcolm, 1984; Masson, 1985; Miller, 1985; Search, 1988). What is the answer? *State-dependent memory!* I hypothesize that the partial, fragmentary, easily reversible recall of early traumatic memories corresponds exactly with the reversible and partial character of SDMLB when we measure it under controlled conditions in the laboratory (Izquierdo et al., 1988b). Under the mild *"abaissement du niveau mental"* of "free association" in a light trance, patients can reactivate, at least in part, the information substances that encode their early sensory-perceptual-emotional processes that, in turn, reactivate their early traumatic memories. When the patient stands up and unwittingly returns to normal everyday consciousness, however, the "reality sense" (Janet's *fonction du réel*) of delicately encoded state dependent memories of the past tends to vanish and many patients say, "Oh, well, I probably just made it all up!"

But not only are stress, symptoms, and the psychopathology of everyday life encoded by ultradian related SDMLB, I believe that most of the normal associative processes of everyday consciousness (Erickson, Rossi, & Rossi, 1976) and peak experiences of everyday life can be accounted for on the same psychobiological basis. I have described how healing facilitated by Erickson's utilization approach operates by accessing the state-dependent memories encoding problems and submitting them to the patient's own inner resources for problem solving (Rossi, 1986; Rossi & Cheek, 1988; Rossi & Ryan, 1986). I hypothesize that meditation, ritual, and all manner of spiritual practices may be activating the same psychobiology of SDMLB (Kiefer & Cowan, 1979). On the molecular level they are all methods for turning on and turning off the information substances that modulate memory, learning, and behavior for healing as well as for illness.

THE BRAIN-BODY CONNECTION

A curious feature of Figure 1 is that it does not show any nerves connecting the brain with the body. How can this be correct? Up to now, we believed that nerves were like telephone wires connecting all our sensory-perceptual apparatus with our brain. Sensations came in through the nerves, and the brain made some conscious and unconscious connections and then sent out other impulses through the nerves to move our motor (muscles) apparatus. The first 100 years of research in psychophysiology has been primarily an investigation of such sensory-motor, stimulus-response processes.

For obvious reasons, however, most psychotherapists are nonplussed by all this research. It seems irrelevant to the main work of understanding a patient's *emotional states* and *psychological processes*. Nerves, however, are relatively big compared to molecules and the methods of microscopic anatomy developed before our current methods of molecular biology. It is therefore only natural that the first model of mind-body information transduction used nerves as the basic communication link.

It turns out, however, that the nervous system is only the "Johnny Come Lately" of communication on an evolutionary scale. Single-cell organisms do not have nerve cells. How does communication take place in single-cell forms of life? The obvious answer is via messenger molecules—the same information substances we have found as the modulators of memory, learning, and emotions. When life evolved into multicellular forms, it developed specialized cells to facilitate communication between one end of the organism and the other. These specialized cells are the nerves. They are something like telephone wires—they are very good for fast communication (on the order of milliseconds) for the type of fast stimulus-response mechanisms that are required to deal with the dangers of the environment.

Our emotional and psychological life, however, doesn't zip by in milliseconds. An emotion takes a few minutes to be fully experienced. Moods and psychobiological states can last for minutes, hours, days, half a lifetime. What is the cause of these enduring states over time? *Information substances!* Information substances that are constantly released on the cellular level and constantly modulate the messages and states of the nervous sytem. The nervous system has been called the hardware of the mind; the information substances are the software that actually encodes experience and tells the hardware how to operate and process mind-body information transduction.

Having said this, however, I must now backtrack a bit. Nerves are, of course, an important component in the messages that modulate mind/body communication. The distinguished neurosurgeon Richard Bergland (1979) has been a pioneer in research that indicates how neurons can serve as conduits for producing and transporting informational molecules (Bergland & Page, 1979; Bergland et al., 1980). In his recent "entry level" book that is excellent reading for psychotherapists, he summarizes the situation as follows (Bergland, 1985, p. 114):

The science of neuroendocrinology—the brain-to-pituitary link that was discerned by Hinsey, Wislocki, du Vigneaud, and Harris—is dependent upon hormones flowing within nerve axons. This phenomenon, axonal flow, was first noted by Ernst and Barta Scharrer, who suggested that hormone "managers" were being sent by the brain to peripheral organs through nerve fibers. For many decades it was assumed that axonal flow was always "down," that is, it moved away from the brain.

In the past decade it has become clear that hormones also move "up" nerve fibers from the body to the brain. This was noted using many different experimental techniques: hormones injected into the eye are carried back to the brain, tracers injected into the tongue are carried back to the brainstem and, most remarkably, substances injected into the thigh muscle may be carried into the spinal cord. The best-studied such molecule is "nerve growth factor."

It is now well known, for example, that a downward brain-body communication link takes place via the autonomic nervous system which can modulate the activity of lymphoid tissue; this is one of the basic mechanisms of psychoneuroimmunology (Bulloch, 1985). In addition, however, an upward communication link from the body to the brain takes place via informational molecules produced in white blood cells that modulate the brain (Pert, Ruff, Weber, & Herkenham, 1985).

The Neuropeptide Hypothesis of Consciousness and Catharsis

The most vivid demonstration of how informational substances produced by many neurons—often called "neuropeptides"—may be involved in psychotherapy in general and Ericksonian hypnotherapy in particular, is in the so-called catharsis reactions. You will recall that catharsis, the dramatic emotional release of suppressed and usually traumatic state dependent memories of significant life events, was regarded by the early Freud as the most significant turning point in his "talking cure." Most classical forms of psychotherapy from the rituals of native healers and shamen to modern encounter groups and psychoanalysis usually involve two stages: (1) an initial stage of symphathetic systems arousal with elevated heart rate, respiration, sweating, shouting, and tears that is typical of the emotional catharsis phase that can last from a few minutes to hours but usually requires around 20 or 30 minutes; (2) a relaxation phase then follows with feelings of comfort and gratitude for the new insights received and the emotional blocks worked through.

The initial catharsis phase can be so alarming that even audiences of professional psychotherapists who have observed my work have been concerned lest the patient somehow incurs serious or permanent emotional harm rather than therapy. Yet the patient invariably experiences the second phase of emotional insight, comfort, and well-being. Although a great deal of professional skill is in fact required to facilitate such a satisfactory therapeutic outcome, my personal sense of confidence is supported by what I presume to be one of mother nature's laws: "The Neuropeptide Hypothesis of Consciousness and Catharsis— The arousal and relaxation phases of cathartic psychotherapy and emotional insight are mediated by the release of ACTH and B-endorphin from their mother molecule, POMC (proopiomelanocortin), via the basic process of mind-body information transduction in the limbic-hypothalamic pituitary system (the funnel in Figure 1)."

Support for this neuropeptide hypothesis of consciousness and catharsis comes from the incredible recent developments in psychoendocrinology (Brush & Levine, 1989; de Wied, 1987) over the past decade. Most recently, for example, researchers (Iranmanesh et al., 1989) documenting the ultradian and circadian rhythms of hormone and neuropeptide informational substances have said, "... cortisol was considered to lead B-endorphin by 20 or 30 minutes. We conclude that B-endorphin is released physiologically in a pulsate manner with circadian and ultradian rhythmicity and a close temporal coupling to cortisol." (p. 1019) Since cortisol is part of the informational cascade that begins with the release of ACTH, this research provides at least indirect support for the neuropeptide hypothesis of psychotherapy. More direct support would require that we continuously monitor the release of ACTH, B-endorphin, cortisol, and related informational substances during the two-step process of arousal and relaxation in cathartic psychotherapy.

Another mechanism illustrating how nerves modulated by information substances can modulate memory, learning, and behavior as the basis of psychological experience is the recent report of how the information substance cholecystokinin (CCK-8S), a gastrointestinal hormone that is released when a good meal has been eaten, encodes memory. The researchers (Flood, Smith, & Morley, 1987) summarize their findings as follows (p. 834):

> Our data show that both feeding and peripherally administered CCK-8S enhance memory in mice. This gastrointestinal hormone seems to produce its effect on memory by activating ascending vagal fibers. Further studies are necessary to determine if CCK-8S is responsible for the entire effect of feeding on memory, or, as appears to be the case in the regulation of feeding, if a combination of gastrointestinal hormones act synergistically to produce this effect. The concentrations of CCK-8 achieved after administration of the optimum memory enhancing dose would be well within the physiological range seen after feeding in rodents. A link may have evolved between the release of gastric peptides and memory processing in the central nervous system because of the survival advantages for an animal to remember the details of a successful food-foraging expedition.

Memory, learning, and behavior associated with the presence of the information substance CCK in the mind-body are therefore state-dependent. The association of this state-dependent learning with evolutionary processes of survival has profound implications for a new theory of the evolution of memory, learning, and, ultimately, consciousness itself! Who will pursue these suggested links for creating a new view of the evolution of consciousness, meaning, and well-being? This has echoes for me in my pragmatic psychotherapeutic definition of "consciousness or mind as a process of self-reflective information transduction" (Rossi, 1986, p. 34).

Sex, Brain and Personality

In Figure 1, I emphasize SEX as another clear illustration of how the mind-body-cellular-genetic process of information transduction works. The sexual steroid hormones operate as primary messengers from the limbic-hypothalamic-pituitary system and pass right through the cell walls of the body to eventually turn on certain genes. These genes, in turn, produce messenger RNA, which transmits gene information to the protein factories of the cell (the ribosomes on the endoplastic reticulum) to produce proteins and other information substances that will eventually circulate back to the brain and modulate at least 50 different brain cites, including the locus ceruleus, which is implicated in dreaming. The sexual hormones that process information transduction from mind to gene comprise the most complete cybernetic psychobiological system known to date. Since psychotherapy and hypnosis are well known for their use as modulators of sexual behavior, I would expect that the crucial experiments relating sexual imagery to molecular responses at the cellular level could be most easily validated in this area.

As I mentioned earlier, 1988 was the year when the role of sexual hormones on behavior reached the headlines. Ben Johnson was caught using male steroids illegally to enhance his athletic performance in the 100-yard dash in the Olympics at Seoul, Korea. Of the hundreds of articles published about this incident around the globe, however, not one referred to this as an example of state-dependent memory, learning, and *behavior.* But a moment's reflection will confirm this: When the male steroids are injected into the body, not only is athletic performance temporarily enhanced, but there are also significant changes in mood, memory, and behavior: more aggression, sex, and all sorts of high and low moods and patterns of personality change. When the steroids are metabolized out of the body, the mood, personality, and performance changes return to normal; all the changes were reversible because they were state-dependent or the presence or absence of excess steroids.

The other headline-grabbing report on sexual steroids was the finding of Kimura and Hampson (1988) that women's mental skills are modulated by the monthly shifts in their estrogen levels. The *Science News* report of their work runs in part as follows (Weiss, 1988, p. 341):

The researchers back up with scientific rigor what until now was accumulated anecdotal evidence: that a woman's monthly ebb and flow of gender-related biochemicals has predictable cognitive and behavioral effects. The results were not related to mood changes and have nothing to do with premenstrual syndrome, they say.

Doreen Kimura and Elizabeth Hampson of the University of Western Ontario in London, Canada, found that when a woman experiences low estrogen levels—during and immediately after menstruation—she excels at tasks involving spatial relationships but performs poorly at complex motor tasks, including some involving speech.

In contrast, peak estrogen levels are associated with improved performance of motor and verbal tasks but difficulty with problems involving spatial relations. Peak estrogen levels occur briefly just before ovulation and again in the last 7 to 10 days before menstruation.

"This is the first demonstration of a reciprocal change in how one functions at given levels of sex hormones," Kimura says. "My guess is that this also happens in males."

She and other researchers plan similar studies on men, she said in Toronto at the annual meeting of the Society for Neuroscience. In addition to other, less documented male hormonal cycles, men's testosterone levels rise and fall every 24 hours.

The new research advances a long history of scientific inquiry into the neurological and behavioral effects of sex hormones on the brain. Animal studies confirm that the relative concentration of male or female hormones in utero significantly alters the neuronal organization of the fetus' developing brain. Apparently these differences in structure affect the brain's response to those hormones later in life. But in part because researchers have until now failed to look at the most relevant behavioral variables, Kimura says, documenting these effects in adult humans has proved difficult. The new research "supports the idea that male-female differences in cognitive patterns in humans are originally organized—and are still mediated by—sex hormones," she says.

... "Certainly there are gender differences on the average," says Estelle Ramey, professor emeritus at Georgetown University in Washington, D.C., a pioneer in the study of how sex hormones influence behavior. "The differences make it possible for the species to survive, among other things. If you take large groups of females and large groups of males and test them on a variety of traits, you'll find some [traits] that are socially induced and some biological."

. . . Finally, Kimura and others warn that there is little basis for assuming that women's behavior fluctuates more than men's just because women's cycles may be more biologically apparent. "There are cycles in the male, also," Ramey says, citing several studies of male behavioral periodicity. "Everything cycles that is living. Onions cycle, potatoes cycle, rats cycle. And men fall into that category also."

These experimental findings come as a striking confirmation of my extensive discussion of the relationship of Is-receptors, state-dependent memory, learning, and behavior, and women's consciousness in a recent volume (Rossi & Cheek, 1988). As in the case of Ben Johnson's lost gold medals, none of the published reports mention how these significant gender issues are examples of SDMLB in everyday life. All these conceptual connecting links are important for us as psychotherapists to understand, however, if we are to avoid the "Reductionistic Trap" mentioned earlier and achieve a more specific and effective focus in our daily work. Ericksonian approaches involve something more than "talking therapy" and "suggestion": We presume to access and facilitate the state-dependent Is-receptor communication systems at a molecular/genetic level that are the basis of psychobiological problems.

Far more difficult to establish within the bounds of current knowledge (although this is shifting very rapidly, of course) is how psychotherapy can facilitate healing in more controversial areas such as cancer and AIDS. To understand these we must look to the final bottom line of the cellular-genetic level: the protein kinases. The protein kinases are an important intracellular link in mind-body communication. The relationship between primary messengers of the body (like hormones) and secondary messengers of the cell (like cAMP), genes and protein kinases that are the bottom line in producing the actual metabolic changes that are needed for life and healing, is lucidly outlined by Wallace, King, and Sanders (1986, p. 862):

Apparently, at least a dozen other hormones stimulate the production of cAMP and use it as a second messenger. The list includes glucagon, ACTH, LH FSH, TSH, PTH, ADH, and calcitonin. But the question arises: How is the activity of so many hormones regulated if they all activate the same second messenger? The answer incorporates a number of important points. For instance, each cell has specific receptor sites and

462

thus are target cells to specific hormones (although they may contain receptor sites for more than one hormone). But equally important, cAMP, perhaps in all cases, activates a specific starting enzyme called a protein kinase. Protein kinases are a class of enzymes that activate other enzymes through the transfer of phosphate from ATP to that enzyme. So, in a sense, the situation is a "set-up"; that is, the specificity of hormonal action depends on which protein kinases are present in the cell. This ultimately depends on which structural (enzyme-encoding) genes are active. Because of these factors, a number of hormones can utilize cAMP as a second messenger.

It is facinating to realize that most of these hormones that serve as primary messengers between the brain and the secondary messengers of the cells of the body are released in ultradian and circadian rhythms (Iranmanesh et al, 1989; Veldhuis & Johnson, 1988). An *Ultradian-Circadian Theory of Therapeutic Hypnosis* that encodes SDMLB thus has a deep reach into the cell and its secondary messengers that signal genes into expression. This completes the cybrenetic flow of information among mind, brain, and body to the bottom line of all healing that I call "The Cell-Gene Connection."

THE CELL-GENE CONNECTION

The third level of mind-body communication in Figure 1 is what I call the *cell-gene connection*. Herein, I believe, the true genius of our age is becoming manifest. We are now on the threshold of understanding the molecular informational systems that are the ultimate basis of the life process itself. Please note once again that this is not a process of reductionism—we are not simply reducing the processes of life and mind to the molecular level. That is the most common misconception and source of "resistance" to be found within the psychological community today. The molecular biology of life cannot make do with purely reductionist and mechanistic concepts! As I mentioned earlier, the major leading texts in biochemistry, biology, and genetics are now using essentially *mentalistic* concepts such as "signaling, signal recognition particles, communication, information, sentient molecules, symbolic system, and metabolic codes" to conceptualize activity on the molecular level. To illustrate this, let us focus briefly on the role of "secondary messengers" that operate within all cells transmitting the primary signal (hormones, or as we now say, information substances) received by the cell receptor (the doorway to the interior of the cell) to the cytoplasm, the nucleus, and genes. The best known of these secondary messengers is cyclic AMP (cAMP). The significance of the evolutionary role of cAMP was discussed by Stryer (1988) in his highly regarded text on biochemistry (p. 983):

> Cyclic AMP has a regulatory role in bacteria, too, where it stimulates the transcription of certain genes. *It is evident that cycle AMP has a long evolutionary history as a regulatory molecule.* In bacteria, cyclic AMP is a hunger signal. It signifies an absence of glucose and leads to the synthesis of enzymes that can exploit other energy sources. In some mammalian cells, such as liver and muscle, cyclic AMP retains its ancient role as a hunger signal. However, it acts by stimulating a protein kinase rather than by enhancing the transcription of certain genes. Another difference is that *cyclic AMP in higher organisms mediates intracellular signaling rather than intercellular signaling.* The role of cyclic AMP in the life cycle of the slime mold *Dictyostelium discoideum*, a simple eucaryote, is especially interesting. When food is abundant, *Dictyostelium* exists as independent cells. When food becomes scarce, cyclic AMP is secreted by the free-living amoebae. Cyclic AMP serves as a chemoattractant that leads to the aggregation of *Dictyostelium* into a slug and to major changes in the gene expression.

Understand what is being said here. When food is abundant, this slime mold exists as a free-living, single-celled ameba. When food is scarce, each ameba sends out cAMP as a signal into the environment. When other free-living amebas receive this signal, they are attracted to its source. In this way, these amebas "find each other." They then clump together to form a multicellular organism—the slug—which can then survive in the changed environment to eventually produce spores that can resist even complete drying out and survive until it rains again. In the presence of water, each spore then becomes a free-living, single-cell ameba again until the environment dries out, again forcing the development of a multicellular slug for survival. What we are seeing here is a critical evolutionary step between single and multicellular life. cAMP is the signaling molecule that makes it possible.

Now this same cAMP molecule is still active as a secondary messenger within every cell of our bodies. George Engle, a pioneer in mind-body theory with over 300 publications to his credit, speculates about the role of cAMP in human psychology as follows (1985, pp. 16-17; quoted in Foss & Rothenberg, 1987, pp. 272-273):

For me, not only were the "supplies" that I lost upon my father's death multiplex and peculiar for me, but also their internal representatives derived not just from my father-relationship but from the whole history of my social relationships since birth. But note that my social relationships actually had their beginnings in a biological context, in the transition at birth from the biologic mutuality of transplacental nutrition to the social mutuality of oral feeding at my mother's breasts. In that process the recurring cycles of hunger-feeding-satiation that I experienced as a neonate not only were regulators of my earliest social relations, they also established a permanent linkage between processes implicated in maintaining cellular nutrition and processes implicated in sustaining human relationship, literally linking cAMP and feelings that reflect human ties....

The very fact that my apprehending of my father's death includes use of symbolic processes historically connected since my birth with regulation of biological supplies in itself predetermines that connections could exist even at the level of molecular symbols. Obviously our inner world of symbols is not a separate world unto itself, as Cartesian dualism would have us believe; it is an integral part of a complex multi-layered network intimately involved in biological regulation even at the cellular level.

How is this related to cancer? When we use hypnosis and imagery to facilitate healing in cancer, what are we actually trying to do? In brief, many genes (about 80 are commonly known) are involved in regulating normal growth processes of the cell. These are now sometimes called *protooncogenes*. When these normal gene activities are interfered with by, say, a foreign virus, their action may be accelerated out of control so that they become oncogenes; that is, they are now responsible for the wild, out-of-control growth we call cancer. The actual mechanism by which this out-of-control growth takes place is at the enzymatic level of protein kinases (Hunter, 1987a). How do these protein kinases operate? Tony Hunter, a molecular biologist at the Salk Institute in La Jolla, California, hypothesizes that they operate as transistors for the signals regulating cellular processes at the molecular level (Hunter, 1987b, p. 826):

... A reasonable answer to the question of why there are so many protein kinases would be that they serve as major components of the essential regulatory circuitry of the cell. To draw an electronic analogy, one might term them the transistors of the cell. In electronic circuits transistors are used either as simple on/off switches or as amplifiers for an electric current. Transistors commonly have two inputs, which regulate current flow and gain, and a single output. Protein kinases share many properties with transistors that make them ideal components of biological feedback and amplification pathways, as well as switching or signalling systems.

To pursue this analogy, the ability of protein kinases to phosphorylate other proteins can be considered the basis for signal (current) transmission, with phosphorylated substrates being the output. This basic transmission activity can be regulated positively or negatively by several types of input such as specific ligands or by phosphorylation of the protein kinases themselves. In this manner the phosphorylation signal (enzymatic activity) can be turned on and off, and the "gain" of amplification of the signal can be regulated as the specific activity of the enzyme is changed. In some ways, however, protein kinases are more sophisticated control units than single transistors, being more akin to integrated chips.

Although we currently know of only 100 protein kinases, Hunter predicts that their number will soon reach 1,000. What do we as psychotherapists know of the protein kinases we are modulating when we attempt to facilitate healing of cancer by use of imagery, symbols, and metaphors? Is it any wonder that our results in this area are so notoriously unreliable?

To enhance the reliability of our approaches to mind-body healing at the cellular-genetic level we need to understand the fundamental difference between *alterations in the structure of genes* and the *modulation of gene expression.* Alterations in the structure of genes is a evolutionary event based upon chance errors in copying the chemical structure of the gene; Western science maintains that mind has absolutely nothing to do with such changes in the structure of genes. The modulation of gene expression, however, involves the turning on and off of certain genes by many of the same hormones and secondary messengers that encode the state dependent processes of mind and behavior. Western science maintains the possibility of mind-gene communication by this path. The most articulate expression of this possibility comes from Eric Kandel (1989) who has done some of the most innovative research on the molecular basis of mind, memory and learning at the genetic level.

The genetic data on schizophrenia and on depression indicate that these diseases involve alteration *in the structure of genes*. By contrast, the data now emerging on learning suggest that neurotic illnesses acquired by learning, which can often respond to psychotherapy, might involve alterations *in the regulation of gene expression*. In this context, it is important to realize, as I have emphasized earlier, that genes have two regions: a regulatory region and a coding region. The *regulatory region* usually lies upstream of the coding region and consists of two types of DNA elements. One type of DNA element is called the promoter. This is the site where the enzyme RNA polymerase binds before it reads and transcribes the gene into messenger RNA. The second type of DNA region is called the *enhancer region*. It recognizes protein signals that determine in which cells, and when, the coding region will be transcribed by the polymerase. Whether the RNA polymerase binds and transcribes the gene and how often it does so in any given period of time is determined by a small number of proteins, transcriptional regulators that bind to different segments of the upstream enhancer region. Development, hormones, stress, and learning are all factors that can alter the binding of the transcriptional regulator proteins to the regulatory regions of genes. I suggest that at least certain neurotic illnesses (or components of them) represent a reversible defect in gene regulation, which is produced by learning and that may be due to altered binding of specific proteins to certain upstream regions that control the expression of certain genes.

According to this view, schizophrenia and depression would be due primarily to heritable genetic changes in neuronal and synaptic function in a population carrying one or more mutations. By contrast, *neurotic illnesses might represent alterations in neuronal and synaptic function produced by environmentally induced modulation of gene expression. Insofar as psychotherapy works and produces long-term learned changes in behavior, it may do so by producing alterations in gene expression.* Needless to say, psychotic illness, although primarily caused by inherited alterations in gene structure, may also involve a secondary disturbance in environmentally acquired gene expression. (pp. 122-123) (Italics ours)

Humans have about 100,000 genes. Approximately 30,000 of these are called "Housekeeping Genes" because their expression is regulated every moment of our lives by the continuous messages they receive from mind and brain via the primary hormonal signaling system. I would therefore speculate that about one third of our genes are available for modulation by mind methods. How can we turn such speculations into verifiable experimental designs?

A NEW RESEARCH PROGRAM

Obviously what we desperately need is a new kind of research program to explore the incredibly rich and varied experimental designs suggested by the hypothesis of a psychobiologically oriented form of therapeutic hypnosis that facilitates healing via the *mind–Is–receptor–gene* connection. Table 1 outlines four levels of research ranging from the sociocultural to the cellular-genetic. I have cited a few basic research designs that can serve as heuristic models for future research on each level. A more detailed outline of 128 research designs can be found in Rossi and Cheek (1988). I am currently serving as a consultant to a few research groups that are moving into this area; I would be happy to facilitate and coordinate any others who are fired with enthusiasm. I believe our therapeutic approaches to mind-body healing will continue to be unreliable and unbelievable until we actually demonstrate by controlled experiment just how our mind methods are facilitating information transduction by modulating molecular processes at the cellular-genetic level.

A new possibility for investigating how mind methods may modulate gene expression is suggested by the recent finding that the psychosomatic problem of psoriasis is mediated at the genetic level. Elder et al. (1989) have been able to document that psoriasis is mediated on the molecular-genetic level by an *informational substance* called "Transforming Growth Factor alpha" (TGF-a) interacting with the Epidermal Growth Factor receptor. They relate this to the genetic level as follows: "Results demonstrate quantitatively that the TGF-a gene is over-expressed in lesional psoriatic epidermis and show that TGF-a is a potential mediator of the epidermal and angiogenic components of the inflammatory hyperproliferative response" (p. 812).

It now remains for an enterprising mind-body research team to explore the hypnotherapeutic healing of psoriasis to determine if the cases that respond with healing do, in fact, evidence a reduction in the over expression of the TGF-a gene. An interesting control would be easy to incorporate into this research. We would expect, as is typical of most clinical work with hypnosis, that there would be some cases that will not respond with healing. The mind-gene connection will not be successful in these instances, and we would expect in these "control cases" that the patient would evidence no reduction in the over-expression of the TGF-a gene. Once we establish the validity of the mind modulation of gene expression in this way we will be in a position to systematically explore other variables we can use to enhance the reliability of mind-body healing.

SUMMARY

The psychobiological theory outlined in this chapter has traveled far indeed beyond the limits of current clinical practice. How can we reconnect this evolving psychobiological theory with Ericksonian approaches to psychotherapy in general and hypnotherapy in particular? I believe this point of connection can be found in what Erickson called his "naturalistic" (Erickson, 1958/1980) or "utilization" (Erickson, 1959/1980) approach.

It was my effort to update Erickson's understanding of the psychoneurophysiological basis of hypnosis that originally led to my current studies in the psychobiology of mind-body healing (Rossi & Ryan, 1986). I regard the information-receptor system on the molecular level, together with its phenomenological manifestation in state-dependent memory, learning, and behavior, as the most current update of what Erickson called the "psychoneurophysiological basis of hypnosis." This is a vision we can carry into the future when we will be able to say of our work that it is "more than a metaphor."

REFERENCES

Abramovitz, R. (1974). *Cybernetics of Cybernetics*. Urbana: University of Illinois.

Aldrich, K., & Bernstein, D. (1987). The effect of time of day on hypnotizability. *International Journal of Clinical & Experimental Hypnosis, 35*(3), 141-145.

Bergland, R. (1979). Neurosecretory bodies within the median-eminence in association with pituitary tumors. *Lancet, 2*(8155), 1270-1272.

Bergland, R. (1985). *The Fabric of Mind*. New York: Viking.

Bergland, R., & Page, R. (1979). Pituitary-brain vascular relation: New paradigm. *Science, 204* (4388), 18-24.

Bergland, R., Blume, H., Hamilton, A., Monica, P., & Paterson, R. (1980). Adrenocorticotropic hormone may be transported directly from the pituitary to the brain. *Science, 210*(4469), 541-543.

Brush, F., & Levine, S. (Eds) (1989). *Psychoendocrinology.* New York: Academic Press.

Bulloch, K. (1985). Neuroanatomy of lymphoid tissue: A review. In R. Guillemin & M. Cohn (Eds.), *Neural Modulation of Immunity* (pp. 111-141). New York: Raven Press.

Darnell, J., Lodish, H., & Baltimore, D. (1986). *Molecular Cell Biology.* New York: Scientific American Books.

de Wied, D. (1983). Neuropeptides and behavior. In M. Parnham & J. Bruinvels (Eds.), *Discoveries in Pharmacology. Vol. I. Psycho-and Neuro-pharmacology.* New York: Elsevier Science.

de Wied, D. (1987). The neuropeptide concept. In E. de Kloet, V. Wiegant, & D. de Wied (Eds.), *Progress in Brain Research, 72.* New York: Elsevier Science.

Elder, J., Fisher, G., Lindquist, P., et al. (1989). Overexpression of Transforming Growth Factor a in Psoriatic Epidermis. *Science, 243,* 811-814.

Erickson, M. (1943a/1980). Experimentally elicited salivary and related responses to hypnotic visual hallucinations confirmed by personality reactions. In E. Rossi (Ed.), *The Collected Papers of Milton H. Erickson on Hypnosis. Vol. II. Hypnotic Alteration of Sensory, Perceptual, and Psychophysical Processes* (pp. 175-178). New York: Irvington.

Erickson, M. (1943b/1980). Hypnotic investigation of psychosomatic phenomena: A controlled experimental use of hypnotic regression in the therapy of an acquired food intolerance. In E. Rossi (Ed.), *The Collected Papers of Milton H. Erickson on Hypnosis. Vol. II. Hypnotic Alteration of Sensory, Perceptual, and Psychophysical Processes* (pp. 169-174). New York: Irvington.

Erickson, M. (1943c/1980). Hypnotic investigation of psychosomatic phenomena: Psychosomatic interrelationships studied by experimental hypnosis. In E. Rossi (Ed.), *The Collected Papers of Milton H. Erickson on Hypnosis. Vol. II. Hypnotic Alteration of Sensory, Perceptual, and Psychophysical Processes* (pp. 145-156). New York: Irvington.

Erickson, M. (1943d/1980). Hypnotic investigation of psychosomatic phenomena: The development of aphasialike reactions from hypnotically induced amnesias. In E. Rossi (Ed.), *The Collected Papers of Milton H. Erickson on Hypnosis. Vol. II. Hypnotic Alteration of Sensory, Perceptual, and Psychophysical Processes* (pp. 157-168). New York: Irvington.

Erickson, M. (1958/1980). Naturalistic techniques of hypnotherapy. In E. Rossi (Ed.)., *The Collected Papers of Milton H. Erickson on Hypnosis. I. The Nature of Hypnosis and Suggestion* (pp. 168-176). New York: Irvington.

Erickson, M. (1959/1980). Further clinical techniques of hypnosis: Utilization techniques. In E. Rossi (Ed.), *The Collected Papers of Milton H. Erickson on Hypnosis. I. The Nature of Hypnosis and Suggestion* (pp. 177-205). New York: Irvington.

Erickson, M., Rossi, E., & Rossi, S. (1976). *Hypnotic Realities.* New York: Irvington.

Fischer, E., & Lipson, C. (1988). *Thinking About Science: Max Delbruck and the Origins of Molecular Biology.* New York: Norton.

Fischer, R. (1971a). Arousal-statebound recall of experience. *Diseases of the Nervous System, 32,* 373-382.

Fischer, R. (1971b). The "flashback": Arousal-statebound recall of experience. *Journal of Psychedelic Drugs, 3,* 31-39.

Fischer, R. (1971c). A cartography of ecstatic and meditative states. *Science, 174,* 897-904.

Flood, J., Smith, G., & Morley, J. (1987). Modulation of memory processing by cholecystokinin: Dependence on the vagus nerve. *Science, 236,* 832-834.

Foss, L., & Rothenberg, K. (1987). *The Second Medical Revolution: From Biomedicine to Infomedicine.* Boston: Shambhala.

Frank, J. (1963). *Persuasion and Healing.* New York: Shocken Books.

Goelet, P., & Kandel, E. (1986). Tracking the flow of learned information from membrane to receptors to geneome. *Trends in Neurosciences, 9*(10), 492-499.

Gold, P., Weinberger, N., & Sternberg, D. (1985). Epinephrine-induced learning under anesthesia: Retention performance at several training testing intervals. *Behavioral Neuroscience, 99*(4), 1019-1022.

Hunter, T. (1987a). The role of phosphorylation in growth control and malignant transformation. In L. Heilmeyer (Ed.), *Signal Transduction and Protein Phosphorylation* (pp. 329-344). NATO ASI Series A: Life Sciences, Vol. 13.

Hunter, T. (1987b). A thousand and one protein kinases. *Cell, 50,* 823-829.

Iranmanesh, A., Lizarradle, G., Johnson, M., & Veldhuis, J. (1989). Circadian, ultradian, and episodic release of Bendorphin in men, and its temporal coupling with cortisol. *Journal of Clinical Endocrinology and Metabolism, 68*(6), 1019-1025.

Izquierdo, I. (1984). Endogenous state dependency: Memory depends on the relation between the neurohumoral and hormonal states present after training and at the time of testing. In G. Lynch, J. McGaugh, & N. Weinberger (Eds.), *Neurobiology of Learning and Memory* (pp. 333-350). New York: Guilford Press.

Izquierdo, I. (1989). Different forms of post-training memory processing. *Behavioral & Neural Biology, 51,* 171-202.

Izquierdo, I., Netto, C., Chaves, M., Dalmaz, C., Pereira, M., Ferreira, M., & Siegfried, B. (1988a). The organization of memories into "files." In J. Delacour & C. Levy (Eds.), *Systems with Learning and Memory Abilities.* Amsterdam: Elsevier.

Izquierdo, I., Netto, C., Dalmaz, C., Chaves, M., Pereira, M., & Siegfried, B. (1988b). Construction and reconstruction of memories. *Brazilian Journal of Medical and Biological Research, 21,* 9-25.

Janet, P. (1925). *Psychological Healing: A Historical and Clinical Study. Vols. 1 and 2.* Translated by Eden & Cedar Paul. London: George Allen & Unwin.

Kandel, E. (1976). *Cellular Basis of Behavior.* San Francisco: Freeman.

Kandel, E. (1983). From metapsychology to molecular biology: Explorations into the nature of anxiety. *American Journal of Psychiatry, 140*(10), 1277–1293.

Kandel, E., & Schwartz, G. (1985). *Principles of Neural Science* (Third Edition). New York: Elsevier.

Kandel, E. (1989). Genes, verve cells, and the remembrance of things past. *Journal of Neuropsychiatry, 1*(2), 103–125.

Kiefer, C., & Cowan, J. (1979). State/context dependence and theories of ritual. *Journal of Psychological Anthropology, 2*(1), 53–58.

Kimura, D., & Hampson, E. (1988). Reciprocal effects of hormonal fluctuations on human motor and perceptual skill. *Behavioral Neuroscience, 102*(3), 456–459.

Lippincott, B. (1990). A pilot study of the ultradian theory of therapeutic hypnosis. Paper presented at the thirty second annual scientific meeting of the American Society of Clinical Hypnosis, Orlando, March 27, 1990.

Lydic, R. (1987). State-dependent aspects of regulatory physiology. *FASEB Journal, 1*(1), 6–15.

Malcolm, J. 1984. *In the Freud Archives.* New York: Knopf.

Masson, J. (1985). *The Assault on Truth.* Neww York: Penguin Books.

McGaugh, J. (1983). Preserving the presence of the past: Hormonal influences on memory storage. *American Psychologist, 38*(2), 161–173.

McGaugh, J., Liang, K., Bennett, C., & Sternberg, D. (1984). Adrenergic influences on memory storage: Interaction of peripheral and central systems. In G. Lynch, J. McGaugh, & N. Weinberger (Eds.), *Neurobiology of Learning and Memory* (pp. 313–332). New York: Guilford Press.

Miller, A. (1985). *Thou Shalt Not Be Aware.* London: Pluto Press.

Newsweek. (1988). The doped-up games. October 10, pp. 54–57.

Pert, C., Ruff, M., Weber, R., & Herkenham, M. (1985). Neuropeptides and their receptors: A psychosomatic network. *Journal of Immunology, 135*(2), 820s–826s.

Pert, C., Ruff, M., Spencer, D., & Rossi, E. (1989) Self-refective molecular psycholog. *Psychological Perspectives, 20*(1), 213–221.

Reus, V., Weingartner, H., & Post, R. (1979). Clinical implications of state-dependent learning. *American Journal of Psychiatry, 136*(7), 927–931.

Rigter, H., & Crabbe, J. (1979). Modulation of memory by pituitary hormones. *Vitamins and Hormones, 37.* New York: Academic Press.

Rossi, E. (1982). Hypnosis and ultradian cycles: A new state(s) theory of hypnosis? *The American Journal of Clinical Hypnosis, 25*(1), 21–32.

Rossi, E. (1986). *The Psychobiology of Mind-Body Healing: New Concepts in Therapeutic Hypnosis.* New York: Norton.

Rossi, E. (1986a). Altered states of consciousness in everyday life: The ultradian rhythms. In B. Wolman & M. Ullman (Eds.), *Handbook of Altered States of Consciousness* (pp. 97–132). New York: Van Nostrand.

Rossi, E. (1986b). Hypnosis and ultradian rhythms. In B. Zilbergeld, M. Edelstien, & D. Araoz (Eds.), *Hypnosis: Questions and Answers* (pp. 17–21). New York: W. W. Norton.

Rossi, E., & Smith, M. (1990a). The eternal quest: The hidden rhythms of stress and healing in everyday life. *Psychological Perspectives, (22),* 1.

Rossi, E. (1990b). A clinical experimental assessment of the ultradian theory of therapeutic hypnosis. Paper presented at the Thirty second annual scientific meetings of the American Society of Cinical Hypnosis, March 27, 1990.

Rossi, E., & Cheek, D. (1988). *Mind-Body Therapy: Methods of Ideodynamic Healing in Hypnosis.* New York: Norton.

Rossi, E., & Ryan, M. (1986). *Mind-Body Communication in Hypnosis. Vol. 3. The Seminars, Workshops, and Lectures of Milton H. Erickson.* New York: Irvington.

Rossi, E., & Ryan, M. (1990). *Creative Choice in Hypnosis. Vol. 4. The Seminars, Workshops, and Lectures of Milton H. Erickson.* New York: Irvington.

Schmitt, F. (1984). Molecular regulators of brain function: A new view. *Neuroscience, 13,* 991.

Schmitt, F. (1986). Chemical information processing in the brain: Prospect from retrospect. In L. Iversen & E. Goodman (Eds.), *Fast and Slow Signalling in the Nervous System* (pp. 239–243). New York: Oxford University Press.

Search, G. (1988). *The Last Taboo: Sexual Abuse of Children.* New York: Penguin Books.

Stryer, L. (1988). *Biochemistry* (Third Edition). New York: Freeman and Company.

Veldhuis, J., & Johnson, M. (1988). Operating characteristics of the hypothalamo-pituitary-gonadal axis in men: Circadian, ultradian, and pulsatile release of prolactin and its temporal coupling with luteinizing hormone. *Journal of Clinical Endocrinology and Metabolism,* 67(1), 116–123.

von Foerster, H. (1984). *Observing Systems.* Seaside, CA: Intersystems Publications.

Wallace, A. (1966). *Religion: An Anthropological View.* New York: Random House.

Wallace, R., King, J., & Sanders, G. (1986). *Biology of the Science of Life* (Second Edition). Glenview, IL: Scott Foresman & Company.

Watson, J., Hopkins, N., Roberts, J., Steitz, J., & Weiner, A. (1985). *Molecular Biology of the Gene* (Fourth Edition). Menlo Park, CA: Benjamin/Cummings.

Weingartner, H. (1978). Human state dependent learning. In B. Ho, D. Richards, & D. Chute (Eds.), *Drug Discrimination and State-Dependent Learning* (pp. 361–382). New York: Academic Press.

Weingartner, H. (1986). Memory: The roots of failure. *Psychology Today,* January, 6–7.

Weiss, R. (1988). Women's skills linked to estrogen levels. *Science News,* 134(22), 341.

Zornetzer, S. (1978). Neurotransmitter modulation and memory: A new neuropharmacological phrenology? In M. Lipton, A. di Mascio, & K. Killam (Eds.), *Psychopharmacology: A Generation of Progress.* New York: Raven Press.

CHAPTER 34

Modeling and Role-Modeling with Psychophysiological Problems

Helen L. Erickson

Discussions describing the link between mind and body have repeatedly surfaced in society. The ancient Greeks argued that physical illness was caused by evil spirits and healed by divine or sacred interventions. Later, the work of Hippocrates and Plato emphasized factors internal to the individual. In *The Republic,* Plato defined health as a harmony between mind and body. Subsequently, others have proposed various types of linkages. Some, such as Freud (1924) and Dunbar (1935), suggested that specific emotions were related to specific cell and tissue responses, proposing that biophysical behaviors were symbolic of psychological needs or conflicts that were linked to specific organic systems. Others (Alexander, 1950; Cannon, 1918) supported the view that a mind-body linkage existed but argued that the relationship was more generalized and less symbolic. Unmet or repressed needs were identified as stimuli related to biophysical responses by way of the autonomic nervous system. From this frame of reference, somatic symptoms had no specific psychic meaning but were considered to be the end result of prolonged physiological states which were the biophysical companions of unmet needs.

Selye's (1956) work provided further evidence that a *reactive* process between mind and body could result in physiological outcomes which, when prolonged, could produce tissue change and disease. The adrenal gland played a key role in the processes described by Selye. Others have studied the hypothalmus-pituitary-adrenal linkage (also known as the HPA axis). For example, during the seventies, the work of Friedman (1977) linking the Type A personality to cardiovascular disease stimulated considerable research. Most recently, considerable research has developed from the work initiated by Ader (1981) that linked the immune system to the HPA axis. The current thrust of investigations is to consider the feedback loop (body to mind) as well as the direct effects of mind on body.

Interestingly, recent literature describes reactive processes with the outcome of tissue damage, disease, or ailment. That is, emphasis has been placed on studying the relationship between psychosocial stimuli and *negative biophysical responses*—responses that interfere with the health and growth of humans. Stated in another way, this literature primarily addresses how psychosocial stressors might serve as stimuli to initiate biophysical responses which (over time) result in biophysical ailment and/or disease. This work provides an understanding of what might go wrong, but contains little information for therapists who intend to help people *regain health or prevent disease proactively*.

In contrast, the work of Milton Erickson (c.f. Rossi & Ryan, 1986) was built on an assumption that mind-body linkages existed and that they provided a means for designing *proactive interventions aimed at building resources, facilitating growth, restoring holistic health, and assisting the client in achieving maximum potential*. An additional underlying assumption was that these linkages were both psychophysiological and physiopsychological. That is, the mind can produce stimuli that affect the body, and vice versa. The recent work of Rossi (1986) has provided both the theoretical explanations and elaborations of the multiple pathways between mind and body. More important, it has provided a fundamental understanding of the potential for proactive therapeutic interventions as well as implications for reactive therapeutic interventions. Rossi has taken the step to link the most finite constituents of the mind with the most finite components of the body. Investigators may thus be able to find an interaction between "learned responses" and genetic bases. Scientists often view these two factors as dichotomous, and therefore treat them in a reductionist manner. The attitude has been, "It's in your genes; therefore you are helplessly at high risk." Or, "It is learned and therefore we should be able to affect new learning without consideration of the genetic factors." Rossi's work provides a new way to think about this problem. He provides a basis for understanding the *mechanisms* of mind-body linkages and therefore the basis for planning clinical care.

Two major difficulties I've found in working with people who have biophysical problems as a result of prolonged psychosocial stressors are that they have learned to compartmentalize the various subsystems (i.e., psychosocial, cognitive, and biophysical), and thus they isolate their psychosocial needs, or they have learned that the only way to get psychosocial needs met is through biophysical illness. In the first instance, excessive stress in one subsystem effects a strain in another. This can go either way—psychosocial stressors producing biophysical responses, or biophysical stress producing psychosocial responses. Such responses reduce the tension created by the original stressors and thus produce primary gain. Simply stated, these individuals get physically ill because they are unable to mobilize resources needed to contend with psychosocial stressors. Treatment focuses on reducing the stressors and increasing the resources.

Secondary gain is more difficult to manage. Those who have learned that psychosocial needs can be met through physiological illness experience secondary gain. They have limited resources due to prolonged unmet needs, morbid grief, and long-standing developmental deficits. Because of these major deficits, these people have great difficulty in giving up inadequate and/or inappropriate coping processes. Secondary gain processes can be either conscious or unconscious.

Both types of process need to be considered when working with people who have psychophysiological problems, i.e., people who have physical illness due to psychosocial deficits. My intention in this chapter is to present modeling and role-modeling as a paradigm that facilitates working with such people. This model is based on two major assumptions: First, mind and body relationships exist. Therefore, emotions affect the biophysiological functioning of the body and both disease *and* healing processes; second, information regarding the potential effects of these linkages requires that the assessment process start with an understanding of the client's model of the world.

MODELING AND ROLE MODELING

When I asked what I could do to help people, Milton Erickson often responded with a simple comment, "Model and role-model." When I asked him to explain what this meant, a story was told, an assignment was given, or experiences in daily life were presented. Over a number of years I came to a personal understanding of the phrase "model and role-model" (Erickson, 1984, 1988; Erickson, Tomlin, & Swain, 1988). *Modeling* is the process of stepping into the world of another in order to build a mirror image of that unique world. This requires that the therapist use every sense possible when assessing the situation. That is, the therapist assimilates cues through all senses (e.g., seeing, smelling, hearing, touching) in order to fully *model the client's perceptions* and the *context* of those perceptions. Modeling also requires interpreting and analyzing both the perceptions and their contexts.

Once the client's world has been fully modeled, role modeling can occur. *Role-modeling* is the process of designing strategies to help clients attain a maximum level of satisfaction in carrying out the various roles they perceive as important. Thus, role modeling involves helping clients redesign their model of the world so that they are able to live happy, fulfilling lives.

The focus of my practice is both psychophysiological and physio-psychological. This distinction is simple: In the former, psychosocial stimuli effect physiological responses; in the latter, physiological stimuli effect psychological responses. In either case, the feedback loop of mind to body to mind is assumed. Furthermore, the explicit linkages described by Rossi (1986) (e.g., mind to body, brain to body, and brain to cell) are accepted.

There are several additional assumptions that provide a base of reference for modeling and role-modeling. While these have been described in detail in other sources (Erickson, 1984, 1988; Erickson, Tomlin, & Swain, 1988) I will cite here five specific concepts and their application to practice: *holism, inherent potential for growth, affiliated individuation, lifespan processes,* and *self-care knowledge*. The assumption that people are composed of multiple subsystems that interface and interrelate is akin to holism. *Holism* is defined as the whole that is greater than the sum of the parts. This is basic to mind-body linkages and implies that the mind has the potential for cognitive learning as well as multiple emotions.

The notion that people have an *inherent potential for growth* implies that growth *can and will* occur if the environment is conducive to growth. That is, when basic, instinctual needs are satisfied, the individual is inherently driven toward growth.

The need for affiliated individuation is also instinctual. *Affiliated individuation* is a need or desire for a sense of affiliation or connection with a significant other that is constantly balanced with a sense of individuation or autonomy from that significant object. The degree of affiliation to individuation varies given different lifespan tasks.

Lifespan processes also are assumed. People are challenged continuously with the tasks of normal development. These tasks are sequentially ordered, epigenetic, and chronologically based. Residual from each task provides a base for management of the next. This residual is psychological, physiological, and cognitive. Thus, biophysical and cognitive development is directly linked to psychosocial assets or deficits.

Self-care knowledge provides insights regarding such residual; self-care knowledge (Erickson, 1984; Erickson, Tomlin, & Swain, 1988) is the primary source of information for therapists. Simply stated, self-care knowledge means that the individual knows (at some level) what has interfered with his growth processes and what will help him be healthier.

Implications for the therapist using modeling and role-modeling are that: (1) they must accept the person's state of development with the understanding that growth will occur if a therapeutic environment can be established; (2) the emphasis of the treatment is on the strengths and worthiness of the individual, rather than the weakness or deficits; (3) need satisfaction, coupled with continuous developmental processes, is based on the lifespan process of object attachment, loss, grief, and reattachment; and (4) interventions must be designed to match the need status, developmental residual, and object attachment-loss processes. This means that interventions are designed to specifically match the developmental task at hand regardless of the individual's chronological age. Thus, a 65-year-old adult who is working on the developmental tasks of the first three years of life while challenged by the task of middle age will need assistance with both age-related tasks.

CASE EXAMPLES

The following cases illustrate how I have used modeling and role-modeling to help people build, reframe, and mobilize psychosocial resources needed to effect healthy bodies.

Case One

Along with colleagues at a midwestern university, I conducted an outpatient research study on the effects of modeling and role-modeling on subjects with hypertension. The consent form stated that I was interested in helping people with hypertension to identify their concerns, worries, and needs and to find alternative ways to manage these. The language had been purposefully designed to imply that hypertension could be caused by psychosocial stressors and to indicate that with assistance, healthier ways to manage *normal stress* responses could be found by the subjects themselves. The goal of the consent form was to indirectly imply that my concern was with the person, not the disease, and that I would focus on those aspects of everyday life that could be linked to physiological responses gone awry. Furthermore, I wanted to suggest that individuals know what is wrong and what will help build or mobilize resources needed to deal with the stress of life. Thus, emphasis was placed on the client's perceptions of cause and solution, rather than a reductionistic approach emphasizing treatment of the symptom.

Mr. M., a 53-year-old scholar and full professor at a large university, presented himself for the study. He lingered outside the door. His physical stance indicated that he was guarded and uncertain about entering my office. While his attire suggested individuality, his motor responses indicated conservatism. As he introduced himself, he extended his right hand, glanced up, briefly making eye contact, and then slouched into himself. He stated that he had been under medical care for two or more years for hypertension and was currently taking medication four times a day. In spite of this, his blood pressure ran between 160/95 and 180/105 so he had decided to see me. I stated that I was interested in people who had hypertension and that I believed that at some level they knew what was related to such symptoms and what would help them be healthier. I told him that I believed that all people had needs that motivated their behavior, that unmet needs affected them as people, and that they wanted to get these needs met in a way that would be acceptable to others. I then asked him if he would like to participate in the study and stated that if he did he would have to come in, fill out some forms, and have his blood pressure taken. I indicated that he could select any one of a number of chairs in the room near a table, and I placed the forms on the table near my choice of seat. He immediately sat down, completed the forms and handed them to me. At this point I rolled up his shirtsleeve and placed the blood pressure cuff, while talking quietly about the importance of knowing what we know, even though we aren't always sure we know it. I recorded his vital signs, including blood pressure, pulse, and respirations. As I talked with him, I paced my respirations with his respirations and paced my rate of speech with his pulse. I asked him to sit back in his chair, make himself as comfortable as possible, and when he was ready, to tell me whatever he would like. I mentioned that at first he might notice the light coming in the windows and/or the sounds in the hall, but soon those probably would not be noticeable. I also suggested that he might begin to notice a change in his pulse rate or depth of respirations or other aspects of his body *as he became more and more comfortable and relaxed.* I did not specify what he should talk about or when he should start—only that he knew things that he didn't even know he knew, and the more he attended to this knowledge, the more he would know what he wanted to know. As he settled in I used nonverbal pacing to model his world. *That is I matched his breathing, imitated his body posture, position, movements, and facial affect as much as possible. I also continued to pace his voice tones, pitch, and rhythm during our opening interactions.* His initial description of the situation was that he was "hypertense" all of the time because his wife nagged him continuously. While he loved her and wanted to remain married, she never seemed to approve of him or the decisions he made. Her complaints ranged from the way he took out the garbage to his lack of productivity in scholarship. She complained about the way he drove the car, what he bought at the grocery store, the clothes he wore, and how he interacted with their three children. She stated that he sometimes acted like one of the kids, rather than the father. He tended to agree with her assessment. While he had acquired an international reputation for his scholarship, he constantly felt gloomy and depressed; he knew that his job was secure, but he always felt insecure. He could not see a change in the future. He stated that he wanted to feel more closely linked to his wife, to enjoy her company. He assured me that she was really a bright, charming woman, and that he felt guilty for even thinking about her like this, but he simply couldn't feel happy when she constantly reminded him that he used poor judgment and made bad decisions. He went on to say that he felt confused about the entire situation.

Modeling his world indicated that he was chronologically working on the task of intimacy and struggling to avoid isolation. This was particularly difficult as he was heavily burdened with shame and doubt residual related to the task of autonomy. His interest in an intimate relationship with his wife was perfectly normal, but could not be achieved satisfactorily when he was confronted with such extensive residual of insecure attachment (from task of trust), shame and doubt (autonomy), guilt (initiative), inferiority (industry), and role confusion (identity), all symptomatic of difficulty in resolving developmental crises from infancy to middle age (Erikson, 1963).

Interventions were initially designed to address insecure attachment. Verbal and nonverbal communications were selected that were consistent with communication in the first three years. Nonverbal considerations included eye contact, mild motor movements that were open in stance, and gentle touch. Verbal considerations included messages that could be assimilated or accommodated into sensorimotor, pre-operational, and early concrete schema. Direct hypothetical messages were avoided initially, although metaphors were used as indirect messages. Pacing, reframing, indirect suggestions, and embedded commands were used extensively.

Initially Mr. M. stated that if he was really going to get into this, he needed to see me "regularly" and asked if he could come twice a week. As the consent form had indicated that subjects in the study could have one hour of time each week, I considered this an important question.

One way to interpret it was that I was being tested—Did I really mean that I cared about him and would I really help him by giving him more time? Another possible interpretation was that his cognition regarding these issues was so immature that he couldn't remember the object from week to week. After balancing the alternatives, we agreed that he could come twice a week as he *felt* the need and as he *envisioned* himself getting to *know* himself better.

During the next month Mr. M. visited twice a week, then he gradually decreased his visits to once a week, then once every other week. During the early sessions, his body stance opened and straightened, his eye contact increased, and he began to report interactions with his colleagues that were satisfying. About the fourth week two things happened. First, as he entered he handed me a book he had written several years before and stated that this would explain everything I needed to know about him. The second occurred as he prepared to leave: He proclaimed that he couldn't get too healthy or he wouldn't be able to come see me. I responded that I was interested in all of him, and that he could get as healthy as he wanted and still come see me. At this time, I told him that I had a gift for him that would remind him I knew he was wise, and I gave him a small rock (earlier he told me he collected rocks). The following week his blood pressure was within normal range. He began to take initiative for more positive interactions with his wife and children and to take pleasure in his achievements. Within four months he was able to identify experiences that were sufficiently stressful so that they would elevate his blood pressure unless he changed the experience. At this point he would place his hand on the telephone (his link to me), review his newly discovered "wisdom," and avoid an elevated blood pressure. Since he had his own sphygmomanometer at home, he was able to document these processes.

I was curious to see what would happen as he approached the developmental task of industry. Since his first experience with this task had resulted in his avoiding multiple psychosocial stressors by focusing on cognitive learning—but learning for *external rewards*, not internal rewards—I wondered how he would restructure his entire frame of reference. Several things happened during this phase of the treatment. First, while he no longer taxed his peripheral vascular system in order to contend with the psychosocial system, he methodically taxed one after another of the biological systems. He had an episode of pleurisy, then *Salmonella*-like gastrointestinal disturbance, then cystitis, followed by two stress fractures, and two severe episodes of hyperventilation. The final episode was his admission to the hospital with myocardial infarct symptoms. At this point I said that we had to have a contract (which I wrote on a piece of white paper) that stated he would not do anything

more to hurt himself, including having a heart attack or choking in a restaurant. He agreed, signed the contract, and placed it in his left breast
pocket.* At the next visit Mr. M. reported a dream: He was running
through a house, going from one room to another, and being chased by
two witches brandishing brooms. The rooms looked very much like the
organs in his body, while the witches looked remarkably like his mother
and wife. It was rather terrifying until he got to the last room, where he
noticed that the entire room was a version of the house, only the rooms
had been reorganized and the two witches had turned into two ordinary
women. At this point he invited them to join him in his garden for tea. I
commended him for knowing what he knew, for his wisdom, and for his
willingness to take *healthy* risks. I also commented that it would be interesting to learn what else he knew.**

At the following visit Mr. M. stood outside the door, body slouched,
obviously tense, hesitating to enter. When encouraged to come in and
"make himself *even more comfortable than ever before and start where
he wanted but to learn what he needed to know*," he immediately
launched into his "deepest fear": He thought that he might be homosexual. The perceived implications were devastating. He was married, had
three children, and worked closely with several male graduate students
and male colleagues. If he were homosexual, he thought, he would be
ostracized. He went on to explain that as a youth he had wanted to be a
Boy Scout and had been told that the Boy Scouts were all "a little
strange," and besides, he had a lot of homework so he did not have time
for such nonsense.

Mr. M. was told that wanting to have friends and experience adven-
ture did not mean that one was homosexual. In fact, it meant that one
was perfectly normal. He was then advised to search the community for
three to four different types of groups, and select "one or two, or two or
three, or more," that he wanted to further explore. He was to have fun
searching and exploring, and to learn something new about himself with
each group.

Mr. M. canceled the next two visits. When he returned, he was quite
pleased that he had joined three groups. The first was the university
faculty club, the second was a group interested in family camping, and
the third was a group studying the classics. He had tried two others—
both all-male groups—but they seemed boring, so he had decided not to

---

*I consulted Milton Erickson at this time to validate my assessment and verify my
therapeutic plan.
**At this point I made my second contact with Milton Erickson to describe what had
transpired and to explore whether alternative actions should be taken. After I gave him a
thorough account of this visit, he responded with a single comment, "I know."

join. He commented that he had no idea why he had suddenly gotten interested in exploring group membership, and he hoped that I wasn't upset that he had canceled his last two appointments. He then commented that it was interesting to him that his sexual relationship with his wife had really improved and that he guessed that it was all related somehow, but he didn't care. He also asked if it would be ok if he called when he thought he needed to see me again rather than immediately making another appointment.

Approximately five months later, Mr. M. called and asked if he could come in for about 15 minutes. He was preparing to leave the country for about six months on a research project. When he arrived, he informed me that he was fine, his blood pressure had been normal for months, he was no longer taking any medication, and he just wanted to check in before he left the country. As he exited, he turned around, pulled his contract from his pocket, and commented with a smile that he guessed his umbilical cord wasn't cut yet. I told him that it sure could stretch a long way, and that he would know when it was ready to be cut.

One year later, I received a notice from Mr. M. that he was presenting an expensive piece of art to the museum in my name. The 16th-century picture shows a male emperor looking into a mirror. The caption states that a female friend had helped this important man see his own reflection. In doing so, he had been able to go on to other things in life. Interestingly, self-reflection in a mirror symbolizes renewal of life in the culture where the painting originated—and Mr. M. was a scholar of this culture.

Mr. M. had entered treatment with insecure attachment in infancy and morbid grief due to perceived loss in toddlerhood. This had resulted in diminished psychosocial resources needed to work through subsequent life tasks. His presenting crisis was due to inability to work through the task of intimacy (as defined by Erikson, 1963). As a result he perceived additional losses, felt anxious, and had hypertension due to multiple psychological stressors.

Treatment was based on the epigenetic model of development with consideration for necessary attachment objects at each stage. Initially, treatment was designed to facilitate secure attachment. Interventions appropriate to facilitate attachment in infancy were designed; various hypnotherapeutic techniques were used in these interventions. All interventions were designed within the context of the client's world.

As Mr. M. presented evidence of growth within a stage, movement into a new stage, growth through a stage, and movement into another, appropriate attachment objects (including transitional objects) were identified and attachment encouraged. During each stage, issues generally encountered in the normal growth processes emerged. At the conclusion of treatment, Mr. M. had moved from the tasks of infancy and toddlerhood to those of middle-aged adulthood. He was beginning to discuss the overall merit of his life and to focus on the future. His blood pressure was within normal range, and he described himself as feeling alive and healthy. During the next several years he published several articles, wrote two books, and reinvested in this family. Subsequently, his scholarship was recognized by his university as making an outstanding contribution to society.

Case Two

Mrs. T., a masters-level health care provider, called for an appointment, stating that her physician had informed her that she must get help or he would not continue to see her. She had experienced two myocardial infarcts and two coronary bypass surgeries. She was being treated for recurring angina, extreme fatigue, and intolerance to exercise. A cardiac catheterization had shown that three of her coronary vessels were 80% occluded. She entered my office with an unlit cigarette in one hand and a cup of coffee in the other. She immediately stated that she knew the doctor didn't want her to indulge in caffeine or cigarettes, but that she was stuck. She didn't know how to stop.

Her social history revealed that she had recently married for the third time. Her relationship with her current husband was deteriorating rapidly owing to her physical condition, though this didn't seem to seriously bother her. In addition, she was having trouble with her three grown children. However, her greatest problem was a deep sense of emptiness, futility, and darkness. She was unable to put additional words to her feelings. She poured out a life review: She was sick a great deal of the time as a child and had to be hospitalized. While she was able to recall feelings of anger and sadness when hospitalized for rheumatic fever at the age of six, her current feelings were much less focused and quite pervasive. She pinpointed the onset of the current feelings to three years earlier, when her second husband had died of cancer. She described his death as a terrible loss, stating that he had been wonderful to her. He had courted her, attended to her needs, cared for her, and made her feel important. However, he had not been financially solvent, so his death had left her in debt and without means of compensation. While she appeared to overcome her feelings and refocus her energies onto her children and her current husband, she had continued to feel a "deep sense of darkness and gloominess inside."

Shortly after her current marriage, she had an acute myocardial infarct that required emergency surgery. This was followed by a second attack and a second surgery in less than a year. Since that time she had not recovered. She had some signs of free-floating anxiety and was unable to return to work or resume her familial roles. She stated that she needed to have a nightlight on in her bedroom so that she could sleep at night and the only thing that she could do during the day was to go to her garden and pull a few weeds, pick a few vegetables, and smell a few flowers. She informed me that she had seen two other therapists and that they had been unable to help her. I responded that we would both be *interested and curious* to see *how* I was going to *help her help herself gain without losing.*

As we talked about the relationships among basic needs, developmental tasks, loss, and grief, I drew an analogy between a stairway and life. I suggested that we start life on a flat plain and as we go through life, we build foundations and new plains. After a while we have a series of plains that are similar to a series of steps. The nature of each step is determined by the quality of the products used to build it. Each step provides foundation for the next. I also suggested that our steps were set in a context, perhaps like a hill, so that we soon have more than several steps; we have a *stairway* that helps us get from one point to another. We can go up and down the stairway when we want; we can stop on any one step at a time, and we can step off the stairway and onto the hillside at any time. I suggested that whenever we choose to step off the stairs onto the hill, we can go up or down a number of different paths to explore gardens or other *interesting or curious* things that might help us better understand what we want to know. I encouraged her to imagine that she had a light that she could carry with her so she could see better. We practiced seeing the light and then feeling the light's warm glow. We discussed how nice it was to have control over the light by turning it off and on, or up and down. I suggested that the more we know, the more we can explore, that knowing is like discovering that a can of worms is really a can of caterpillars waiting to become beautiful butterflies. I emphasized that no matter where we choose to explore, we will always know our way back to the top step.

Mrs. T. was told to find a most comfortable seat, completely relax, and begin to be aware of her body's responses to the room *where she and I were sitting quietly together.* I suggested that the more she attended to how she was breathing *so quietly*, how her heart was beating *so regularly*, how her skin seemed to *feel comfortably* warm, but not too warm, the more she would relax. I also suggested that as she paid more attention to these signs of her healthy body, she would become more aware of other signs that her body was working well and she might gain new insights as well. I suggested that she might be able to see her stair steps, but that for the time being, we would focus on the top step. I wanted her to develop healthy physiological responses before discussing earlier developmental issues. As she moved into a deeper trance, I suggested that she move onto the path next to the top step and that she move along the path and toward the garden. I suggested that she might envision her body as though it were a lovely garden with many healthy vegetables and flowers growing in their proper place with multiple *rivers and streams running freely* in order to feed her vegetables and flowers. I further suggested that she might want to watch for rocks in her riverbeds, rocks that blocked the flow of nutrients to the vegetables and flowers, and that she *might want to move or remove some of those rocks* that interfered with the flow. I also reminded her that I was there in the room with her, that she was a special person, and that she would never be alone again because my voice would always be with her. I suggested that she might be interested in finding this special garden at other times and knowing that as she found it, my voice would be with her.

My initial assessment indicated that for unknown reasons, Mrs. K. had a strong sense of abandonment in infancy and this had left her with extensive insecure attachment. This had resulted in difficulty in each developmental stage from autonomy to her current stage. Her need for affiliated-individuation was similar to that of an infant. While she had been able to compensate for unmet psychosocial needs fairly well, the process had taxed her body excessively. Suggestions that she should take care of herself (e.g., stop smoking) only reinforced her sense of abandonment. The health care providers were telling her to take care of herself, by herself; by doing so they inadvertently pushed her farther into the "black chasm" that was engulfing her.

My goals for these sessions were to build a secure attachment as it related to the stage of trust and to begin to build an awareness of self-control over the body. During the stage of infancy, the developmental task is to learn that dependent needs will be met, and a major challenge is to gain a sense of healthy stability in the biophysical mechanisms of the body. Since there are significant linkages between mind and body, it is important to anchor healthy physiological responses with feelings of security to the maximum extent possible. If this could be accomplished, I might be able to address some of the early developmental factors without risking untoward physiological responses.

As her adverse cardiovascular symptoms subsided, concurrent evidence of secure attachment emerged. About the fifth week in treatment, Mrs. T. stated that she wanted to know more about her feelings of desertion. She stated that cognitively she knew that people cared about her, but that she didn't feel cared about. Hypnosis was used, and as she entered a trance state, I suggested that she might first want to go up one more step and that in order to do this, she would need to build the framework. I suggested that she might see herself in the future, that she might be able to see herself happy, working, and living a full, satisfying life. As her ideomotor and verbal responses validated that she was able to envision herself in this way, she was told that she could choose to go back down the stairs, one step at a time, that she would remember *that my voice would go with her*, and that her body would remember that it was able to maintain steady, strong functioning processes.

As she regressed, one step at a time, she described key events in her life, most of which symbolized fear of abandonment and multiple actions directed toward avoiding such an outcome. When she reached the age of five, she described her hospitalization, her parents leaving her, and the nurses' failure to respond to her cries of distress. In an earlier session I had asked her to bring a picture of her parents to a session. At this time, I stated that she was very small, that it is natural for small children to want their parents, and that her desire to have her parents nearby was a healthy thing for this wise little girl. I then suggested that it was also very smart of her to have her parents with her, and to remember that she could always have them with her and that she could know that they were there. I then told her that it was also natural for small children to want to have their nurse with them when they were frightened (and even when they were not frightened) and now that she knew that her parents were with her and that she could hear her nurse's voice go with her, she would also know that she would not be left alone again. I suggested that she might want to think about this for a few minutes and enjoy the comfort and security that was related to knowing that she would *never be left alone again*, and as she experienced such feelings she would note that her *body* was feeling more secure as well. After several minutes she decided to come out of the trance. Upon awakening she commented that she felt better, that she was more hopeful, and that she wanted to return the following week.

When she arrived for her next appointment, she went directly into a trance and regressed to an even earlier age. Curling her body inward, she placed both hands to the left side of her neck and began to cry like a small child. When asked to tell me where she was and what she was experiencing, she described being in a large room that was very black. There were many beds with bars on them and they were filled with little children. She said that her neck hurt badly, that it was dark and frightening, and that no one would come to her. I reminded her that I was there, that my voice would always be with her, and that she had her small flashlight that I had given her in an earlier session. She was to remember that this light could be turned off completely so that it would be very dark; it could be turned on a little so that there was a little light; or it could be turned on fully so that there was a lot of light. I suggested that she imagine turning her light on full so that she could feel safe, and that she might then want to practice feeling safe with and without her light fully on. I also suggested that as she turned her light on and off, she could hear my voice and know that I was there and that she would notice that even when she turned the light off, a little light remained with her. I told her that when she was finished practicing she could go up the stairway to the top step and remember only what she wanted to remember, but that she would always know that she had control over *turning her parts on and off,* making them work for her, and making them help her help herself. After she awakened from the trance, she remarked that she had always wondered why she had a scar on the left side of her neck, but had never asked. She said that she intended to ask her mother. As she left, she commented that she felt pleasantly warm as though she had a soft glow inside her.

The following week Mrs. T. arrived early, arranged herself comfortably, and said that she had talked with her mother about her scar. Her mother told her that she had been born with a huge hematoma that had been surgically removed when she was 11 months old. She was told that the surgery was difficult and required a prolonged hospitalization. Since the mother had two other children at home, Mrs. T. had been left to fend for herself and to deal with her own pain and anxiety. She discussed the linkage between that experience and what she had observed as a health professional when small children were left in hospitals. She commented that she felt less anxious now than she had before we began to work together. I commented on how much *I valued her ability to know what she wanted to know when she was ready to know it, and that as time went by, she would not need me to know how to know.*

The next visit she reported that she had been to her gynecologist and that she had a large ovarian cyst that required surgery and that her physician had insisted she have a cardiac catheterization to determine whether she could tolerate surgery. She stated that she was reluctant to have another catheterization, because she felt that there was more risk than benefit. I encouraged her to discuss her concerns with her physician and reminded her that she had great control over her body. She called me a few days later and stated that she had convinced the physician that she could have the surgery without catheterization. Later that week she underwent surgery, recovered without event, and returned home four days later. She called to tell me that she had been up and down her stairway several times over the last four days, and it had worked very well for her.

During the next few weeks Mrs. T. worked intensively to prepare for my departure. While she had been informed that I was moving out of state, she had not accepted the possibility of adapting to this loss until she gained insight about feelings of abandonment. At this point she began to accumulate transitional objects. She took pictures, made audiotapes, and used homework assignments to prepare herself. Although her situation with her grown children continued to be difficult, she showed continuous improvement in her relationship with her husband. They decided to take a two-week trip to "reestablish their relationship." When they returned from their trip, the two of them came in for several appointments. While they were both reluctant to face our last appointment, they commented that they were greatful that Mrs. T. was feeling so much better, and that they were able to enjoy one another again.

Three weeks after we moved, I received a telephone call from Mrs. T. She had felt well enough to return to work several months before. However, she still tired after a full day's work. She had been in to see her physician who had recommended that she have a cardiac catheterization to monitor her progress, and she had agreed. She was thrilled to report that two of her coronary vessels were completely clear, and the third was only 50% occluded. We agreed that she had done very well indeed, and that with a little more time, she might be able to *remove the rocks from that river* too. We talked about fatigue as a healthy sign that indicates that *rest and comfort is needed*, and that we can often overcome fatigue by going to a place or space that is comforting. I commended her for knowing where her comforting spots were and knowing how to get there and how long she needed to stay. I also reminded her that she could always take her special helpers (her light and my voice) with her wherever she went.

Mrs. T. entered treatment with insecure attachment and morbid grief from infancy, which was potentiated by additional loss during the stage of initiative. These multiple experiences of abandonment resulted in a coping pattern similar to that seen in highly stressed children aged three to seven. That is, they develop patterns of physiological responses to psychosocial stressors. Mrs. T.'s difficulty culminated in a crisis when challenged by normal stages of intimacy. At this time, her coping style threatened her life. Since she had inadequate psychosocial resources to contend with the task of intimacy, she was at risk for a life-threatening myocardial infarct.

Since Mrs. T.'s initial loss was during a preverbal stage in life, she was unable to put words to her experience; instead she defined it as a "black chasm." Language used in hypnotic induction and therapeutic interventions were initially designed to establish secure attachment and, therefore, to facilitate her development of ego boundaries. As she produced evidence of movement into subsequent stages, the language and interventions were adapted according to the developmental stage. Continuous emphasis was placed on filling the "black chasm" with light symbolic of attachment (stage of trust), *gaining* control over bodily functions in a healthy manner (stage of autonomy), and *taking* control over herself physiologically and psychologically (stage of initiative).

At the end of treatment, Mrs. T. was working on a healthy relationship with her husband which symbolized movement into the stage of intimacy. Her cardiovascular risk factors had been decreased considerably. She had returned to work in a professional role that was satisfying and she was beginning to plan for the future. She had gained considerable control over her body and was learning how to take control proactively so that she might be able to *prevent* further physiological distress.

SUMMARY

The two cases presented here have been used to demonstrate the effect of planning psychosocial interventions to deal with physiological problems. Several others have been presented elsewhere (Erickson, 1984, 1988; Erickson, Tomlin, & Swain, 1988). Major considerations in these cases were that psychosocial factors were directly linked to physiological outcomes. However, the opposite also holds true. The effects of altered blood glucose, oxygen, drugs, extreme physical trauma, and so forth on the mind are well substantiated. The question that has to be asked is which comes first. In a study with a sample of people who have diabetes we learned that people have at least two different reactions to insulin overdose. The first is a sense of being out of control; the second is a sense of floating free. The first is described as being frightening and something to avoid; the second is described as relaxing, and something that is enjoyed. Many questions have come from this discovery. Key among them is the notion that Rossi (1986) raises when he says that there are linkages among the mind, the brain, and the body. Where does it start, and where do we start our interventions? After many years of experience as a private clinician, as well as a consultant to many medical-surgical units in major hospital systems (including intensive care units), I have come to believe that the mind's effects on the brain and thus the body are more powerful than the body's on the mind. However, since the reverse cannot be ignored, a multifront approach is often indicated.

REFERENCES

Ader, R. (Ed). (1981). *Psychoneuroimmunology*. New York: Academic Press.

Alexander, F. (1950). *Psychosomatic Medicine: Its Principles and Application.* New York: Norton.

Cannon, W. (1918). *Bodily Changes in Pain, Hunger, Fear, and Rage: An Account of Recent Researces into the Function of Emotional Excitement.* New York: Appleton.

Dunbar, F. (1935). *Emotions and Bodily Changes.* New York: Columbia University Press.

Erickson, H. (1984). Self-care knowledge: Relations among the concepts support, hope, control, satisfaction with daily life, and physical health status. *Dissertation Abstracts International, 46,* 06B. (University Microfilms International, No. 84-12,-136)

Erickson, H. (1988). Modeling and role-modeling: Ericksonian techniques applied to physiological problems. In J. K. Zeig & S. Lankton (Eds.), *Developing Ericksonian Therapy: State of the Art.* New York: Brunner/Mazel.

Erickson, H., Tomlin, E., & Swain, M. A. (1988). *Modeling and Role-Modeling: A Theory and Paradigm for Nursing.* Lexington, SC: Pine Press of Lexington.

Erikson, E. (1963). *Childhood and Society.* New York: Norton.

Freud, S. (1924). *Collected Papers.* New York: International Psychoanalytic Press.

Friedman, M. (1977). Type A behavior pattern: Some of its pathophysiological components. *Bulletin of the New York Academy of Science, 53,* 593.

Rossi, E. (1986). *The Psychobiology of Mind-Body Healing: New Concepts of Therapeutic Hypnosis.* New York: Norton.

Rossi, E., & Ryan, M. (Eds.) (1986). *Mind-Body Communication in Hypnosis: The Seminars, Workshops, and Lectures of Milton H. Erickson, Volume III.* New York: Irvington.

Selye, H. (1956). *Stress of Life.* New York: McGraw-Hill.

Contributors

Joseph Barber, Ph.D., Department of Psychiatry, UCLA School of Medicine, Los Angeles, CA

Joel Bergman, Ph.D., Ackerman Institute for Family Therapy, New York, NY

Simon Budman, Ph.D., Harvard Community Health Plan and Innovative Training Systems, Newton Center, MA

Gianfranco Cecchin, M.D., Centro Milanese di Terapia della Famiglia, Milan, Italy

Nicholas Cummings, Ph.D., American Biodyne, Inc., South San Francisco, CA

Steve de Shazer, Brief Family Therapy Center, Milwaukee, WI

Albert Ellis, Ph.D., Institute for Rational-Emotive Therapy, New York, NY

Betty Alice Erickson-Elliot, M. S., private practice, Dallas, TX

Helen L. Erickson, R.N., Ph.D., School of Nursing, University of Texas at Austin, Austin, TX

Allen Fay, M.D., Department of Psychiatry, Mount Sinai School of Medicine, City University of New York, New York, NY

Richard Fisch, M.D., Mental Research Institute, Palo Alto, CA

Stephen G. Gilligan, Ph.D., private practive, San Diego, CA

David Gordon, M.A., private practice, Oakland, CA

Mary McClure Goulding, M.S.W., Western Institute for Group and Family Therapy, Watsonville, CA

James Paul Gustafson, M.D., Department of Psychiatry, University of Wisconsin, Madison, WI

Jay Haley, M.A., Family Therapy Institute of Washington, D.C., Rockville, MD

Leslie Kadis, M.D., private practice, Santa Cruz and San Francisco, CA

Roxanna Erickson Klein, R.N., M.S., Dallas, TX

Carol Lankton, M.A., Center for Personal and Family Development, Pensacola, FL

491

Stephen Lankton, M.S.W., private practice, Gulf Breeze, FL

Arnold A. Lazarus, Ph.D., Graduate School of Applied and Professional Psychology, Rutgers University, Piscataway, NJ

Herbert Lustig, M.D., Private practice, Ardmore, PA

Cloé Madanes, Family Therapy Institute of Washington, D.C., Rockville, MD

Ruth McClendon, M.S.W., private practice, Santa Cruz and San Francisco, CA

William Hudson O'Hanlon, M.S., The Hudson Center for Brief Therapy, Omaha, NE

Peggy Papp, A.C.S.W., Ackerman Institute for Family Therapy, New York, NY

Erving Polster, Ph.D., Gestalt Training Center, San Diego, CA

Sidney Rosen, M.D., private practice, New York, NY

Ernest Rossi, Ph.D., private practice, Los Angeles, CA

Peter Sifenos, M.D., Department of Psychiatry, Harvard University Medical School, Boston, MA

Hans H. Strupp, Ph.D., Department of Psychology, Vanderbilt University, Nashville, TN

Kay F. Thompson, D.D.S., private practice, Pittsburgh, PA

Paul Watzlawick, Ph.D., Mental Research Institute, Palo Alto, CA

John Weakland, Ch.E., Mental Research Institute, Palo Alto, CA

Michael D. Yapko, Ph.D., private practice, San Diego, CA

Jeffrey K. Zeig, Ph.D., The Milton H. Erickson Foundation, Phoenix, AZ